The Governance, Security and Development Nexus

Kenneth Omeje
Editor

The Governance, Security and Development Nexus

Africa Rising

palgrave
macmillan

Editor
Kenneth Omeje
Manifold Crown Research and Training Consult
Bradford, UK

Addis Ababa University
Addis Ababa, Ethiopia

ISBN 978-3-030-49347-9 ISBN 978-3-030-49348-6 (eBook)
https://doi.org/10.1007/978-3-030-49348-6

This Palgrave Macmillan imprint is published by the registered company Springer Nature Switzerland AG
The registered company address is: Gewerbestrasse 11, 6330 Cham, Switzerland

Preface

This book explores the nexus between governance, security and development in Africa as it relates to the narrative that contemporary Africa has made remarkable progress over the past one and half decades, a phenomenon captured in influential sections of international media and academic and policy discourses as "Africa rising." The book investigates and interrogates the discursive assumptions and empirical indicators of the Africa rising narratives. The Africa rising debate is a controversial discourse postulating that contemporary Africa has made a substantial leap from the longstanding Valhalla of underdevelopment and its negative governance and security correlates to the trajectory of sustainable progress. Is continental Africa finally witnessing what the famous American post-war economist W. W. Rostow called the "preconditions for take-off" or probably his actual "take off of self-sustaining economic growth?" In what specific empirical forms and ways have Africa recorded the highly publicised rising progress or take-off? What are the local, regional and international factors that have enabled Africa to rise and to what extent are African states and institutions in command of these variables? Seriously speaking, what specific countries are rising in Africa—arguably Ethiopia, Rwanda, Ghana, Tanzania, Mozambique, DRC, Zambia, Uganda, Niger and Burkina Faso? How well and how fast are they rising? Can we by any stretch of the imagination justifiably brand any assemblage of the rising countries the "African tigers"—a conceptual mimicry of the "Asian tigers," the countries that engineered the competitive and rapid ascendancy of the South Asian economies on the global stage over the past 30 years? What is the cumulative national and regional impact of the rising of any of the African countries said to be on the rise? To what extent have the ordinary citizens, as well as vulnerable social groups, communities and states empirically felt the impact of the Africa rising narratives? Where do we place countries like Somalia, Sudan, South Sudan, Eritrea, Cameroun, Central African Republic and Eswatini (to mention but a few of the countries that seem stuck in a protracted limbo) in the Africa rising debate? How can the continent build on any recorded performance successes to leverage the governance, security and development nexus for the overall benefit and well-being of the African people and states? These are some of the questions explored in this edited volume with incisive contributions from experts in African economics, politics, conflicts, security, peacebuilding, development and international relations.

This book comprises a total of 19 commissioned chapters, structured into five thematic parts. Part I explores the conceptual issues and interrogates the empirical indicators of the governance, security and development nexus in the context of Africa rising as reflected and debated in extant literature. Part II is a critical assessment of the global dimensions of "Africa rising," examining the trends and dynamics of Africa—EU (European Union) relations, Africa—US relations, Africa—China relations, as well as the cumulative direction and impact of foreign direct investments in Africa. Part III analyses the regional imperatives of Africa rising, the empirical trends, challenges and opportunities of intra-African trade, as well as the politics of regional development and economic integration. Part IV discusses specific national contests of Africa rising, taking a case study of a few states believed to be on the "rise" and conversely examining a few other states that represent "the forgotten Africa"—countries that are seemingly trapped in the doldrums and therefore hardly discussed in the overall debate.

The book is concluded in Part V, which examines the empirical realities and macroeconomic imperatives of how Africa can overcome present obstacles to make more meaningful progress within the prevailing regional and global economic framework. Overall, the narratives that Africa is rising on the neoliberal path of development discussed in the various chapters of this book present mixed results of euphoria versus dysphoria, success versus failure and triumphalism verses cautious optimism. The book ends with a set of policy-relevant measures and strategies articulated into a coherent vision that can help Africa to arise or rise sustainably.

I wish to observe that the last set of this book's manuscripts were completed during the first quarter of 2020 while the world grappled with the destabilising scourge of the COVID-19 popularly known as Coronavirus (the name of the causative virus). Because the "pandemic" was still unfolding at the time of completing the manuscripts, it is important to mention that its impact on the economies of the various African countries and the overall discourse of "Africa rising" has not been captured in this volume. I imagine that this will be the subject of many future researches on this subject whenever the scourge settles, hopefully, not too long from now.

I greatly commend the passionate commitment of all the chapter contributors, especially those that were invited at the "eleventh hour" and had the unenviable challenge of navigating through the logistical nightmares occasioned by the Coronavirus-instigated lockdown. To the Palgrave Macmillan Editor of Regional Politics and Development Studies, Ms. Alina Yurova, I render my unreserved appreciation for your professional guidance and goodwill. I cannot end this preface without gratefully acknowledging the unflinching support, prayers and understanding of my loving wife, Ngozi, and children, Rejoicing, Chibia and Ifediche. I am blessed to have a wonderful family in you four. To the entire members of the Crown of Christ Gospel Church in Bradford, my brethren and family in Christ, I convey my profound gratitude for your spiritual support and solidarity.

Bradford, UK Kenneth Omeje

Contents

Notes on Contributors

Samuel Baba Ayegba is a Lecturer in the Department of Defence and Security Studies, Nigerian Defence Academy, Kaduna, and a Research Fellow at the Centre for Defence Studies and Documentation (CDSD), Nigerian Defence Academy, Kaduna. He completed his M.Sc. degree in Defence and Strategic Studies from the Nigerian Defence Academy, Kaduna. Samuel is currently a doctoral candidate in Defence and Strategic Studies at the Nigerian Defence Academy, Kaduna and has published in several peer-reviewed platforms. His area of scholarly interests includes security and strategic studies, gender, environmental politics, and peace and conflict studies.

Bashir Bala is a Captain in the Nigerian Army. A graduate of the Nigerian Defence Academy, Capt. Bala was commissioned at the Royal Military Academy Sandhurst, United Kingdom, and thereafter attended Shijiazhuang Mechanised Infantry Academy for Basic and Advanced Special Operations Courses in China. He was formerly a tactical commander in several critical Counter-Insurgency Operations in the Northeast Region of Nigeria. His is co-author (with Prof. Usman Tar) of *New Architecture for Regional Security in Africa: Counter-Terrorism and Counter-Insurgency in the Lake Chad Basin* (Lexington Books, Lanham MD, USA, 2020). Captain Bala is a doctoral candidate at the Security and Strategy Institute, University of Exeter, United Kingdom. His doctoral research is titled: *The Role of the Armed Forces of Nigeria in Providing Security Support to*

Transnational Oil Companies, and Its Effects on Nigerian Defence and Economic Security.

Ibrahim Bangura has worked extensively in the fields of Disarmament, Demobilisation and Reintegration of Ex-Combatants, Security Sector Reform, Sustainable Livelihoods, Gender and Conflict Resolution in Africa. He holds a Bachelor's degree in Political Science and History and a Master's degree in Gender Studies from University of Sierra Leone; another Master's degree in International Development Studies from the University of Amsterdam; and a Doctorate degree in Economics from the Leipzig Graduate School of Management in Germany. He currently works as an independent consultant and also lectures at the Peace and Conflict Studies Programme, Fourah Bay College, University of Sierra Leone.

Redie Bereketeab, Ph.D. is an Associate Professor of Sociology and currently works as a Senior Researcher at the Nordic Africa Institute, Uppsala, Sweden, where he spearheads research projects on (i) conflict and state-building in the Horn of Africa (Sudan, South Sudan, Somalia, Ethiopia, Eritrea and Djibouti); and (ii) the role of regional economic communities (RECs) in peacebuilding in Africa (AMU, ECCASS, ECOWAS, IGAD and SADC). His areas of research interest are political sociology, development, peace and conflict studies, state-building, nation-building, identity, democracy and governance in Africa. He has authored several books, book chapters and articles in referred journals published by Routledge, James Currey, Pluto Books, Palgrave Macmillan and The Red Sea Press. Among the journals where his articles have been published in include *Studies of Ethnicity and Nationalism*, *African Studies*, *Journal of Civil Society*, *African Studies*, *African Studies Review*, *African and Asian Studies*, and *South African Journal of International Affairs.*

Asebe Regassa Debelo is an Associate Professor at Dilla University, Ethiopia and was a postdoctoral fellow at the University of Zürich, Switzerland (2015–2016). Dr. Debelo has also served as Director Research and Dissemination office, Dilla University. He extensively published papers on various themes including the high-modernist developmentalism, land grabbing, indigenous peoples' right, conflict and peacebuilding and Africa–China relations in peace and security. Dr. Debelo's research interest includes indigenous peoples' right to resources, large-scale development projects and impacts on indigenous peoples, nature–culture relations and peacebuilding with specific geographical areas on Eastern Africa.

Hilde Geens (Belgium) is a Programm and Policy Officer for a medical NGO Artsen Zonder Vakantie. She is interested in development cooperation, capacity development, societal change and resistance in developing countries.

Hamdy A. Hassan, Ph.D. is a Professor of Political Science at the College of Humanities and Social Sciences in Zayed University in Dubai. He is also a member of the advisory board of the Swedish Network of Peace, Conflict and Development Research. In 1999, Professor Hassan was granted the Egyptian State award in Political Science for his book *Issues in the African Political Systems* published by the Center for African Future Studies, Cairo. From 2001 to 2005, Professor Hassan served as an elect Vice President of the African Association of Political Science (AAPS), based in Pretoria, South Africa. He is the founder and Director of the Centre for African Future Studies, Cairo, since 1996. From 1999 to 2000, he served as a Director of the UNESCO Human Rights Chair located in Jordan. His research focuses on democratisation and development in Africa and the Arab world, Islamic Discourse in Africa and Conflict management. He has published many books and journal articles in both Arabic and English, including Hassan, H. et al. (2018) *The Road of Soft Power: UAE and Africa*. Abu Dhabi: Abu Dhabi Tourism and Culture Department; and, Hassan, H. (2018) "The Security and Military Relations Between UAE and Egypt." In Hassanein Ali (ed.) *The UAE—Egyptian Relationship*. Sharjah: Gulf Centre for Studies.

Joseph Lansana Kormoh is a Senior Lecturer in the Department of History and African Studies at Fourah Bay College, University of Sierra Leone and also a Commonwealth Scholar at the University of Bradford. He led the teaching of general African history and the history of the United States for more than a decade before he relocated to the UK for his Ph.D. studies in Peace Studies at the University of Bradford. Joseph holds a Postgraduate Diploma in Research Methods from the University of Bradford and presently works as a UK-based freelance researcher. He completed his undergraduate studies at the Fourah Bay College, University of Sierra Leone where he graduated with a B.A. (Hons.) degree in History and later obtained an M.A. degree in History from the same

University. Since his graduation, Joseph has been involved in university teaching, research and consulting for the government of Sierra Leone and international organisations such as the UNDP. He has also been hugely involved in the formation and training of Catholic priests at the St. Paul's major seminary in Sierra Leone. His book chapters have been published by Palgrave Macmillan and Routledge and he has also published a book with Arthur House UK, among other reputable publishing houses. In 2008, Joseph was a visiting scholar at the New York University (NYU) during which he held a series of seminars in various universities in the USA.

Anne Kubai is Associate Professor of World Christianity and Interreligious Studies. Currently, she is a researcher at the School for Historical and Contemporary Studies at Södertörn University, Sweden. Kubai is also a research associate at the Research Institute for Theology and Religion (RITR) at the University of South Africa, Pretoria. Kubai is a visiting professor at the Institute for Women and Gender Studies at Egerton University, Kenya. Her research interests include genocide, mass violence, religion in peace and conflict, gender-based violence, transitional justice, international migration, applied development and psychosocial studies. In addition, she has a keen interest in the humanitarian-development-peacebuilding nexus. Kubai worked with different universities and organisations in Kenya and Rwanda for many years. She worked as Research Director for Life & Peace Institute, an International Ecumenical Centre for Peace Research and Action in Uppsala, Sweden. Kubai also worked as Senior Social Scientist at the Division of Global Health (IHCAR), Department of Public Health Sciences at Karolinska Institute in Stockholm, Sweden. Until recently she was a researcher at the Centre for Multidisciplinary Research on Racism (CEMFOR) at the Department of Theology, Uppsala University. Kubai has published numerous peer-reviewed journal articles, contributions to anthologies, co-edited anthologies, research reports, popular science articles and two documentaries.

Temitope J. Laniran earned a B.Sc. degree in Economics from Bowen University Iwo in Nigeria and M.Sc. and PhD in Economics and Development Studies from the Bradford Centre for International Development (BCID), University of Bradford. During his M.Sc. degree course, Temitope was awarded an Erasmus grant of the European Union Lifelong

Learning programme to study Human Development and Food Security at the Roma Tre Universita Degli Studi Rome, Italy. He has previously worked with the Centre for Petroleum, Energy Economics and Law, (CPEEL) at the University of Ibadan, as well as Equilibra Consulting—both in Nigeria. He currently teaches Economics at the University of Bradford and was previously a Research Associate at the University's John and Elnora Fergusson Centre for African Studies. His research interest is focused on economic growth and development issues of resource-rich countries and fragile states.

Nolubabalo Lulu Magam, Ph.D. holds an undergraduate degree in Peace Studies, a Master's in International Relations from the North-West University (South Africa) and a Ph.D. in International Relations from the University of KwaZulu-Natal (South Africa). Nolubabalo is a Political Science and Conflict Transformation and Peace studies Lecturer at the University of KwaZulu-Natal and has taught Political Science and International Relations at the University of Pretoria and North-West University in South Africa. She has published in the area of alternative energy and climate change adaptation as a means to peace and security, as well as immigration policies in South Africa. Her current research interest is in exploring the potential of paradiplomacy in Africa's development, which derives from his doctoral research.

Uchenna A. Nnamani is an early career development economist with strong interest in development finance. He desires a career in development researcher and practice. Nnamani is currently a Ph.D. degree candidate at the Institute for Development Studies, University of Nigeria (Enugu Campus). He holds a Master's degree in Development Studies, and a Bachelor of Science degree in Economics. Nnamani has been working with the Development Strategy Centre (a Nigerian-based research think tank) since 2015. Working with the think tank while doing his Ph.D. research has helped him gain reasonable research experience in the area of international finance, trade, policy analysis and impact assessment. His experience in international finance includes being part of an AERC-funded research project titled "Asymmetric Shocks, Real Exchange Rate Distortions and Options for the Second Monetary Zone in West Africa." Nnamani has presented papers at International Conferences, and workshops of African Economic Research Consortium.

Aymar Nyenyezi Bisoka is currently a lecturer and postdoctoral researcher. He earned his Ph.D. degree from the School of Political and Social Sciences of the Catholic University of Louvain, Belgium, with a background in legal and political studies. His postdoctoral researches focus on issues of power and resistance in relation to access to natural resources in the Great Lakes Region. Nyenyezi is involved in teaching and coordinating research-action projects in Belgium (UCLouvain), Burundi (University of Burundi), DRC (Catholic University of Bukavu and the Higher Institute of Rural Development) and Rwanda.

Abdullahi Mohammed Odowa is the Ambassador of the Federal Government of Somalia to the State of Kuwait, and a doctoral candidate at the Africa Programme of the United Nations-Mandated University for Peace in Costa Rica. Previously, Ambassador Odowa worked as a Senior Political Advisor to the Office of the Prime Minister of the Federal Government of Somalia, General-Director of Somali Observatory of Conflict and Violence Prevention (OCVP), and the Director of Institute for Peace and Conflict Studies (IPCS) at the University of Hargeisa in Somalia. Ambassador Odowa holds a Bachelor's degree in Human Anatomy from the University of Maiduguri in Nigeria, M.A. in Natural Resources and Peace from the United Nations Mandated University for Peace in Costa Rica, and M.A. in Peacebuilding from the Centre of Trust, Peace and Social Relations at Coventry University in the United Kingdom. Prior to his appointment to lead the Somali Diplomatic Mission to the State of Kuwait, Ambassador Odowa developed and implemented numerous field research projects on issues of security, peacebuilding, governance and development in the Somali regions with support from major international development partners and academic institutions. His current areas of research interest include traditional peacebuilding, state-building and security governance in the Horn of Africa.

Kenneth Omeje is Director, Manifold Crown Consulting in Bradford, UK; Visiting Professor at the Institute for Peace and Security Studies (IPSS) in Addis Ababa University, Ethiopia; and Visiting Professorial Fellow at the Nigerian Defence Academy in Kaduna, Nigeria. He has previously held the positions of Professor of International Relations at the United States International University in Nairobi, Kenya; Senior Research Fellow at the John and Elnora Ferguson Centre for African Studies, University of Bradford, UK and Senior Research Associate at the University of Johannesburg, South Africa. Kenneth is the author of *Peacebuilding* *in Contemporary Africa: In Search of Alternative Strategies* (edited, London: Routledge, 2019), *The Crises of Postcoloniality in Africa* (edited, Dakar: CODESRIA, 2015), *Conflict and Peacebuilding in the African Great Lakes Region* (co. ed. Indiana: Indiana University Press, 2013), *High Stakes and Stakeholders: Oil Conflict & Security in Nigeria* (Aldershot: Ashgate, 2006); etc. He has more than 90 publications, including books, book chapters, contributions to international encyclopedias and articles in well-regarded journals. Kenneth has previously held visiting research fellowship positions at the Centre for African Studies, University of Florida, Gainesville, USA (Spring, 1992); Law Department, Keele University, UK (Spring, 2000); Institute of Higher Education, Comprehensive University of Kassel, Germany (Summer, 2000); Department of International Politics, University of Wales, Aberystwyth (Spring, 2001); and Georg Eckert Institute (GEI) in Braunschweig, Germany (Autumn 2014). He is a Fellow of the West Africa Institute (WAI) in Praia, Cape Verde and a member of the Advisory Board of the African Peacebuilding Network (APN) of the Social Science Research Council (SSRC) of New York.

Onyukwu E. Onyukwu is a Development Economist and thoroughbred academic with over twenty-five years of professional experience. He was formerly the Head of the Department of Economics, University of Nigeria, Nsukka. He is an alumnus of the Cambridge University Advanced Programme on Rethinking Development Economics (CAPORDE). He has taught Development Economics at both undergraduate and postgraduate levels among other undergraduate courses for several years. He is a Senior Fellow at the Institute for Development Studies (IDS) of the same University where he teaches graduate courses in theories of development and development policy, as well as supervises Master's and Doctoral students' theses. He is a development policy expert and professional trainer. His professional experiences cut across organisational capacity development, policy research and advocacy capacity building, strategy development, performance monitoring and evaluation, organisational assessment, governance research designs and implementation. He has done extensive evaluation work in the area of public expenditures and public policy development. For many years, he has been engaged in grassroots community advocacy and sensitisation activities for various civil society network organisations. He has held several short-term consultancy positions funded by different international organisations such as DFID,

UNDP, USAID-DAI and the World Bank, and also different government institutions in Nigeria, including the Central Bank of Nigeria (CBN).

Taiwo Owoeye, Ph.D. is a 2018 grantee of the African Peacebuilding Network (APN) of the New York-based Social Science Research Council (SSRC). He is a Senior Lecturer in the Department of Economics, Ekiti State University, Ado-Ekiti, Nigeria. He is an Alumnus of the American Political Science Association (APSA) African Methodological Workshop 2013. He was also a co-recipient of 2014 American Political Science Association Methodological Workshop Alumni Networking Grant. Taiwo's research interest is in how politics, institutions and history drive economic decisions in Africa. His publications have appeared in diverse reputable journals.

Sabastiano Rwengabo is a Ugandan Political Scientist and Independent Consultant in the areas of Fragility and Resilience Assessments, Political Economy Analyses and Institutional Assessments. He is a Country Expert with the Varieties of Democracy (V-Dem) Project of the Department of Political Science, University of Gothenburg. He was formerly a Research Fellow with the Advocates Coalition for Development and Environment (ACODE), a Kampala-based regional policy research and advocacy think tank. He completed the History Makers Training (HMT) and Oakseed Executive Leadership Course (OELC) with the Institute for National Transformation (INT). Dr. Rwengabo holds a Ph.D. degree from the National University of Singapore (NUS), where he was a Research Scholar, President's Graduate Fellow and Graduate Teacher, 2010–2014. His scholarly interest focuses on areas of International Politics and Security, Regionalism, Civil—Military Relations (CMR), Post-Conflict Transformation and Democratisation. One of Dr. Rwengabo's latest research products is a book on Security Cooperation in the East African Community (Trenton, New Jersey: African World Press, 2018).

Usman A. Tar (Ph.D.) is Endowed Professor of Defence and Security Studies at the Nigerian Defence Academy, and Director of the Academy's flagship Centre for Defence Studies and Documentation (CDSD). Prof Tar has held professional academic positions in Africa, United Kingdom and the Republic of Iraq. He is a Member of the Board of Social Science Research Council's African Peacebuilding Network (SSRC/APN), New York, USA. He has previously held the positions of Associate Research Fellow at the John and Elnora Ferguson Centre for Africa Studies

(JEFCAS) at the University of Bradford, and Assistant Professor at the Department of Politics and International Relations and Director of Postgraduate Studies at the University of Kurdistan-Hewler, Northern Iraq. Prof. Tar is the author of *The Politics of Neoliberal Democracy in Africa* (London/New York: I.B. Tauris, 2009); *Globalization in Africa: Perspectives on Development, Security, and the Environment* (Lexington Books, Lanham MD, USA, 2016); *Defence Transformation and the Consolidation of Democracy in Nigeria* (Kaduna: Academy Publishers, 2018); *New Architecture for Regional Security in Africa: Counter-Terrorism and Counter-Insurgency in the Lake Chad Basin* (Lexington Books, Lanham MD, USA, 2020), and the *Routledge Handbook of Counter-Terrorism and Counter-Insurgency in Africa* (Routledge, forthcoming, Autumn 2020). Prof. Tar was a member of Presidential Committee to Review Nigeria's National Defence Policy (2014–2015) and currently sits on the High-Powered Ministerial Think Tank established by Nigeria's Federal Ministry of Defence to monitor and review threats to national security in Nigeria. Prof. Tar has consulted for the *Westminster Foundation for Democracy* (WFD, Nigeria), *United Nations Development Programme* (UNDP, Nigeria), *United States Institute for Peace* (Nigeria Office) and *Konrad Adaneur Stiftung* (German Development Fund, Nigeria). He also serves as visiting professor and external examiner to several institutions of higher learning in Nigeria.

Yohannes Tekalign earned a B.A. degree in Political Science and International Relations, and Master's and Ph.D. degrees in Peace and Security Studies from Addis Ababa University. He has over ten years' experience in teaching and research in Ethiopia's higher education institutions. His research focus is on regional peace, conflict and security. Presently, Dr. Yohannes is an Assistant Professor of Peace and Conflict Studies at the Federal Meles Zenawi Leadership Academy in Addis Ababa, Ethiopia.

Abbreviations

ACAs	Anti-Corruption Agencies
ACP	African, Caribbean and Pacific
AfCFTA	African Continental Free Trade Area
AfDB	African Development Bank
AFRICOM	Africa Command
AGOA	African Growth Opportunity Act
AMU	Arab Maghreb Union
APF	African Peace Facility
APSA	African Peace and Security Architecture
AQAP	Al-Qaeda in the Arabian Peninsula
AQIM	Al-Qaeda in the Islamic Maghreb
ARII	Africa Regional Integration Index
ASF	African Standby Force
ATA	Agricultural Transformation Agenda
AU	African Union
AUPSC	Africa Union Peace and Security Council
BHTs	Boko Haram Terrorists
BOA	Bank of Agriculture
BOI	Bank of Industry
CAADP	Comprehensive Africa Agriculture Development Programme
CADSP	Common African Defence and Security Policy
CEN-SAD	Community of Sahel-Saharan States
CET	Common External Tariff
CFA	Communauté Financière Africaine
COMESA	Common Market for Eastern and Southern Africa
CPI	Corruption Perception Index

CPIA	Country Policy and Institutional Assessment
CT-COIN	Counter-Terrorism and Counter-Insurgency
DRC	Democratic Republic of Congo
EAC	East African Community
EALA	East African Legislative Assembly
EASF	East African Standby Force
ECCAS	Economic Community of Central African States
ECLAC	Economic Commission for Latin America and the Caribbean
ECOMOG	ECOWAS Ceasefire Monitoring Group
ECOWAS	Economic Community of West African States
ECSC	European Coal and Steel Community
EDF	European Development Fund
EEBC	Eritrea Ethiopia Border Commission
EEC	European Economic Community
EPLF	Eritrean People's Liberation Front
EPRDF	Ethiopian People's Revolutionary Democratic Front
EPRP	Ethiopian People's Revolutionary Party
ESF	ECOWAS Standby Force
ETLS	ECOWAS Trade Liberalisation Scheme
EU	European Union
FDI	Foreign Direct Investment
FFP	Fund for Peace
FGDP	Federal Gross Domestic Product
FOCAC	Forum on China-Africa Cooperation
FOMAC	*Force Multinationale de l'Afrique Centrale*
FSI	Fragile State Index
G7	Group of 7
GDP	Gross Domestic Products
GLR	Great Lakes Region
GNI	Gross National Income
HDI	Human Development Index
HIPC	Heavily Indebted Poor Countries
HRW	Human Rights Watch
ICGLR	International Conference on the Great Lakes Region
ICT	Information and Communications Technology
IDA	International Development Association
IDPs	Internally Displaced Persons
IEDs	Improvised Explosive Devices
IGAD	Intergovernmental Authority on Development
IMF	International Monetary Fund
ISIS	Islamic State in Iraq and Syria
ISWA	Islamic State in West Africa
JAES	Joint Africa EU Strategy

LCB	Lake Chad Basin
LCBC	Lake Chad Basin Commission
LDCs	Least Developed Countries
LIC	Low Income Country
MDAs	Ministries, Departments and Agencies
MDGs	Millennium Development Goals
MIC	Middle Income Country
MJTF	Multinational Joint Task Force
MNCs	Multinational Corporations
NAOs	National Authorisation Offices
NARC	North African Regional Capability
NATO	North Atlantic Treaty Organisation
NEDC	North East Development Commission
NEEDS	Economic Empowerment and Development Strategy
NIRP	Nigeria Industrial Revolution Plan
NLM	National Liberation Movement
NNPC	Nigerian National Petroleum Corporation
NPIRD	National Policy on Integrated Rural Development
NPLF	National Patriotic Front of Liberia
NSIA	Nigerian Sovereign Investment Authority
OAU	Organisation of African Unity
OCTs	Overseas Countries and Territories
ODA	Overseas Development Aid
OECD	Organisation for Economic Cooperation and Development
PEDI	Presidential Economic Diversification Initiative
PFI	Presidential Fertiliser Initiative
PSC	Peace and Security Council
PWD	People with Disability
REC	Regional Economic Community
ROM	Result Oriented Monitoring
ROO	Rules of Origin
RPF	Rwandan Patriotic Front
RUF	Revolutionary United Front
SADC	Southern African Development Community
SALW	Small Arms and Light Weapons
SAP	Structural Adjustment Programme
SDGs	Sustainable Development Goals
SEZ	Special Economic Zones
SMEs	Small and Medium Size Enterprises
SSA	Sub-Saharan Africa
SSF	SADC Standby Force
TCC	Troop Contributing Country
TFs	Trust Funds

TI	Transparency International
TSA	Treasury Single Account
TSCTP	Trans-Saharan Counterterrorism Partnership
UAE	United Arab Emirate
UN	United Nations
UNCTAD	United Nations Conference on Trade and Development
UNDP	United Nations Development Programme
UNGA	United Nations General Assembly
UNODC	United Nations Office on Drugs and Crime
UNSC	United Nations Security Council
USA	United States of America
USSR	Union of Soviet Socialist Republics
WAEMU	West African Economic and Monetary Union
WTTC	World Travel and Tourism Council

List of Figures

List of Tables

PART I

Conceptual and Contextual Background

CHAPTER 1

Exploring the Governance, Security and Development Nexus: Africa Rising?

Kenneth Omeje

Introduction

This edited book is concerned with the nexus between governance, security and development in Africa. Specifically, it is conceived to interrogate the debate and politics of "Africa rising," a contemporary catchphrase for what many proponents perceive as the fast-moving economic, development and governance transformations of the continent. From all intents and purposes, the discourses on "Africa rising" presuppose the occurrence of a planned, sustained and systematic change in the governance, security and development landscape of the continent capable of empirically redefining and repositioning Africa away from its vulnerable subaltern status in the global political economy. This book offers a searching critique and assessment of the Africa rising discourses. Has Africa been rising as many proponents of the euphoric discourses have claimed? If indeed Africa is rising, how much of the impact is reflected in the living conditions and well-being of the citizens? Is Africa uniformly rising or are there just a few countries on the rise while the rest stagnate or

K. Omeje (✉)
Manifold Crown Research and Training Consult, Bradford, UK
e-mail: komeje@manifoldcrown.org

K. Omeje (ed.), *The Governance, Security and Development Nexus*,
https://doi.org/10.1007/978-3-030-49348-6_1

even probably regress? Is there any osmotic resonance between the rising African states and their "non-performing" counterparts? Using a nexus of context-specific, regional and international data, the various chapters of this book have been structured to shed light on these intellectual puzzles with a view to enunciating policy-relevant visions, interventions and strategies on how Africa can arise or rise sustainably.

Africa entered the 2000 millennium as a heavily beleaguered continent marked by a post-colonial history of massive governance, security and development deficits. Decades of states' policy failures and neopatrimonial plunder in a bunch of dysfunctional neo-colonial economies that are overly dependent on production and export of primary commodities have exposed many countries on the continent to an erratic balance of payment deficits, rising external borrowing and debt crisis, skewed and unsustainable development, massive youth unemployment, high poverty levels and ultimately armed rebellion and civil wars. In its worst post-independence economic crisis of the 1980s and 1990s, the situation was evidently exacerbated by the inappropriate therapy of Structural Adjustment Programme (SAP) foisted on most countries of Sub-Saharan Africa by the World Bank, IMF and the US Treasury Department, three powerful global financial institutions based in Washington and altogether known as the Washington Consensus. SAP placed emphasis on stringent credit financing that attracted conditionalities, such as huge debt service obligations, currency devaluation, dismantling of state's social development obligations, privatization of public enterprises and massive deregulation of the economy (Dibua 2006; Moghalu 2014). The unbearable external debt overhang and debt service obligations associated with the SAP regime bankrupted African economies and ruptured their political systems. At the turn of the last century, Sub-Saharan Africa's twenty years economic and political crisis had generated about two dozen armed conflicts of varied intensities which prompted the London-based magazine *The Economist* to portray Africa in its May 2000 edition as "The Hopeless Continent." The latter was the controversial title of the magazine's cover story. Despite the apparent hopelessness of the African long-drawn-out crisis, many African intellectuals, policy practitioners and statesmen were visibly offended by this pessimistic castigation of the continent as "the hopeless continent."

Fast-forward to 2005, the security and economic development conditions and prospects of many hitherto marooned African countries were looking a lot more optimistic. Many warring parties of the 1980s and

1990s in countries devastated by armed conflicts had laid down their arms or been defeated in the battlefield to make way for a return to peace. The civil wars and armed conflicts in Liberia, Sierra Leone, Cote d'Ivoire, Angola, Mozambique, Uganda, Southern Senegal and Rwanda were all brought to an end. Africa emerged from two decades of war and political turbulence and profited massively from a long boom in commodity prices as well as peace, improved governance and a better investment climate (Grynberg 2016). In recent years, significant de-escalation of hostilities relative to the peak years of war has occurred in some of the tinderbox areas marked by persistent armed violence, notably Northern Mali, South Sudan, Libya, Darfur-Sudan, Eastern Congo, Central African Republic, Somalia and North-East Nigeria.

Since the 2000s, liberal democracy has spread on the continent like wildfire, bringing an end to diverse shades of civilian and military dictatorships. Through the political conditionalities of SAP, a strong impression was created in the late-1980s by the leading international financial institutions (World Bank and IMF) bankrolling economic recovery on the continent that dismantling authoritarian governance structures and replacing them with liberal democratic institutions (notably multi-party electoral system, parliamentary structures and debate, independent judiciary, free press and respect for human rights and civil societies) would facilitate economic transformation, growth and development. Instead of the Bretton Woods institutions accepting responsibility for drawing Africa into deeper crises through the introduction of SAP, the World Bank produced a document entitled *From Crisis to Sustainable Growth* in 1989, in which they blamed lack of good governance and policy reform as the cause of economic crisis and lack of development in Africa in the 1980s (Ndlovu-Gatsheni 2018: 29). By the 1990s, the ideological prescription of political reform as a prerequisite for economic development canvassed by the Bretton Woods institutions had gained strong currency in international development quarters and among African civil society organisations leading to a united pressure on African governments to embrace liberal democratic institutions and practices. By courtesy of this induced pressure to democratize the political space as necessary precondition for economic growth, Africa witnessed a rapid resurgence, spread and consolidation of the Western neo-liberal model of development throughout the continent. It is this neo-liberal model of development, which is essentially rooted in post-Keynesian economic theories of the relationships between monetary policies, growth, trade and development, that takes the credit for what has been popularised as "Africa rising." To put it more bluntly, Africa is ultimately rising due to the final conquest and consolidation of the Western neo-liberal model of development throughout the continent. This is the disguised ideological underpinning of the Africa rising narrative.

According to IMF data, between 2008 and 2017, a number of African countries such as Ethiopia, Rwanda, Ghana, Tanzania, Mozambique, DRC, Zambia, Uganda, Niger and Burkina Faso recorded an average annual GDP growth rate of between 5.6 and 10%, with Ethiopia recording an impressive growth rate of roughly 10%, making it the world's second fastest growing economy over the 10 year period (Global Finance 2018). With this fantastic economic growth performance, it seemed that Sub-Saharan Africa (SSA) was finally witnessing what in mainstream modernisation paradigm could be termed "the preconditions for take-off" if not the actual "take off of self-sustaining economic growth." According to the chief proponent of this economic growth theory, Walt Whitman Rostow, "take-off is an industrial revolution, tied directly to radical changes in methods of production, having their decisive consequences over a relatively short period of time" (cited in Goalstone 2007: 216). The term "take off" implies three things in Rostow's conceptions of five stages of modernization-oriented growth: "first, the proportion of investment to national income must rise from 5% to 10% and more so as to outstrip the likely population growth; secondly, the period must be relatively short so that it should show the characteristics of an economic revolution; and thirdly, it must culminate in self-sustaining and self-generating economic growth" (Guru, n.d.).

Compared to Sub-Saharan Africa, the seemingly more insulated Arab Maghreb Union countries of North Africa had for decades enjoyed better economic performances and political stability in spite of their repressive autocratic regimes, leading many analysts to postulate that the Arabs had a pathological antipathy to democracy, and at any rate, had no need for democratic reforms to achieve far-reaching and sustainable economic and political development (cf. *The Economist* 2014, 5 July; Monshipouri 2014). In the aftermath of the 9/11 2001 terrorist attacks in America, the US government nonetheless significantly increased its international development assistance to North African and Middle Eastern NGOs working for de-radicalisation of Islam, women empowerment and sundry political reforms short of regime change (Hamid 2011).

When the Arab Spring broke out in December 2010, overthrowing three longstanding dictatorships in the North African Maghreb region

(Tunisia, Egypt and Libya) and unravelling the dominant discourses of governance and stability in the Arab world, the immediate reaction to the "revolution" was a mix of cautious euphoria and hope that the youth-led clamour for change would almost certainly break the limits to political and economic development in the Arab world.

It was little wonder that while the Arab Spring still unfolded in North Africa and the Middle East, *The Economist* magazine took a courageous step to atone for its sin of over ten years by publishing an optimistic narrative of Africa in December 2011 with a cover page story titled "The Hopeful Continent: Africa Rising." This rather bullish narrative which was welcomed by many African policy experts and sympathisers around the world chronicled the fast-moving positive changes of the preceding decade on the continent, remarking that:

> After decades of slow growth, Africa has a real chance to follow in the footsteps of Asia. ... Over the past decade six of the world's ten fastest growing countries were African. In eight of the past ten years, Africa has grown faster than East Asia, including Japan. ... The commodities boom is partly responsible. In 2000–08 around a quarter of Africa's growth came from higher revenues from natural resources. ... But the growth also has a lot to do with the manufacturing and service economies that African countries are beginning to develop. (*The Economist* 2011, 3 December)

Clearly, as a philosophical vision "Africa rising" would unmistakably excite most Afro-optimists, but many well-meaning optimists would more significantly like to see the vision translated to evidence-based forms, and not championed as figments of the imagination and bare-faced exaggerations of protagonists. Africa rising in concrete sustainable forms would be a welcome agenda that holds promise to lift over half of the African population from the trap of poverty and hopelessness into the safety nets of the middle class. In the African context, the middle class has been defined by the African Development Bank (AfDB) as those with a per capita daily consumption level of $2–$20 [further subcategorised into "floating class" with a consumption level of $2–$4 per day; "lower middle class" with a consumption level of $4–$10 per day, and "upper middle class" with a consumption level of $10–$20 per day] (AfDB 2011: 2; Wadongo 2014). The AfDB's threefold conception of the African middle class is similar to the threefold classification of the middle class in the United States based on income levels by the US News and World Report, among other similar studies (see Livingstone 2015). According to the US Report, the American middle class comprises:

1. **Working Class**: People in this group typically have blue-collar jobs – the kind where you work with your hands – and are paid on an hourly rather than a salaried basis. They also tend to have low levels of education.
2. **Lower-Middle Class**: The article defines this group as "lower-level, white-collar workers": office workers with lower income and little authority. It says most of them have college degrees, but not advanced degrees, and their income ranges from $32,500 to $60,000 ($33,670 to $62,150 in 2015 dollars).
3. **Upper-Middle Class**: This group, also called the professional class, fills the upper ranks of offices. Workers in this group often have post-graduate degrees and can earn as much as $150,000 ($155,390 in 2015 dollars). (ibid.)

Interestingly, the AfDB's seminal research found that the size of the African middle class has tripled over a space of three decades to 313 million which equates to 34% of the population or roughly "one in three Africans" (AfDB 2011; *African Business* 2015, 8 September). In a 2017 Report, AfDB estimated Africa's so-called expanding middle class to be 350 million (AfDB 2017: 29). The AfDB claims particularly reinforce the viewpoint of "Africa Rising" protagonists and their narrative that the continent has "a bulging middle class" with a surge in consumer demand and promising consumption power. In his masterful critique of the AfDB report, Patrick Bond (2018: 478) describes the Bank's claim that "one in three Africans is middle class" "a hoax-type claim," arguing that the consumption levels of $2–$20 per day depicted by the bank as middle class are all "poverty levels in most African cities, whose price levels leave them among the world's most expensive."

The Protagonist School: Neo-Liberal Political Economy

The neo-liberal political economy school of Africa rising is an off-shoot of the brand of post-Keynesian economics promoted by advocates and sympathisers of the Western development orthodoxy who share the triumphalist narrative that the political conditionalities of SAP and the external aid-driven post-SAP development interventions in Africa have yielded fantastic dividends. Most of the post-SAP development interventions in Africa approved by the Bretton Woods institutions and supported by the West are mainly focused on pro-growth policies, conditional debt relief within the Heavily Indebted Poor Countries (HIPC) initiative, promoting private sector investment and partnerships, and market-oriented pro-poor reforms particularly those linked to the defunct Millennium Development Goals (MDGs) of 2000–2015. MDGs were replaced in January 2016 by Sustainable Development Goals (SDGs, 2016–2030), with its 17 points agenda and prolific targets. The idea of sustainable development which tries to reconcile the demands of economic growth with concerns of environment protection and human security needs of ordinary people have become a popular mantra since the Rio global Earth Summit of 1992. Having said that, at a more philosophical and ideological level, as Tony Binns and Etienne Nel (2018: 275) have argued, the hegemonic neo-liberal discourse that have fundamentally shaped Africa's position in the world economy and determined its future prospects is all part of the neo-liberal internationalism championed from the early 1980s by the then UK Prime Minister Margaret Thatcher and American President Ronald Reagan.

Evaluating Africa's development performance in 2010, the World Bank (2010: 1) reported that Africa had in the preceding five years recorded acceleration in growth; declining poverty, child mortality and HIV/AIDS rates; success in ICT especially mobile phone penetration, a rising private sector that increasingly attracts investment flows at rates higher than official development assistance, as well as a high rate of returns on investments that is among the highest in the world. Putting all these factors together, the World Bank (2010: 1) concluded that Africa could be on the brink of an economic take-off, much like China was 30 years ago, and India 20 years ago. To sustain and scale up the momentum for economic take-off, the World Bank pledged to mobilise the development community to support a "Marshall Plan for Africa," aimed at relaxing the financing constraint to Africa to reach the MDGs (and beyond), ... and to use all possible partnership platforms (such as the G-20) to promote the idea of "Africa as an investment proposition"—a promising investment opportunity for both public and private actors (World Bank 2010: 13). Even though the World Bank was cautious in its report not to take open credit for its Africa rising narrative, the Bank unmistakeably used the report to reassert itself as the "essential partner" and "linchpin to African development," "willing and ready to exercise its comparative advantage," particularly with regard to promoting private sector linkages, strategic partnerships, technical knowledge and development financing (*The Guardian* 2010).

Besides its 2010 Report heralding a rising Africa, the World Bank has published many other studies that more or less buttress the narrative that neo-liberal policies have turned African economies around, the most prominent perhaps being the Bank's annual Country Policy and Institutional Assessment (CPIA) report that is used in determining African countries that are eligible for support from the International Development Association (IDA), the concessional financing arm of the World Bank Group. Fundamentally, this report analyses the annual progress made by IDA-eligible African countries in strengthening the quality of their development policies and institutional frameworks to enhance expected outcomes. "The CPIA evaluates countries on a scale of 1–6 (with 6 as the highest and 1 as the lowest) using 16 indicators in four areas to determine a country's final score. These areas include economic management, structural policies, policies for social inclusion and equity, and public sector management and institutions" (World Bank 2016).

The CPIA Report published by the World Bank in July 2018, which is based on a performance assessment of 38 Sub-Saharan Africa countries reveals the following reassuring portrait:

- The average quality of policies and institutions in Sub-Saharan Africa's International Development Association (IDA)–eligible countries was broadly unchanged in 2017, representing a shift from the deterioration observed in the previous year. A more favourable global environment in 2017 eased policy constraints, providing countries with space to implement reforms. The regional Country Policy and Institutional Assessment (CPIA) score was 3.1.
- Reflecting an encouraging trend, nearly 30 percent more countries strengthened their policy and institutional quality in 2017 compared with 2016, and 40 percent fewer countries had a weakening trend. The downside movement in aggregate scores was concentrated in fragile countries, attesting to the difficult enabling environment in fragile countries and the high risks of conflict, commodity price shocks, or climate threat that they face, which can translate into rapid deterioration in policy performance.
- Country-level policy and institutional quality varied widely across the region. Rwanda continued to lead at the regional level and globally, with a CPIA score of 4.0. Other countries at the high end of

> the regional score range were Senegal, with a score of 3.8, closely followed by Cape Verde, Kenya, and Tanzania, all with scores of 3.7. Overall, slightly more than half (20) of the region's IDA borrowers posted relatively weak performance — that is, a score of 3.2 or lower (World Bank Group 2018: 4).

It is interesting to note that an African country Rwanda has for many years held the best performance in the World Bank's global CPIA scores. The AfDB publishes a biannual CPIA (published annually between 2012 and 2016). With limited originality and preponderantly imitative of the World Bank's assessment, the CPIA of the AfDB is "designed to assess the performance of countries' policy and institutional frameworks in terms of their capacity to ensure the efficient utilization of resources for achieving sustainable and inclusive growth" (AfDB 2018: 3).

Without doubt, it is in the strategic interest of the World Bank to portray an image of a rising Africa given the massive reputational battering and damage it has suffered in the developing world where the Bank is essentially regarded as a Western front for economic recolonisation and development reversal, especially through the notorious role it played in the ill-fated SAPs. Therefore, regardless of any empirical validity it might have, something that is highly questionable, the World Bank's narrative, cannot be dissociated from the Bank's politics of striving to acquit itself from all the damage its policies and programmes have been credited with causing in Africa over the years, and if possible to see how it can earn some credit for any post-SAP economic reconstruction and development discernibly reported in any country on the continent.

To buttress the neo-liberal narrative of a rising Africa beyond the World Bank's strategic claim, influential publications, international conferences and seminars have blossomed like Spring flowers showcasing the bests of the "African renaissance" in arts, music, poetry, fashion, governance, entrepreneurship, development and tourist attraction. Many promotional advertisements, special documentaries and editorials have been featured in international media such as CNN, BBC, Al Jazeera, CNC World, *The Economist, New African Magazine* and *Wall Street Journal*, highlighting different countries of Africa as new favourable destinations for Foreign Direct Investment (FDI) and tourism. Reputable Western public relations firms such as the London-based Bell Pottinger and Washington-based Levick have been hired by African businesses and governments for international reputation laundering and to promote a favourable image that African states, firms and business community are ready for business (Wilson 2014; *The Guardian* 2017, 10 July; 2017, 5 September). The enormous opportunities and prospects for doing business in Africa are vigorously promoted by "investment promotion agencies" to eclipse all the hitherto acknowledged deficits and obstacles.

Renowned global business consultant and University of Texas' Professor of Marketing Vijay Mahajan in his highly acclaimed book titled *Africa Rising: How 900 Million African Consumers Offer More Than You Think* published in 2008 eulogises Africa as "a remarkable market-place with massive needs and surprising buying power." Writing with a density of anecdotal and ethnographic insight, Mahajan (2008) tells the riveting story of how home-grown entrepreneurs and global companies are succeeding in Africa, even in the most challenging locations, specifically detailing how Indian and Chinese investors and the African Diaspora are extraordinarily driving investments and development on the continent. Mahajan argues, quite controversially, that the average Gross National Income (GNI) per capita across Africa has already surpassed that of India, and that a dozen African countries have a higher GNI per capita than China, thereby demonstrating the far-reaching investment and consumer opportunities available in Africa, especially for multinational companies facing shrinking profits from other emerging markets in the aftermath of the global financial crisis (ibid.).

In 2010, the McKinsey Global Institute (MGI) published a report in which they described the potential and progress of African economies as "lions on the move," (World Economic Forum 2016), implying that the world is about to witness the "Africa Lions" which could predictably surpass the "Asian Tigers." Reflecting on some of the well-known existential and circumstantial challenges, the World Economic Forum (2016) argues that despite the collapse of global commodity prices which has adversely affected many countries of Sub-Saharan Africa and the political shocks that have slowed growth in North Africa, "Africa's economic lions" are still moving forward, affirming that the continent is still on the rise.

With these interesting developments, it seems an opportune time to take a strong analytical stock of the "Africa Rising" discourses. Has Africa really been sufficiently positioned to rise and is it indeed rising? Are we already witnessing the "African Tigers" (akin to the Asian Tigers) or "the African Lions," and if so, who are they and how are they performing? What are the empirical indicators that Africa is rising or perhaps the converse indicators that as opposed to rising, Africa is apparently convulsing, crawling and intermittently slumbering? If indeed Africa is rising, what can the region do to maximise and expand the benefits of such a positive transformation to ensure that no sections of its over one billion people disproportionally distributed into 54 sovereign states are left out? This edited book argues that some core issues of governance must be addressed to expand growth and development in a sustainable way that will not predictably unravel security.

Hopes have long waned and even evaporated about the Arab Spring in North Africa, trends that have apparently excluded the region from the profile of most discussions on "Africa Rising." The expectation in 2011 that the "People Revolution" was going to generate a significant transformation in the region has long been replaced by the grimmer reality that the revolution was wasted and has practically left the region worse off. In Libya, the "Arab Spring Revolution" backfired and rapidly fragmented into militia insurgency and fratricidal war; in Egypt the revolution was hijacked and stolen by a status quo-oriented faction of the military, while in Tunisia the Arab Spring has literally opened a Pandora's Box of reactionary Islam, terrorist infestation and simmering discourses of anti-Westernisation. The Arab Spring has impacted negatively on the economic performance of the affected countries. The economies of Egypt, Libya and Tunisia did not grow at all between 2010 and 2015, in stark contrast to average annual growth among the three economies of 4.8% in the previous decade; the annual rate of productivity growth in the Arab Spring countries fell from 1.7 to 0.6% (World Economic Forum 2016).

The Critical Political Economy School

The critical political economy school in the African rising debate spans from the centre-right to the left of the ideological spectrum, but fundamentally are critical of the euphoric narrative that post-SAP neo-liberal development intervention policies in Africa have generated internal seismic transformations capable of repositioning the continent in the global political economy. A leftist variant of the critical political economy school attributes African development setbacks to the economic structures, political institutions and persistent conflicts rooted in colonial legacies (Taylor 2014; Ndlovu-Gatsheni 2018). Other mixed perspectives that may not strictly emphasise colonial legacy tend to blame the neo-liberal model of development foisted by the West on African post-colonial states, the obfuscating structures of international political economy and the bad policy choices made by the states' governing elites for the unsatisfactory political, economic and social outcomes, with the result that neo-liberal top-down policies seem not to have benefitted the bulk of African populations (Lyons and Jolley 2018; Binns and Nel 2018: 283). Many proponents are of the view that the neo-liberal export-oriented strategy designed to keep most African economies as a peripheral appendage in the international division of labour dependent on primary products export, especially minerals and oil, have done enormous damage to genuine and beneficial popular development (Bond 2018: 477; Ndlovu-Gatsheni 2018: 31).

Critics of the "Africa Rising" narrative argue that much of the "over-hyped" economic growth statistics is fuelled by the exploitation of oil and gas reserves, investment in telecommunication industry, and infrastructural development, and that most of the profits and benefits from this growth go into the pockets of investors, shareholders and government officials with the result that the living conditions of average citizens have not necessarily improved and poverty levels remain palpably high (Wadongo 2014; Taylor 2014). A pan-African NGO formed in 2016 known as *Africans Rising for Justice, Peace and Dignity* or *Africans Rising* for short has used online and social media platforms to actively challenge the narrative of Africa Rising as a story of "uninclusive development." According to *Africans Rising* (2016), the increases in GDP of some selected African countries brandished to celebrate the economic growth story of Africa portray a growth story that is in many instances characterised by the devastation of Africa's natural environment, the displacement of multiple communities, major land grabs and massive illicit financial flows that deprive the government the necessary resources to ensure service delivery. "The celebration of this economic growth story," laments the regional NGO, "takes place while the majority of people on the continent continue to suffer marginalisation, deep poverty and effects of the rise in inequality" (Wadongo 2014).

In his damning critique, leading international strategist and political economist Kingsley Moghalu (2014: 6) lampoons the Africa Rising narrative as an exaggerated bubble, asserting that despite the economic growth hype, Africa's share of world trade is a minute 3%, with less than 5% of FDI flows. According to global investment trends published by UNCTAD in 2018, Africa has disproportionately continued to receive the least FDI flows among the developing regions netting a share of

$42 billion in 2017, a paltry share when compared to the FDI flows of $476 billion to the developing economies of Asia and the FDI flows of $151 billion to Latin America and the Caribbean (UNCTAD 2018: 4 and 38). The top FDI host economies in Africa in 2017 are Egypt, Nigeria, Ghana and Mozambique, Ethiopia and Morocco—most of them commodity-exporting economies. Moghalu (2014: 6) further argues that:

> In 2010, the combined GDP of the 54 countries that make up the *"celebrated rising"* continent of Africa was just barely equal to that of India, and just 100,000 individuals accounted for 80% of Africa's GDP, while the continent's share of global poverty rose by 8% between 1999 and 2008. The GDP of the entire Sub-Saharan Africa, including South Africa, is just about equal to that of Belgium or that of metropolitan Chicago, a city in the United States. And all the electricity produced in Sub-Saharan Africa, half of which is, in fact, produced by South Africa, is equivalent to that of Spain, which has 20 times fewer people than Africa.

With a population of 1.2 billion, cumulative GDP of the 54 African countries in 2018 is about $2.5 trillion (AU 2019), whereas the GDP of the US State of California which has a population of 40 million is $2.8 trillion (Kiersz 2019).

In his critique, British Professor of International Relations and African Politics Ian Taylor (2014: 3–4) observes that many of the stellar economic indicators in the Africa Rising narrative have been possibly exaggerated so as to lure investors, and this is emblematically revealed by the fact that UNCTAD reported that Africa's total foreign investment inflow in 2011 was $42.7 billion, but the London-based accounting firm Ernest & Young put the figure at more than $75 billion; coincidentally Ernest & Young at the same time opened their new Africa Global Tax Desk in Beijing which offered Chinese companies a helping hand in their investments in Africa. Taylor is of the view that the nature of growth and investment promoted by the politics of "Africa Rising" deepens Africa's inveterate and deleterious terms of integration within the global political economy—terms which continue to be characterised by external dominance and socially damaging forms of accumulation (ibid.: 4).

Given the enormous excitement, fuss and controversy the discourses have generated, the need to rigorously interrogate the debate and politics of "Africa rising" has never been more urgent. If indeed Africa is rising, how much of the impact is reflected in the living conditions and well-being of the citizens? Is Africa uniformly rising or are there just a few countries on the rise while the rest stagnate or even probably regress? Is there any osmotic resonance between the rising African states and their "non-performing" counterparts? This book is conceived to shed light on these intellectual puzzles with a view to enunciating policy-relevant visions, interventions and strategies on how Africa can arise or rise sustainably.

The Governance, Security and Development Nexus

Areas of Progress

It can hardly be disputed that compared to the massive economic and political development setbacks of the 1980s through the 1990s, Africa has made some progress in the new millennium. As already highlighted in the foregoing sections, Africa's progress since the early 2000s could be seen in at least three broad interrelated aspects: security, governance and development. In the security sector, the continent has witnessed a successful resolution of many civil wars and armed conflicts that engulfed different countries in the 1980s and 1990s, and the rebuilding of state institutions and reconciliation of diverse hitherto bitterly divided communities and states. One of the most intriguing post-war reconciliations in contemporary African history is the restoration of peace and normal relations in July 2018 between protracted arch-rivals Ethiopia and Eritrea. The peace treaty between Ethiopia and Eritrea was made possible by the emergence in April 2018 of a new dynamic Prime Minister in Ethiopia Dr Abiy Ahmed who took bold steps to reach out to the Eritrean President Isaias Afwerki, offering to implement the UN-backed peace agreements that ended two years of trench warfare between the two countries (1998–2000), including the controversial ruling on the location of the border, without preconditions (*The Economist* 2018, 17 July).

Another interesting development in the African security sector is the systematic reformation of African regional institutions (the African Union and the various regional economic communities) which has enabled them to more effectively take on security challenges in member states through robust interventionist actions, notably peacekeeping deployment. By courtesy of the new interventionist disposition and action of the African regional institutions, a number of major political conflicts have been ended or averted in several countries (sometimes with the help of the international community) including countries like Burundi, Guinea Bissau, Cote d'Ivoire, Mali, The Gambia and The Central African Republic.

In the area of political governance, Africa has made substantial progress in the stabilisation of countries emerging from war to avoid a relapse to hostilities, as well as in facilitating transition from dictatorships and war to civilian democratic rule. The majority of African countries have made the transition from dictatorship and war to multi-party civilian democracy since the 1990s with the result that there are fewer than six surviving unelected governments in Africa today. There are no doubt concerns about the contextual relevance, quality and impact of the type of democracy (western-style liberal democracies) that have become dominant in Africa. Adetula (2011: 11) has argued that the democratic experiments in several African countries have recorded unimpressive results despite the introduction of neo-liberal constitutions, legislatures and electoral systems with the result that most of them have been labelled by the west as "incomplete democratic transitions" and "illiberal democracies." Some scholars have argued that liberal democracy is infeasible in Africa because of cultural incompatibility—an allusion that foisting liberal democracy on indigenous political institutions in Africa has profound pathological effects (Chabal and Daloz 1999; Ellis 2005).

There are other scholars like French political scientists Jean-François Bayart (1996) and Daniel Bach (2011) who have blamed the dysfunctioning of African liberal democracies on the pervasiveness of neopatrimonial institutions and systems of governance in many post-colonial states. In political science literature, experts use the concept of neopatrimonialism to describe the confusion observable in many developing countries between the public and private spheres; between public office and the office holder in a typical state characterised by a paradoxical coexistence of formal legal-bureaucratic institutions of the modern states and the informal affective practices of indigenous societies. The theory further argues that the African governing elite use public bureaucratic institutions as a façade, while in reality actual political authority for the day-to-day running of the state lies with a small oligarchy controlled by a ruling strongman or network of strongmen whose support bases are sometimes rooted in their primordial groups and communities. Bach (2011) has re-theorised the familiar concept of neopatrimonialism by classifying it into two forms, the regulated neopatrimonialism and predatory neopatrimonialism. According to Bach, the regulated neopatrimonial state is characterised by a combination of personal rule, elite co-optation and a policy of re-distributing resources to ensure ethno-regional balance. Under regulated neopatrimonialism, there is a significant institutionalisation of the state bureaucracy that enables the government to formulate and pursue well-meaning development policies and programmes. The examples of regulated neopatrimonial states given by Bach in Africa are all early post-independence regimes: Kenya under Jomo Kenyatta and Cote d'Iviore under Félix Houphouët-Boigny. On the other hand, predatory neopatrimonialism is a ruthless model where there is extreme personalization of the state and looting of its resources by the governing elite, with the result that there is a loss of any sense of public space or public policy (Bach 2011: 279). The example of predatory neopatrimonialism provided by Bach is former Zaire under Mobutu Sese Seko. Predatory neopatrimonialism is profoundly anti-development, anti-democracy and a fundamental threat to the coherence and internal sovereignty of the state.

Commenting on the partial infeasibility of liberal democracy in Africa, the former Ghanaian President John Mahama has argued that dictatorships and authoritarian systems of government are needed in some African countries to facilitate their development as democracy is "an expensive ritual" (referring to the enormous cost of holding periodic elections) that "encourages slow decision- making processes" (*General News* 2017, 3 November). Despite the controversy surrounding the suitability of liberal democracy in Africa and the challenges of democratic consolidation it is observable that a few stable liberal democracies have emerged on the continent notably in Botswana, Mauritius, Senegal, Tanzania, Zambia, South Africa and Ghana. There are also some emerging democracies with variants of the Asian developmental state model and some African "indigenous palaver" colouration. The latter is typified by the democracy models in Rwanda and Ethiopia, to a lesser extent (albeit, Prime Minister Abiy Ahmed seems keen to reform the Ethiopian state along a neo-liberal trajectory).

In the area of development, two key aspects of progress have been reported, economic growth and infrastructural development. While economic growth has been mostly tied to primary commodity exports (including solid minerals and crude oil), infrastructural development has been largely associated with foreign aid, especially aid from sources outside the traditional western capitalist economy, notably China. Since the establishment of the Forum on China–Africa Cooperation (FOCAC) in October 2000 to strengthen development cooperation and trade between the two sides, China has advanced progressively to become Africa's largest infrastructural development funder and trading partner. Between 2000 and 2014, Chinese banks, contractors and the government loaned more than $86 billion to Africa, about 61% of which were used for infrastructure construction, 16% are for industrial development and a small portion of the remaining allocations was channelled to health, general budget support and education (Zhang 2016; Albert 2017). Over the same period it is estimated that China funded about 1700 official assistance projects in 51 African countries (only the four countries that did not have diplomatic relations with China—Gambia, Swaziland, Burkina Faso and São Tomé and Príncipe—were left out) (ibid.; The Conversation 2016). Similarly, over the same 14 years period, merchandise exports from Sub-Saharan Africa to China (mostly primary commodities) increased from $4.0 billion to $68.1 billion, before decreasing significantly because of the fall in commodity prices (Langdon et al. 2018: 543). By the end of 2018, SSA's debt to China stood at about US$154 billion (Green 2019; World Bank 2019a). Brookings has criticised Chinese massive loans to Africa on account of being "lent generally on commercial terms," arguing that "in a poor governance environment, projects are less likely to proceed well and to generate growth, creating repayment difficulties" (World Economy 2017).

Progress and Contradictions: Empirical Trends and Concluding Remarks

Generally, while many analysts would accept that progress has been made in various key sectors and probably overall, what is however contestable is how significant, widespread and sustainable the recorded progress has been. There are no easy answers to this puzzle because of the fundamental differences in the worldviews of contestants and pundits concerning the path to genuine and sustainable development, as well as how the latter interfaces with the imperatives of governance and security.

In the highly inveighed but resilient neoclassical economistic approaches, there is an overwhelming emphasis on achieving and maintaining economic growth with the assumption that if national output grew faster than the population, income per capita would increase and the well-being of people would improve (Langdon et al. 2018: 65). To achieve growth, policies that aim to reduce taxes on businesses and the wealthy, encourage domestic and foreign savings, capital accumulation and investments, and as well as enhance efficient technology have to be actively promoted. The real conundrum in this assumption is the view that growth is a necessary and sufficient condition for sustainable development and that issues of unemployment, education and skills training, income redistribution, poverty reduction and the likes will logically be sorted by sustaining growth. In other words, growth has the capacity and elasticity to generate a paradigm of trickle-down economics beneficial to all and sundry. The trickle-down economic theory was heavily influenced by the economic thoughts of the nineteenth-century French economist Jean-Baptiste Say, among other eminent thinkers.

For proponents, trickle-down theory is based on the premise that within an economy, giving tax breaks to the top earners makes them more likely to earn more and to invest their surplus money in productive activities or to spend more of their time in high paying productive ventures, which ultimately reinvigorates the economy, creates jobs and generates more tax revenues from all taxable income earners (Mcgrath 2009). In this way, it is believed that tax breaks for the rich fosters a supply-side driven economic growth pattern (increased outputs and production) that benefits all through a trickle-down logic. Hence, as growth policies stimulate supply, demand logically follows. This was the dominant economic growth model of the President Ronald Reagan years in the 1980s and George W. Bush in the early 2000s in the United States, which also had resonance with many developing countries because of the global influence of the US government and the Washington Consensus it unofficially heads. Writing from a Keynesian approach (the theory credited to the erudite British economist John Maynard Keynes), critics of trickle-down economics argue that governments should rather promote consumer demand (as opposed to supply-side entrepreneurial production which ultimately results in overproduction) because when people consume more they create more jobs and production (Mcgrath 2009). An influential school of post-Keynesian economics amplifies the argument of Keynes that governments should adjust monetary policies (interest rates and availability or amount of money in circulation) and fiscal policies (government spending and taxes) to boost demand (Mcgrath 2009; Aboobaker et al. 2016).

In practice, the much-trumped benefits of trickle-down economics have not been the experience of most growing economies where the benefits of growth have seldom been evenly distributed (Jafar 2015). In fact, in many African countries that have maintained an impressive economic growth rate of 5.6–10% over the past ten years, there has not been any demonstration of corresponding outcome trends in poverty reduction, service delivery and reduction in unemployment levels, especially for the youth populations—e.g. countries like Ethiopia, Ghana, Tanzania, Mozambique, Zambia and Uganda. Perhaps the only rare exceptions on the continent where growth has been associated with qualitative improvements in service delivery, public infrastructures and high levels of human capital development and youth employment, are Mauritius, Seychelles and Botswana and Rwanda, to a lesser extent. Most significantly, institutional economists have largely explained the observed positive developments in these relatively thriving countries from the standpoint of the overall institutional frameworks (over and above growth-oriented policies), notably the nature of political institutions, governance policies and the security context (Acemoglu and Robinson 2012; AfDB 2018).

The horrendous failure of strategies that are largely supply-side growth-oriented, which in the African context is best exemplified by the first phase of SAP in the 1980s and early 1990s, ultimately necessitated deliberate multi-dimensional policies that aim to support growth while at the same time reduce poverty, create jobs and strengthen the overall governance framework to mitigate corruption and foster inclusiveness, popular participation and more efficient service delivery.

The failure of SAP and the brand of neoclassical economics philosophy championed by the Washington Consensus in Africa led the World Bank in particular to embrace and promote the view of institutional economists that the outcome of economic policies is heavily dependent on the nature of a state's political institutions. Proponents of this view believe that liberal democratic institutions are more conducive to good governance, the latter being regarded as a necessary condition for economic development (Langdon et al. 2018: 70–73). Among other things, good governance, believed to be best fostered by liberal democratic institutions, matters for economic growth and development because of the predilection of liberal democracy to openness, constructive parliamentary debate, accountability and checks and balances among the various arms and agencies of government. Little wonder, exponents have argued, that the growth turnaround in the African context since the late 1990s coincided with a period of increasing democratisation across the region (ibid.).

Scholars across the ideological spectrum who espouse the view that the Africa rising discourse is a sham point to Africa's abysmal position in all the established global ranking for security, development and governance performances. The performance ranking of the African region has not made any significant improvement over the years and countries of the African region are consistently the worst regional clusters at the bottom of the ladder. In the 2018 and 2019 "fragile state index" (FSI) published by the US think tank Fund for Peace, which measures the different pressures faced by states that impact their levels of fragility using empirical indicators such as security threats, economic implosion, human rights violations, refugee flows, etc., seven of the ten most fragile states in the world are in the African region (FFP 2018, 2019). These include: South Sudan, Somalia, Central African Republic, DRC, Sudan, Chad and Zimbabwe. The only three non-African countries in the bottom 10 of the list are war-torn Yemen, Syria and Afghanistan. It is indicative that Africa's largest economy (in terms of GDP) Nigeria, is ranked the 14th most fragile country in the world over the two years while the continent's fastest growing economy Ethiopia, is ranked the world's 15th most fragile country in 2018 and 23rd in 2019. The best ranked or least fragile African country is the small island of Mauritius which is ranked No. 151 and No. 150 out of 178 countries in 2018 and 2019. Mauritius is followed by the island of Seychelles on No. 125 and No. 126 most fragile country in 2018 and 2019. The Southern African mainland state of Botswana is ranked No. 120 most fragile state or No. 58 from the top over the two years.

Similarly, the 2018 and 2019 Corruption Perception Index (CPI) published by Berlin-based Transparency International which ranks 180 countries and territories by their perceived levels of public sector corruption according to experts and business people, indicates that seven of the ten most corrupt countries in the world in 2018 and five in 2019 are in the African region (TI 2018, 2019). The most culpable African countries in 2018 are: Somalia, South Sudan, Sudan, Guinea Bissau, Equatorial Guinea, Libya and Burundi. Libya and Burundi jointly occupy the 10th position from the bottom. The five most corrupt African countries in the bottom 10 of the league table in 2019 are: Somalia, South Sudan, Sudan, Equatorial Guinea and Guinea Bissau.

The five African countries with the best performance records in 2018 and 2019 are Seychelles (No. 28 and 27 from the top), Botswana (No 34 from the top), Cape Verde (No. 45 and 41 from the top), Rwanda (No. 48 and 51 from the top) and Namibia (No. 52 and 56 from the top). Africa's second largest economy South Africa is ranked the No 73 and 70 least corrupt country in the world while Nigeria, Africa's largest economy is ranked as the 26th most corrupt country in the world over the two-year period. The CPI 2018 report classifies only two African countries, Cote d'Ivoire (No. 105 from the top) and Senegal (No. 67 from the top) as improvers in the CPI ranking relative to their previous positions in the corruption league table, and Cote d'Ivoire even made further progress in 2019 (TI 2018, 2019).

It is remarkable that the poor ranking of the African region in the global CPI is in spite of the fact that several African countries have over the past two decades established national Anti-Corruption Agencies (ACAs) to fight corruption and economic crimes (including money laundering), sometimes because of pressure from international financial institutions (Langdon et al. 2018: 76). ACAs exist today in the majority of African countries in various forms, but available evidence suggests that they are still largely ineffective due to the fact that most of them are under-resourced and highly politicised as instruments to witch-hunt and persecute political opponents (ibid.).

In the 2018 and 2019 global Human Development Index (HDI) published by the UNDP, which ranks 189 countries of the world according to HDI's measurement of national achievements in health, education and income, with the exception of war-torn Yemen, it is indicative that 19 of the 20 poorest countries in the world in terms of HDI indicators are all in Africa. These countries include the following: Niger, Central African Republic, South Sudan, Chad, Burundi, Sierra Leone, Burkina Faso, Mali, Liberia, Mozambique, Eritrea, Guinea Bissau, DRC, Guinea, Gambia, Ethiopia, Djibouti and Malawi. It is remarkable that Ethiopia, which is reputed to be the world's second fastest growing economy over the preceding 10 years was still ranked as one of the 20 poorest countries in the world in 2018 and 2019 (UNDP 2018: 8–11; 2019). Ethiopia's impressive economic growth has managed to reduce the country's poverty rate from 44% in 2000 to about 23.5% since 2015; more than 70% of Ethiopia's population is still employed in the agricultural sector, but services have surpassed agriculture as the principal source of GDP (Looney 2015; *Economy Watch* 2015; CIA 2019). In exploring the various development failures of the Ethiopian state in Chapter 12 of this volume, Yohannes Tekalign argues that in spite of the significant economic boom the country has experienced in more than 10 years, about 20 million Ethiopians (one fifth of the national population) still live below the poverty line. Among the world's three least developed regions, the UNDP report shows that South Asia has had the fastest growing HDI value over 1990–2017, at 45.3%, followed by East Asia and the Pacific at 41.8%, while Sub-Saharan Africa lags behind with 34.9% (UNDP 2018: 2).

The World Bank's compiles a Doing Business index of 190 countries and ranks them on a set of 10 indicators that cover different aspects of the business cycle such as: starting a business, dealing with construction permits, getting electricity, registering property, getting credit, protecting minority investors, paying taxes, trading across borders, enforcing contracts and resolving insolvency (World Bank 2018, 2019b). The 2018 and 2019 doing business reports indicate that seven of the ten countries with the most cumbersome record of doing business are in Africa, and they are: Somali, Eritrea, Libya, South Sudan, DRC, Central African Republic and Chad. The only non-African countries in the bottom 10 over the two years are Venezuela, Yemen and Haiti/Timor-Leste. The three best performing African countries in the 2018 and 2019 Doing Business Index are Rwanda, Morocco and Kenya. Over the two years, Nigeria, Africa's largest economy is placed No. 146 and 131 on the list while Ethiopia, Africa's fastest growing economy is No. 159. Five African countries (Djibouti, Togo, Kenya, Cote d'Ivoire and Rwanda) are listed by the World Bank's reports among the 10 economies with the most notable improvement in Doing Business 2019 relative to the preceding year.

Beyond Africa's poor performance records on the global governance, security and development indexes, it is worrisome that several African countries remain dependent on development assistance or foreign aid and many critics have argued that apart from humanitarian aid given as a response to short-term emergencies such as natural disaster, long-term development aid has produced deleterious effects on African economies (Moyo 2009; Langdon et al. 2018: 501). Making a case in favour of fair trade as against development assistance in her controversial book *Dead Aid*, Dambisa Moyo (2009) argues that foreign aid has aggravated the syndromes of dependency, corruption, consumerism, clientelism and tokenism in post-colonial Africa, and is sometimes diverted to military aid in times of conflict. While fair trade with the developed world has continued to remain elusive to Africa because of the powerful vested interests in the asymmetrical structures of global trade, African states have in recent years been exploring opportunities to expand the volume of intra-African trade, investment and movement of people and services. The boldest project in this new direction is the African Continental Free Trade Area (AfCFTA) treaty signed by 44 African states at the African Union Summit in Kigali, Rwanda in March 2018. The prospects and potential challenges of AfCFTA are discussed in Chapter 19 of this volume.

Africa's poor HDI performance is against the backdrop of the significantly high level of external development assistance and rising sovereign debt levels. Africa's sovereign debt-to-GDP ratio has been on the increase over the past decade rising from 34% in 2010 to 44% in 2015, and 53% as at April 2019 (Tshabalala 2015; Adegoke 2019). As at the end of 2018, Sub-Saharan Africa's "external debt stock" stood at US$524 billion (that of North Africa is about US$151 billion); this external debt profile excludes debt owed by countries of SSA to the Chinese (mostly tied to infrastructural development), which stands at about US$154 billion (Green 2019; World Bank 2019a). In all, the governance, security and development interface in Africa doesn't seem to portray the robust picture of a substantially transforming continent even though it may not be denied that some progress has been made. The portrait is still one of an unsettling mixed grill.

References

Aboobaker, Adam, et al. 2016. Post-Keynesian Economics. Exploring Economics, 18 December. https://www.exploring-economics.org/en/orientation/post-keynesian-economics/.

Acemoglu, Daron, and James A. Robinson. 2012. *Why Nations Fail: The Origins of Prosperity, Power and Poverty*. New York: Crown Publishers.

Adegoke, Yinka. 2019. When It Comes to Africa's Growing Debt, Size Doesn't Matter. Yet. Quartz Africa, 9 April., https://qz.com/africa/1588751/the-size-of-africas-growing-debt-isnt-its-biggest-problem/.

Adetula, Victor A.O. 2011. Measuring Democracy and Good Governance in Africa: A Critique of Assumptions and Methods. In *Governance in the 21st Century*, ed. Kwandiwe Kondlo and Chinenyengozi Ejiogu, 10–25. Cape Town: HSRC Press. https://www.academia.edu/790041/Measuring_democracy_and_good_governancein_Africa_A_critique_of_assumptions_and_methods.

AfDB. 2011. The Middle of the Pyramid: Dynamics of the Middle Class in Africa. Africa Development Bank (AfDB) Market Brief, 20 April. https://www.afdb.org/fileadmin/uploads/afdb/Documents/Publications/The%20Middle%20of%20the%20Pyramid_The%20Middle%20of%20the%20Pyramid.pdf.

AfDB. 2017. Africa Economic Outlook 2017. Africa Development Bank (AfDB). https://www.afdb.org/en/knowledge/publications/african-economic-outlook/.

AfDB. 2018. 2018 Country Policy and Institutional Assessment: CPIA Questionnaire. Africa Development Bank (AfDB), July. https://cpia.afdb.org/documents/public/cpia2018-questionnaire-en.pdf.

African Business. 2015. How Big Really Is Africa's Middle Class? 8 September. https://africanbusinessmagazine.com/region/continental/how-big-really-is-africas-middle-class/.

Africans Rising. 2016. A Vision for Africans Rising—The Rationale for a Pan-African Movement. September. https://www.africans-rising.org/vision/.

Albert, Eleanor. 2017. China in Africa. Council on Foreign Relations, 12 July. https://www.cfr.org/backgrounder/china-africa.

AU. 2019. African Continental Free Trade Area. African Union Documentary, 28 January. https://www.bing.com/videos/search?q=africa+continental+free+trade+areadocumentary&&view=detail&mid=7EE60C60564E73FF591B7EE60C60564E73FF591B&&FORM=VRDGAR.

Bach, Daniel C. 2011. Patrimonialism and Neopatrimonialism: Comparative Trajectories and Readings. *Commonwealth & Comparative Politics* 49 (3) (July): 275–294.

Bayart, J. 1996. *The State in Africa: The Politics of the Belly*. London: Longman.

Binns, Tony, and Etienne Nel. 2018. African Development: Hopeless Africa, Africa Rising. In *The Routledge Handbook of African Development*, ed. Tony Binns, Kenneth Lynch, and Etienne Nel, 273–285. London: Routledge.

Bond, Patrick. 2018. Africa's Extreme Uneven Development Worsening During Global Economic Turmoil. In *The Routledge Handbook of African Development*, ed. Tony Binns, Kenneth Lynch, and Etienne Nel, 477–491. London: Routledge.

Chabal, Patrick, and Jean-Pascal Daloz. 1999. *Africa Works: Disorder as Political Instrument*. Oxford: James Currey.

CIA. 2019. Ethiopian Economy 2019. US Central Intelligence Agency (CIA), 8 February. https://theodora.com/wfbcurrent/ethiopia/ethiopia_economy.html.

Dibua, Jeremiah I. 2006. *Modernization and the Crisis of Development in Africa*. Aldershot: Ashgate.

Economy Watch. 2015. Can Ethiopia's "Economic Miracle" Continue? 20 April. http://www.economywatch.com/news/Can-Ethiopias-Economic-Miracle-Continue.04-20-15.html.

Ellis, Stephen. 2005. How to Rebuild Africa. *The New York Times*, 13 October. https://archive.nytimes.com/www.nytimes.com/cfr/international/20050901faessay-v84n5_ellis.html.

FFP. 2018. Fragile States Index 2018—Annual Report. Fund For Peace (FFP), 24 April. http://fundforpeace.org/fsi/2018/04/24/fragile-states-index-2018-annual-report/.

FFP. 2019. Fragile States Index 2019—Annual Report. Fund For Peace (FFP), 10 April. https://fundforpeace.org/2019/04/10/fragile-states-index-2019/.

General News. 2017. Some Nations Need Dictatorship—Mahama. 3 November. https://www.ghanaweb.com/GhanaHomePage/NewsArchive/Some-nations-need-dictatorship-Mahama-597050.

Global Finance. 2018. Countries with Highest GDP Growth 2017. 12 November. https://www.gfmag.com/global-data/economic-data/countries-highest-gdp-growth-2017.

Goalstone, David. 2007. *Macrofoundations of Political Economy and Development*. New York: Palgrave Macmillan.

Green, Duncan. 2019. From Poverty to Power: How Active Citizens and Effective States Can Change the World. https://oxfamblogs.org/fp2p/africa-in-2019-7-trends-to-watch-by-apollos-nwafor/.

Grynberg, Roman. 2016. Africa: 'Hopeless Continent' to 'Africa Rising ...' The Need to Try Harder. The Namibia, 1 March. http://allafrica.com/stories/201603011227.html. Accessed on 12 November 2018.

Guru, Supriya. n.d. Rostow's Five Stages of Growth—Explained! http://www.yourarticlelibrary.com/economics/rostows-five-stages-of-growth-explained/38235.

Hamid, Shadi. 2011. The Struggle for Middle East Democracy. 26 April. https://www.brookings.edu/articles/the-struggle-for-middle-east-democracy/.

Jafar, Badr. 2015. Why Trickle-Down Economics Won't Eliminate Poverty. World Economic Forum, 12 April. https://www.weforum.org/agenda/2015/10/why-trickle-down-economics-wont-eliminate-poverty/.

Kiersz, Andy. 2019. This Map Shows That Each US State Is Basically Its Own Country. *Business Insider*, 29 March. https://www.businessinsider.com/state-vs-country-gdp-map-2019-3?r=US&IR=T.

Langdon, Steven, Achibald R.M. Ritter, and Yiagadeesen Samy. 2018. *African Economic Development*. London: Routledge.

Livingstone, Amy. 2015. What Is Considered Middle Class in America?—Definition, Income Range and Jobs. https://www.moneycrashers.com/middle-class-america-definition-income-range-jobs/.

Looney, Robert. 2015. Ethiopia's Economic Miracle Is Running Out of Steam. *Foreign Policy*, 16 April. https://foreignpolicy.com/2015/04/16/ethiopias-economic-miracle-is-running-out-of-steam-east-africa/.

Lyons, Tanya, and David Jolley. 2018. Post-independence Africa: Challenges and Opportunities. In *The Routledge Handbook of African Development*, ed. Tony Binns, Kenneth Lynch, and Etienne Nel, 49–67. London: Routledge.

Mahajan, Vijay. 2008. *Africa Rising: How 900 Million African Consumers Offer More Than You Think*. Philadelphia: Wharton School Publishing.

Mcgrath, Jane. 2009. How Trickle-Down Economics Works. https://money.howstuffworks.com/trickle-down-economics4.htm.

Moghalu, Kingsley C. 2014. *Emerging Africa: How Global Economy's 'Last Frontier' Can Prosper and Matter*. London: Penguin Books.

Monshipouri, Mahmood. 2014. *Democratic Uprising in the New Middle East: Youth, Technology, Human Rights and US Foreign Policy*. Boulder, CO: Paradigm Publishers.

Moyo, Dambissa. 2009. *Dead Aid: Why Aid Is Not Working and How There Is Another Way for Africa*. New York: Farrar, Straus and Giroux.

Ndlovu-Gatsheni, Sabelo J. 2018. The African Idea of Development. In *The Routledge Handbook of African Development*, ed. Tony Binns, Kenneth Lynch, and Etienne Nel, 19–34. London: Routledge.

Taylor, Ian. 2014. *Africa Rising? BRICS—Diversifying Dependency*. Woodbridge: James Currey.

The Conversation. 2016. How and Why China became Africa's Biggest Aid Donor. 26 April. http://theconversation.com/how-and-why-china-became-africas-biggest-aid-donor-57992.

The Economist. 2011. The Hopeful Continent: Africa Rising. 3 December. http://www.economist.com/node/21541015. Accessed on 12 November 2018.

The Economist. 2014. The Middle East: The Tragedy of the Arabs. https://www.economist.com/leaders/2014/07/05/the-tragedy-of-the-arabs.

The Economist. 2018. How Ethiopia and Eritrea Made Peace. 17 July. https://www.economist.com/the-economist-explains/2018/07/17/how-ethiopia-and-eritrea-made-peace.

The Guardian. 2010. What Role Does the World Bank Have in Africa's Future? 17 November. https://www.theguardian.com/global-development/poverty-matters/2010/nov/17/world-bank-africa-strategy.

The Guardian. 2017. British PR Firm Bell Pottinger Apologizes for South Africa Campaign. 10 July. https://www.theguardian.com/uk-news/2017/jul/10/bell-pottinger-pr-firm-apologizes-south-africa-campaign.

The Guardian. 2017 'Reputation Laundering' Is Lucrative Business for London PR Firms. 5 September. https://www.theguardian.com/media/2017/sep/05/reputation-laundering-is-lucrative-business-for-london-pr-firms.

TI. 2018. Corruption Perception Index 2018. Transparency International (TI). https://www.transparency.org/cpi2018.

TI. 2019. Corruption Perception Index 2019. Transparency International (TI). https://www.transparency.org/cpi2019.

Tshabalala, Sibusiso. 2015. Africa's Crippling 20th Century Debt Trap Could Be on Its Way Back. Quartz Africa, 5 November. https://qz.com/africa/541126/africas-crippling-20th-century-debt-trap-could-be-on-its-way-back/.

UNCTAD. 2018. *World Investment Report 2018: Investment and New Industrial Policies*. Geneva: United Nations. https://unctad.org/en/PublicationsLibrary/wir2018_en.pdf.

UNDP. 2018. *Human Development Indices and Indicators 2018 Statistical Update*. UNDP. http://hdr.undp.org/sites/default/files/2018_summary_human_development_statistical_update_en.pdf.

UNDP. 2019. *Human Development Indices and Indicators 2019 Statistical Update*. UNDP. http://hdr.undp.org/en/content/2019-human-development-index-ranking.

Wadongo, Evans. 2014. Africa Rising? Let's Be Afro-Realistic. *The Guardian*, 7 November. https://www.theguardian.com/global-development-professionals-network/2014/nov/07/africa-rising-lets-be-afro-realistic.

Wilson, Megan R. 2014. Nigeria Hires PR for Boko Haram Fallout. 26 June. https://thehill.com/business-a-lobbying/210635-nigeria-hires-pr-for-boko-haram-fallout.

World Bank. 2010. Africa's Future and the World Bank's Role in It. http://siteresources.worldbank.org/INTAFRICA/Resources/Africa_s_Future_and_the_World_Bank_s_Role_in_it.pdf.

World Bank. 2016. Development Policies, Institutions Improve in Few African Countries. 28 June. http://www.worldbank.org/en/region/afr/publication/development-policies-institutions-improve-in-few-african-countries.

World Bank. 2018. Doing Business: Training and Reforms. The World Bank. http://www.doingbusiness.org/content/dam/doingBusiness/media/Annual-Reports/English/DB2019-report_web-version.pdf.

World Bank. 2019a. 2019 International Debt Statistics. The World Bank. http://datatopics.worldbank.org/debt/ids/region/SSA.

World Bank. 2019b. Doing Business: Training and Reforms. The World Bank. https://www.doingbusiness.org/en/rankings.

World Bank Group. 2018. *CPIA Africa, July 2018: Assessing Africa's Policies and Institutions*. Washington, DC: World Bank. https://openknowledge.worldbank.org/handle/10986/30155.

World Economic Forum. 2016. Three Reasons Things Are Looking up for African Economies. 5 May. https://www.weforum.org/agenda/2016/05/what-s-the-future-of-economic-growth-in-africa/.

World Economy. 2017. Five Charts That Show How China Is Spending Billions in Foreign Aid. 13 October. https://www.cnbc.com/2017/10/13/china-development-aid-how-and-where-beijing-is-spending-its-cash.html.

Zhang, Junyi. 2016. Chinese Foreign Assistance Explained. 19 July. https://www.brookings.edu/blog/order-from-chaos/2016/07/19/chinese-foreign-assistance-explained/.

CHAPTER 2

Interrogating the Political Economy of Africa Rising: Who Are the "African Tigers"?

Temitope J. Laniran

Introduction

In post-colonial history, Sub-Saharan Africa (SSA) has for the most part been the least developed and perhaps, the most potentially volatile region of the world. The region is often easily dismissed as backward and unable to channel its potentials to actual progress. At the wake of the new millennium, *The Economist* (2000) regarded Africa as "the hopeless continent", illustrated with a map of the continent with an arm bearing young man at its heart as the cover page. Around the same period, it was highlighted that the continent has been wracked by armed conflicts and dictators (Brooks 2000). According to Collier and Gunning (1999): "It is clear that Africa has suffered a chronic failure of economic growth". Recent periods have, however, seen the SSA region record some consistent and impressive economic growth. The immediate past one to two decades has witnessed a gradual change in narrative. *The Economist* (2011, 3

T. J. Laniran (✉)
Institute of Development Studies, Brighton, UK

Centre for Petroleum Energy Economics and Law, University of Ibadan, Ibadan, Nigeria

K. Omeje (ed.), *The Governance, Security and Development Nexus*,
https://doi.org/10.1007/978-3-030-49348-6_2

December) wrote a lead editorial titled "The Hopeful Continent: Africa Rising". In a later issue of *The Economist* (2013, 2 March) it published an editorial titled "Aspiring Africa". The "Africa Rising Narrative" presents an optimistic standpoint on the economic prospects of Africa based on the assumption that the region is on a verge to take-off and perhaps become the "21st Century Asia". Other editorials that have featured this changing narrative include the *Time Magazine* (2012) "Africa Rising" and the *Financial Times* (2013) "Africa Calling" among others.

The change in narrative propelled quite a lot of the SSA countries to revisit their gross domestic product (GDP) and entire national accounting process. In 2010, Ghana pioneered this GDP rebasing process, its GDP almost doubled and as such graduated into middle-income status. Nigeria rebased its GDP in 2014, to account for new sectors which prior to 1990 were not in existence and were not accounted for prior to 2014. The rebasing exercise saw an almost doubling effect on Nigeria's GDP and as such the country overtook South Africa to become the continent's largest economy. Kenya rebased its GDP in 2013 and recorded an estimated 25% increase in the size of its economy. Other countries that have rebased their GDP include Tanzania, Zambia and Uganda with an estimated 27.8, 25.2 and 13.1% change in the size of their economy, respectively. While this rebasing exercise has largely been carried out in some of the African countries in a quest to find evidence of structural transformation[1] in their economies, however, this does not mean citizens welfare in these countries has suddenly improved overnight. It only shows that the size and composition of these economies have changed over the years and the basis of calculation of GDP needed a review to represent the current composition.

In reviewing the detailed analysis of the rebased economies, changes in the composition of their economy by sector became visible. While the change in contribution of sector to GDP varied across countries, however, a common noticeable trend is that the services sector is the single largest component of African economies (accounting for half or more of total GDP), while the manufacturing and agriculture sectors remain essentially unchanged or have shrunk (World Bank 2014). These rebasing exercises have helped to clarify the diversity within selected African economies, providing policymakers with a better fundamental understanding of the structural changes their economies have undergone over the years. For example, the rise in the services sector's share of GDP, together, with gradual or no increases in the shares of industrialisation and agriculture may have significant implications for sustaining the region's growth (Rodrik 2016).

The changing narrative on Africa which presently exudes the optimism that Africa is on the rise could not go unnoticed as the continent had previously and for far too long been known for increasing debt profiles despite its huge levels of resource deposits, conflicts driven by ethnic heterogeneity and resources, as well as an abysmal quality of life for a larger percentage of its population among other issues. As a result of the change in narrative, there has been a gradual renewed interest by investors, businesses and multinational companies which had hitherto withdrawn or completely stayed away from the region. This recent development, therefore, necessitates a closer examination of the changing narrative and the nature of the economic growth experienced by the region. In this chapter, we trace the economic growth trajectory of the continent from 1960. The chapter proceeds to interrogate the inclusiveness and productivity, as well as try to identify the economies driving the changing narrative in subsequent sections.

Economic Growth Timeline of the SSA

The post-colonial growth pattern and trajectory of the SSA has been characterised by quite a lot of fluctuations, looking at economic growth time-series data from 1961 to 2017 as depicted in Fig. 2.1.

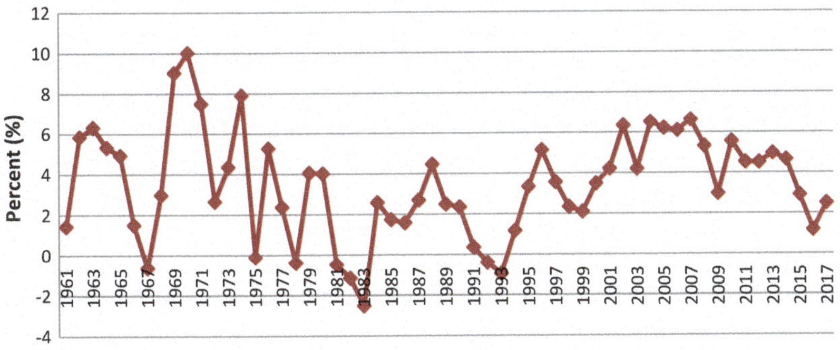

Fig. 2.1 GDP growth in Sub-Saharan Africa (1961–2017) (annual %) (*Source* World Bank, World Development Indicators 2018)

The period 1961–1963 witnessed significant growth trend for the largely newly independent SSA, 1964–1967 which coincides with a significant global recession saw the region experience steady economic downturn. The period 1968–1973, however, had significant levels of recovery. On the broader scope, the immediate post-independence period 1961–1973 witnessed significant growth averaging about 6% on the SSA region. Indeed, the immediate post-colonial period saw the SSA experience relatively significant growth that could raise expectations and impose some elements of prospect on the region. For example, when compared with the South East Asia region, which at the time was largely undergoing a wave of conflict and severe poverty, the African development prospect seemed imminent.

The commodity price crash of the 1970s had adverse economic implication for the SSA. The impressive performance of the immediate post-colonial periods came to an abrupt decline from the mid-1970s through mid-1990s. This period is often referred to as the "lost decades". This period signified a two-decade time span of abysmal economic performance for the region. Given this protracted economic stagnation and low economic output compared to other regions, it appeared the continent was doomed to an unending spiral of underdevelopment and all immediate post-colonial optimism fizzled out. The hypothesis as to the cause often clustered around three factors: geographical conditions, the slave trade legacy and colonisation (Zamfir 2016). The assumption is that one of these initial factors led African countries on an institutional path that was not on any real development trajectory. The prevailing weak institutional framework coupled with the commodity price shock would not make economic underperformance of the mid-1970s surprising.

In response to the prevailing economic and institutional conditions in the region, the international economic development community among others suggested development strategies to address the situation. For example, the World Bank in 1981 issued an influential report titled: Accelerated Development in Sub-Saharan Africa: An Agenda for Action, known as the Berg Report. The report was prepared at the request of the African Governors at the World Bank. It unveiled the World Bank's recommendation for a new strategic approach that emphasised the need for policy and structural adjustments. Throughout the 1980s and early 1990s, African governments reluctantly accepted what was known as the Structural Adjustment Programmes (SAP) that came with conditions for financial assistance. Many African governments, with limited alternative options, embarked on reforms under the auspices of the World Bank and the IMF (Toh 2016).

By the early 1990s, the inability of SAP to achieve the expected outcomes had become quite clear, leaving the region with massively inefficient, ineffective and unmanageable debt profile. By the end of the 1990s, a gradual shift in the trend which by the turn of the new millennium had fully manifested, thereby changing the narrative of the continent positively became visible. A sustained and speedy growth of more than 5% was largely witnessed across the region with some African countries being some of the fastest growing economies in the world. The 2008 global financial crisis dealt its fair share on the changing narrative of Africa. The above 5% growth trend the continent had maintained in the early periods of the millennium slowed down significantly. However, the continent recovered rather faster than anticipated, showing decent levels of resilience. The resilience exhibited in the aftermath of the crisis has been linked to two factors: good fiscal situation and low real economic inter-connectivity with the real global economy (Zamfir 2016). Zamfir, however, noted that the fiscal situation across the region had recently begun deteriorating with visibility of deficits (current account and government budget) as against surpluses that helped in originally withstanding the crisis.

The World Bank (2015) forecasts that the region will continue to be among the fastest growing regions even in the face of declining commodity prices among other unfavourable financial and economic exogeneities. Growth in the region has in recent times slowed down with growth levels largely below 5%. For example, growth in 2015 declined to 2.9% from 4.6% in the previous year, signifying almost 20% decrease in growth. In 2016, there was a further slowdown in growth to about three decade's low of 1.2%. Growth has gradually picked up again by 2017 to 2.5%. Swaniker (2013) in discussing factors driving Africa's rising economies argued that the trend of the economic performance of Africa can be divided into various generations and the narrative can be discussed along three generational lines and groupings. A critical look at Fig. 2.1, for example, presents a scenario where the narrative of the performance of African economies can be discussed along the three generations:

> The first generation emerged in the 1950s, with leaders such as Kwame Nkrumah of Ghana and Julius Nyerere of Tanzania. This generation can be referred to as the "immediate post-colonial era".

While that generation had its limitations, it must be credited for leaving behind a legacy of independence, and ambitious growth trajectory.

The second generation of leaders had leaders such as Liberian President Samuel Doe, Ugandan President Idi Amin and Congolese President Mobutu Sese Seko. This generation can be referred to as the "autocratic takeover". This generation seized power from the first generation largely between the mid-1960s and the mid-1980s. They claimed their actions were largely as a result of the flaws of the first generation which they argued included incompetence. That generation left a terrible legacy for the continent: one of incessant warfare, corruption, gross human rights abuses and general political instability. The period also has been described as "the lost decades".

The third generation of leaders started emerging largely since the mid-1990s. This period accounts for the changing narrative of the region's economic performance. This generation of leaders are largely civilian and have also focused on achieving political and macroeconomic stability for their countries. While conflicts still occur, in selected parts of the region, it is no longer full-blown like the periods where there were widespread civil wars and conflicts. The number of autocratic regimes in Sub-Saharan Africa fell from a peak of 36 countries in 1989 to only five in 2004. Liberian President Ellen Johnson-Sirleaf, Rwandan President Paul Kagame and President Goodluck Jonathan of Nigeria, among others, typify this third generation.

How Inclusive Is "Africa Rising"?

The SSA region is expected to continue to experience economic growth, with the increasing privatisation and democratisation of the region. Whether this growth is accompanied by poverty reduction and reduced inequality gaps remains probable.

Generally, there has been a recent economic ascension of the developing world, with GDP growth rates in a surplus of those obtained in the developed world. This progression has been particularly evident since the mid-1990s. With tremendous global poverty reduction, largely attributable to China, Chen and Ravallion (2008), suggest that even when China is omitted from the sample, poverty reduction is still considerable. This attainment, however, remains far from homogeneous, with many

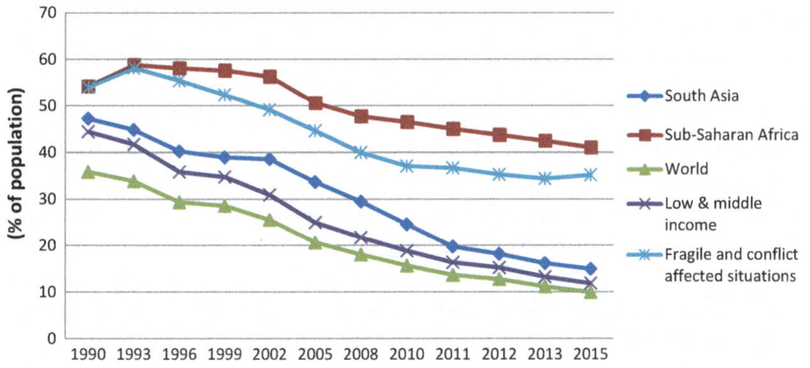

Fig. 2.2 Poverty headcount ratio at $1.90 a day (2011 PPP) (% of population) (*Source* World Bank, World Development Indicators 2018)

countries, largely in SSA, experiencing abysmal levels of poverty reduction or even increasing poverty. Figure 2.2 presents the trend of poverty headcount ratio for different regions across the globe.

Generally, poverty reduction in the world has experienced a significant fall. While the slope of poverty reduction in South Asia and low and middle-income countries can be seen to be converging with that of the world, the case of SSA and fragile states present a rather different narrative with almost divergent trends when compared to the rest of the world. This is a contrast with the economic growth trajectory of the region.

The first Millennium Development Goal (MDG) which aimed at halving the proportion of the world's population living in extreme poverty by 2015 was met five years early. It is, however, crucial to note that a huge chunk of this success can be in no less attributed to China, which alone accounted for about half of the decline in the extreme poverty rate worldwide. It has also driven significant gains across its region. In the early 1980s, Asia had the highest extreme poverty rate in the world, with more than three in four people living on less than $1.25 a day, but by 2010, just one in eight were. It is argued that two developing giants, India and China, are alone responsible for three-quarters of the reduction in the world's poor witnessed over the period 2005–2015. This has culminated into the current emerging narrative on the changing face of global poverty. Asia's share of global poverty fell from about two-thirds to one-third, while Africa's share more than doubled from 28 to 60%.

Poverty is, therefore, becoming a majorly African problem despite the growth the continent has witnessed in recent periods. Although some African Countries including Angola, Nigeria, Ethiopia and Rwanda have been among the fastest growing economies of the past decade, MDG Report (2014) suggests that Africa constitutes the largest deficit to MDG 2015 achievement.

This rapid growth has led to the graduation of about seven Sub-Saharan Africa economies, including Angola and Nigeria to middle-income economy status, (although the middle-income class is now further divided into upper and lower middle income, and most of the upgraded African countries are in the lower middle-income category). The experience of these fast-growing economies is mostly consistent with the economic concepts of "convergence" (or the "catch-up effect") and "post-conflict growth rebound" (Staines 2004; UNDP BCPR 2008). The convergence notion explains the faster growth experienced in poorer economies compared to economies that have achieved a high-income level. The post-conflict growth rebound explains the fast growth that follows sharp drops in GDP, Liberia being an important example of this phenomenon (Radelet 2007). Other countries that experienced highly disruptive and destructive conflicts after the end of the Cold War have experienced notable economic rebounds after hostilities ceased (e.g. Angola, Mozambique and Sierra Leone).

With the graduation of some of these countries into Middle-Income Country (MIC) status, albeit mostly lower middle-income category, poverty is gradually no longer only concentrated in SSA Low-Income Countries (LIC). Large chunks of poverty clusters are now located in these upgraded countries with particular significant clusters in the fragile ones.[2] For example, by mid-2018, the World Poverty Clock reflected that Nigeria, one of the largest economies on the continent with a total population of about 200 million people had overtaken India with a total population of about one billion as the country with the largest number of people living in extreme poverty. By the end of 2018, an estimated 90 million Nigerians were living in poverty accounting for about half of the country's population, and a quarter of the total poor in the region.[3] It is important to note that Africa currently accounts for about two-thirds of the global poor. 14 out of 18 countries where poverty is rising are in Africa. By the end of 2018, there were over 400 million Africans living in poverty, with the figure projected to continue to rise. If the current trends persist and the economic growth remains non-inclusive, it is expected that by 2030 Africa will account for 90% of the world's poor, hence, the emergence of the changing face of global poverty narrative.

The trend in the emerging face of poverty presents a rather more complex situation. With fast growth experienced in developing economies (fragile and non-fragile), the face of global poverty has changed over the years. Poverty is increasingly becoming a fragility issue[4] (Chandy 2011; Sumner 2012). In 2008 "barely 7 per cent of world poverty existed in developing non-fragile, low-income economies" (Sumner 2012). Aptly put by the World Development Report 2011 "the gap in poverty is widening between countries affected by violence and others" (World Bank 2011). Using the World Bank's data, Chandy and Gertz (2011) revealed that about 30 fragile states experienced a doubling of poverty concentration from 20 to 40% between 2005 and 2010. They argued further that with the ascension of some of the fragile states from low income to middle income, the world's share of the poor living in middle-income countries increased from 26 to 65%.

Perhaps the problem with these economies may not necessarily be the inability to grow, but the lack of effective institutions to efficiently allocate and distribute resources. The growing concentration of global poverty in fragile states suggests that fragility presents one of the biggest challenges to development policy and particularly the efforts to reduce poverty. Fragile states have significantly greater difficulties in achieving the development goals than non-fragile developing countries and their vulnerability to violent conflict makes them not only a threat to their populations but also to the stability of their regions (Chandy 2011).

Given the trends, the poverty trajectory is evolving from that of poor people in poor economies to that of poor people living in middle-income economies. In 2005, 73% of the world's poor lived in low-income countries; by 2010, 65% of the world's poor lived in middle-income economies, largely from the SSA region. The concentration of poverty in middle-income countries tends to suggest that these upgraded fragile economies only moved up in size but still accommodate large chunks of the world's poor. Perhaps the preponderant prevalence of poverty in these economies may be a function of fragility. Poverty in itself may be a cause of their fragility. While the evidence of the impact of growth on poverty remains heterogeneous, growth is not always matched by a proportionate measure of poverty reduction. Income levels of the poorest of the poor in an economy often rise at a slower pace (Sumners 2012).

While economic growth remains a crucial first-order condition in achieving this target, concerted efforts aimed at institutional strengthening in the region remains crucial in achieving somewhat equitable redistribution of wealth needed to make the growth more inclusive.

How Productive Is "Africa Rising"

The changing face of global poverty and the emergence of about half of the fragile states from low-income to middle-income economies only illustrate the arduous task involved in reducing poverty. While China and India that accounted for the larger chunk of success achieved in halving global poverty were not commodity-dependent economies, the middle-income fragile states, particularly those of SSA currently housing a larger proportion of global poor are commodity-dependent. The non-inclusive and volatile natures of the commodity market are common knowledge and can largely explain the economic performance pattern of these states. The difficult policy environment and institutional weakness that characterise fragile states, however, explain their inability in achieving wealth redistribution, hence, inequality and large chunks of poverty concentration.

Economic performance in natural resource states can be driven by their endowments and not necessarily productivity as seen in the case of most of the upgraded countries. Growth owed to natural resource endowment often tends to be non-inclusive. The non-inclusivity is attributable to the fact that the natural resource sector does not employ much of the population and hence does not affect the lives of the large sections of the citizenry and sometimes even leaves them worse as natural resource exploration has a considerable negative impact in circumstances where there are no strong institutions to ensure best practices (Sachs and Warner 2001). Kolstad and Soreide (2009) have stressed the importance of strong governance in the management of natural resources, while Hausmann et al. (2005) have argued that corruption is a bane in any society, not least in fragile states endowed with enormous natural resources. This, therefore, suggests that natural resource-driven growth in fragile states mainly widens the gap of inequality, ipso facto aggravating structural poverty.

Many countries in Africa are endowed with natural resources. At least, there are about 17 resource-rich countries in SSA: eight oil exporters (Angola, Chad, and Republic of the Congo, Equatorial Guinea, Gabon, Nigeria, South Sudan and Sudan) and nine metals and mineral exporters

(Botswana, Democratic Republic of the Congo, Guinea, Liberia, Mauritania, Namibia, Niger, Sierra Leone, Zambia) (Zamfir 2016). Two of the SSA oil exporters are also members of OPEC, namely Angola, and Nigeria. Among the SSA countries which are not resource-rich, some have the potential to become resource-rich in the near future: for instance, Mozambique and Uganda have in recent years discovered significant oil and gas reserves; Liberia has exploitable offshore oil and Malawi large uranium deposits they could extract. Deplorably, most resource-rich countries in Africa are characterised by dependence on one or a few export commodities, exposing their economies to periodic external shocks. The linkage of the extractive sector with the rest of the economy has also remained low and resource-rich countries have usually failed to diversify their economies. Thus, the jobs generated by the extractive industries have been few. This deplorable trend characterises oil export in Nigeria, gold mining in Ghana, the copper economy in Zambia, cobalt in the Democratic Republic of Congo, uranium in Namibia and Niger, bauxite in Guinea and until recently diamond in Botswana. The situation is similar for agricultural exporters like Kenya, the third largest tea exporter in the world after China and India, and Ethiopia, a major coffee producer. The exported agricultural products are mostly unprocessed.

There are gains for having a diversified economy, notably, it would help SSA resource-dependent economies to maximise their potentials (Bhorat and Tarp 2016). Countries that are resource-rich are more likely to be poorer than those that are not, a paradox that has been widely referred to as the resource curse (Sachs and Warner 2001). Proponents of the resource curse have written on diverse ways by which over-reliance on natural resource export can adversely affect a country's economy.

Firstly, natural resource over-dependence, it is argued, affects a country's terms of trade in the sense that the relative price of primary commodities to manufactured products follows a downward trend over time and as such economies that depend on natural resources are more likely to experience declining terms of trade (Prebisch 1959). Secondly, over-reliance on resource export has been linked to the crowding out of the manufacturing sector. Proponents argue that a boom in the commodity market would lead to a growth in the domestic resource sector that ultimately crowds out the domestic manufacturing sector (Sachs and Warner 2001). Thirdly, natural resource boom can inhibit growth and development by promoting a rent-seeking behaviour often characterised by widespread mismanagement, waste and corruption (Caselli and Cunningham 2009; Robinson et al. 2006; McGuirk 2013). The literature on the political economy of resource rents shows that the abundance of natural resource revenue increases the appetite of the governing elite to perpetuate themselves in power for their self-serving advantages and as such perpetuate a destructive pattern of activities that weaken state institutions (Laniran 2017). The tendency further leads to a misallocation of resources to power-preserving activities rather than increasing expenditures that could improve institutions, economic capacity and development (Robinson et al. 2006; Caselli and Cunningham 2009; Ajala 2018). Karl (2007) describes this mechanism as the participation deficit, arguing that this deficit as one of the most significant challenges natural resource-abundant states face.

The resource curse hypothesis has however been widely critiqued. Mehlum et al. (2006) propose a "conditional resource curse", which argues that institutional quality determines the ability of a country to gainfully exploit its natural resource endowments. The scholars found evidence that resource endowments with weak institutional quality are associated with low growth, while resource endowments with strong institutional quality are associated with high growth. Others have linked levels of human capital in a resource-abundant country to its ability to gainfully exploit its natural resource for growth (Bravo-Ortega and Gregorio 2007). However, there tends to be a relationship between institutional quality and human capital quality in a country as suggested by (Jalilian et al. 2007). Sachs and Warner (2001) have proffered evidence to suggest that resource-dependence can have undermining impact on SSA countries, thus providing supportive evidence for the curse in SSA. Lederman and Maloney (2008), however, using larger samples found little evidence for the curse and as such proposed "a curse of concentration". The curse of concentration argues that countries that are solely dependent on natural resource exports are associated with negative growth effects. In essence, the presence of natural resource in a country does not necessarily hinder the growth and development of the country. The ability of a country to gainfully exploit its natural resource or otherwise depends on the presence or absence of other growth determinants such as institutional quality and a diversified economy. A diversified economy is ultimately essential for sustainable economic growth and management in resource-rich countries. Among other things, it strengthens the capacity of the economy to absorb external shocks because commodity prices tend to exhibit high levels of volatility that, coupled with an export concentration in natural resource-based exports, result in broader macroeconomic volatility (Bhorat and Tarp 2016). It is argued that the type of products the economy diversifies towards matters as well in providing the necessary and adequate economic base to shield it from commodity market fluctuations.

While economic growth has been significant for most countries in SSA, gauging the degree to which effective economic transformation for sustaining the observed growth has taken place may be rather challenging. In the 1970s, manufacturing in SSA boomed due to import substitution industrialisation. However, when economic liberalisation and the privatisation of state enterprises became rampant under stabilisation and structural adjustment in the 1980s, African manufacturing went into circular decline, as the continent could not compete with low wage Asian countries (Bhorat and Tarp 2016). Import competition led to the contraction of many domestic industries, resulting in a structural change where labour moves towards less productive sectors, such as the service sectors and small firms operating in informal sectors. The even worse news for African manufacturing is the degree to which it is dominated by small, informal firms that are not particularly productive (Rodrik 2016). Taking a clue from Rodrik (2016): "The evidence on informality suggests few small, informal firms eventually grow out of informality. So, informality is a drag on overall productivity, and this plays a large part in explaining why not just services but also manufacturing in Africa has been falling behind the productivity frontier, even in recent years with high growth". This is depicted in Figs. 2.3 and 2.4.

Figure 2.3 makes obvious how at independence Africa's manufacturing productivity was above that of Asia, however, within half a decade Asia caught up and superseded Africa. In the 1970s there was an industrialisation drive as discussed earlier that almost brought Africa on par, however that lost its initial inertia by the middle of the decade and since then, Africa has continued to fail in improving its manufacturing productivity.

African countries were not well prepared for import competition due to the fact that state-led import substitution created high protection and heavy import dependency. Other factors, such as weak institutional capacity and infrastructural deficit were also at play. An understanding of the performance of sectors of an economy may, however, be unable to explain how a developing economy's service sector would continue to grow without an initial and sustained growth in other tangible sectors.

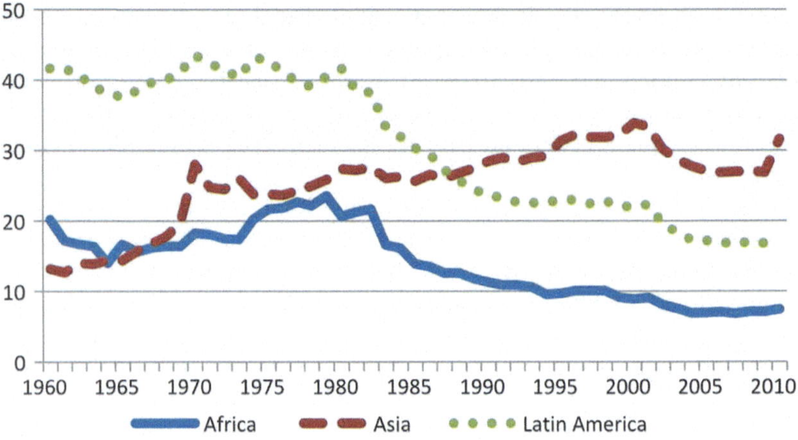

Fig. 2.3 An international perspective on productivity (USA = 100): manufacturing (*Source* De Vries et al. 2015)

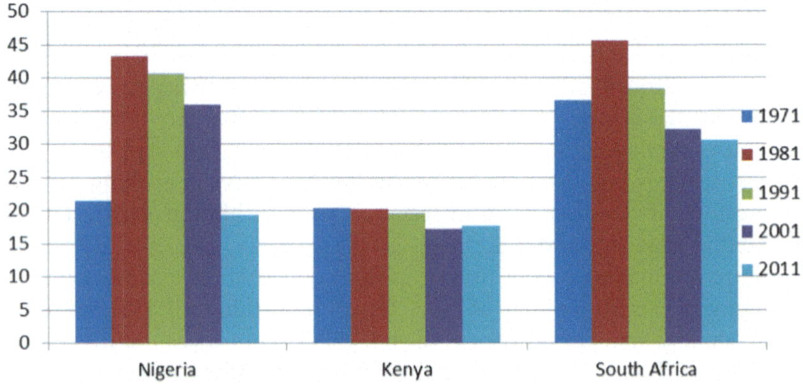

Fig. 2.4 Industrial output as percentage of GDP (*Source* World Bank, World Development Indicators 2018)

Structural changes in most advanced economies come as a result of the transfer of resources from the primary to secondary sector, and ultimately tertiary sector. In the process, high productivity and wealth redistribution is achieved. It, however, appears that the SSA region bypassed the secondary sector to service sectors. The manufacturing sector that necessitates growth in value addition and ultimately helps in job creation has not grown with the African growth narrative. What has however been noticeable is that a de-industrialisation trajectory is observable in most of the countries in the region as seen in Figs. 2.3 and 2.4. According to Zamfir (2016), the failure of industrialisation on the continent can be explained by a multiplicity of inhibiting factors: insufficient infrastructure (mainly electricity supply and transport), lack of skills, small purchasing capacity; most African countries are small economies with significantly dysfunctional institutions. Productivity has also remained low and prices are above the level expected given the low-income level, further hindering international competitiveness. There are other necessary factors largely absent in the region, which are also vital for successful industrialisation, namely companies' orientation towards exports, industrial clusters and firm capabilities. According to Cadot et al. (2016), cases of countries that have achieved development "without factories" are too scarce and idiosyncratic to serve as a model. However, given the technical progress in services and the lack of plausible alternatives in manufacturing, the question remains openly contemplative, whether it is a plausible model for SSA to achieve sustained and efficient growth without a strong manufacturing sector.

Who Are the "Africa Rising" Drivers? A Tale of the Big, Small and Fast Cats

The Africa rising narrative refers to a period of fast and impressive economic performance in Africa, which was visible across the continent largely over the period 2000–2014 as discussed earlier. The fast pace growth in the region, however, witnessed a slowdown from 2015, although, more recent periods are witnessing a gradual return to a growth trajectory. Key measures that drove the change in the growth narrative were largely dependent on the economic performance of the region which was mainly quantified with the use of growth in the GDP as portrayed in Fig. 2.1. For example, from 2002 to 2008 the region grew at about 5.93%, meaning that the continent as a whole was the second fastest growing region, only behind Asia. According to the United Nations Economic Commission for Africa (2012), seven of the fastest growing economies in 2011 were in Africa.

Weak economic growth for SSA since 2015, along with continued commodity market volatility, the sustainability of the promising narrative has been doubtful and highly critiqued, as the growth rate has reduced since 2015 when the commodity market started slowing down. Sceptics downplay several important factors. For example, the aggregate growth rate in the region is mostly driven by the three largest economies: Angola, Nigeria and South Africa. These three economies alone accounted for more than 60% of the regions GDP from 2000 to 2014. A fluctuation in the income of either Nigeria or South Africa which each individually account for over a quarter of the regions GDP will, therefore, have a very significant impact of the regional performance. When Sudan and Kenya are added, over 70% of the region's economy is already accounted for. These five countries can be referred to as the "big Cats" of the region. The remaining over 40 countries only account for about 30% of the region's economy. In global discussions on emerging economies, the two SSA countries that have often come up are Nigeria and South Africa. While Nigeria has come up in the MINT[5] as well as the Next 11,[6] South Africa has come up in the BRICS.[7] The criteria used have largely depended on macroeconomic stability, political maturity, openness and investment policies (Lo and Hiscock 2014). This tendency, therefore, raises concerns on the role of size in growth and if growth figures cannot be trusted should size be an alternative?

Also, the relationship between SSA countries and their development partners became healthier, since the early 2000s. Country-led poverty reduction strategies replaced SAP at the centre of policymaking, providing a stronger basis for international financial flows to bolster future development efforts. The region witnessed a significant boost in the inflow of foreign capital (including portfolio investment, direct investment and remittances, among others). The level of aggregate inflow into the region which stood at US$20 billion in 1990 rose to US$120 billion by 2012. Other factors such as improvements in governance, macroeconomic management and business environments as well as a rise in small-scale enterprises are expected to sustain growth. It is, however, important to note that the potentials of the small-scale enterprises to optimise their capacity in driving economic performance are not guaranteed (Rodrik 2016).

In an earlier study by Bhorat and Tarp (2016), a group of six countries (Ethiopia, Ghana, Kenya, Mozambique, Nigeria and South Africa) were referred to as "the African Lions". While clear criteria for the selection of these countries were not provided, they argued that these six fast-growing and/or economically dominant African countries depicted as Africa's

Lions will largely shape the continent's future. However, a careful examination at the selected countries presents a mix of the largest/dominant economies (Nigeria and South Africa) as depicted in Fig. 2.5 and some of the fastest growing economies in the region (Ethiopia, Ghana, Kenya, Mozambique).

The fact that the commodity (oil) market shock of 2014 affected many SSA countries calls for concern. Aggregate growth declined from 5.11% for 2004–2014 to only 2.22% in 2015–2017, a rate that barely keeps up with population growth. The most recent economic underperformance (2015–2017) of some of the "big cat" economies is particularly disturbing. They have performed largely below the regional average for the recent period. For example, South Africa has in recent times continued to witness structural issues that have almost stagnated its economy. In the case of Nigeria, the country witnessed its first economic recession in over two decades in 2016 resulting from an initial slowdown in 2015 and merely recovered in 2017. The average growth rate for Nigeria for the period 2015–2017 was a meagre rate of 0.6% which was below the country population growth rate (3.6%) and sub-regional growth rate. The case of Angola mirrors that of Nigeria as the country recorded negative growth of −0.59% for the 2015–2017 periods. The period 2000–2014 saw about 15 countries including the lead "big three" growing above 5% and the regional average of 5.11% as presented in Fig. 2.6.

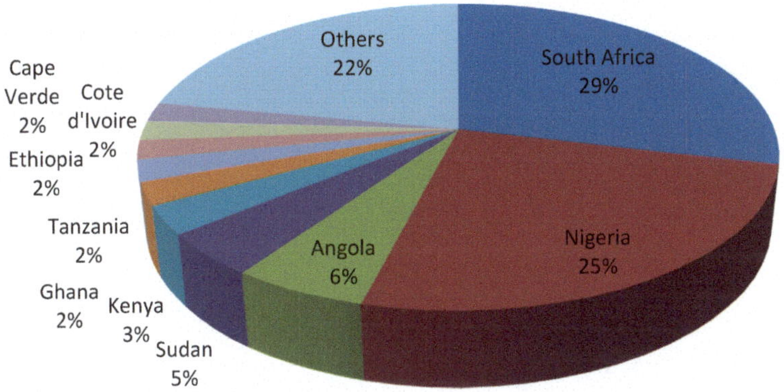

Fig. 2.5 Share of average annual GDP (US$) 2000–2014 (*Source* World Bank, World Development Indicators 2018)

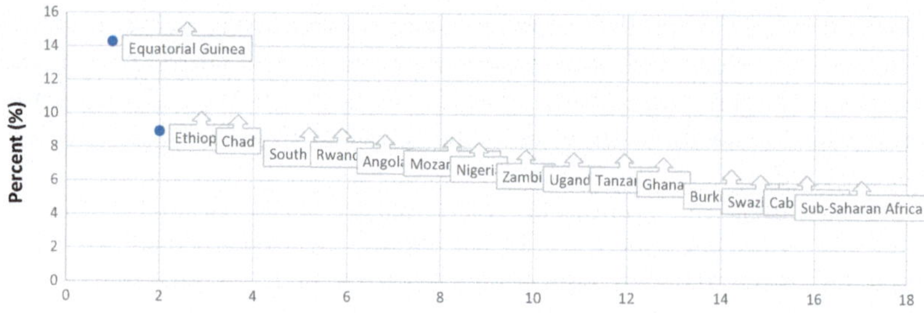

Fig. 2.6 Average annual GDP growth (%) 2000–2014 >5% (*Source* World Bank, World Development Indicators 2018)

A closer inspection of the growth and development indicators suggests the need for a more cautious approach in understanding the recent growth, as well as persistent capital accumulation and the structural transformation challenges the region has been faced with (Bush 2018). While the region had about 15 economies (including its largest economies) growing above 5% average from 2000 to 2014, the post-2015 performance presents a situation where only 11 countries out of the entire region grew above 5% as portrayed in Fig. 2.7. The outlook for the region still calls for some concern with growth remaining significantly below the pre-2015 crisis average.

The 11 post-2015 thriving economies are for the most part neither oil-producing nor post-conflict states with the exception of Cote d Ivoire,

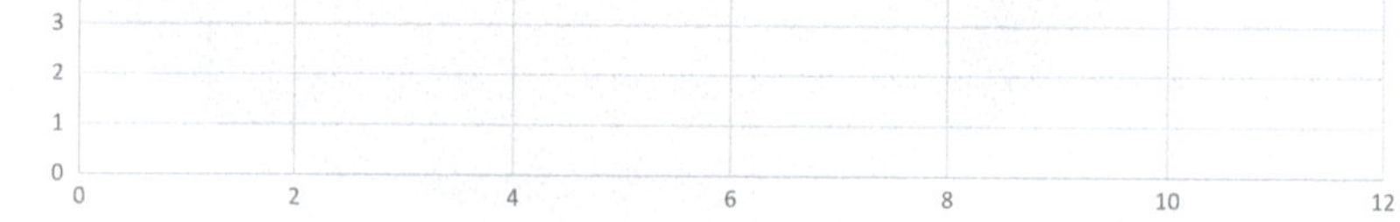

Fig. 2.7 Average annual GDP growth (%) 2015–2017 >5% (*Source* World Bank, World Development Indicators 2018)

thus underscoring the importance of a diversified and stable economy. The 11 thriving economies mainly fall into the categories of non-oil or landlocked states. Metaphorically, these post-2015 thriving economies can be referred to as the "small cats" (Table 2.1).

Apparently, a more interesting observation is that out of the 11 countries that grew above 5% post-2015, only four (Ethiopia, Tanzania, Rwanda and Burkina Faso) grew above 5% in the 2000–2014 period, three of which are members of the East African Economic Bloc. In essence, only these four countries have been able to maintain a growth rate above 5% since the birth of the "Africa rising" narrative and using our cat metaphor, these countries can be referred to as "the fast ones". This, therefore, suggests that the rise of the SSA region remains largely susceptible to fluctuations in the commodity market, despite the evidence found for structural transformation during the rebasing exercise. The countries that have been able to exhibit this growth resilience are only a very minute fraction of the region's economy and account for approximately less than 7% of the region's economy.[8] Also, these four states have civilian democratic rule, albeit with peculiar variations. The incumbent regimes in some of these countries have been criticised as civilian regimes and democracies with autocratic tendencies. Some political scientists have attributed the autocratic credentials of some of these regimes to the political imperatives of the developmental state model of national development they have chosen.[9] For example, Nwapi and Andrews (2017) have rationalised how Tanzania and Rwanda have pursued some of the vigorous policy and legal interventions aimed at strengthening their domestic capacity for national development. However, in an article titled "Democracy under assault" *The Economist* Magazine of 15 March 2018 highlighted how Tanzania's "rogue president" has hidden under the guise of policies of national transformation and development to steer Tanzania from a flawed democracy to a brutal dictatorship.

It is important to note that the growth narrative reported in the Africa rising discourse has mainly been triggered by GDP growth and therefore not necessarily representative of changes in the living standards of the people. For example, when GDP per capita (a mere division of GDP by population size) which is a rather very vague proxy for quality of life is examined, a different picture is observed.

Table 2.1 How widespread is the "Africa rising" narrative?

Growth > regional average (2000–2014)				*Growth < regional average (2000–2014)*			
Non-oil exporting	*Oil exporting*	*Post-conflict*	*Landlocked*	*Non-oil exporting*	*Oil exporting*	*Post-conflict*	*Landlocked*
South Africa	Equatorial Guinea		Ethiopia	Namibia	Congo, Rep.	Congo, Dem. Rep.	Niger
Mozambique	Chad		Rwanda	Senegal	Mauritania	Burundi	Mali
Tanzania	Angola		Zambia	Malawi	Cameroon	Liberia	Botswana
Ghana	Nigeria		Uganda	Mauritius	Sudan	Sierra Leone	Zimbabwe
Cape Verde			Burkina Faso	Guinea-Bissau	Gabon	Cote d'Ivoire	Central African Republic
			Swaziland	Benin			
				Lesotho			
				Seychelles			
				Guinea			
				Togo			
				Comoros			
				The Gambia,			
				Madagascar			
				Kenya			
				Eritrea			

Source Adapted from Toh (2016)

Conclusion

The beginning of the new millennium saw an SSA region where the average economic growth exceeded the observable growth rate in the rest of the world. Average growth for almost a decade and a half across the region exceeded 5%. This gave birth to the "Africa rising" narrative that has engaged and excited public discourse in remarkable ways. However, the sustainability and efficiency (qualitative impact) of this growth remains to be seen.

Among the growth drivers were a commodity boom that fuelled the economies of resource-endowed countries. Moreover, political gains informed by what many scholars have dubbed "the third wave of democratization", as well as economic reforms such as liberalisation have opened doors for increased foreign capital inflows (Howard and Hussain 2013; Ngwafu 2016). The economic optimism of the past two decades has, however, been tempered by a combination of contradictory factors, notably a worldwide decline in commodity prices and climatic changes. Although the region still has some of the fastest growing economies (Burkina Faso, Ethiopia, Tanzania, and Rwanda) which have proven to be resilient, commodity market fluctuations still have a great impact on the region's economic performance. For example, some of the economic giants, particularly Nigeria and Angola have been hit hard and have witnessed recession since the recent commodity crisis. It is important to note that the crisis did not have a homogenous impact across the region. For example, Kenya which mainly imports its fuel has gained from the crisis in terms of cheaper fuel to drive its economy. For the Africa Rising story not to be a story of "growth for growth" sake, there is a need for a strong focus on a paradigm of growth reliant on structural transformation where the contribution of value addition plays a more significant role in economic performance. The growth model of the past two decades has not necessarily been efficient in ensuring improved living standards for the vast majority of the African people.

Moving forward, a strong lesson from the present growth model is that SSA countries must as a matter of necessity liberate their economies from their natural resource reliance. They must prioritise domestic production and consumption, export promotion, value addition and diversification. Achieving this will require, among other things, modernising agricultural production and an extractive industry that contributes to local industrial processing. While the primary sector, including agriculture and extractive industries, remains pivotal for most SSA countries, growing the region's industrial base is vital to economic transformation and job creation, which will greatly benefit the burgeoning middle class and the rapid urbanisation sweeping across the region. Also, for more qualitative growth, a mere introduction of electoral democracy is not sufficient. There is the need to strengthen African democracies by strengthening all the relevant institutions of the state and society, and building resilience against fragility. Current conflict trends have clearly revealed that contemporary dimensions of poverty are, for the most part, a fragility challenge, which among other things is manifested in the absence of strong institutions to ensure efficient allocation and distribution of wealth. Tackling the foundation and challenges of institutional fragility is important in ensuring that the African region fulfils its vast untapped potential.

Notes

1. Structural transformation is the reallocation of economic activity away from the least productive sectors of the economy to more productive ones. It is one fundamental driver of economic development. It contains two elements: the rise of new, more productive activities and the movement of resources from traditional activities to these newer ones, raising overall productivity. Without the first, there is little that propels the economy forward. Without the second, productivity gains are not diffused to the rest of the economy. See McMillan, M.S. and D. Rodrik, Globalisation, structural change and productivity growth, NBER Working Paper No. 17143, 2011.
2. Given the multiple sources of fragility and the reinforcing interactions among them, fragile countries find it very difficult to build resilience. Many of them seem to be caught in what can be termed a "fragility trap". This fragility trap refers to a closely interlinked circle of underdevelopment, political instability or conflict, and ineffective state capacity. This makes the transition out of fragility neither simple nor rapid: for instance, it is estimated that of the 26 Sub-Saharan African countries identified as fragile, only 12 could be expected to become more resilient by 2039 (Cilliers and Sisk 2013).
3. Other countries in Africa on the list of countries with the poorest people: include the Democratic Republic of Congo, with 60 million people out of 81.3 million people; Ethiopia with 23.9 million people out of 105 million people; Tanzania with 19.9 million out of 57.31 million people; Mozambique, with 17.8 million people out of 29.67 million people; Kenya, with

14.7 million people out of 49.7 million people; and Uganda, with 14.2 million out of 42.86 million people.
4. It is important to note that Africa accounts for the more than half of fragile states across the globe (OECD 2013).
5. MINT economies (Mexico, Indonesia, Nigeria, Turkey).
6. Next 11 economies (Bangladesh, Egypt, Indonesia, Iran, Mexico, Nigeria, Pakistan, Philippines, Turkey, South Korea, Vietnam).
7. BRICS economies (Brazil, Russia, India, China, South Africa).
8. Tanzania (2.7%), Ethiopia (2.4%), Burkina Faso (0.66%) and Rwanda (0.40%).
9. For a more robust debate on developmental states in Africa, see Routley (2014).

References

Ajala, O. 2018. Formation of Insurgent Groups: MEND and Boko Haram in Nigeria. *Small Wars & Insurgencies* 29 (1): 112–130.

Bhorat H., and F. Tarp. 2016. The Pursuit of Long-Run Economic Growth in Africa: An Overview of Key Challenges. In *Africa's Lions*, 1–36. Brookings Institution Press.

Bravo-Ortega, Claudio, and Jose de Gregorio. 2007. The Relative Richness of the Poor. Natural Resources, Human Capital and Economic Growth. In *Natural Resources: Neither Curse Nor Destiny*, ed. D. Lederman and W.F. Maloney. Palo Alto: Stanford University Press and Washington, DC: World Bank.

Brooks, D. 2000. Hope for the 'Hopeless Continent': Mercenaries. *Traders: Journal for the Southern African Region* 3: 1–9.

Bush, R. 2018. Africa: A Political Economy of Continued Crisis. *Afrika Focus* 31 (2): 23–46.

Cadot, O., J. de Melo, P. Plane, L. Wagner, and M.T. Woldemichael. 2016. Industrialisation et transformation structurelle: l'Afriquesubsahariennepeut-elle se développer sans usines? *Revue d'economie du developpement* 24 (2): 19–49.

Caselli, F., and T. Cunningham. 2009. Leader Behaviour and the Natural Resource Curse. *Oxford Economic Papers* 61 (4): 628–650.

Chandy, L. 2011. Ten Years of Fragile States: What Have We Learned? Global Views Policy Paper 2011-12, The Brookings Institution, Washington, DC. Available at www.brookings.edu/~/media/research/files/papers/2011/11/fragile%20states%20chandy/11_fragile_states_chandy.pdf.

Chandy, L., and G. Gertz. 2011. *Poverty in Numbers: The Changing State of Global Poverty from 2005 to 2015* (pp. 8–10). Washington, DC: Brookings Institution.

Chen. S., and M. Ravallion. 2008. The Developing World Is Poorer Than We Thought, but No Less Successful in the Fight Against Poverty. Policy Research Working Paper 4703, World Bank, Washington, DC.

Cilliers, J., and T. Sisk. 2013. Assessing Long-Term State Fragility in Africa: Prospects for 26 "More Fragile" Countries. ISS Monograph No. 188. Pretoria. Available at http://pardee.du.edu/assessing-long-term-state-fragility-africa-prospects-26-%E2%80%9Cmore-fragile%E2%80%9D-countries#sthash.L7BXF58U.dpuf.

Collier, P., and J.W. Gunning. 1999. Why Has Africa Grown Slowly? *Journal of Economic Perspectives* 13 (3): 3–22.

De Vries, G., M. Timmer, and K. De Vries. 2015. Structural Transformation in Africa: Static Gains, Dynamic Losses. *The Journal of Development Studies* 51 (6): 674–688.

The Economist. 2000. Hopeless Africa. May 11.

The Economist. 2011. Africa's Hopeful Economies: The Sun Shines Bright. December.

The Economist. 2013. Africa Rising: A Hopeful Continent. March 3.

Hausmann R., D. Rodrik, and A. Velasco. 2005. Growth Diagnostics. John F. Kennedy School of Government, Harvard University, Cambridge, MA.

Howard, P.N., and M.M. Hussain. 2013. *Democracy's Fourth Wave? Digital Media and the Arab Spring*. Oxford: Oxford University Press.

Jalilian, H., C. Kirkpatrick, and D. Parker. 2007. Impact of Regulation on Economic Growth in Developing Countries: A Cross-Country Analysis. *World Development* 35 (1): 87–103.

Karl, T.L. 2007. Ensuring Fairness: The Case for a Transparent Fiscal Contract. In *Escaping the Resource Curse*, ed. M. Humphreys, J. Sachs, and J. Stiglitz, 256–285. New York: Columbia University Press.

Kolstad, I., and T. Soreide. 2009. Corruption in Natural Resource Management—Implications for Policymakers. *Resources Policy* 34 (4): 214–226.

Laniran, T.J. 2017. Fiscal Regimes in Resource-Dependent African States: A Political Economy Game. AGDI Working Paper No. WP/17/037.

Lederman, D., and W. Maloney. 2008. *In Search of the Missing Resource Curse*. Washington, DC: World Bank.

Lo, V.I., and M. Hiscock (eds.). 2014. *The Rise of the BRICS in the Global Political Economy: Changing Paradigms?* Cheltenham: Edward Elgar.

McGuirk, E.F. 2013. The Illusory Leader: Natural Resources, Taxation and Accountability. *Public Choice* 154 (3–4): 285–313.

McMillan, M.S., and D. Rodrik. 2011. Globalization, Structural Change and Productivity Growth. National Bureau of Economic Research No. w17143.

MDG Report. 2014. Assessing Progress in Africa Toward the Millennium Development Goals. Addis Ababa.

Mehlum, H., K. Moene, and R. Torvik. 2006. Institutions and the Resource Curse. *The Economic Journal* 116 (508): 1–20.

Ngwafu, P.A. 2016. US Support for Democracy in Africa: Discrepant Orientations of Anglophone and Francophone Africa Towards Democratic Practices, Good Governance & Human Rights. *African Social Science Review* 8 (1): 23–48.

Nwapi C., and N. Andrews. 2017. A New Developmental State in Africa: Evaluating Recent State Interventions Vis-a-Vis Resource Extraction in Kenya, Tanzania, and Rwanda. *McGill Journal of Sustainable Development and. Law* 13 (2): 223–267.

OECD. 2013. Fragile States 2013: Resource Flows and Trends in a Shifting World. OECD Publishing, Paris and International Monetary Fund (IMF), Washington, DC. Available at www.imf.org/external/pubs/ft/wp/2004/wp0495.pdf.

Prebisch, R. 1959. Commercial Policy in Underdeveloped Countries. *The American Economic Review* 49 (2): 251–273.

Radelet, S. 2007. Reviving Economic Growth in Liberia. Centre for Global Development (CGD) Working Paper, No. 133, CGD, Washington, DC. Available at www.cgdev.org/files/14912_file_Liberia_Growth.pdf.

Robinson, J.A., R. Torvik, and T. Verdier. 2006. Political Foundations of the Resource Curse. *Journal of Development Economics* 79 (2): 447–468.

Rodrik, D. 2016. An African Growth Miracle? *Journal of African Economies* 27 (1): 10–27.

Routley, L. 2014. Developmental States in Africa? A Review of Ongoing Debates and Buzzwords. *Development Policy Review* 32 (2): 159–177.

Sachs, J., and A. Warner. 2001. The Curse of Natural Resources. *European Economic Review* 45 (4–6): 827–838.

Staines, N. 2004. Economic Performance over the Conflict Cycle. IMF Working Paper No. WP/04/95.

Sumner, A. 2012. From Deprivation to Distribution: Is Global Poverty Becoming a Matter of National Inequality? IDS Working Papers, 2012(394), 1–36.

Swaniker, F. 2013. Africa's Rising Economies. *Survival* 55: 129–142.

Toh, K. 2016. Emerging Growth Economies in Sub-Saharan Africa. *The American Economist* 61 (2): 229–244.

UNDP BCPR. 2008. Post-Conflict Economic Recovery; Enabling Local Ingenuity. Crisis Prevention and Recovery Report 2008, UNDP BCPR (Bureau for Crisis Prevention and Recovery) New York. Available at www.undp.org/content/dam/undp/library/crisis%20prevention/undp-cpr-post-conflict-economic-recovery-enable-local-ingenuity-report-2008.pdf.

UNECA. 2012. *Unleashing Africa's Potential as a Pole of Global Growth*. Addis Ababa: United Nations Economic Commission for Africa (UNECA) and Africa Union.

World Bank. 2011. *Word Development Report 2011: Conflict, Security, and Development*. Washington, DC: World Bank.

World Bank. 2014 Decades of Sustained Growth Is Transforming Africa's Economies. *Africa Pulse* 10 (October).

World Bank. 2015. *The Economic Outlook for the Middle East and North Africa*. Washington, DC: The World Bank.

World Bank. 2018. *World Development Indicators*. Washington, DC: The World Bank.

Zamfir, I. 2016. *Africa's Economic Growth: Taking Off or Slowing Down?* Members' Research Service, Directorate-General for Parliamentary Research Services, European Parliament.

PART II

Interrogating the Global Dimensions of Africa Rising

CHAPTER 3

Africa-EU Relations and the Politics of International Development

Ibrahim Bangura

Introduction

The First and Second World Wars had devastating consequences for Europe and other parts of the world. They were characterised by a massive loss of human lives and the devastation of countries within and outside of Europe. Europe alone lost over 39 million people to the war and political and economic systems in many countries were permanently altered (Kesternich et al. 2012: 1). With the end of World War II in 1945, an ideological struggle referred to as the Cold War ensued between the two major powers, the United States of America (USA) and the defunct Union of Soviet Socialist Republics (USSR). The USA wanted to contain the spread of communism by USSR and it degenerated into a "global conflict that affected many countries, particularly the continent of Europe. Indeed, Europe, divided into two blocs, became one of the main theatres of the Cold War. In Western Europe, the European integration process began with the support of the United States, while the countries

I. Bangura (✉)
Department of Peace and Conflict Studies, Fourah Bay College, University of Sierra Leone, Freetown, Sierra Leone

K. Omeje (ed.), *The Governance, Security and Development Nexus*,
https://doi.org/10.1007/978-3-030-49348-6_3

of Eastern Europe became satellites of the USSR" (Virtual Centre for Knowledge about Europe 2016: 3).

The need for integration was predicated on the desire to strengthen security and trade relations among European nations, especially in the aftermath of the two World Wars and the immediate challenges posed by the Cold War. The decision to pool the coal and steel industries of six European countries (France, Italy, Belgium, Netherlands and Luxembourg and West Germany) to establish the European Coal and Steel Community (ECSC), brought into force by the Treaty of Paris in 1951, marked the first step towards European integration. The Treaties of Rome of 1957 further strengthened the foundations of integration and the notion of a common future for the six European countries (European Parliament 2018: 3). Increased interest on the part of other European countries to be part of such security and trade arrangements gradually culminated into an expanded integration, with the signing of the Treaty on the European Union (EU) by twelve countries[1] in Maastricht, the Netherlands on 7 February 1992. Key objectives of the Treaty include:

> - [T]o promote economic and social progress which is balanced and sustainable in particular through the creation of an area without internal frontiers, through the strengthening of economic and social cohesion and through the establishment of economic and monetary union, ultimately including a single currency in accordance with the provisions of this Treaty;
> - To assert its identity on the international scene, in particular through the implementation of a common foreign and security policy including the eventual framing of a common defence policy, which might in time lead to a common defence. (European Union 1992: 7–8)

What started off with twelve countries in 1992 now has a membership of twenty-eight.[2] Since its establishment, the EU has strategically positioned itself as a vital development partner to Africa. According to the EU, its "aid represents more than 50% of global aid. €21 billion in development aid was provided to Africa in 2016 by the EU and its member states, additionally, one third of the overall foreign direct investment in Africa comes from the EU with €32 billion invested in Africa by EU companies in 2015, €1.4 billion are committed to educational programmes in Africa from 2014 to 2020" (European Union 2019).[3] The EU Delegations in the respective countries support and oversee the implementation of aid-related activities, with the aim of promoting the expected impact and sustainability of the initiatives undertaken.

Maurizio Carbone (2012) states that the EU's importance goes well beyond the monetary commitment it has towards Africa's development. The EU through its soft power, as a norm maker introduced concepts such as complementarity and division of labour, has also partaken in the discursive charge towards enhancing aid effectiveness (Carbone 2012: 7–8). In addition to the claim by Carbone, supports provided by the EU are usually geared towards strengthening systems and structures geared towards promoting good governance and safe and secure societies.

In contrast to the claims above, analysts such as Huigens and Niemann (2011) have argued that the EU's role in development is much more complicated than it might first appear, and that to avoid casual and incomplete understanding of the Union and its actions, one must first problematise the driving motive of the EU in the development field (2011: 635). Similarly, writers such as Bountagkidis et al. (2015) have questioned both the intentions and nature of the EU-Africa relationship. The criticisms are based on claims that what exists between the two is an uneven donor–recipient based relationship, with the intentions of Europe being unclear and not well-defined which disadvantages Africa.

To further deepen the understanding of and perspectives related to EU-Africa relations, the chapter critically examines the evolution of the relationship and priorities of EU's support to Africa and scepticisms related to the relationship. It provides suggestions and recommendations on how EU-Africa relations could be re-modelled to positively support Africa's desire to rise from the trajectory of an underdeveloped and poverty-stricken continent.

The methodological approach employed was based on key interviews done with 82 (63 males and 19 females) experts in the fields of international development and politics. They were largely drawn from relevant Ministries, Departments and Agencies (MDAs), EU funded projects and academic institutions in Nigeria, Sierra Leone, Guinea, Ghana, Somalia and Cote d'Ivoire. A significant number of interviews were done with the use of telephone and Skype, while the rest were done during field consultations in some of the countries listed above.

The Politics of International Development and Development Aid in a Changing World

While a good number of African countries had strong and stable economies during independence, factors such as political instability, corruption, mismanagement of state resources, coupled with subsequent stringent economic recovery programmes instituted by the Bretton Woods Institution, plunged many African countries into indebtedness. Thus, development assistance emerged as an avenue to address economic challenges African countries were contending with (Koroma 1996).

This donor–recipient relationship was initially mostly tied to former colonial masters or in cases where such ties were severed; new development partners were sought. By then, the understanding of development aid as a concept was very limited. The International Monetary Fund (IMF) defines Overseas[4] Development Aid (ODA) as:

> Flows of official financing administered with the promotion of the economic development and welfare of developing countries as the main objective, and which are concessional in character with a grant element of at least 25 percent (using a fixed 10 percent rate of discount). By convention, ODA flows comprise contributions of donor government agencies, at all levels, to developing countries ("bilateral ODA") and to multilateral institutions. ODA receipts comprise disbursements by bilateral donors and multilateral institutions. Lending by export credit agencies—with the pure purpose of export promotion—is excluded. (IMF 2003)

Though there is extensive literature on the definition and origin of development aid, President Harry S. Truman of the United States is often credited with the introduction of the terminology as a concept, during his inaugural speech in 1949. He referred to development aid as "a bold new programme for making the benefits of our scientific advances and industrial progress available for the improvement and growth of underdeveloped areas" (Truman 1949). Truman's test came with the delivery of the Marshall Plan, a massive aid package that "pulled Europe from the abyss of economic collapse and political chaos" after the Second World War (Wilson 1977: 5).

While Western Europe was able to recover through American aid, the eruption of the Cold War at the end of the Second World War had both direct and indirect effects on the nature and types of relationships that existed between post-independence emerging states and their Western/Eastern partners until the early 1990s. A Cold War Historian and a former Foreign Minister of Sierra Leone[5] commented on the interaction between Western and Eastern powers with Sub-Sahara Africa:

> Development aid was tied to the support for the USA, Russia or their allies. It was very political and military in nature. It benefited the elites but deprived the masses, which led to the eruption of several military coups and civil wars, with devastating long term effects. For both the US and Russia and their allies, it was about strategic positioning. Western interests were pushed by Bretton Woods institutions such as the World Bank and the IMF were used to economically strangulate African countries using development aid and loans with conditionalities that no country could meet. They further plunged Africa into significant economic clutter that most countries have never recovered from.

With the end of the Cold War in 1989, the drive towards globalisation has "spurred economic convergence, upending the 20thcentury economic balance and creating a smaller world where both problems and solutions spill across national borders more readily. This has given rise to a legion of new development actors—including emerging economies, non-governmental organisations, private businesses and coordinating networks" (Brookings 2011: 1).

Increasing number of development partners rather provides countries with more options to choose from, thus, an opportunity to assess the true intentions of donors. Coupled with this, it becomes challenging for the countries to own and lead the process of setting the agenda and priorities to foster the efficient and effective use of aid secured. To minimise challenges related to development aid, several initiatives have been introduced including the Paris Declaration on Aid Effectiveness 2005, the Accra Agenda for Action, 2008 and the Busan Partnership for Effective Development Cooperation, 2011. Additionally, in September 2015, the Sustainable Development Goals (SDGs) were adopted by the United Nations General Assembly (UNGA) with the 2030 Agenda for Sustainable Development. This was done out of the recognition of the fact that ending poverty must go hand-in-hand with strategies that build economic growth and address a range of social needs including education, health, social protection and job opportunities while tackling climate change and environmental protection (United Nations 2019).

Inasmuch as the initiatives listed above are meant to promote aid effectiveness and development in targeted countries, unhealthy competition, leadership and coordination challenges, alongside the security and political interests of donors continue to undermine the development.[6] A development expert working in Puntland, Somalia[7] claims that:

> There are usually strong links between political, economic and security interests when it comes to the provision of aid to countries in need. Countries such as Somalia, Central African Republic, Niger and Chad will never get the kind of aid they require, they are of no strategic interest to any major power. Even when aid is provided in some cases, the process is completely owned and driven by donors; the poor countries are left to fit into the priorities of the donor. There has to be an interest on the part of international actors to change the approach to aid. It has to be meant to make a positive difference in the lives of people. Aid should have a human face.

To overcome some of the challenges stated above, United Nations Economic Commission for Latin America and the Caribbean (ECLAC) and the Development Centre of the Organisation for Economic Cooperation and Development (OECD) proposed five pillars to improve development cooperation:

> [F]irst, international cooperation for development should measure development beyond per capita Gross Domestic Product (GDP). Second, the cooperation strategies and focus of development should be linked to national strategies and reflect a multidimensional approach. Third, the focus of the multilateral agenda should be based on the 2030 Agenda for Sustainable Development promoting better global public goods. Fourth, the governance and financing approach to cooperation should look beyond official development assistance (ODA) and be multilevel in nature.... Finally, international cooperation should go beyond traditional instruments and include such modalities as innovative instruments of knowledge-sharing, capacity-building and technology transfers. (ECLAC and OECD 2018: 7)

The proposed pillars point at the need for more strategic and unorthodox approaches geared towards strengthening local capacity to promote sustainable development.

The Evolution of EU-Africa Relations

The EU and Africa have succeeded in maintaining a relationship that goes as far back as the late 1950s when the Europeans were seeking to establish a common union to overcome the historical legacies of World War II. Describing the history of EU-Africa relations, Bossuyt (2017: 1) states that:

> Following the wave of independence, African countries became the main beneficiaries of Europe's first steps into foreign policy. Developmental goals were only part of the story behind the 'association' offered to the European project through the so called 'Yaoundé Conventions' (1963-75). For France in particular, it was critical to bring its overseas territories on board to protect its markets, maintain its political influence and ensure a 'burden sharing' of the ensuing bill (i.e. the aid provided through the so-called European Development Fund, EDF) with the other European Economic Community (EEC) members.

The relationship between the EU and Africa, however, gained firmer and more formal roots with the establishment of the Africa-EU Partnership at the first Africa-EU Summit in Cairo, Egypt in 2000. According to the African Union (AU 2019): "The Africa - EU Partnership strives to bring Africa and Europe closer together through strengthening economic cooperation and promoting sustainable development, with both continents co-existing in peace, security, democracy, prosperity, solidarity and human dignity." Seven years into the partnership, it was concluded that to ensure a much more strategic and efficient relationship, it was essential for the partners to develop a strategic framework to guide the partnership and as such, the Joint Africa-EU Strategy (JAES) was developed and subsequently adopted during the second EU-Africa Summit in Lisbon, Portugal in 2007.

As indicated under Sections 10 and 11 of the JAES:

> The four main objectives of this long-term strategic partnership set the comprehensive framework within which specific strategies will have to be put in place in the following areas: (a) peace and security, (b) governance and human rights, (c) trade and regional integration and (d) key development issues.
>
> In the implementation of this new partnership, the principle of policy coherence for development will be applied by both African and EU

> partners by identifying and promoting interactions and positive complementarities between sectoral policies and strategies, while ensuring that measures taken in one policy area do not undermine results in other areas. (JAES 2007: 4)

Responding to questions on the JAES, a senior staff of the African Union[8] described the transitional phases of the Africa-EU relationship:

> The relationship between EU and Africa was initially not well defined and coordinated. There were significant suspicions and doubts and it was necessary for the two to come up with a framework that will guide the evolving relationship. The JAES symbolises an attempt on the part of the EU to have an open and better-defined relationship with Africa.

A staff of the EU in Brussels[9] indicated that:

> Discussion around the development of the JAES commenced out of the need on the part of the EU to develop a long-term political vision that would shape its relationship and interaction with Africa. There was the need for a shift from the EU being looked at as a donor to a much more credible relationship based on true partnership and effective collaboration between two continents which are neighbours. We share common challenges and have common interests and by working together we strengthen each other.

It appears that both institutions were keen on having a framework that would foster effective coordination of activities and a stronger working relationship. While Africa's reliance on the EU's aid may not dwindle in the coming years, it will be more productive if the aid provided is better coordinated and complemented. Additionally, with a clearly defined road map, gains made in one area would not be undermined by investments by the EU in other areas. Thus, the JAES was meant to provide both a political platform for constructive engagement and the means to ensure efficient and effective use of resources provided.

Since 2007, the process of implementing the JAES "has benefitted from a number of different financial instruments developed by the EU to support its external partners. Among them, the European Development Fund (EDF) – including its African Peace Facility (APF) component –is the EU's main instrument for supplying development aid to African, Caribbean and Pacific (ACP) countries as well as other Overseas Countries and Territories (OCTs). In addition, Trust Funds (TFs) totally or partially funded through the EDF have been created" (European Parliament 2017: 14).

With its massive investments in Africa, the EU is the biggest donor to Africa, with African states receiving direct EU funding, especially under the EDF. To ensure their buy-in, leadership and ownership of the process on the part of member states, European Union Delegations (EUDs) work with the National Authorisation Offices (NAOs) and the relevant line ministries during the implementation of programmes and projects. This is complemented by the EU sending external monitors to conduct Result-Oriented Monitoring (ROM) Missions to assess the impact created by activities implemented.

Few years after 2007, developments in both Africa and Europe pointed at the need for a shift in approach. Key issues that motivated the need for a shift in approach included the rise in the activities of terror-related groups on the continent such as Al Qaeda and Boko Haram; the fall of the Muammar Qaddafi's regime in Libya; increase in irregular migration among young people; the "youth bulge" and massive unemployment and poverty among youth and women across Africa. These challenges have a direct impact on not just Africa but also Europe, which is the principal target of both terror groups and impoverished young people seeking to migrate out of Africa. In making a case for a shift in approach, the European Parliament states:

> The objectives identified in 2007 still remain valid but concrete priorities need to be adapted to the new reality. Moreover, refinement of the Africa-EU partnership's strategic vision has become urgent following adoption of the Agenda 2063 and the EU Global Strategy, new strategic frameworks for the African continent's socio-economic transformation over the next 50 years and the EU's foreign and security policy, respectively. (European Parliament 2017: 7)

Consequently, 10 years after Cairo, the EU, AU and other partners agreed on the need to critically re-examine the relationship between the two and come up with pragmatic approaches to dealing with existing and emerging challenges. In 2017, during the 5th African Union-European Union Summit in Abidjan, Côte d'Ivoire, a joint declaration outlined four common priorities for the future of the Africa-EU partnership: (i)

Investing in people—education, science, technology and skills development; (ii) Strengthening Resilience, Peace, Security and Governance; (iii) Migration and mobility; (iv) Mobilising Investments for African structural and sustainable transformation.[10] The four priority areas were deemed to be crucial to the strengthening of peace, stability and development in Africa. According to a participant[11] in the summit working at the Foreign Ministry in Côte d'Ivoire:

> The Summit was a success and it brought together leaders from both the EU and Africa, with them having clear and frank discussions on what was needed to have less 'political' but more meaningful dialogues on the future of the relationship between the two continents. The priority areas arrived at stretches across the core of the challenges and difficulties in Africa, that also have implications for Europe. The Summit also created an opportunity for the EU to commit itself to further strengthening its investment in Africa.

Out of the 82 interviewees, 43 indicated that the Abidjan Summit was very positive and had good outcomes that favoured Africa, particularly the commitments related to the increase in aid and promotion of effective coordination of activities. The other 39 interviewees were mostly critical of the Summit and claimed that it was business as usual. They argued that African leaders were only interested in getting additional aid, while the Europeans were keen on having African leaders commit to curbing irregular migration and combating terror-related groups that have the potential of affecting European business interests in the continent. One of the 39 critical respondents who is a development expert working in Libya[12] had this to say:

> The Summit was a summit of 'unequal partners' and both sides went there with clear agendas. One wanted more money and the other wanted to provide aid, with the aid tied to European interests such as migration and security. Furthermore, the Europeans went to Abidjan, with the scar of Libya on their conscience and focusing on having African leaders work on dealing with the use of Libya as a route to Europe. Thus, it came as little surprise that a joint statement on migration by EU-AU leaders was released before the end of the Summit. While the Summit was designed to appear as if EU leaders respect the views and aspirations of Africa, the earlier disregard by the EU of the position of the AU on the Libyan crisis was a show of utter disrespect to the continent and its leaders. When the Summit came, all African leaders could think of was more money and not

how to re-engineer the relationship between them and European leaders to ensure that they are respected and treated with dignity.

Similar sentiments were expressed by a senior lecturer at the University of Ghana, Legon[13]:

> When it comes to issues such as security, the opinion of Africans and their leaders do not matter to Europeans. The true test of whether our views as Africans matter or not comes into play when the EU or institutions that its Member States are part of such as the North-Atlantic Treaty Organisation (NATO) are interested in undertaking security measures that the AU is against. The approach to the Libyan crisis was not respectful to the AU, the relationship we have is based on the politics of development aid. Africans are perceived to be poor and voiceless and that is also how our leaders portray the continent. The Abidjan Summit was the same as all other summits. At the end, it all boiled down to how much money will come in and the donor-recipient relationship continues.

Whatever the case may be, as indicated above, it is clear that the EU remains one of the largest donors in Africa and the EU's support remains vital to both government and non-governmental actors. The reliance on donor support makes it very difficult for the relation to be a relationship of equals. Some of the interviewees accused the EU and some of its members of interfering in the internal politics of countries, especially that of Sub-Sahara Africa.[14] However, one may argue that the relationship between some member states of the EU such as the British, French and Portuguese, with African states transcends that of the EU as a bloc. As such, the activities of member states should not necessarily be interpreted as actions of the EU. This line appears to be blurred to some of the interviewees, which resulted in the perception that the EU unduly influences political and electoral processes in African countries.

In a study done in 2015 on EU and development aid in Sub-Saharan Africa, Bountagkidis et al. (2015: 1) state that "The evidence found indicates that in certain instances, aid allocation contradicts the normative rhetoric that the EU uses to describe its development policy, as the donor's own interests in the region seem to supersede priority given to the needs of the aid recipient states." This may lay credence to some of the claims by interviewees of the relationship between the EU's interests, politics and aid in Africa. The European NGO Confederation for Relief and Development-CONCORD (2014) similarly indicated that "the EU-Africa relations are still built on an unfair relationship that needs change." The section below provides arguments on what could be done to change the character of the existing relationship.

Promoting a Mutually Beneficial Relationship for Sustainable Growth and Development in Africa

Among 82 interviewees, 67 indicated that Africa's relationship with the EU is uneven and that the high reliance of the continent on European aid undermines any potential for a relationship that is mutually beneficial and that can lead to sustainable growth and development in Africa. This, they indicated could be changed if there is reduced need or reliance on aid on the part of African states. In recent years, the realisation of the need for a shift from Western aid has played into the hands of the Chinese, who in a bid to expand their influence in Africa offer terms and conditions that focus less on the need to strengthen good governance and human rights in the continent. Such an approach seems favourable to African elites who rush to China to avoid the scrutiny of Western donors such as the EU.

The switch to China does not provide the answers that Africa is seeking but rather exposes the continent to more foreign exploitation and abuse. Providing suggestions on what Africa needs to improve its relationship with the EU, a political scientist at the University of Sierra Leone[15] noted:

> Africa needs to be sincere with itself, its leaders need to invest in strengthening its governance system, fight corruption, provide effective and result oriented leadership, use the limited resources available to improve human resource capacity, upscale industrialization processes, reduce import and improve on export of finished products, expand on employment and livelihood opportunities and strengthen social cohesion and security. This is do-able if corruption and bad governance are checked. Developing and using home-grown and owned solutions are the answer and we need to begin working on them.

Corruption and bad governance are among the greatest challenges that Africa contends with. While the continent has an abundance of resources, it remains among the poorest in the world according to the World Economic Forum "Today, extreme poverty is mostly around Africa, where

23 of the world's 28 poorest countries are found. These countries have poverty rates above 30%. Poverty projections up to the year 2030 (the end of the Sustainable Development Goals) suggest that even under the most optimistic scenario, over 300 million people in sub-Saharan Africa will still be in extreme poverty" (World Economic Forum 2019).

Similar to the proposal of the interviewee at the University of Sierra Leone, the World Economic Forum asserts that:

> Sub-Saharan African states often suffer from limited institutional capacity to carry out policies that deliver benefits and services to citizens. In other words, they have limited state capacity. Building state capacity depends on many variables. It is greater when ruling elites are subject to effective limits on the exercise of their power through institutionalised checks and balances. (World Economic Forum 2019)

Inasmuch as the focus has to be on Africa fixing its internal challenges to strategically position itself as a credible partner, the EU should also play a role in supporting Africa's drive to establish itself as a credible partner. One way this could be done is in promoting the region's trade potentials, especially in industrialisation, value chain development, expanding export opportunities and credible trade opportunities. This would go alongside working with the AU, Regional Economic Communities and the Member States to strengthen governance and effective service delivery to citizens of the respective countries. Such efforts would go a long way in promoting growth and development in targeted countries, thereby opening the socio-economic and political space for vulnerable groups such as youth, women and People with Disability (PWD). The availability of education, employment and livelihood opportunities would go a long way in mitigating irregular migration and its potential terror-related and other transnational threats, which both continents have been seeking to overcome in the last decade, albeit unsuccessfully. Such approaches if adopted would promote a mutually beneficial and respectful relationship, which is essential for sustainable growth and development in Africa.

A senior policy analyst[16] at the Ministry of Finance in Conakry, Guinea summed up her thought on a change in approach to EU-Africa relationship:

> There is a need for the relationship between the EU and Africa to be revisited, with both sides working on genuinely inspiring and encouraging

Africa's transition to a stable and progressive continent. The shift from reliance on aid to contributing on a fair basis to addressing issues affecting both continents would go a long way in enhancing Africa's respect and global voice. While this may take years to happen, that journey needs to begin as soon as possible. EU's investment should be geared towards strengthening good governance and reducing the continent's reliance on aid.

Conclusion

For several decades, the EU has remained a close partner to Africa and is the largest aid contributor to the continent. Through aid delivery, it has succeeded in assisting governments to deliver much-needed services to their people. Since 2002, there have been efforts made by the two partners to further strengthen their relationship through seeking to shift from ad hoc approaches to the adoption of concrete strategies for the delivery and use of financial and technical support to the continent. This has led to the 2007 and 2017 summits, alongside other initiatives in the two continents. Consequently, the EU has steadily increased its support to the continent, with EU member states also providing bi-lateral support to countries they have bi-lateral relationships with.

However, inasmuch as the tremendous effort has gone into improving EU-Africa relationship, there is the perception among my fieldwork respondents that it is an unequal and unbalanced relationship between a donor and an aid recipient. The conclusion of the respondents is in line with those presented by both CONCORD and Bountagkidis et al. (2015). The EU continues to have tremendous political leverage, with African countries and the AU continuously being the underdog. A typical example provided by interviewees is the Libyan crisis and the dismissal on the part of EU member states of the protests by the AU against military intervention by NATO. Furthermore, the relationship is believed to be specifically focused on largely addressing only issues of immediate importance to the EU's agenda such as migration and the fight against terror than promoting long-term sustainable growth and development in Africa.

It is the view of most respondents that there has to be an African solution to addressing the continent's challenges. However, this change process has to come from the willingness on the part of the continent's political leaders to strengthen good democratic governance, human security, invest in economic growth and development and open the socio-economic and political space for women, youth and other vulnerable groups. The EU could shift its support from "small" projects to investing in more tangible and productive economic initiatives which would stimulate development in the true sense of the word. Such initiatives should include investing in industrialisation with the aim of reducing import and improving on export, the development and adoption of favourable trade agreements, promotion of democratic good governance and citizens' participation in leadership and decision-making processes. Such investments would lead to a win–win situation for both Africa and Europe.

Notes

1. Britain, France, Germany, the Irish Republic, Spain, Portugal, Italy, Greece, Denmark, Luxembourg, Belgium and the Netherlands were the twelve countries that signed the Maastricht Treaty in 1992.
2. This number will be reduced to 27 when Britain eventually leaves the Union in October 2019 as a result of its citizens voting in a referendum to leave the EU. The referendum which is now referred to as the Brexit referendum was held on 23 June 2016 and 51.9% of the voters voted for Britain to leave the Union.
3. See https://ec.europa.eu/europeaid/regions/africa/africa-eu-continental-cooperation_en (Accessed 21 May 2019).
4. This chapter uses International Development Aid rather than Overseas Development Aid.
5. Interview conducted in Freetown, Sierra Leone on 21 May 2019.
6. Based on interviews conducted for the chapter.
7. Interview conducted in Puntland, Somalia on 16 January 2019.
8. Interview conducted via Skype on 14 May 2019.
9. Interview conducted via Skype on 21 April 2019.
10. See https://www.africa-eu-partnership.org/en/our-events/5th-au-eu-summit.
11. Interview conducted on 13 March via Skype.
12. Interview conducted via telephone on 15 February 2019.
13. Interview conducted in Accra, Ghana on 20 February 2019.
14. Based on interviews conducted for this chapter.
15. Interview conducted in Freetown, Sierra Leone on 12 May 2019.
16. Interview conducted in Conakry, Guinea on 1 March 2019.

References

African Union. 2019. The Partnership and Joint Africa-EU Strategy. https://www.africa-eu-partnership.org/en/partnership-and-joint-africa-eu-strategy. Accessed 18 April 2019.

Bountagkidis, Georgios K., Konstantinos C. Fragkos, and Christos C. Frango. 2015. EU Development Aid Towards Sub-Saharan Africa: Exploring the Normative Principle. *Social Sciences* 4: 85–116.

Bossuyt, Jean. 2017. Can EU-Africa Relations be Deepened? A Perspective on Power Relations, Interests and Incentives. Briefing Note No. 97. The European Centre for Development Policy Management (ECDPM). The Netherlands.

Brookings. 2011. From Aid to Global Development Cooperation. The 2011 Brookings Blum Rountable Briefs. USA.

Carbone, Maurizio. 2012. Between EU Actorness and Aid Effectiveness: The Logics of EU Aid to Sub-Saharan Africa. Paper presented at the annual meeting of the Società Italiana di Scienza Politica (SISP), University of Rome III.

ECLAC and OECD. 2018. Emerging Challenges and Shifting Paradigms: New Perspectives on International Cooperation for Development. United Nations Economic Commission for Latin America and the Caribbean (ECLAC) and the Development Centre of the Organisation for Economic Cooperation and Development (OECD), Santiago, Chile.

European NGO Confederation for Relief and Development-CONCORD. 2014. EU-Africa: An Unfair Relationship That Needs Change. Brussels, Belgium. https://concordeurope.org/blog/2014/04/03/eu-africa-an-unfair-relationship-that-needs-change/.

European Parliament. 2017. The Joint Africa-EU Strategy. Directorate-General for External Policies- Policy Department, Brussels, Belgium.

European Parliament. 2018. The Historical Development of European Integration. Brussels, Belgium.

European Union. 1992. The Treaty on European Union. Brussels, Belgium.

European Union. 2019. Africa-EU Cooperation. https://ec.europa.eu/europeaid/regions/africa/africa-eu-continental-cooperation_en.

Huigens, Judith, and Arne Niemann. 2011. The G8 ½: The EU's Contested and Ambiguous Actorness in the G8. *Cambridge Review of International Affairs* 24(4): 629–657.

International Monetary Fund. 2003. *External Debt Statistics: Guide for Compilers and Users*. Washington, DC: IMF.

European Union and African Union. 2007. The Africa-EU Strategic Partnership: A Joint Africa-EU Strategy. Portugal. https://africa-eupartnership.org/sites/default/files/eas2007_joint_strategy_en_0.pdf.

Kesternich, Iris, Bettina Siflinger, James P. Smith, and Joachim K. Winter. 2012. The Effects of World War II on Economic and Health Outcomes Across Europe. RAND Labour and Population Working Paper Series, USA.

Koroma, Abdul Karim. 1996. *Sierra Leone: The Agony of a Nation*. Freetown, Sierra Leone: Andromeda Publications.

Truman, Harry. S. 1949. Inaugural Speech as President of the United States of America. https://avalon.law.yale.edu/20th_century/truman.asp.

United Nations. 2019. Sustainable Development Goals. New York, USA. https://www.un.org/sustainabledevelopment/.

Virtual Centre for Knowledge about Europe. 2016. The Cold War (1945–1989). University of Luxembourg, Luxembourg.

Wilson, Theodore A. 1977. The Marshall Plan an Atlantic Venture of 1947–1951 and How It Shaped Our World. Headline Series 236, Foreign Policy Association, USA.

World Economic Forum. 2019. Here's How We Can Eradicate Poverty in Africa Faster. Geneva, Switzerland.

CHAPTER 4

Africa–US Relations: The Politics of Trade, Investment and Security

Taiwo Owoeye

Introduction

This chapter discusses the changing nature of Africa–US relation and America's interpretations of its role in Africa with respect to security, trade and investment. It starts from America defining the continent from the prism of its NATO allies during the struggle for independence to considering Africa as an ideological battleground during the Cold War era, and as a potent land for the spread of Islamic extremism during the post 9/11 era. This chapter argues that while the security concern of the United States is legitimate, the best strategy to reduce the danger of Africa as a global security threat is to help the continent integrate into the global production process through trade and investment. It therefore reviews the flagship trade preference scheme introduced by the United States in 2000 known as African Growth Opportunity Act (AGOA), which aims at opening the massive and lucrative US market to Africa exports and help the continent on the path to sustainable economic growth. It argues that the trade preference scheme has been less successful than expected

T. Owoeye (✉)
Department of Economics, Ekiti State University, Ado Ekiti, Nigeria

K. Omeje (ed.), *The Governance, Security and Development Nexus*,
https://doi.org/10.1007/978-3-030-49348-6_4

for two reasons. First, African exports to United States have been dominated by energy and other natural resources and not manufactured goods. Second, the scheme has not attracted massive private foreign investment to the manufacturing sector from the OECD and Asia as anticipated. Yet, Africa's hope of rising lies in diversifying its exports base away from natural resources to manufactured goods. This chapter concludes that, for Africa to truly rise, the United States needs to help the region breaks into the global manufacturing chain, like it did for Asia after the Second World War.

The euphoria of 'Africa Rising' that dominated global developmental discourse in the first one and half decade of the twenty-first century is understandable because Africa has been tagged the 'hopeless continent' at the turn of the century (*The Economist* 2000). The narratives of wars (Sierra Leone, Liberia, Angola, Congo, Cote d'lvoire, Mozambique), famine (Ethiopia), genocide (Rwanda, and Burundi), that came out of Africa in the last two decades of the twentieth century were so depressing that any form of good news coming out of the continent has the tendency to be overhyped, and economic indicators for the period 2000–2014 have been very encouraging for Africa. Some African economies were among the fastest growing in the world within this period, driven largely by high commodity price, good macroeconomic management and democratic wave (IMF 2017). According to data from African Development Bank, average annual economic growth rate in Africa was 6% for the period of 2008–2014 and this is very encouraging compared to an average of 1.5% for 1960–2000 (Collier and O'Connell 2007). The conflicts that dominated Africa during the 1980s and 1990s have reduced significantly and some of those countries dominated by conflicts are now among the fastest growing economies in the world and these include Rwanda, Ethiopia and Angola (World Bank 2011; AfDB 2017).

The consistently high annual economic growth rate of 6% that dominated the first fifteen years of the twenty-first century came to abrupt halt in 2016 when it declined to 2.2% (AfDB 2017). This reinforces the concerns of those who have argued that Africa Rising was fuelled by commodity price boom and has very little to do with fundamental changes in the structure of the economy (Fiormonti 2017; Moghalu 2014). The narrative of Africa Rising has therefore taken a hit and doubts have begun to emerge about whether the celebration of the rise of Africa is rather not too early. At the same time, development indices coming out of different international agencies have reinforced the position of Africa as the poorest region in the world. For example the two most populated countries in Africa, Nigeria and Congo, are leading Africa as the home to two-third of the world poorest, while Nigeria, its biggest economy by size and population was infamously dubbed the poverty capital of the world (Kharas et al. 2018). The region is expected to be home to 90% of the poorest people in the world by 2030, while 14 out of the 18 countries with the poorest people in the world will be in Africa by that year (Kharas et al. 2018). The euphoria of Africa Rising has therefore been disputed by poor human development indicators, commodity price shocks and persistent structural weaknesses of African economies. For example, it is the structural weakness that has made it difficult for Africa to integrate into the global economy as its share of global trade has remained around 3% for more than 50 years (World Bank 2011). There is the need, therefore, to re-evaluate the idea that Africa has reached the path of sustained economic growth and this requires an interrogation of the relationship between Africa and the United States. This interrogation is important for three reasons.

Firstly, the long period of commodity price rally behind the impressive economic performance that produced the narrative of Africa rising was essentially driven by the economic transformation of two Asian powerhouses, China and India, and their insatiable demand for natural resources (AfDB 2017; Arieff et al. 2019). It is not by accident that during the period of the Africa rising euphoria, China displaced the United States as Africa's biggest trading partner (AfDB 2017). In other words, the African commodity export boom occurred when the influence of the United States in Africa was declining. Secondly, the transformation of Asia as the global workshop was supported, in part, by massive US investment over the last 70 years since the end of the Second World War as the world relocated its factories from Europe and North America to Asia. The first wave was America investment in Japan following the Second World War, followed by another round of investment in the Asian Tigers (South Korea, Hong Kong, Singapore and Taiwan), and the third wave was massive investment by Western firms in China and other emerging Asian economies. For example, Foreign Direct Investment, FDI, inflow to Asia was US$527 billion in 2015 led by investment from United States, while that of Africa was only US$51 billion during the same period (UNCTAD 2016). Africa FDI inflow was dominated by extractive industry, while Asia was dominated by manufacturing sector (IMF 2017). Thirdly, Africa has always been considered by the richer global North as a basket case of misery, poverty and conflicts and one of the most important questions for development experts is whether the euphoria of the period of Africa rising has changed that perception by convincing the developed countries to invest in Africa instead of sending aid and grants. For example, the US engagements with Africa have been dominated by humanitarian grants and a national security imperative concerned with counterterrorism (Harris 2017). Yet, Africa needs trade and investment from the West like Asia to transform itself and integrate into the global production process, expand its economy and improve the welfare of its people (Collier 2007). The United States is important to achieving these objectives because of its influence and pre-eminent position in global economic and political relations.

This chapter, therefore, interrogates the international dimension of the Africa rising narratives by evaluating the engagements between Africa and the United States in relation to trade, investment and security. It starts by tracing how the relationship between the United States and Africa has evolved overtime from struggle for independence through post-9/11 war on terror. It then evaluates US trade and investment relations with Africa using the flagship preference trade scheme, African Growth Opportunity Acts (AGOA). The study analyses the security dimension of Africa–US relation, showing how improving trade and investment is key to securing Africa and reducing its potential capacity as breeding ground for terrorism. The next section discusses the declining influence of the United States in Africa relative to the rising influence of China, while the final section concludes by briefly outlining how the United States can help Africa to rise.

A Short History of Africa–US Relation

The interest of America in Africa is limited by its lack of colonial connection with the region. It was the Europeans that partitioned Africa among themselves during the nineteenth century and it was through the prism of its European NATO allies that America largely defined Africa during the struggle for independence that spread through the continent after the Second World War. In an essay published in The Foreign Affairs in 1962, Rupert Emerson, one of the then leading American experts on African Affairs critiqued Africa–US relations and argued that as Africa moves towards total independence from European colonialists, America can consider the region as a new book and deals with it within that context. He argued that the relationship between the two regions has been defined by Europe because the Americans respect the imperial interests of their NATO allies, but as the continent struggled off the chain of colonial rule, it is important for the Americans to chart a new path in their relationship with Africa.

The reality of the Cold War changed the attitude of the United State as Africa became an ideological battleground between the Americans and USSR as they struggled for global domination in a bipolar world. America thereafter defined its relationship within the struggle to stop newly independent African states from falling into the communist bloc. The main strategy of US foreign policy during the independence wave of the early 1960s was that Africa in its parts and as a whole be preserved from joining the communist camp (Emerson 1962) Yet, for many newly independent African countries in the 1960s, the United State represented the imperialist NATO-oriented oppressors akin to the colonial powers from whom they just gained independence, whereas the USSR and China were considered allies who are champions of the underdogs like them. The United States, in the opinion of many Africans, was too close to their European colonial oppressors to be considered good allies (Emerson 1962).

To make matter worse, the United States sided with its European allies when the General Assembly debated the Declaration on Colonial Independence in 1960. The Soviet bloc in contrast supported immediate freedom for all colonies. This was an indication of how far the United States went with its European allies to spite Africa. As the American fear of developing countries drifting towards communism deepened, the United States forged an alliance with many right-wing and authoritarian regimes around the world that visibly opposed to communism. In Africa where newly independent states were just emerging, the United States supported local opposition groups hostile to any pro-communist newly installed governments in the global South (Emerson 1962). The alleged complicity of the America's CIA in the assassination in 1961 of Congolese Prime Minister Patrice Lumumba and in the overthrow of Ghana President Kwameh Nkrumah in 1966 was all part of the US anti-communist foreign policy strategy in the developing world.

This anti-communist strategy continued well into the 1980s until after the collapse of the Soviet Union and the end of the Cold War when the American policy towards Africa changed to a perception of the region as a major source of energy and recipient of humanitarian aid. The policy of the United States towards Africa was to further undergo a change in the post-9/11 2001 era as the United States confronted the menace of global Islamist terror. In recent years, different American Presidents have come up with diverse initiatives for African–United States relations. The Bill Clinton administration focused on trade and investment through AGOA, the George W. Bush administration on counterterrorism and combating HIV/AIDS, and major epidemiological diseases, the Obama administration prioritised access to electricity, while the Trump administration is focusing on combating terrorism and countering China's influence on the continent (Signe and Allen 2018).

Trade and Investment: Evaluating the Africa Growth Opportunity Acts (AGOA)

In May 2000, President Bill Clinton signed into law the Trade and Development Act with a preferential trade agreement focus on Africa called the AGOA. The main objective of the Act is to increase both trade and investment between United States and eligible African countries (AGOA 2013). To achieve this objective, the Act proposed the opening up of the US market by reducing and eliminating tariffs for some African exports of different products. It is also aimed at promoting economic development and reform in Africa (AGOA 2013). This flagship trade preference scheme with Africa has been re-authorised and re-ordered four times since the promulgation of the Act, the most recent one being in 2015, and it extended the scheme till 2025. AGOA operates under the Generalised System of Preference (GSP), a programme that applies to exports from most developing countries. It provides access for African exports to the US market. Although, the GSP expired in 2013, AGOA is to remain in operation until 2025 and covers more than 6400 product lines from 38 African countries (Meltzer 2016). The scheme has helped in expanding the African-US trade volume. According to recent estimates by United States Office of Trade Representatives, between 2001 and 2013, exports under AGOA increased from US$7.6 billion to US$24.8 billion but decline by over 50% to US$11.6 billion in 2016 due to the declining oil prices. AGOA has helped in stimulating foreign investment in Africa and some US firms, especially retailers in apparels, are taking advantages of AGOA to produce in Africa, notably in Mauritius and Ethiopia (USTR 2018).

The trade scheme also helps in promoting economic growth and good governance by attaching some conditions to granting market access. This includes progress towards a market-based economy, reduction in trade barrier, commitment to rule of law, as well as fight against corruption and improved workers' conditions (Meltzer 2016). Beneficiary countries must not partake in any activities that may undermine the national security of the United States and should not violate human rights. These constraints were introduced to strengthen democracy and promote good governance. They are also expected to lead to reforms in the business environment of beneficiary's countries. This seems to be working as the recent World Bank 'Ease of Doing Business' Report of 2018 shows that African countries dominate the group of countries that have made the most progress in the index (World Bank 2018). There are concerns at the early stage of the scheme that some of the restrictions may also work against the success of AGOA (Matto et al. 2002).

An important challenge of AGOA is the compositions of African exports to the United States as it is dominated by crude oil exports which accounts for about 70% of the exports to the United States (USTR 2018; Schneidman and Lewis 2012; Jones and William 2012). An important issue with this is that the impact of the preferential treatment on duty for crude oil exports on African countries has been limited since crude oil was also under GSP agreement (Jones and Hornbeck 2013; Brenton and Hope 2006). However, the dramatic growth in shale oil production has reduced the volume of African crude oil to the United States, and trade volume between the United States and Africa has been decreasing, with the possibility that the trend will continue into the nearest future (IMF 2017). This therefore calls for urgent need of encouraging non-oil exports under AGOA. There has been some progress made in this respect. For example, the most important impact of AGOA is that the fastest expansion has been made in apparel exports, which has increased from US$355 million in 2001, the first full year of AGOA, to US$1.13 billion in 2008 before declining to US$907 million in 2013 as Asian competitors slashed African share of the lucrative US market (USTR 2018). Also, empirical studies show a positive and very significant impact of AGOA on garment and apparels exports to the United States (Condon and Stern 2011; Asmah and Taiwo 2010; Tadesse and Fayissa 2008)

However, getting African manufactured goods to the United States through AGOA has been difficult because of the limited capacity of Africa for manufactured goods. The little progress that has been made in this regard has been from motor vehicle exports from South Africa (the region's most industrialised country) to the United States. This is however limited both in volume and scope and does not reveal the capability of a vast majority of African countries. To some extent, it looks like two advanced countries trading between themselves. With regard to agricultural exports, the story is more pathetic; while agricultural exports grew from US$59 million in 2001 to US$201 million in 2014, agricultural produce as a share of total Africa exports declined from 6.2% in 2001 to 2.2% in 2014 (USTR 2018). In other words, agricultural exports are becoming increasingly insignificant as a component of Africa exports to the United States. This is also true of all other non-oil exports under AGOA as the limited success of the scheme has been driven by massive crude oil exports to the United States.

The above observations notwithstanding, there is room for more growth in Africa–US trade relation. One way of achieving this is to expand trade in agriculture. Presently the main agriculture products exported by Africa to the United States are cocoa powder and paste, fruits and nuts, as well as tobacco and vegetables—there is therefore the need to expand the scope of these products (Charles and Carol 2011). Expanding the scope of agriculture exports from Africa to the United States has the potential of reducing unemployment in Africa and improving the condition for inclusive growth since agriculture accounts for 30% of GDP and 50% of employment on the continent. It also has the potential to reduce poverty and address youth unemployment since Africa has a youth bulge. Agricultural exports through AGOA may have been limited by lack of diversifications in products and little or no investment in agricultural productivity and processing (Lionel and Anne-C'elial 2007). Agricultural exports from Africa can also be expanded by eliminating high tariff on sugar and cotton and removal of Tariff Rate Quota (TRQs) on seven commodities—tobacco, dairy, beef, peanuts, cotton, peanuts and green olive. It has been estimated that complete removal of tariff on some agricultural exports to the United States can increase by over US$100 million the value of agricultural exports by 2025 (Mevel et al. 2013). The United States can also help Africa to strengthen its capability through the African Continental Free Trade Zone (AfCFTA), a new trade policy that Africa's hope could expand intra-regional trade in manufacturing as a prelude to breaking into the global market.

The AfCFTA which was established with a treaty in May, 2018 will cover a market of 1.2 billion people with a combined GDP of US$2.5 trillion and potential consumer and business spending of more than US$4 trillion (Fofack 2018). It has the potential to transform Africa from passive globalisers and suppliers of raw materials to active globalisers with a definite path for effective integration into global economy provided the treaty can overcome the challenges of its implementation (Signe and van der Ven 2019; Fofack 2018). The United States can also help in this process by harnessing the opportunities provided by this trade agreement to improve its trade and investment relations with Africa in several ways. First, the United States can align the opportunities provided by AfCFTA to achieve the objective of The Trump Administration Africa Strategy, which was unveiled in December, 2018, with the sole aim of enhancing America's economic ties with Africa through trade and investment and reducing the inflow of aids (Hammond 2019). Second, the United States can imports its low valued goods from Africa, rather than producing them at home and then focus on the production of high value, specialised goods and services in which it has comparative advantages (Hammond 2019). This will create a win-win situation as Africa earns income from these exports and the United States gets low price goods and services due to cheap labour cost. Third, negotiating trade agreements between Africa and the United States will be cheaper and faster with AfCFTA because it will involve a single trading bloc instead of 55 different countries. The United Trade Representative has always complained about the time-consuming and costly nature of trade negotiation with numerous Africa countries (USTR 2018).

Paul Collier and Tony Venables, in a 2007 review of AGOA identified two elements in the schemes: The first is trade preference which grants market access at reduced tariff rates and with less restrictive quotas for market access. The second is the constraints on participation. These two schemes define eligible countries and products and also impose 'rules of origin' (ROO). Considering the contrasting tendency of these two elements, they noted that while the scheme has improved trade and investment relationship between Africa and the United States, it has not achieved much due to some important reasons. First, the constraints on participation define eligible countries and products and impose ROO. These constraints have overwhelmed the access, with ROO placing more restrictions on African exports because of difficulty in defining the origin of a value-added product in a fragmented global manufacturing sector.

Second, the production of manufactured goods for export has the greatest potential to expand employment and economic growth in Africa because it can overcome the diminishing returns of traditional agricultural and resource exports. Resource endowment tends to diminish as population expands, while land become unsustainable as population pressure increases, especially with limited attempt at improving land productivity. Manufacturing exports, on the other hand, are subject to scale threshold and can generate multiple equilibria through external economies. Third, modern manufacturing process requires many complementary inputs that are frequently supplied by different countries, and this includes, design, engineering, marketing and components production occurring at different locations. This is known as fragmentation of production and it has the potential of increasing return to scale and making cluster more productive. It also means that comparative advantages are now defined within some narrow tasks. The real problem is that tightly defined ROOs under AGOA make it difficult for African countries to participate in this type of modern production process and break into global value chain. Fourth, African countries can develop clusters in Export Processing Zones, where infrastructure could be localised, and later expanded through learning by overcoming their lack of infrastructure. Collier and Venables concluded their review by advocating for a special trade waiver by OECD countries that will help Africa break into the manufacturing value-added, especially in labour-intensive activities.

Security

The US engagement with Africa can be divided into three phases. The first was during the Cold War when the America's strategy was to prevent Africa from falling into the Soviets' Communist camp. The second was the post-9/11 phase when the strategy was making sure the region does not become a breeding ground for Islamist terrorism. The third is the current phase of the President Trump administration (since 2017) aimed to reduce the influence of China in Africa as part of the efforts by the United States to curtail the global influence of China. To achieve its security objectives in Africa, the United States established its first and only military base in Africa in Djibouti in 2006 and it is currently home to some 4000 permanently stationed US troops (Harris 2017; Signe and Allen 2018). The United States is also Africa's largest supplier of military hardware and biggest supporter of peacekeeping operations. It also recently promised nearly US$533 million to combat famine and enhance food security in war-torn regions of Africa (Signe and Allen 2018). The main security concern of the United States in recent years is how the

Islamic State of Iraq and al-Sham (ISIS) and other terrorist groups are expanding their reach in Africa (Harris 2017).

However, scholars have critiqued attempts by the United States to militarise its relationship with Africa, arguing that Africans must define security engagements with the United States in their own humanist terms (Campbell 2017). Specifically, African scholars have been encouraged to probe deeper into the underlying reasons for the establishment of AFRICOM to coordinate military operations in Africa and in the process unravels the unstated intention of the United States (Bellamy 2015; Campbell and Murrey 2014). Three prominent features of AFRICOM that seem to have raised the suspicions that the United States may have other ulterior motives for setting up the military base has been identified (Campbell 2017). First, the emphasis on gathering information on strategies used by African military elites is dangerous in an era when modern conflicts are based on information and cyber warfare. Second, the structure of AFRICOM with its limited personnel and reliance on private military contractors can expose African military system to the parochial influence of these military contractors rather than the common good of a public-driven military system. Third, the danger that the US AFRICOM Social Science Research Platform may not provide independent intellectual research output because of the circumstances of its emergent is real and not good for Africa (Campbell and Murrey 2014). It is therefore important that African elites note these features of AFRICOM and constantly push for a military relation with the United States that will improve the security situation in Africa without undermining the sovereignty of African countries.

Additionally, the foundation of political instability and conflicts in Africa is poor economic conditions and this means that for the United States to improve the security of its citizens both at home and abroad there is the need to strengthen partnership with Africa to promote local economies, support good governance and address conflicts in the region (Harris 2017). For example, recent studies have identifies financial incentives as one of the major reasons why new recruits join Boko Haram in north eastern Nigeria, indicating that it actually costs on the average US$60 to entice a new recruit in West Africa (Ewi and Salifu 2017; IEP 2016). The core security strategy of the United States in the post-9/11 era is the realisation that weak and failed states incubate instability and this has extensive implications for its national security. The need to stop these states from serving as the sources of transnational threats is therefore of uttermost importance for policymakers in the United States. Sadly, African countries dominate the global club of failed and fragile states, with nineteen slots out of twenty-five (Fund for Peace's Fragile State Index 2019). Terrorist groups in Africa are expanding on a daily basis with Boko Haram becoming the second most lethal terrorist group in the World, while Al-Qaeda in the Islamic Maghreb (AQIM) are spreading anti-American ideologies in the continent. In recent years, many attacks have been carried out by these terrorist groups against Western targets in Africa, including the bombing of United Nations Building in Abuja by Boko Haram in 2011, and the attacks by AQIM on hotels in Mali (2015), Burkina Faso (2016), Cote d'Ivoire (2010) (Harris 2017).

The United States has responded to these emerging forms of security threats by taking some unprecedented drastic and direct actions. These include the establishment of the first and only US military base on the continent in Djibouti and the scaling up of its operations against Al-Shabaab in Somalia and Al-Qaeda in the Arabian Peninsula (AQAP) (Harris 2017). The United States has also increased its security partnership with different governments in Africa. For example, in 2015 alone, AFRICOM conducted seventy-five joint operations, twelve major joint operations and four hundred security cooperation activities (Harris 2017). The foregoing shows how serious the United States has taken the terrorism threats from Africa. However, to effectively combat terrorism requires less of a military approach. It requires addressing the underlying reasons for extremism, notably the development challenge facing most African countries. It is therefore important to address the structural and governance environment creating the incentives for individual radicalisation, which is the trigger for violent acts. In partnership with African countries and regional institutions, the United States needs to develop a new strategy that will help poor African countries to alleviate the despair that creates extremism in the first instance. In the words of President George W. Bush 'It is in the best interest of our nation to alleviate the despair that can allow extremism to take hold by fighting hunger and disease, supporting basic education initiatives and advancing global economic development' (George Bush's Freedom Agenda as cited in Harris 2017). The best way to advance global economic development is to integrate Africa into the global economy through trade and investment and by helping the region to improve its capacity to effectively govern itself (Collier 2007).

Trade and Investment: The Declining Influence of the United States

Increasingly, the influence of the United States in trade and investment in Africa is declining despite the introduction of AGOA in 2000 and its recent renewal till 2025. African trade geography is shifting from United States and Europe to Asia. According to data from IMF, in 2000, the United States was Africa's biggest trading partner followed by France while China and India were in 8th and 9th position, but by 2015 China and India have jumped to 1st and 2nd position while United States and France have declined to 3rd and 4th position. This geographic shift reveals how the influence of America has declined overtime. Although the EU still remains Africa's biggest trading partner accounting for 30% of trade value in 2015, this is down from 40% in 2000. It should be noted however that EU bloc consists of many former imperial powers that have colonial ties to Africa.

To put the decline of US trade relation with Africa in perspective requires some comparative analysis with Asia giants, China and India. By 2016, trade between the United States and Africa declined for the sixth straight year due mainly to increased production of oil and gas in the United States. In contrast trade between Africa and Asia expanded five folds to reach a quarter of Africa's merchandised trade between 2000 and 2015. In quantitative terms, China total trade with Africa increased from US$7.3 billion in 2000 to US$93.3 billion and US$135.9 billion in 2010 and 2015, respectively. Also, during the same time India increased its trading position with Africa as its trading figures jumped from US$6.9 billion in 2000 to US$37.5 billion and US$51.1 billion in 2010 and 2015, respectively (UNCTAD 2017; AfDB 2017). In contrast, the US total value in trade increased from US$33.3 billion in 2000 to US$98.4 billion in 2010 before declining to US$45.3 billion in 2015. The figure for 2016 is as low as US$22 billion indicating how trade relation between Africa and the United States has declined overtime. In the same vein, France, Africa's traditional friend also posted fluctuating trade figures with Africa during this period with trade figures first increasing from US$27 billion to US$53 billion from 2000 to 2010 but declining to US$50 billion in 2015 (UNCTAD 2017; AfDB 2017).

The deteriorating trade relation between Africa and the United States can be attributed to many reasons. The first is the nature of African exports; they are dominated by natural resources, especially oil and gas, precious stones and metals. In recent times the United States has ramped up its oil production with improved technology and it is becoming less dependent on oil and gas imports from Africa. The second is the rise of Asian powerhouse, China and India and their willingness to trade with Africa because the continent satisfies their insatiable appetite for natural resources as their economy grew dramatically over the last three two to three decades. The third is the component of Africa's global trade, which is dominated by exports of very few natural resources and imports of merchandised goods and food, especially from Asia and specifically from China. The US export of merchandised goods to Africa is limited by high cost of America products and the relatively small size of Africa market for such high-cost exports, China has no such limitations. In summary, the United States despite AGOA does not consider Africa as strategic and important for both growth enhancing trade and investment relation as it does for Asia in the second half of the twentieth century. It considers the continent as supplier of natural resources and receiver of foreign aid to tackle poverty and health challenges.

While it is fashionable to blame the United States declining influence in trade and investment ties with Africa on its inability to see the region beyond recipient of aid and exporters of natural resources, Africa's problem lies in its inability to diversify its exports. Out of the 53 African countries survey by AfDB, more than half rely on between 1 and 4 commodities for more than 75% of their exports, and these include Angola, Nigeria and Congo among others. However, the volume of Africa share in global trade has increased dramatically between 1995 and 2015 from US$197 billion to US$825 billion, its share of global trade remains on the average between 2% and 3% over the same period. In the same vein, African imports of goods and services from the rest of the world have increased 4.7 times during the same period, while its sales of goods and services to rest of the world has quadrupled (AfDB 2017).

A key worry for Africa–US relation watchers is how the Trump administration's Trade Protectionist Policy will affect Africa. According to African Development Bank, this policy may have limited effects on African economy for several reasons. Firstly, AGOA, which drives African trade with the United States, is dominated by exports of natural resources to the United States and not manufactured goods that are focus on the American First slogan of the Trump Administration. The share of non-oil exports, like cocoa and cocoa products, fruits and nuts, prepared vegetable and cut flowers, foot wares and apparels, is still small compared to oil. Secondly, the size of African trade with United States is so small, at 3%, that even when it results in trade deficit, the Americans are not bothered. Thirdly, the Trump administration's withdrawal of the United States from Trans-Pacific Partnerships and the formation of AfCFTA have the potentials to improve United States trade relation with Africa by making African exports more competitive in the United States. The flip side is that this could also discourage the United States from expanding AGOA beyond 2025, and this could have grave implications for Africa exporters in Kenya and Mauritius who needed long-term trade preference scheme with the United States to become mature and competitive.

Foreign Direct Investment to Africa is still led by the United States and Europe, although this is driven essentially by extractive FDI. According to figures from United Nations Conference on Trade and Development (UNCTAD), Foreign Direct Investment to Africa fell by 21% in 2017, while the United States led the FDI stock in Africa at USD57bllion in 2016, maintaining the same figure from 2011. The United States is followed by United Kingdom at US$55 billion up from US£54 billion in 2011, while the corresponding figure for France is US$52 billion and US$40 billion 2016 and 2011, respectively. China which makes up the fourth of the top five saw the biggest increase in FDI stock growing from US$10 billion in 2011 to US$40 billion in 2016 (UNCTAD 2016). However, apart from China, South Africa, India, Singapore and Hong Kong are becoming increasingly important in the FDI stock in Africa. As for the pattern of FDI inflows to Africa, it tracks the volatility of commodity price during the 2015–2016 oil price shocks and dropped by 8% in 2015. It recovered in 2016 increasing at about 10% to US$56.5 billion before dropping by 21% to US$42 billion in 2017 (IMF 2018; UNCTAD 2017).

According to an analysis by KPMG, the bulk of FDI inflow to Africa is linked to the extractive industries, notably in Algeria and Egypt in North Africa, Ghana and Nigeria in West Africa, Chad and Congo in Central Africa and Angola, Mozambique and South Africa in Southern Africa. The United States through its large MNCs and IOCs play a central role in these investments (KPMG 2016). Increasingly, however China is emerging as the biggest investors for Greenfield investment in Africa as measured by capital investment. In 2015–2016, China led capital investment with US$34 billion investment and this was followed by United Arab Emirates with US$14.9 billion; Italy with US$11.6 billion, while the United States came 4th with US$10.4 billion. China's investments represent about 24% of the total Greenfield capital investment, while that of the United States stood at 6.5% (FDi Markets 2016). An analysis of the top fourteen capital investment firms in Africa between January 2015 and December 2016 shows that the firms are dominated by Chinese firms just as China dominates the size of the total Greenfield capital investment (FDi Markets 2016). This is an indication of the receding influence of the United States in Africa and the increasing influence of China.

Conclusion

Over and above the points explored in the preceding sections of this chapter, Africa should matter to the United States for many additional reasons. According to Grant Harris of the Think Tank, Atlantic Council, the US engagement with Africa should be based on three important considerations. Firstly, Africa's weak states are a direct threat to global peace, as they can spread instability through terrorism, war and pandemic diseases as witnessed during the Ebola crisis in West Africa in 2014–2016. Secondly, Africa has a potential market that the United States cannot ignore. The region is expected to be home to a quarter of global population by 2050, and a majority of this population are projected to be youths. This means Africa has the potential to drive the global economy in the nearest future and the United States needs to reposition its engagement with Africa so that the Chinese will not displace it from a prosperous Africa of the future. Thirdly, the United States has the moral obligations to help Africa overcome its humanitarian, health and conflicts problems so that the world can become a safer place for all. This moral argument has been the central thesis of Paul Collier book, *The Bottom Billion* (2008), where the need for the United States and its allies in G7 to help Africa integrate into the global economy for sustainable development has been well analysed.

The United States has through the years seen Africa as a basket case of misery and a breeding ground for terrorism and political instability. The US strategy has been to approach these problems from the standpoint of humanitarian interventions. This has instead plunged Africa into deeper economic uncertainties and impaired its ability to attain the goal of sustainable development as most of Asia presently enjoys. It has also made the continent's economy so structurally weak that the initial hope of Africa rising has ostensibly waned due to commodity price volatility. Consequently, the prevailing global trade rules as well as the international economic and political order are bias against Africa. One of the key ways the United States can help Africa to rise is to develop a new strategy, in partnership with other developed countries, to enable Africa break into the global economy through massive foreign investment and preferential trade schemes. This will help the African manufacturing sector to develop and integrate into global production networks.

References

Africa Development Bank. 2017. African Economic Outlook. Retrieved on 27 March 2019, https://www.afdb.org/fileadmin/uploads/afdb/Documents/Publications/African_Economic_Outlook_2018_-_EN.pdf.

AGOA. 2013. African Growth and Opportunity Act Website. Retrieved on 15 March 2019, https://agoa.info/about-agoa.html.

Arieff, Alexis, Martin A. Weiss, and Vivican C. Isles. 2019. *The Global Economic Crisis: Impact on Sub-Saharan African and Global Policy Perceptive*. Washington, DC: Congressional Research Service.

Asmah, E., and O. Taiwo. 2010. AGOA and the Africa Agriculture Sector in AGOA at 10: Challenges and Prospects for US-Africa Trade and Investment Relations. Brookings, 2010.

Bellamy, F.J. 2015. The New Imperialism of Globalised Monopoly Finance Capital. *Monthly Review* 67 (3) (July–August).

Brenton, P., and M. Hope. 2006. The Africa Growth and Opportunity Act, Exports and Development in Sub-Saharan Africa. World Bank Policy Research Working Paper (3996).

Campbell, H.G. 2017. The United States and Security in Africa: The Impact of the Military Management of the International System. *Africa Development* 62 (2): 45–71.

Campbell, H.G., and M. Murrey. 2014. Culture-Centric Pre-emptive Counterinsurgency and US Africa Command: Assessing the Role of the US Social Science in US Military Engagements in Africa. *Third World Quarterly* 35 (8): 1457–1475.

Charles, E., and C. Carol. 2011. *US Agricultural Trade: Trends, Composition, Direction and Policy*. CRS Report for Congress.

Collier, P. 2007. *The Bottom Billion: Why the Poor Countries Are Falling and What Can Be Done About It*. Oxford: Oxford University Press.

Collier, P., and S.A. O'Connell. 2007. Opportunities and Choices. In *The Political Economy of Economic Growth in Africa, 1960–2000*, ed. B.J. Ndulu, S.A. O'Connell, R.H. Bates, P. Collier, and C.A. Soludo, 76–136. Cambridge: Cambridge University Press.

Collier, P., and A.J. Venables. 2007. Rethinking Trade Preferences: How Africa Can Diversify It Exports. *The World Economy* 30 (8): 1326–1345.

Condon, N., and N. Stern. 2011. The Effectiveness of African Growth and Opportunity Act (AGOA) in Increasing Trade from Least Developed Countries: A Systematic Review. EPPI Centre, Social Science Research Unit. Institute of Education, University of London, London.

Emerson, Rupert. 1962. American Policy in Africa. *Foreign Affairs*, January.

Ewi, Martins, and Uyo Salifu. 2017. Money Talks: A Key Reasons Youths Join Boko Haram. Institute of Security Studies Policy Brief 98. Retrieved on 22 March 2019, https://frantic.s3-eu-west-1.amazonaws.com/kua-peacemakers/2016/07/Money-talks-A-key-reason-youth-join-Boko-Haram.pdf.

FDi Markets. 2016. Investment Reports. Retrieved on 20 March 2019, https://www.fdiintelligence.com/Investment-Promotion-Services/fDi-Markets.

Fiormonti, P. 2017. The Myth of Africa Rising. The Conversation. Retrieved on 24 March 2019, http://theconversation.com/the-africa-rising-story-was-based-on-faulty-logic-heres-how-to-fix-it-86327.

Fofack, H. 2018. A Competitive Africa: Economic Integration Can Make the Continent a Global Player. *Finance and Development* 55 (4) (December). IMF, Washington. Retrieved on 18 July 2019, https://www.imf.org/external/pubs/ft/fandd/2018/12/pdf/afcfta-economic-integration-in-africa-fofack.pdf.

Fund for Peace. 2019. Fragile State Index. Retrieved on 2 April 2019, http://fundforpeace.org/wp-content/uploads/2019/04/9511904-fragilestatesindex.pdf.

Hammond, Alexander C.R. 2019. Africa's New Free-Trade Areas Is Great News for America. *The National Interest*, 12 July. Retrieved on 16 July 2019, https://nationalinterest.org/feature/africa%E2%80%99s-new-free-trade-area-great-news-america-62407.

Harris, Grant T. 2017. Why Africa Matters to US National Security. A Report of Atlantic Council Africa Center. Retrieved on 26 March 2019, https://www.atlanticcouncil.org/images/publications/Why_Africa_Matters_to_US_National_Security_0524_web.pdf.

IMF. 2017. *Regional Economic Outlook: Sub-Saharan Africa Restarting the Growth Engine*. Washington, DC: International Monetary Fund.

IMF. 2018. *Regional Economic Outlook: Sub-Saharan Africa*. Washington, DC: International Monetary Fund.

Institute for Economics and Peace. 2016. Global Terrorism Index. Retrieved on 22 March 2019, http://economicsandpeace.org/wp-content/uploads/2016/11/Global-Terrorism-Index-2016.2.pdf.

Jones, V.C., and J.F. Hornbeck. 2013. *Trade Preferences: Economic Issues and Policy Options*. Washington, DC: Congressional Research Service.

Jones, V.C., and B.R. William. 2012. *US Trade and Investment Relations with Sub-Saharan Africa and the Africa Growth and Opportunity Act*. Washington, DC: Congressional Research Services.

Kharas, H., Kristofer Hamel, and Martins Hofer. 2018. The Start of a New Poverty Narratives. Brookings Future Development. Retrieved on 27 March 2019, https://www.brookings.edu/blog/future-development/2018/06/19/the-start-of-a-new-poverty-narrative/.

KPMG. 2016. What Influences Foreign Direct Investment into Africa. Retrieved on 15 April 2019, https://assets.kpmg/content/dam/kpmg/pdf/2016/07/What-influences-FDI-into-Africa.pdf.

Lionel, F.M., and Anne-C'elial. 2007. The Impact of Regulation on Agricultural Trade: Evidence from SPS and TBT Agreement. January, 29.

Matto A., D. Roy, and A. Subramanian. 2002. The Africa Growth and Opportunity Acts and Its Rules of Origin: Generosity Undermined? International Monetary Policy Working Paper, September.

Meltzer, Joshua P. 2016. Deepening the United States-Africa Trade and Investment Relationship Brooking Institutions, January 28. Retrieved on 15 March 2019, https://www.brookings.edu/testimonies/deepening-the-united-states-africa-trade-and-investment-relationship/.

Mevel, S., Z. Lewis, M.S. Kimenji, S. Karinji, and A. Kamara. 2013. The African Growth and Opportunity Act: An Empirical Analysis. Retrieved on 15 April 2019, https://www.brookings.edu/wp-content/uploads/2016/06/130729-AGOA-2013WEBFINAL.pdf.

Moghalu, K. 2014. *Emerging Africa: How the Global Economy's 'Last Frontier' Can Prosper and Matter*. London: Penguin.

Schneidman, W., and Zenca Lewis. 2012. The African Growth and Opportunity Act: Looking Back, Looking Forward. Brooking African Growth Initiative.

Signe, L., and N.D.F. Allen. 2018. Trumps Africa Policy Takes Form with Focus on Security and China. Brookings Institute Blog. Retrieved on 4 April 2019, https://www.brookings.edu/opinions/trumps-africa-policy-takes-form-with-focus-on-security-and-china/.

Signe, L., and Colette van der Ven. 2019. Keys to Success for the AfCFTA Negotiations. Africa Growth Initiative. Policy Brief. Brooking Institute, Washington, May. Retrieved on 17 July 2019. https://www.brookings.edu/wpcontent/uploads/2019/05/Keys_to_success_for_AfCFTA.pdf.

Tadesse, B., and B. Fayissa. 2008. The Impact of African Growth Opportunity Act (AGOA) on US Imports from Sub-Saharan Africa. *Journal of International Development* 20 (7): 920–940.

The Economist. 2000. The Hopeless Continent, May, 11. Retrieved on 24 March 2019, https://www.economist.com/leaders/2000/05/11/hopeless-africa.

United Nations Conference on Trade and Development. 2016. Trade and Development Report. Retrieved on 15 March 2019, https://unctad.org/en/pages/PressRelease.aspx?OriginalVersionID=461.
United Nations Conference on Trade and Development. 2017. Trade and Development Report. Retrieved on 15 April 2019. https://unctad.org/en/Pages/Publications/TradeandDevelopmentReport.aspx.
USTR. 2018. Countries and Regions Report. United States Office of Trade Representatives. Retrieved on 20 March 2019, https://ustr.gov/countries-regions/africa.
World Bank. 2011. *World Development Report*. Washington DC: World Bank.
World Bank. 2018. Doing Business Report on Sub-Saharan Africa. Retrieved on 20 March 2019, https://www.worldbank.org/en/news/press-release/2018/10/31/doing-business-report-sub-saharan-african-economies-set-third-consecutive-record-of-reforms-to-improve-business-climate.

CHAPTER 5

The Political Economy of Africa's Relations with China

Asebe Regassa Debelo

Introduction

In the first decade after the new Millennium, Africa has attracted global attention not least for the fast economic growth of some countries but mainly due to the continent being part of the resource frontier for the major global economies. Resource frontier, in this context can be conceptualized as a geographical imagination of spaces as full of resources but underutilized in terms of converting these spaces into productive resources. The representation of any geographical space as a resource frontier entails discursive and political engagement to convert areas deemed unproductive to productive spaces through technological advancement, modernist discourses, developmental state political economy and consolidation of state power so as to fill political vacuum (Regassa et al. 2018; Korf et al. 2015).

Accordingly, China has chosen Africa as one of its resource frontier areas and designed political, development, and security strategies as pillars of its foreign relations with Africa in general (through regional and continental organizations) and with specific African countries. After

A. R. Debelo (✉)
Dilla University, Dilla, Ethiopia

K. Omeje (ed.), *The Governance, Security and Development Nexus*,
https://doi.org/10.1007/978-3-030-49348-6_5

it established Forum on China–Africa Cooperation (FOCAC) in 2000, China introduced different packages constituting economic aid, loan, and technical support to enhance peace and security initiatives in Africa and expanded its diplomatic engagements with many specific African countries (Leslie 2016). In this chapter, I argue that China's increased diplomatic and economic relations with Africa should be analyzed from a political economy perspective as it renders a comprehensive understanding of power, politics, development, and security nexus.

Over the last half a century, China–Africa relation passed through different ranges of transformation underpinning shifts in ideological, diplomatic, and political economy frameworks (Zeleza 2014). To better grasp the policy change, it is imperative to situate Beijing's contemporary engagement in Africa within historical contexts. China–Africa partnership passed through different ranges of ideological, diplomatic, and economic shifts. According to an official in the AU,[1] China was one of the allies during the liberation movement, and its current partnership can also be seen as a continuation of the past. "The partnership is reciprocal," asserts the official, reiterating the role some African countries played in lobbying for China to become a permanent member of UN Security Council. This seems to have now garnered China the leverage to represent itself as a genuine partner without colonial legacy in Africa (Debelo 2017). With China emerging as the global economic power in the dawn of the twenty-first century and subsequently with its rise as a major actor in the global political dynamics, Africa became an ideal "new frontier" of diplomacy for Beijing to exercise "soft," "hard," and "smart" power. China has recently become Africa's leading partner in the areas of trade, investment, and development. Apart from bilateral relations with African states, China partners with regional and subregional organizations on a growing number of issues. Of note in this bourgeoning relationship is the partnership between China and the African Union (AU) including in the field of peace and security.[2]

China's involvement in peace and security initiatives on the continent signals a policy departure from principles of non-interventionist foreign policy, less conditional support in areas of human rights, and focus on infrastructural development to this emerging era of active engagement. Therefore, Beijing's relationship with Africa can be broadly categorized into ideological, economic, strategic, and global dimensions. In this chapter, I explore the political economy of Africa's relations with China within two broader areas. First, I discuss the economic dimensions of the relationship by critically interrogating how diplomatic relations are framed within the notion of Africa being the resource frontier for China. Second, I critically probe into Beijing's shift in foreign policy from non-interventionism to active engagement particularly in areas of peace and security. This will also be linked to the economic dimension as ensuring peace and security is deemed to (1) secure Chinese investment companies, and (2) ensure China's thrust to resource security—the approach of accessing natural resources in the continent. Finally, I will give brief conclusion.

New Frontier of Diplomacy and Critical Geopolitics as Explanations to China–Africa Relations

Today's shift in Beijing's African policy from non-interventionism to active engagement came as a result of its consideration of Africa as a "new frontier" that encompasses economic, strategic, and geopolitical interests. The notion of "new frontier" constitutes "energy-diplomacy" or "resource-diplomacy" within China's economic interests in Africa, and geopolitical/strategic and security–diplomacy that in turn enhances the achievement of Beijing's economic interests. Therefore, this chapter takes the notions of new frontier of diplomacy and critical geopolitics as conceptual frameworks.

For better understanding of the dynamics in China's relation with Africa, it is also essential to posit the discussion within the context of geographical and political imaginaries and representations of Africa historically in Western popular culture, academia, and media. Since recently, China also joined the West in representing the continent as a new frontier awaiting its companies, technologies, and firms to be used for its domestic economic growth. Beginning from the colonial era, European explorers, colonial authorities, scholars, and the media ambivalently represented Africa as backward, uncivilized, and wild but as resourceful space awaiting the hands of civilized nations (Adams and McShanne 1996; Mawdsley 2008). Such ambivalent representation of Africa has reinforced the portrayal of European and eventually American engagement in Africa through what modernist scholars and development practitioners consider as a civilizing mission "once through Christianity, commerce and (in the case of the UK) 'Pax Britannica', now through good governance and development" (Mawdsley 2008: 512). Different scholars argue that the West's encroachment upon Africa during the colonial period and their continued influence on African politics, economy, and culture in the post-independence period is a function of African representation in Western popular culture as economic, geopolitical, and cultural frontier (Herbst 2000).

To establish national parks and game reserves in Africa, for example, colonial powers used the notion of "wild Africa," "pristine nature," "the Garden of Eden," and the "natural Africa" (Neumann 1998). Likewise, in their postcolonial diplomatic and political engagement in Africa, the West used notions of "war-torn Africa," "the continent with authoritarian regimes," "the helpless continent," and so on (Mazrui 2002). Scholars on frontier and frontier dynamics argue that representation of certain spaces and states from conflict perspective discursively calls for consolidation of state power upon such local authorities because conflict signals power vacuum to be filled (Korf et al. 2015; Das and Poole 2004).

Herbst (2000) contextualizes the power relations between colonial Africa and their colonial masters, and representation of Africa in western popular culture within the center-periphery relations. According to this perspective, which can be seen within critical geopolitics, "images and representations that circulate and sediment in popular culture, including through film, documentaries, comics, novels and the visual and print media" significantly influence the economic, political, and diplomatic relations between different actors (Mawdsley 2008: 511). By giving meanings or labeling of whatsoever to a certain space, different actors construct discourses of power, resource, and territory that would eventually produce hegemonic regimes of representation. This substantiates the debates on frontier dynamics that entail the geographical and political project of portraying territories as "full of resources" but "empty of people" that awaits technological intervention and political engagement from advanced societies or nations (Korf et al. 2015). This frontier dynamics is often used in describing and analyzing the emerging land grabbing in developing countries particularly following the 2007/2008 global food and energy crisis.

China–Africa relations can also be explained from two perspectives—the critical geopolitics and new frontier dynamics. As it will be discussed later in this chapter, Beijing has found Africa as a new frontier not only for diplomatic relations but also as a resourceful continent to boost its domestic economic development (Shelton 2001; Wang and Zou 2014).

In relation to its active engagement in areas of peacekeeping missions in the continent, the conventional representation of Africa as war-torn continent, conflict-prone region, and a continent that has over the years failed to resolve major wars and conflicts by itself has perpetuated the notion of peaceful development through what some scholars consider as "smart power" (Neethling 2015).

Some scholars claim that China's growing interest in Africa in economic spheres should be analyzed from the perspective of "energy diplomacy" (Wang and Zou 2014), particularly in response to the rise in domestic energy demand. More importantly, China's rapid industrialization process on the one hand, and the government's adherence to the principle of "performance legitimacy"—the notion of garnering public trust by sustainably ensuring economic growth—on the other hand, has prompted China to look for overseas energy sources (Beeson et al. 2011).

From a critical geopolitical perspective, China has also designed a systematic approach of ensuring resource security that encompasses issues of peace and security, and control of resource and strategic bases. Issues of resource security have shaped China's foreign policy over the last two decades entailing the exercise of different forms of power. For example, China has established a major military base in Djibouti countering USA, France, and UAE. As it will be explained later, China's military engagement and peacekeeping missions in Africa should be understood from the country's pragmatic approaches to secure access to natural resources (Beeson et al. 2011).

China from Non-interventionist to Active Engagement in Africa

There is a wide range of debate on the underlying factors behind China's shift from non-intervention to engagement in areas of peacekeeping in general and its involvement in UN peacekeeping missions in particular. Nevertheless, China's active engagement in peacekeeping missions in Africa cannot be separately seen from its economic interests in the continent as discussed above. Moreover, China's growing influence in global political power relations has served as a motivating factor for Beijing to consider itself as a responsible power in ensuring peace and stability overseas. Although this argument is still sound, China's involvement in peacekeeping missions in Africa can be better understood within its growing economic interest in the continent, as a result of which it had to protect the security of its citizens and companies operating in different parts of Africa.

China has recently departed from its long diplomatic strategy of non-interventionism by engaging itself in global peacekeeping missions particularly in Africa. As a global power with growing economic and political interests in Africa, China has become the second largest contributor to UN peacekeeping in terms of human power and the largest in areas of financial contribution. In 2015 for example, China has revealed a new aid package of 60 billion USD for Africa, and also additional 60 million USD for supporting AU's peace and security initiatives (Leslie 2016). Given the country's position as a permanent member of the UN Security Council and its economic and political power, Beijing's strong involvement in peacekeeping missions in particular and its diplomatic shift from non-interventionist to engagement in general would inevitably shape the contours of peacebuilding discourses and practices in the continent. Within this backdrop, this chapter addresses the following fundamental questions: what underlying factors compelled China to depart from its long history of non-interventionism to engagement in peacekeeping missions in Africa? What influences does China's involvement bring to the discourses and practices of peacekeeping and peacebuilding within UN and AU as far as wars and conflicts in the continent are concerned? How is China's involvement in the peacekeeping received by different actors? What challenges has China's involvement faced? The chapter addresses these questions through rigorous analysis of diverse range of works, reports, and information on the subject through document analysis, and empirical study at African Union (AU), department of peace and security.

During the Cold War period, Beijing's policy toward Africa underpinned the support for Africa's anti-colonial and revolutionary movements along Maoist socialist ideological framework. More importantly, China was one of the leading powers in the Non-aligned Movement that promoted the policy of neutrality from the capitalist and socialist rivalries (Shelton 2001). In the 1970s and 1980s, however, China's engagement in political domain subsided while its economic interest in the continent was even much insignificant. As Zeleza (2014) argues, China entered into a new phase of restructuring its relations with Africa from ideological and revolutionary fervor to a pragmatic approach of supporting trade, investment, and aid to Africa to enhance its own domestic economic development in the 1990s. According to Shelton (2001: 113): "In order to promote trade and economic cooperation with

Africa, the central thrust of China's new Africa policy, Beijing set up investment, development and trade centers in a number of African countries, including Egypt, Guinea, Cameroon, Mali, Gabon, Cote d'lvoire, Nigeria, Tanzania, Zambia, and Mozambique." This is considered as a second phase in China–Africa relations, which some scholars label as a restricting phase (Zeleza 2014) that eventually led to the current relationship (post-2000) called the consolidation phase.

With China emerging as a global economic power in the dawn of twenty-first century and subsequently with its rise as a major actor in the global political dynamics, Africa became an ideal "new frontier" of diplomacy for China and an ideal arena where it exercises a combination of both hard and soft power (Neethling 2015). In exercising smart power—the combination of soft and hard power or non-coercive and coercive diplomacy, respectively, China has managed to win the hearts and minds of many African leaders and elites. In doing so, Beijing represents itself as a mutual partner with Africa unlike the Western powers whom Beijing portrays as paternalistic and imperialistic in their relationship with Africa. The consideration of Africa as a new frontier of diplomacy has been built on China's economic and strategic interests in Africa for the realization of which Beijing pragmatically and contextually exercises both categories of power. In terms of soft power, China has embarked on the practice of convincing African leaders to follow its footsteps in their economic policies, trade relations, security relations, and investments to extend its Beijing model of development (Suzuki 2009). This strategy is often considered as diplomatic instrument of countering the US/Western hegemony. This is evident in China's increasing engagement in Africa in terms of diplomatic ties, economic relations, and more recently in areas of peace and security.

In areas of hard power, China has recently been expanding its areas of engagement in Africa including peacekeeping operations, which has marked radical policy rapture in its foreign policy from non-interventionism to active engagement. In this regard, it is very essential to highlight the underlying factors for the shift in China's policy with Africa. First, in the 1990s, China massively expanded trade and investment in Africa to boost its domestic economy. In 1996 for example, Chinese President Jiang Zemin visited six African countries namely, Kenya, Ethiopia, Egypt, Mali, Namibia, and Zimbabwe during which he emphasized the "Beijing's new 'Economics first' foreign policy paradigm" (Shelton 2001:

113). Shelton further describes that President Jiang also addressed OAU in Addis Ababa cementing Sino–Africa relationship to be based on:

- Fostering a sincere friendship; respecting each other's sovereignty, and refraining from interfering in each other's internal affairs;
- Keeping common development on the basis of mutual benefit;
- Increased consultation and cooperation in international affairs; and
- The establishment of a more peaceful world (Shelton 2001: 113).

It has become logically inevitable for China, as a fast-growing economy in the world, to grapple with high demand for energy and other raw materials. Concomitantly, Chinese industries and companies have also been in strong demand for markets for their products—in which the growing demand for cheap Chinese products in Africa also produced the convergence of supply and demand. From the mid-1990s, China has rediscovered Africa as a "new frontier" for its economic interests while at the same time it partially used the opportunities also for other non-economic interests (strategic, global diplomacy, and political). Since early 2000s, China made a policy of "exporting" its companies and investors to Africa for many reasons. First, it would ease pressure on internal economy and secondly, it would pave the way for Chinese growing demand for resources. Therefore, China's economic interest in Africa grew more than ever in the last nearly one decade or so. In this line, China came to realize that only the soft power (resource diplomacy alone) would not guarantee its economic security, and access to resources. Peace and security in Africa remain critical issues for China's economic interests in the continent.

This, according to some scholars, has compelled the Chinese government to protect its companies, individuals, and institutions in Africa particularly in conflict zones such as South Sudan, Mali, Sudan, and other crisis-prone regions of Africa (Mawdsley 2008; Zeleza 2014). Since the early 2000s, many African countries, at least in principle, turned their political economy toward the Chinese model (i.e., the Beijing model) of "developmental state" model. According to the late Ethiopian Prime Minister, Meles Zenawi, who was the fervent advocate of the Beijing Model, the neoliberal approach of development is a dead end for Africa while the Beijing model is the new beginning to which all African leaders should direct their economic policies (Zenawi 2006). This evidently substantiates the argument that China is able to attract African leaders to "want what it wants."

Secondly, China's growing influence on international stage compels it to assume some responsibilities in protecting human rights wherever there are such violations through intergroup conflict or wars between different groups and authoritarian regimes (Zeleza 2014). As emerging global power, China uses its engagement in international organizations as a gateway to global stage (to influence global politics, and regional political dynamics). In the post 9/11, USA has increased its military engagement in Africa in the name of "war on terror" and this has given a warning signal to China that a Cold War style of partitioning Africa (ideologically) might sideline Chinese economic and strategic interests.

Thirdly, Africa is geopolitically strategic from many dimensions. In the fight against piracy, for example, it is almost impossible to successfully control pirates on Indian and Atlantic Oceans without securing maritime and land military bases in Africa. Therefore, China inevitably shifted its non-interventionist policy to secure its geopolitical and strategic interests.

However, Beijing's shift in its Africa policy should not be construed as a full exercise of hard power and negation of non-coercive diplomacy. Rather, China pragmatically employs Smart power contextually using both categories of power in order to ensure its interests. In this context, the establishment of the Forum on China–Africa Cooperation (FOCAC) in 2000 laid a fundamental cornerstone in cementing China's influence in Africa in all spheres. In 2006, China listed four major areas of engagement in areas of China–Africa peace and security cooperation; these consist of, military cooperation, conflict settlement and peacekeeping operations, judicial and police cooperation, and non-traditional security cooperation. In terms of financial assistance, President Xi announced in 2015 that China would provide $100 million in free assistance to the African Union (AU) to support the building and operation of the African Standby Force and an African Capacity for the Immediate Response to Crisis.[3] Apart from direct financial assistance, China provides technical support, capacity-building trainings, and technologies to combat piracy, terrorism, riot, and generally to equip African organizations to be in a better position to respond to security challenges. In this regard, China plays a positive role in Africa's continental and regional peace and security architecture building, including the AU's Peace and Security Council (PSC) and regional Peace Support Operations by financing AU missions in different

African countries, such as Somalia and Sudan. It has also provided equipment to some regional economic communities for the establishment of their logistics base like ECOWAS. Over the last two decades, China has sent personnel to peacekeeping operations in over a dozen African countries. While all these efforts are laudable, it is still crucial to put China's increasing engagement in peacekeeping missions in Africa within a critical frame that allows us to understand how it can best enhance African peacebuilding policies as discussed below.

Some Chinese analysts downplay the notion of Chinese soft power in Africa and whether China would use that its economic and political leverage as a global power to propagate the "Beijing model" (Suzuki 2009; Wang and Zou 2014). However, it is undeniable fact that many Africa leaders began opting the Chinese model of economy through a top-down authoritarian approach mainly as a counterbalance to the US/Western liberal approach that ties some strings to economic relations. Apart from expanding its influence through economic ties in the form of investment, trade, and resource extraction, China has recently become the major contributor of troops to UN peacekeeping missions in the continent (Neethling, n.d.). As a major economic and political power at the global stage, Chinese engagement through a mixture of soft and hard power would inevitably shape the contours of peace and security in the continent.

Africa's Relations with China and Its Implications

A critical interrogation of China's growing interest and engagement in Africa indicates that China has swiftly responded to the euphoria of "Africa Rising" that is also intertwined with the geographical and political representation of the continent as a new frontier. With radical departure from its classical representation as a backward, helpless, and conflict-prone part of the world, the last two decades of the twentieth century and the first decade into the twenty-first century have brought Africa to the global stage as a new frontier that can be captured for its resource abundance and strategic significance. Global dynamics have also reinforced China to increase its diplomatic and economic interests, as well as its growing involvement in peace and security in the continent. Although China's engagement in Africa was not new, the 2007/2008 global food and fuel crisis has given an alarm to Chinese government and its business companies about the future of its domestic energy demand and supply and consequentially the sustainability of its economic growth. As Beeson et al. (2011) succinctly argue, the global rise in energy price has prompted China to introduce a policy of "Going Global" through which it designed different incentive packages to its companies in encouraging them to invest overseas. Such "going global" policy had also included peacekeeping missions.

Since 2013, China became the second largest contributor of troops to UN peacekeeping missions in Africa next to Ethiopia, contributing over 2000 troops (Neethling 2015). In areas of financial contribution as well, it stood the second next to USA in 2016.[4] In this regard, it can be argued that the coming of China to the scene in areas of peacekeeping and security in Africa would possibly produce two different circumstances. Firstly, it provides alternative opportunities for African leaders and elites and reduces their dependence on western powers. In this case, China might play a positive role in creating balance of power and could potentially transform conflicts into peace mainly because its companies, firms, and institutions demand peaceful environment for successful business (Agubamah 2014). On the other hand, according to my informant from peace and security department in AU,

> China might become another hegemonic power in Africa through its military muscle. As we suffered and still suffer from western interference in African conflicts, China is also likely taking the same contour of intervention because its primary interest is economic advantage. Wherever it thinks its economic interest would be at risk, China would take military intervention in the name of peacekeeping mission. What we need as Africa from our Chinese partners is not in areas of peace and security. We, Africans should solve our problems by ourselves. Rather, we want our Chinese partners to provide us with skills in areas of infrastructure. We need the technology and other sorts of economic partnership. We don't want to see another hegemonic power in the continent.[5]

Ostensibly, Chinese peacekeeping mission in Africa might potentially produce a power of domination on the one hand, and a power of peace and stability on the other hand, depending on how both China and African actors manage the partnership. It should also be recognized that despite its recent engagement in direct peacekeeping operations in Africa, China hasn't fully dropped the fundamental principle of respecting the sovereignty of states. Rather, it believes in "solving African problems by Africans," which many African leaders applaud. The rhetoric of peacekeeping operations by African regional and sub-regional organizations (AU, IGAD, ECOWAS, SADC) subscribes to this principle of "African solutions to African problems." Thus, China is more engaged in supporting these regional and sub-regional organizations (economic communities) in the practices of peace and security, capacity-building, and other related aspects. The views from AU Department of Peace and Security subscribe to two competing perspectives. On the one hand, the officials have the opinion that China might play a positive role in ensuring peace and security in Africa because of its strong commitment to provide financial and technical expertise to African organizations, institutions, and countries to boost their capacity. Conversely, there are some skepticisms in China's involvement associated with the fear of Beijing becoming another hegemonic power in the continent. This fear and skepticism is generated from China's strong economic interest in Africa on the one hand, and thus, it's potential to possibly undertake future military intervention in favor of its interests, on the other hand. The outcome, according to the AU official would "depend on how African leaders and institutions utilize the partnership." Nevertheless, China will remain a strong actor in Africa with some adverse political, economic, and security implications as a result of the asymmetrical power relations between the two sides—China as a rising global power versus the politically disorganized, institutionally weak, and economically poor African countries.

Conclusion

China's shift in African policy is part of Beijing's broader economic, strategic, and political interests in Africa, as well as at the global level. Building on historical advantages as non-colonial power, which garnered China the leverage of presenting itself as a genuine partner to Africa, Beijing has recently combined both diplomatic and active engagements in areas of peacebuilding in the continent. This provided African leaders and organizations such as AU and regional institutions an alternative arena to get financial and technical support in their endeavor to promote economic development, infrastructural provision, and ensure peace and security in the continent. In the areas of Foreign Direct Investment and overseas trade, China has become the leading partner to some African countries, particularly to the natural resource rich countries such as Angola, Democratic Republic Congo, Sudan, South Sudan, South Africa, and

Zambia. Alongside its economic engagement, China also provides technical support, capacity-building trainings, and technologies to combat piracy, terrorism, riot, and generally to equip African organizations to be in a better position to respond to security challenges. In this regard, China plays a positive role in Africa's continental and regional peace and security architecture building, including the AU's Peace and Security Council (PSC) and regional Peace Support Operations by financing AU missions in different African countries, such as Somalia and Sudan.

However, it is pertinent to note that the underlying factors in all these advances are the economic transformations and interest of China that made it to consider Africa as a new resource extraction frontier for the benefit of its companies and institutions. As a result of the asymmetrical power relations between China and Africa, and the pattern of trade relations between the two partners—Africa is exporting raw materials to China and importing Chinese manufactured goods. This asymmetrical economic relation has made some critics to consider China as a powerful neocolonial actor that makes Africa dependent on its largesse for its economic and security interests.

Notes

1. Interview with an Official at AU department of Peace and Security (25 February 2017, Addis Ababa).
2. Giuseppe Crisafulli (2018) China–Africa Trade to Benefit from Growing Economic Cooperation, China Briefing, https://www.china-briefing.com/news/china-africa-trade-to-benefit-from-growing-economic-cooperation/. Accessed on 13 March 2019.
3. Paul Nantulya (2019) Chinese Hard Power Supports Its Growing Strategic Interests in Africa, African Center for Strategic Studies, https://africacenter.org/spotlight/chinese-hard-power-supports-its-growing-strategic-interests-in-africa/. Accessed on 13 March 2019.
4. Institute for Security and Development Policy (2018) "China's Role in UN Peacekeeping" http://isdp.eu/publication/chinas-role-un-peacekeeping/. Accessed 10 May 2019.
5. Anonymous informant in AU (Addis Ababa, 20 June 2017).

References

Adams, Jonathan, and Thomas McShane. 1996. *The Myth of Wild Africa: Conservation Without Illusion*. Los Angeles: University of California Press.

Agubamah, Edgar. 2014. China and Peacekeeping in Africa. *International Journal of Humanities and Social Science* 4 (11): 193–197.

Beeson, Mark, Mills Soko, and Wang Yong. 2011. The New Resource Politics: Can Australia and South Africa Accommodate China? *International Affairs* 87 (6): 1365–1384.

Das, Veena, and Deborah Poole. 2004. State and Its Margins: Comparative Ethnographies. In *Anthropology in the Margins of the State*, ed. Veena Das and Deborah Poole, 3–34. Oxford: James Currey.

Debelo, A. Regassa. 2017. The African Union's Peace and Security Partnership with China. APN Policy Briefing Note, Number 12 (https://s3.amazonaws.com/ssrc-cdn1/crmuploads/new_publication_3/the-african-union-s-peace-and-security-partnership-with-china.pdf).

Herbst, Jeffrey. 2000. *States and Power in Africa: Comparative Lessons in Authority and Control*. Princenton, NJ: Princeton University Press.

Korf, Benedikt, Tobias Hagmann, and Rony Emmenegger. 2015. Re-Spacing African Drylands: Territorialization, Sedentarization and Indigenous Commodification in Ethiopia's Pastoral Frontier. *The Journal of Peasant Studies* 42 (5): 881–901.

Leslie, A. Ngoma. 2016. Introduction China-Africa Relations: Political and Economic Engagement and Media Strategies. *African Studies Quarterly* 6 (3–4): 1–6.

Mawdsley, Emma. 2008. Fu Manchu Versus Dr Livingstone in the Dark Continent? Representing China, Africa and the West in British Broadsheet Newspapers. *Political Geography* 27: 509–529.

Mazrui, Ali A. 2002. Who Killed Democracy in Africa? Clues of the Past, Concerns of the Future. *Development Policy Management Network Bulletin* IX (1): 15–23.

Neethling, Theo. 2015. China's International Peacekeeping Contributions: Towards the End of China's Non-Intervention Policy? *Strategic Review for Southern Africa* 37 (2): 7–28.

Neumann, Roderick. 1998. *Imposing Wilderness: Struggles Over Livelihood and Nature Preservation in Africa*. Berkeley, CA: California State University Press.

Regassa, Asebe, Yetebarek Hizekiel, and Benedikt Korf. 2018. 'Civilizing' the Pastoral Frontier: Land Grabbing, Dispossession and Coercive Agrarian Development in Ethiopia. *The Journal of Peasant Studies*. https://doi.org/10.1080/03066150.2017.1420060.

Shelton, Garth. 2001. China and Africa: Building an Economic Partnership. *South African Journal of International Affairs* 8 (2): 111–119.

Suzuki, Shogo. 2009. Chinese Soft Power, Insecurity Studies, Myopia and Fantasy. *Third World Quarterly* 30 (4): 779–793.

Wang, Jianwei, and Jing Zou. 2014. China Goes to Africa: A Strategic Move? *Journal of Contemporary China* 23 (90): 1113–1132.

Zeleza, Paul. 2014. The Africa-China Relationship: Challenges and Opportunities. *Canadian Journal of African Studies / Revue canadienne des études africaines* 48 (1): 145–169.
Zenawi, Meles. 2006. African Development: Dead Ends and New Beginnings. Unpublished Monograph (http://www.meleszenawi.com/african-development-dead-ends-and-new-biginnings-by-meles-zenawi/).

CHAPTER 6

Foreign Direct Investments and Africa Rising: A Critical Assessment

Onyukwu E. Onyukwu and Uchenna A. Nnamani

Introduction

The Africa rising narrative is not a bare-faced exaggeration of protagonists but largely based on concrete evidence of Africa's improved economic growth record since the turn of the millennium, which nonetheless appears to have plateaued. However, what is the nexus between the African economic growth record and the choice of the continent as a preferred foreign direct investment destination? Has the continent sufficiently achieved sustained high economic growth performance to be able to compete favourably for global FDI flows with other regions of developing economies? Has the FDI attracted by African economies provided the much-desired jobs in the region? These and more are the questions that this chapter seeks to answer.

O. E. Onyukwu (✉) · U. A. Nnamani
Institute of Development Studies, University of Nigeria Enugu Campus, Enugu, Nigeria
e-mail: onyukwu.onyukwu@unn.edu.ng

U. A. Nnamani
Development Strategy Centre, Enugu, Nigeria

K. Omeje (ed.), *The Governance, Security and Development Nexus*,
https://doi.org/10.1007/978-3-030-49348-6_6

Foreign direct investment (FDI) remains one of the most important forms of cross-border capital flow into developing countries including sub-Saharan Africa. Foreign direct investment is different from foreign portfolio investment and does not transmit solely in form of financial capital. Rather, it is a package consisting of not only capital but also technology, management and skill. Ayanwale (2007) defines it as an amalgamation of capital, employment, technology transfers and management competencies. Given the expected high positive net impact of FDI on destination countries, policymakers, particularly in Africa often ascribe an economic miracle performing status to FDI inflows to their countries going by the fanfare that often herald its attraction and the enormous amount of resource giveaways that they are offered. Thus, sub-Saharan African countries tend to have liberal policies favouring inward FDI flows. But has this obviously enticing approach of African countries to FDI flows meant that the region got more than a fair share of global FDI flows? Again, have the FDI flows to African economies always given them the much-anticipated leverage in terms of quantum growth and high employment generation?

FDI inflow to the African continent has increased since the 1980s. This is just as it has increased for all developing economies in Asia, Latin America and the Oceania. For example, FDI inflow into SSA also increased almost sevenfold from US$6.9 billion in 2000 to US$46 billion in 2015. But in terms of global share of FDI flows the continent continues to lag behind in spite of the African rising narrative. Between 1970 and 1979, Africa was receiving 20% of the FDI inflow to the developing world, but fast forward to 2010–2017, the region received only 8% of the inflow to the developing world. However, the character of FDI flows to the continent seems to be changing as the big economies in the region—Nigeria, South Africa and Algeria appear to be finding it difficult lately to attract large FDI relative to the size of their economies. Instead, Egypt, Congo DR, Ethiopia and Ghana appear to be the more preferred FDI destinations. The question is what makes countries preferred destinations of foreign direct investment? Are there different kinds of foreign direct investments? Do they support employment generation differently in their host economies?

In the light of the many unknowns about the size, direction, character and contributions of foreign direct investment to the African rising narrative, this chapter in section "The Role of FDI in the Development of States: A Theoretical Perspective" x-rays the theoretical underpinnings of foreign direct investment. Section "The Contribution of FDI Flows in the Africa Rising Narrative" discusses the nexus between the African economic growth record and FDI inflows to the region both from a region-wide perspective and from country-specific view. Section "Africa's Six Lions" is devoted to discussions around the character of FDI flows to the African continent and the nature of their contributions to the development needs of the region. Section "The Character of FDI to Africa" discusses how African economies can attract large volumes of FDI flows, particularly flows that trigger huge employment opportunities and concludes the chapter.

The Role of FDI in the Development of States: A Theoretical Perspective

It is not an overstatement that foreign direct investment has become an important subject of policy discussions and research across countries of the world, particularly developing states. Despite how important foreign direct investment has become in today's global development discourse, finding a suitable theory that sufficiently explains its character, motivation and impact remain somewhat difficult.

In the classical model of static comparative advantage that underpins international trade, goods are assumed to be completely mobile while factors of production are not. Thus, there is no motivation for foreign direct investment as the classical theory of trade does not anticipate any trade in factor inputs. To derive theories of foreign direct investment, one has to modify the conventional trade theory and consider the dynamic aspects of comparative advantage. Alternatively, one has to look to other branches of economics such as the microeconomics of the firm, industrial organisation theories, location theories, and capital theories for insight. Any satisfactory theory of foreign direct investment, in our view, should be able to offer three important explanations (Chen 1983: 17). First, such a theory must be able to explain why it is worthwhile for firms to invest abroad. There must be certain advantages that the firms can enjoy so that the additional costs of running subsidiaries in the host countries can be more than sufficiently compensated for. Second, any theory of foreign direct investment should be able to explain the country and industry patterns of foreign direct investment. Third, such a theory should also be able to explain the two-way flow of foreign direct investment as it is a common observation that while firms in country A invest in B, firms in country B also invest in A at the same time.

The macroeconomic theory of foreign direct investment assumes a perfectly competitive world in which there is only one commodity and capital (foreign and domestic alike), where international capital flow will occur only where the rate of return to capital is different between countries. With free capital mobility, capital will move from the lower rate of return country to the higher rate of return country, resulting in the international equalisation of rates of return and marginal productivities of capital. The reason for a higher rate of return abroad is simply due to the fact that capital abroad is scarcer and the marginal productivity of capital is therefore higher. In other words, under perfectly competitive conditions, marginal productivity is the only factor which determines the rate of return to capital and it is the pursuance of higher profit which exists in a higher rate of return country that international capital flow occurs. Besides the fact that the theory is based on the rather unrealistic assumption of perfect competition, the MacDougall-Kemp[1] model as it is often referred to, has other shortcomings. First, the analysis does not distinguish between foreign direct investment and foreign indirect portfolio investment. The reasons and effects of such two types of foreign investment must be different. Second, the MacDougall-Kemp model treats foreign investment solely in terms of financial capital, and does not take into consideration the concept of foreign investment (particularly foreign direct investment) as a package consisting of not only capital but also technology, management and skill. Third, the model is a static one in the sense that it does not take into consideration changes in technology, changes in factor prices and the consequential change in comparative advantages. Fourth, the model has rather weak explanatory power for foreign direct investment. The model evidently cannot explain why two-way foreign investment can occur at the same time.

The Contribution of FDI Flows in the Africa Rising Narrative

Foreign direct investment has increased in both size and relevance since 1980s. According to Hirst and Thompson (2000) there has been surge in FDI inflow especially to the developing world. Todaro and Smith (2011), asserts that growth in foreign direct investment (FDI) in the developing world has been rapid, rising from annual rate of $2.4 billion in 1962 to

$35 billion in 1990, $565 billion in 2000 and $670 billion in 2017 (see UNCTAD 2018). Developing economies received 54% of the total world FDI in 2018 (UNCTAD 2019), meaning that for the second time in the last decade, inflows to developing economies outpaced that of developed economies. Transition economies have however consistently received very little FDI.

The bulk of developing economies are in Africa, America, Asia and Oceania. Figure 6.1 shows the FDI inflow to developing economies by region. Developing economies in Asia have consistently received the most FDI since the 1990s. But, a lot has happened between 1980 and 2018,

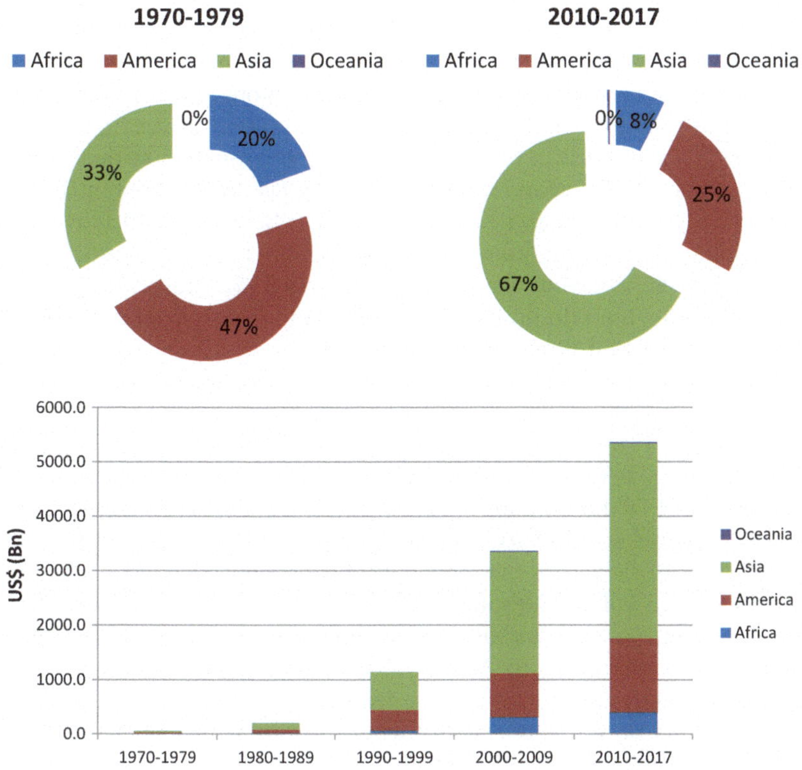

Fig. 6.1 FDI inflow to developing economies (*Source* Authors' computation from UNCTAD [2018] dataset)

leading to the huge gap in the volume FDI to each of these regions. Developing economies of Africa had always lagged behind those in Asia and America, but the gap has also widened since the turn of the millennium. Between 1970 and 1979, Africa was receiving 20% of the FDI inflow to the developing world, but fast forward to 2010–2017, the region received only 8% of the inflow to the developing world. Although inflow has increased across all regions in the developing world, Asia and Latin America have had higher rate of increase hence the higher ratio. This means that Africa's share of global FDI flows has been in decline over the same period that Africa is said to be rising.

Foreign direct investment is an important ingredient for long run sustained economic growth. This is particularly so because of its uniqueness in being an amalgamation of capital, employment and technology transfer. However, FDI flow through multinationals that are largely driven by profit or in recent time possibility of continuous growth. What this implies is that although FDI is an important growth driver, it is motivated by profit and driven by sustained economic growth or strong future growth prospects. An economy that is growing fast, or with potentials for continuous growth is likely to attract more FDI. Between 1980 and 1999, Sub-Saharan Africa only grew by 1.75%. Within the same period, East Asia grew by 4.37%, while South Asia grew by 5.53%. Thus, Africa's weak economic growth no doubt has been largely responsible for the shrinking relative share of FDI flows to the region.

The attraction of investors to Asia is not unconnected to the three decades of growth of the Asian Tigers and recent growth of the cub tigers. African Economy started growing from 2000, sparking the notion of Africa rising. Between 2000 and 2014, Sub-Saharan Africa average 5% growth rate. FDI inflow into SSA also increased almost sevenfold from US$ 6.9 billion in 2000 to US$ 46 billion in 2015. Flows to Eastern and Southern Asia within the same period rose from US$ 138.42 billion to US$ 450.33 billion. Although FDI inflow to SSA grew by more than double the rate of Asia for the period, inflow to SSA in 2017 was just about 10% of the inflow to Asia. In 2018, Africa only received 3.5% of total world FDI. Africa's economic growth no doubt has lost traction since 2015. However, our inability to get the right mix of datasets on Africa's economic growth and FDI flows poses a bit of a challenge to us to further interrogate these issues at the region-wide level, hence shift of focus to specific country flows as shown in Fig. 6.2.

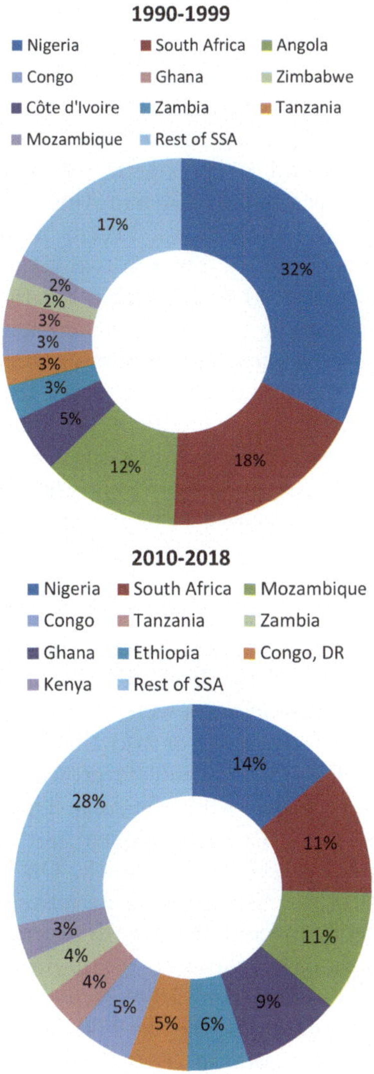

Fig. 6.2 FDI inflow to major destination in SSA 1990–1999; 2010–2018 (*Source* Authors' computation from WDI [2018] dataset)

Perhaps, the flow of investment to SSA can be better explained at the country level of the major players or FDI destination countries. The three largest economies of SSA, namely Angola, Nigeria and South Africa often drive the growth trajectory of the region. FDI seems to have been flowing mainly to the bigger economies of the region in the past. Between 1990 and 1999, Nigeria and South Africa alone received half of the FDI inflow into Sub-Saharan Africa. The top ten recipients of FDI inflow got 83% of the inflows. Recent statistics show that this is changing, albeit not massively. The top two countries for the period 2010–2018 are still Nigeria and South Africa, but they received a combined total of 25% of the inflow to the region (compared to 50% between 1990 and 1999). Also, the top ten destination countries received a total of 72% of the flow to the region. The countries that make up the top ten FDI recipients have changed slightly with Angola giving way for Ethiopia. The overall impression here is that there is high positive correlation between countries' sustained economic growth performance and the volume of FDI flows they are able to attract.

Africa's Six Lions

Ethiopia, Ghana, Kenya, Mozambique, Nigeria and South Africa were dubbed the six lions of Africa in a publication by Bhorat and Tarp (2016). These economies were at the time of analysis either the fastest growing, most advanced, or had the potentials of sustaining growth over time, and probably stimulate growth at the regional scale just like the Asian Tigers. But, while the Asian Tigers had three decades of growth at about 7%, Africa's six lions seem not to be able to sustain at two decades of positive economic growth. On the account of this lacuna, we can say that the 'Africa rising narrative' is not yet anchored on a strong and resilient economic growth experience in Sub-Saharan Africa. Africa's most advanced economy, South Africa, has had less than 4% growth since recovering from 2009 recession. Nigeria, Africa's largest economy had abundant promise, until oil price slump busts her bubble in 2015, leading to a recession in 2016. These two heavyweight countries have continued to dominate the regional economy; hence, their growth seems to mirror the growth of the region. They have also been the dominant destination of FDI in the region (Fig. 6.2).

Nigeria and South Africa are however not all that there is about Africa. Since 2004, Ethiopia has been the fastest growing economy in Africa

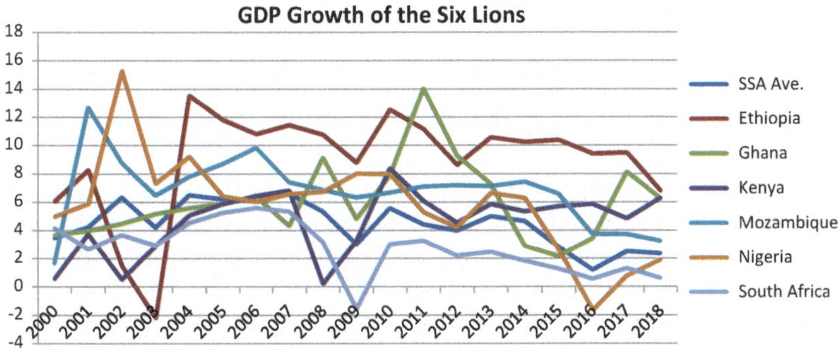

Fig. 6.3 Growth rate of SSA's six lion (*Source* Authors' computation from WDI [2018] dataset)

and one of the fastest in the world. The country averaged 8% economic growth rate between 1998 and 2018 (WDI 2018). This is particularly so important to the 'Africa rising' narrative because the country is non-resource dependent. Mozambique and Kenya have also been relatively stable, while Ghana's growth has fluctuated, while remaining high on the average. The trend of FDI inflow to these countries is interesting and important in understanding the reality of the Africa rising narrative. Flows to these four countries have been growing at varying degrees and have been relatively stable. FDI flows to Ghana and Mozambique have been growing since 2006, while that of Ethiopia has been increasing since 2012 following almost a decade of high growth. FDI flow to Kenya increased and remained stable since 2006 but the increased flow is not as high as the other three countries.

FDI inflows to Nigeria and especially South Africa just like their growth rate are anything but stable. With the return to democracy in 1999, Nigeria witnessed all the economic positives. This was complemented with her exit from the Paris club debt quagmire meaning that from 2006 to 2013, all was well with the Nigerian economy, having an average growth rate of 5% and being a leading destination of investment in Africa. However, this has unfortunately changed since 2015. The economic situation of Nigeria, South Africa and slightly Angola helped to create the Africa rising narrative at the turn of the millennium. This also explains why the mixed performance of these economies appears to be calling the African rising narrative to question. However as can been seen from Fig. 6.3, the stories of the three big economies of SSA are not all that make up the Africa rising narrative. Economic happenings in Ethiopia and some other similar economies really show that Africa (or at least a part of it) is still rising. Yes, it is still rising, although not with the same vigour as at the start or even as desired.

African economies have in the past been driven by natural resources and commodity exports. However, that seems to be changing. In recent times, African economies can be classified into resource intensive and non-resource intensive economies (see IMF 2018). The resource intensive economies are those that depend largely on their natural resources as dominant sources of foreign exchange and government revenue. The resource intensive countries can further be divided into oil exporting countries and other natural resource intensive countries. Among the non-resource intensive economies, some have grown faster than others. Hence, we can have four classifications, namely (i.e. oil exporting countries—OEC; other resource intensive countries—RIC; non-resource intensive high growth countries—NRIC-HG; non-resource intensive low growth countries—NRIC-LG).

FDI inflow into oil exporting countries and other resource intensive countries are very volatile as opposed to that of the NRIC-LG countries that are stable although small in volume(Fig. 6.4). FDI inflow to NRIC-HG countries rose significantly between 2010 and 2013. Although FDI inflow to these countries declined a little between 2013 and 2014, it

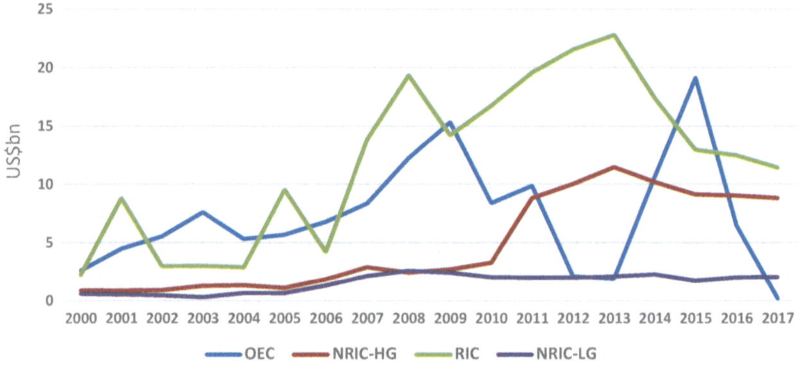

Fig. 6.4 FDI flow to SSA by country group (*Source* Authors' computation from WDI (2018) dataset)

has remained relatively since then. For the NRIC-HG group of countries, economic growth has been rising steadily since 2009, and they are attracting the attention of foreign investors. Ethiopia, Kenya and Mozambique are shining examples of the non-resource intensive high growth countries, particularly with respect to FDI receipts (Table 6.1).

FDI Inflow is becoming more widely distributed across countries on the continent. While the top five country-recipients of FDI inflow got 62% between 1990 and 1999, the top five countries between 2010 and 2018, received 52% of the inflow. The direction of FDI inflow in recent times together with the country-level growth trends suggest that '*a new Africa is rising*' while some of the bigger economies continue to struggle and lag behind. For instance, Nigeria was not among the top five FDI destination countries in Africa in 2018. Smaller economies like Congo, Ethiopia, Ghana and Mozambique in addition to already established bigger economies of Egypt, South Africa and Morocco all received more FDI inflow in 2018 than Nigeria. South Africa was in similar situation in 2016 and 2017. Meanwhile Ethiopia has remained among the top five destination of FDI in the last three years. The foregoing illustrates the changing landscape of FDI inflows in Africa.

Table 6.1 Top ten destination of FDI to Sub-Sahara Africa

		1990–1999		*2000–2009*		*2010–2018*
1	Nigeria	14.94	Nigeria	41.79	Nigeria	45.46
2	South Africa	8.50	South Africa	40.98	South Africa	37.81
3	Angola	5.74	Angola	12.19	Mozambique	34.76
4	Côte d'Ivoire	2.32	Congo	6.61	Ghana	28.56
5	Zambia	1.41	Ghana	6.27	Ethiopia	18.34
6	Tanzania	1.21	Tanzania	6.03	Congo, DR	17.59
7	Congo	1.17	Congo, DR	5.91	Congo	17.23
8	Ghana	1.13	Equatorial Guinea	5.77	Tanzania	12.81
9	Zimbabwe	0.95	Zambia	5.21	Zambia	11.80
10	Mozambique	0.92	Uganda	4.40	Kenya	10.17
	Rest of SSA	7.96	Rest of SSA	54.10	Rest of SSA	92.39

Source Authors' computation from WDI (2018) dataset

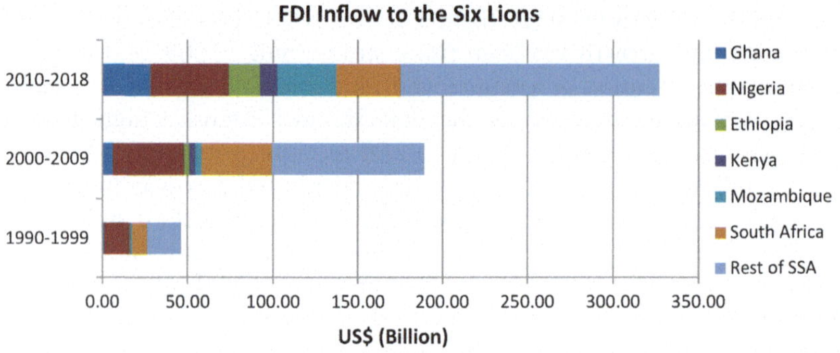

Fig. 6.5 FDI Inflow to SSA's six lions (*Source* Authors' computation from WDI [2018] dataset)

The Character of FDI to Africa

The sentiments that underpin foreign direct investment flows seem to differ from the point of view of the investor and the destination nations. The foreign investor is mainly driven by profitability or its prospects and the security of the investment. By contrast, some recipient country policymakers in Africa seem to ascribe an economic miracle performing status to foreign direct investment. Using the Nigerian experience as an example, often the media is inundated with news headlines of frantic efforts different administrations in the country are making to attract foreign direct investment. The efforts range from well-funded foreign trips of state actors and select businesses and individuals to woo foreign investors into the country. Also governments in Nigeria sometimes appear more willing (if not almost desperate) to give promoters of FDI in the country with such incentives as speedy incorporation of business, import duty waivers, tax holidays and free gift of large expanse of land with title deeds than they would offer similar support to local business initiatives. Thus, many African countries actively shop around for FDI inflows with a variety of incentives from their governments, because rightly or wrongly they view FDI as a quick driver of high economic growth and job creation. However, the patterns of FDI inflows to Africa and in fact the rest of the world seem to suggest that investors are more inclined to move to destinations that are already growing or have prospects for stable and sustained economic growth (Fig. 6.5).

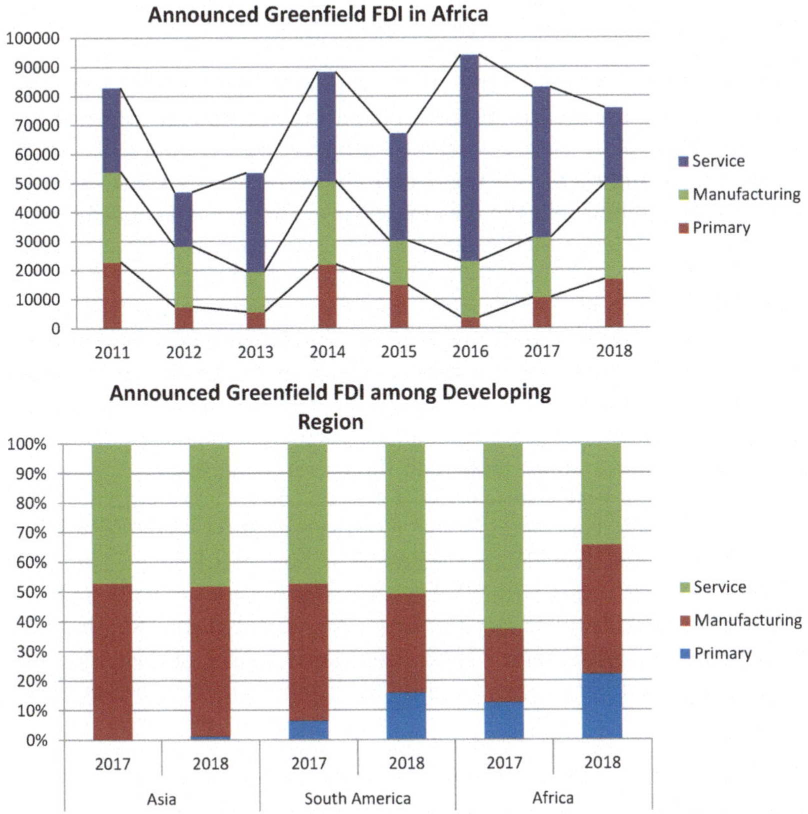

Fig. 6.6 Announced greenfield FDI for Africa and other developing regions (*Source* Authors' computation from UNCTAD [2019] dataset)

Generally, FDI inflows to SSA seem to be a mixed bag in recent times. The service sector dominates the flow but there is also significant flow to the manufacturing sector and primary sector (Fig. 6.6). When compared to other regions, the size of flow to primary sector is higher in Africa. With large volume of flows to the service and primary sectors, Africa has attracted more natural resource-seeking FDI, relative to other regions in recent time. The growth in telecoms across the region also explains the large inflow to the service sector. All sectors of the economy are susceptible to business cycles, but the primary sector is most volatile.

The volatilities of commodity and oil prices have consistently affected the economic growth in most resource-dependent countries of Africa (especially Nigeria and Angola). This is in addition to its limited job-creating capacity when compared to the manufacturing sector. Asia which seems to be the ideal place as it consistently attracts large volumes of FDI to the manufacturing sector. It might therefore be safe to say that flows to Asia, especially China and the Asian tigers are efficiency seeking. By being a destination for efficiency-seeking FDI, Asian countries have become global headquarters of manufacturing activities, leading to export-driven economies. The good news though is that for the first time in 2018, Africa attracted more FDI to the manufacturing sector than service and primary sectors. This is largely due the resurgence of South Africa and increased investment in Egypt and Ethiopia. If the pattern of flows to Egypt, Ethiopia and South Africa is sustained, then manufacturing sector-led growth will be made more feasible in the region (Fig. 6.7).

Market seeking FDI among other thing aim to save cost associated with serving distant markets (Franco and Rentocchini 2008). Hence, it often targets already established big markets. It is largely driven by potentials for high turnover and returns. Recent evidence suggests that big markets in Africa do not always attract the largest inflows. Nigeria, South Africa and Algeria have not attracted large FDI relative to size of their economy in recent time. Rather, Egypt, Congo DR, Ethiopia and Ghana have been

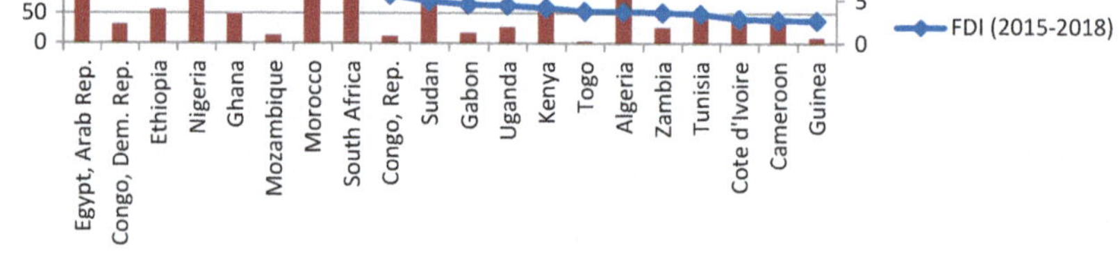

Fig. 6.7 Top 20 destinations of FDI and Africa 2015–2018 (*Source* Authors' computation from UNCTAD (2018) and WDI (2018) dataset)

doing well in recent time in this regard. With the signing of the Africa Free Continental Trade Area, Africa is expected to attract more market seeking FDI going forward. With the free flow of goods expected as an outcome of AfCFTA, Africa would begin to appear as a single market to the rest of the world and particularly foreign investors. As a collective, SSA is larger than Netherland, Brazil and Singapore all of whom received more FDI than all SSA countries combined in 2018. With the signing of the AfCFTA, it is expected that the potentials of economies of scales, and seamless border will attract more market seeking investment into the region. The AfCFTA is not without expected drawback. The most important drawback is that small businesses that are expected to benefit from access to bigger markets will be exposed to very strong competition from abroad.

Recent studies have shown that FDI inflow to Africa has not particularly created the much-desired job. It is important to note here that the sector that creates the most jobs have attracted the least FDI in Africa. According to Wall et al. (2018) the hi-tech sector, which is the smallest sector in terms of FDI attraction in Africa, has the fastest growing FDI-generated employment, followed by manufacturing. These explain why the quest to leverage job creation through FDI inflows has not yielded much results in most African countries.

Conclusion

In conclusion, we hold the view that the Africa rising narrative is not a bare-faced exaggeration of protagonists but largely based on concrete evidence of Africa's improved economic growth record since the turn of the millennium. Regionally, the African Economy started growing from 2000, sparking the notion of Africa rising. Between 2000 and 2014, Sub-Saharan Africa averaged 5% growth rate. However, since 2015 Africa's economic growth has slowed down essentially due to weak or negative growth in most of the big-sized economies on the continent. The verve witnessed in the dominant economies such as Nigeria, South Africa and Angola at the turn of the millennium largely contributed to generating the initial Africa rising narrative. Unfortunately, the vitality experienced by these economies has waned considerably. Similarly, between 2000 and 2015, FDI inflow into SSA increased almost sevenfold from US$6.9 billion to US$46 billion. Although the growth of FDI inflow to the continent has remained positive, SSA countries' relative share in FDI inflows has declined. Somehow, on account of both economic growth and FDI inflows to the continent, the vitality the region has lost as a result of the diminished performance of the dominant economies has been fairly compensated by the strong and enduring performance of few small-size economies on the continent, thereby sustaining the impetus of the Africa rising narrative.

The renewed economic growth in the region brought about renewed prospects of FDI inflows to the continent. The dispersion of economic growth in the region is strongly correlated with the new character and direction of FDI inflows into the continent. FDI Inflow has become more widely distributed across countries on the continent. Thus, from our analysis, there is high positive correlation between countries' sustained economic growth performance and the volume of FDI flows they are able to attract. This should be same for the entire region. Similarly, as the nations' economic growth heightens and endures, the character of FDI attracted to the changes. All FDI inflows do not leave the same effects on their host economies. FDI inflows in natural resource-seeking countries have less job-creating capacity on their host economies than FDI inflows in efficiency-seeking economies, which are mainly attracted by the manufacturing sector. The hi-tech sector, which unfortunately is the smallest sector in terms of FDI attraction to African countries, has the fastest growing FDI-generated employment, followed by manufacturing. Overall, it is instructive for African governments to note that image laundering and incentive giveaways scarcely attract FDI inflows, but rather economic growth prospects or the promise of enduring growth.

Note

1. This analysis of foreign investment was initiated by MacDougall (1960) and elaborated and formalised by Kemp (1961, cited in Chen 1983: 18).

References

Ayanwale, Adeolu B. 2007. FDI and Economic Growth: Evidence from Nigeria. African Economic Research Consortium (AERC) Research Paper 165. Nairobi, Kenya.

Bhorat, Haroon, and Finn Tarp. 2016. *Africa's Lion: Growth Traps and Opportunities for Six African Economies*. Washington, DC: Brookings Institution Press.

Chen, Edward K.Y. 1983. *Multinational Corporations, Technology and Employment*. New York: St Martin's Press.
Franco, Chiara, Francesco Rentocchini, and Giuseppe Vittucci M. 2008. Why do firms invest abroad? *An analysis of the motives underlying Foreign Direct Investments*, Department of Economics Working Papers 0817, Department of Economics, University of Trento, Italia.
Hirst, Paul, and Grahame Thompson. 2000. *Globalisation in Question*, 2nd ed. Malden, MA: Blackwell.
International Monetary Fund. 2018. *Regional Economic Outlook: Sub-Saharan Africa*. Washington, DC, October.
MacDougall, George Donald A. 1960. The Benefits and Costs of Private Investment from Abroad: A theoretical approach. *Bulletin of the Oxford University Institute of Economics & Statistics* 22 (3): 189–211.
Todaro, Michael P., and Stephen Smith. 2011. *Economic Development*, 11th ed. Harlow: Pearson Education Limited.
United Nation's Conference on Trade and Development UNCTAD. 2018. *World Investment Report*. New York: United Nation's Publications.
United Nation's Conference on Trade and Development UNCTAD. 2019. *World Investment Report*. New York: United Nation's Publication.
Wall, Ronald, Poonam Mehta, and Rupinder Kaur. 2018. The Impact of Foreign Direct Investment on Employment in Africa. In *The State of African Cities 2018: The Geography of African Investment*, ed. Ronald Wall, Joseph Maseland, Katharina Rochell, and Mathias Spaliviero, 140–151. UN-Habitat and IHS-Erasmus University Rotterdam.
World Bank. 2018. *World Development Indicators*. Washington, DC: World Bank.

PART III

The Regional Imperatives of Africa Rising

CHAPTER 7

Regional Trade and Security Cooperation: A Case Study of the Economic Community of West African States (ECOWAS)

Ibrahim Bangura

Introduction

The chapter critically examines ECOWAS and its efforts to strengthen regional trade and security cooperation in West Africa. It analyses four key factors: firstly, the trade and security frameworks that ECOWAS has adopted since it was established and how the frameworks are contributing to facilitating regional trade cooperation; secondly, the performance of ECOWAS in preventing and managing conflicts within the region; thirdly, the approaches used in aligning the organisation's trade and security initiatives so that they can mutually reinforce each other and fourthly, the factors that undermine trade and security initiatives in the region and how they could be overcome. The study provides key findings on the challenges that ECOWAS faces and what could be done to overcome them.

I. Bangura (✉)
Department of Peace and Conflict Studies, Fourah Bay College, University of Sierra Leone, Freetown, Sierra Leone

K. Omeje (ed.), *The Governance, Security and Development Nexus*,
https://doi.org/10.1007/978-3-030-49348-6_7

In 1975, fifteen countries in West Africa[1] convened in Nigeria to establish a Regional Economic Community (REC) called the Economic Community of West African States (ECOWAS). Since then, ECOWAS has grown into a formidable organisation comprising of seven institutions and ten specialised agencies. The establishment of ECOWAS was primarily based on the desire on the part of countries in the region to promote regional economic cooperation and integration as indicated in the Multilateral Treaty of ECOWAS of 1975:

> Bearing in mind that effort at sub-regional co-operation should not conflict with or hamper similar efforts being made to foster wider co-operation in Africa;
>
> Affirming as the ultimate objective of their efforts accelerated and sustained economic development of their states and the creation of a homogeneous society, leading to the unity of the countries of West Africa, by the elimination of all types of obstacles to the free movement of goods, capital and persons;
>
> Decide for the purpose of the foregoing to create an Economic Community of West African States ... (ECOWAS 1975: 20)

To achieve its objectives, the Commission adopted several protocols and policies related to economic integration and trade promotion. The focus on economic integration and trade promotion was to a large extent disrupted in the early 1990, with the outbreak of a violent civil war in Liberia in December 1989. To end the war, ECOWAS assembled and deployed a peacekeeping intervention force named ECOWAS Monitoring Group (ECOMOG) and since then has repeatedly used military intervention to backstop diplomatic efforts to restore stability in members states in the region. Typical examples of its interventions are the cases of Sierra Leone, Guinea Bissau and the Gambia, with shuttle diplomacy embarked on in almost every country in the region, especially during electioneering processes.

In the last decades, the Commission has succeeded in strategically positioning itself as an exemplary REC that other RECs, such as the Southern Africa Development Community (SADC), Common Market for Eastern and Southern Africa (COMESA) and the Inter-Governmental Authority on Development (IGAD) could learn from.

Methodologically, this study is based on a qualitative approach, with interviews conducted with staff of ECOWAS, security and trade officials in the governments of Nigeria, Sierra Leone, Liberia, Guinea and Cote d'Ivoire, trade and security experts, academics and civil society actors. A total of 67 people were interviewed (42 males and 25 females). In addition, a comprehensive review of literature was done on trade and security issues related to ECOWAS and its member states.

The chapter is divided into five sections: Section one introduces the chapter; section two critically assesses ECOWAS' drive to promote regional economic integration, notably the development and use of protocols related to the movement of people and goods in the region; section three focuses on the role ECOWAS is playing to strengthen peace and security in the region; section four analyses how regional trade and security initiatives complements each other and also the existing challenges related to how they could overcome; section five is the concluding section.

ECOWAS and Trade Cooperation in West Africa

The decision to pursue greater trade cooperation in ECOWAS resulted from a number of regional and historical factors. Historically, the member states and their populace have long had close trade relations with each other. This was much so the case for the French countries that maintained a stronger relationship with their former colonial masters, France. Of the 15 ECOWAS member states, 6 were former French colonies that shared common institutions such as the West African Communauté Financière Africaine (CFA) Franc and central bank systems (Adkisson 1984: 24–25).

If regional integration was partly inspired by close historic ties, West African states also had material incentives to engage in regional cooperation. As a region, West Africa was characterised by many cross-border initiatives—either in terms of trade among ethno-linguistic groups residing at different sides of the borders, or in massive production and commercial projects (ECOWAS and UNECA 2015: 7). The socio-economic interaction was so intense that interviewees referred to borders as artificial boundaries which only succeeded in dividing ethno-linguistic groups with strong traditional ties. The end of colonialism stimulated a drive for unity and desire for not just state but regional economic integration and harmonisation.

Several political factors also played an influential role towards the establishment of ECOWAS. These include the death of the then President of France Charles de Gaulle in 1970, the resultant relaxation of French control in West Africa, the advent of the Lomé Convention which—for the first time—placed all West African states on equal footing when it comes to trade and development cooperation with the European Economic Community (EEC), the desire of Nigeria to use ECOWAS as a vehicle for repairing relationships with neighbouring states, increasing its sphere of economic influence within the sub-region, and to access the region's market, as well as to counterbalance the influence of former colonial powers (Karaki and Verhaeghe 2017: 4; Adkisson 1984: 26–27).

Article 2(1) of the 1975 ECOWAS Treaty stated that the aim of the Community is "to promote cooperation and development in all fields of economic activities for the purpose of raising the standard of living of its peoples, of increasing and maintaining economic stability, of fostering closer relations among its members and of contributing to the progress and development of the African continent" (ECOWAS 1975). The Treaty further called for the liberalisation of trade—expressed in the abolition of custom duties and quota, establishment of a common custom tariff for goods imported from third countries, as well as freedom of movement and residence for ECOWAS citizens (ECOWAS 1975).

In subsequent years, ECOWAS further developed its trade cooperation scheme through multiple protocols. The free movement of people component, for instance, is supplemented by no fewer than 8 protocols and additional policy documents. These documents include the Protocol on the Free Movement of Persons (1979); Protocol on the Code of Community Citizenship (1982); Resolution on the Implementation of the First stage of the Protocol on Free Movement of Persons, Right of Residence and Establishment (1984); Decision on the Establishment of a Travel Certificate for Member States (1985); Additional Protocols on the Right of Residence (1985) and the Right of Establishment (1989); Decision on the Establishment of a Resident Card for Member States (1990); the Decision on the Establishment of the ECOWAS Passport (2000) and finally the Review of All Protocols on Free Movement (2014).

In principle, protocols and decisions relating to free movement of people are to be implemented in three phases. Phase 1 focused on the right of entry and abolition of visas for a period of up to 90 days and was to be implemented between 1980 and 1985 (ECOWAS 1979: Article 3–5). Phase 2 focused on the establishment of the right of residence in member states and was to be implemented between 1986 and 1990 (ECOWAS 1986: 9–12). The third phase of implementing the freedom of movement revolves around the right of establishment. When properly understood, this particular right allows an ECOWAS citizen to settle or establish in another member state other than his/her state of origin, and to have access to economic activities, to carry out these activities as well as to set up and manage enterprises (particularly in terms of company) under the same conditions as defined by the legislation of the host member state for its own nationals (ECOWAS 1990: Article 1). The protocol provided the option for member states to seek approval from the Community Authority to restrict the application of the right of establishment.

In relation to the free movement of good, the ECOWAS Trade Liberalisation Scheme (ETLS)—seeks to remove tariffs of all kind within the Community. The process would begin with the abolition of tariffs from local products, traditional work of arts and finished goods. This was supplemented by industrial goods which were added in 1990, upon agreements between the member states. Recognising that the removal of tariff will lead to member states losing revenue, in 2004 ECOWAS established a four-year compensation mechanism for countries that dismantle their trade barriers—though hitherto there has been little use of the mechanism due to financial shortfalls.

The Common External Tariff (CET) is one of the three areas of reform requested by the 1975 ECOWAS Treaty. However, it appears that it was only set in 2013 as a result of WAEMU's publication of its tariffs in the early 2000s. The CET is designed primarily as a trade defence measure: consisting of safeguards that temporarily restrict imports of certain products, countervailing duties to counteract the effect of subsidies, anti-dumping measures to counteract unfair practices etc. These measures are especially applicable to agricultural and industrial goods that are sensitive to external competition (Karaki and Verhaeghe 2017: 6). Implementation of the ECOWAS CET started in 2015 with a five-year transition period. As of 2017, 10 out of 15 ECOWAS states have adopted the measure, while the remaining five had failed to do so due to election (Cape Verde), Ebola (Sierra Leone), issues with Portuguese translation and Cote d'Ivoire's hesitation in applying the 35% tariff (Karaki and Verhaeghe, 2017: 6).

In sum, the three main thrusts of ECOWAS trade cooperation initiatives are the free movement of people, free movement of goods and establishment of the CET. When assessing the progress made in each of these areas, it is important to consider ECOWAS' variable-speed approach towards implementation: for it suggests the issue is not so much which countries have adopted a particular measure, but rather how the current state of implementation impacts the long-term success of regional trade cooperation.

When questioned on ECOWAS' trade relations and regional dynamics, a trade expert[2] in Nigeria had this to say:

> ECOWAS means well and has gone a long way in setting policies that could expand on trade opportunities and promote economic development unlike any other region. However, member states have to keep to their commitments and try to be less political about them. Additionally, the Anglophone - Francophone divide continues to negatively affect ECOWAS. The Francophones prefer to stay in their bloc rather than to be fully integrated into the ECOWAS system. This is very clear with the way they guard and direct their economic institutions such as the West African Economic and Monetary Union (WAEMU). Such an approach will continue to undermine ECOWAS' efficacy.

The Anglophone-Francophone struggle appears to have been affecting ECOWAS since its inception and the REC has not succeeded in bridging the divide between the two blocs. This line of argument is reiterated by Jakob Engel and Marie-Agnès Jouanjean who in 2015 stated that though it was intended that ECOWAS would one day subsume WAEMU, both organisations continue to exist and hold very different procedures and approaches to integration (Engel and Jouanjean 2015: 10).

A senior staff of ECOWAS[3] indicated when interviewed that:

> [T]he struggle between the Francophone and the Anglophone countries is not the only challenge in relation to trade that ECOWAS contends with. Individual member states are also very difficult to deal with and they test the patience and limits of ECOWAS by failing to comply with and implement protocols signed. Additionally, there is the perception among smaller states that trade is dominated by countries such as Nigeria and Ghana and tend not to be supportive or compliant to policies agreed on. ECOWAS also lacks the means to ensure that they comply and are punished when they fail to do so. Funds are very limited to adequately monitor and coordinate activities among member states.

Suspicion and rivalry among member states significantly undermines the efficacy of the commission. The recent move in a summit in Abidjan in July 2019 by eight Francophone West African countries to drop their longstanding common currency, the CFA Franc, and adopt the proposed common currency for West Africa, the ECO, without involving their Anglophone counterparts who have been deliberating on adopting the ECO as a common currency since December 2000, have further implications for the relationship between the two sides (Aljazeera News 2019). The Francophone group in their recent summit offered a hand of solidarity to other countries in West Africa to join their new ECO monetary union, a suspicious offer that the Anglophone side (who would ostensibly feel undermined) might be reluctant to accept. The Anglophone member states have repeatedly postponed the date for their adoption of ECO due to the anticipated challenges in ditching their present individual currencies. The latest adoption date they have slated for ECO is 1st January 2020 (*The Sierra Leone Telegraph*, 2019).

The region has better chances of becoming a formidable trade partner to the rest of the world, if the internal challenges—especially the lack of consolidated efforts between the Francophone and Anglophone blocs—are resolved. ECOWAS needs to address this challenge by taking a proactive approach in engaging the Francophone bloc to fully dissolve their sub-regional economic institutions or integrating them into those of ECOWAS'.

ECOWAS should also develop trade policies that would help smaller states have faith in trade relations to assuage their fear and perception that the process is dominated by relatively larger economies such as Nigeria, Ghana and Cote d'Ivoire. This has to be supported with investments by ECOWAS and its development partners in awareness raising and sensitization activities on trade policies in member states.

Regional Security Cooperation in ECOWAS

The eruption of violent and protracted civil wars in West Africa (beginning with Liberia in 1989 followed by Sierra Leone in 1991, Cote d'Ivoire in 2002 and Mali in 2012) had devastating regional consequences. Though inter-state wars have become rare in the post-Cold War dispensation, many ECOWAS countries have experienced insurgencies and low intensity conflict, notably—Mali, Niger, Mauritania, Ghana, Nigeria and Senegal. In total, 7 of the 15 ECOWAS member states have been afflicted with intra-state wars and destabilising forms of violent conflicts such as militia or rebel insurgencies, popular insurrection, etc.

Notwithstanding the substantial loss of lives, destruction of property and hindrance of development that often come with conflicts, history has also demonstrated the risk of one country's conflict triggering further instability and violence in neighbouring countries. This was the case when the National Patriotic Front of Liberia (NPLF) was crossing over from Cote d'Ivoire in a bid to unseat the Liberian government. The NPLF and government of Burkina Faso were also instrumental in triggering and sustaining the Revolutionary United Front (RUF) in Sierra Leone, whose fight against the government would eventually destabilise Guinea and Cote d'Ivoire (Omeje 2007: 16–22). Similarly, the Malian conflict threatens the stability of nearby states—in part because the country has the potential to become a haven and source for violent extremist, and partly because its neighbours are already weakened by "their own share of civil wars, violent extremism, and Islamist jihadist and terrorist activities" (Francis 2013: 9–10).

As it stands, ECOWAS states are subjected to multiple security vulnerabilities. One of these vulnerabilities is the side-lining of youth. Poverty and unemployment, bad governance, exclusion from decision-making processes or a lack of progress towards resolving structural injustices can all have a marginalising effect on young people in West Africa. There are many dangers to this. For one, eeconomic deprivation can lead to a situation wherein the will to survive and achieve social mobility can incentivise young people to secure livelihood opportunities through whatever means necessary—even if it means engaging in crimes or acts of political violence (Bangura 2016: 46; Bangura 2017: 2; Francis 2013: 5; Omeje 2007: 16). Secondly, significant levels of social, economic and political exclusion and lack of opportunities can block young people's transition to adulthood. Should this happen, grievances against structural conditions can lead some young people to engage in violence (Rogan et al. 2016: 11–12).

Bad governance is particularly manifested in the poor relationship between young people and the governing elites in their countries, as well as the harsh reactions by the state when the youth try to express legitimate grievances. Such a state of affair only served to perpetrate young people's marginalisation while hindering progress towards resolving the protracted structural challenges in member states. In countries such as Nigeria and Mali, grappling with protracted security challenges have astronomical effects on their budgets. Additionally, activities of the Islamist terrorist insurgency Boko Haram and militant groups have direct effect on Foreign Direct Investments in the region, which consequently have cumulative impact on trade relations and outcomes. In further analysing issues related to ECOWAS and security in the West Africa region, one can argue that the increasing transnational security threats such as terrorism and piracy has created the need for the Commission to be much more focused on issues related to peace and security in the region.

Some analysts have emphasised the role of Small Arms and Light Weapons (SALW) in precipitating armed conflicts. Recent estimates suggest that West Africa hosts about 7–10 million of the world's illegal SALW; in the African context, the region accounts for 8 million out of the 100 million of SALW circulating in the continent (Edeko 2011: 55–80; Kwaja 2012). According to Nancy Annan (2014), the circulation of this vast stock of weapons fuels political instability, including incidents of insurrection, military coup d'état and insurgency.

Though fully devoted to trade and custom issues during its formative years, by the early 1990s ECOWAS became increasingly concerned with the threat of intra-state conflicts and instability. This is reflected in its establishment of a multilateral military structure named the ECOWAS Monitoring Group (ECOMOG) in 1990 to stop the rebel insurgency in Liberia. ECOMOG became actively involved in the conflict in Liberia and subsequently Sierra Leone, which was devastated by a spill-over effect of the Liberian civil war in 1991.

Expanding its interest in security issues, ECOWAS in Article 58 of its 1993 revised Treaty called upon member states to "safeguard and consolidate relations conducive to the maintenance of peace, stability and security within the region". The scope of this cooperation generally includes the establishment and strengthening of mechanisms for the "timely prevention and resolution of intra-State and inter-State conflicts" (ECOWAS 1993). However, the wording of Article 58 suggests that at that stage, ECOWAS only intended to mount limited interventions vis-à-vis regional conflicts and instability. This is indicated by how the Community framed its perceived roles as that of—observation, examination, consultation and employment of a peacekeeping force when necessary. The measure which was most clearly elaborated was the appropriate employment of "good offices, conciliation, mediation and other methods of peaceful settlement of disputes" (ECOWAS 1993)—which again suggests the Community was content with facilitating reconciliation between conflicting parties rather than addressing the root causes of conflicts.

In 1999, just as conflicts raged across the region with the potential of spreading to affect more countries, ECOWAS member states adopted the 1999 Protocol relating to the Mechanism for Conflict Prevention,

Management, Resolution, Peacekeeping and Security. Significantly more expansive than Article 58 of the 1993 Revised Treaty, the 1999 Protocol started by acknowledging the centrality of peace and security to the eventual achievement of ECOWAS' objectives (ECOWAS 1999: Article 2). The 1999 Protocol also increases ECOWAS' role in conflict management as the Community and its member states were now entitled to "prevent, manage and resolve internal and inter-State conflicts" (ECOWAS 1999: Article 3a). The Protocol further states that this commitment will be achieved through "cooperation in the areas of conflict prevention, early-warning, peacekeeping operations, the control of cross-border crime, international terrorism and proliferation of small arms and anti-personnel mines" (ECOWAS 1999: Article 3d). Further, these activities shall be supplemented by preventive diplomacy and deployment of civilian—military intervention force.

While the 1999 Protocol places much emphasis on conflict mitigation and resolution, the 2001 Supplementary Protocol on Democracy and Good Governance, and the 2008 ECOWAS Conflict Prevention Framework (ECPF) were intended to strengthen the framework for conflict prevention. The Supplementary Protocol, for instance, laid out important principles to be followed by all ECOWAS member states. These include: separation of powers, empowerment and the strengthening of parliament, judiciary independence, freedom of the bar associations' members, free, fair and transparent elections, non-tolerance of power obtained by unconstitutional means and popular participation in decision-making (ECOWAS 2001: Article 1–10).

In the process of implementing these principles, it is the role of ECOWAS to assist, monitor and conduct fact-finding missions in connection with any alleged election irregularities (ECOWAS 2001: Article 13). In the event of violations of the constitutional principles, the supplementary protocol gives ECOWAS the power to impose sanctions on violating parties. There are three different forms of sanctions which ECOWAS can impose: firstly, to refuse candidates access to elective positions within international organisations (ECOWAS included); secondly, to refuse the hosting of ECOWAS meetings within the violating member state; thirdly, to suspend the offending member state from all ECOWAS decision-making bodies with a fine attached (ECOWAS 2001: Article 44–45). The challenge then is how effective these sanctions could be and whether or not they will sufficiently deter violations.

The ECPF, on the other hand, aims to "create space within the ECOWAS system and within member states for cooperative interaction within the region and with external partners to push conflict prevention and peacebuilding up the political agenda of Member States in a manner that will trigger timely and targeted multi-actor and multi-dimensional action to defuse or eliminate potential and real threats to human security in a predictable and institutional manner" (ECOWAS 2008: Article 27). To fulfil its stated purpose, the ECPF specifies 14 broad tasks for the community. These being: (1) early warning; (2) preventive diplomacy; (3) democracy and political governance; (4) human rights and the rule of law; (5) media; (6) natural resource governance and (7) cross-border initiatives. The rest are (8) governance; (9) practical disarmament; (10) women, peace and security; (11) youth empowerment; (12) ECOWAS Standby Force; (13) humanitarian assistance and (14) peace education (ECOWAS 2008: Article 42). Detailed activities, capacity requirement and benchmarks are also provided for in the ECPF. However, the plan of action for the rolling-out of the ECPF was not launched until 25 January 2019—more than 10 years after the adoption of the ECPF (ECOWAS 2019). The long delay in adopting the plan of action signifies lack of efficiency and effectiveness on the part of the organisation to roll-out frameworks that are fundamental to peace and security in the region.

When assessing the effectiveness of ECOWAS' conflict management mechanism, it becomes apparent that the Community is most active in the area where it is given more legal power to intervene namely, the maintenance of peace by upholding democracy and good governance. As Faten Aggad and Luckystar Miyandazi (2017: 11–12) point out, ECOWAS thus far used a combination of military intervention, diplomatic negotiations, sanctions, election observation and legal proceedings to pre-empt a crisis from being born out of a constitutional crisis. A good example of this approach was ECOWAS' use of diplomacy and preparedness to use military option during the post-election crisis in the Gambia in late 2016 and early 2017. Aggad and Miyandazi (2017: 12–13) further argue that ECOWAS' approach to peace and security is usually fraught with challenges including them being reactionary instead of being proactive, having the tendency of compromising with those who remain in power unconstitutionally—as is the case in Togo.

ECOWAS' unwillingness to contemplate the use of force to intervene in certain domestic conflict situations such as was the case with the embattled dictatorship of General Sani Abacha in Nigeria (1993–1998) could be attributed to the military might of Nigeria, the regional hegemon on which ECOWAS heavily relies for leadership and survival. A similar unwillingness for the use of military force happened in connection with the controversial dictatorship of Captain Moussa Dadis Camara in Guinea (2008–2009). ECOWAS' unwillingness to use force to oust the embattled dictatorship of Captain Camara in Guinea could be attributed to certain circumstantial changes and challenges in Nigeria, notably the return to civilian democracy in 1999 which subjects any decision to deploy Nigerian military in regional peacekeeping to parliamentary debate and public scrutiny (as opposed to the preceding dispensation of military fiat), coupled with the spiralling frontiers of insurgency in the Nigerian north-east and Niger Delta, which local politicians and the general public perceived at that time as more pressing priorities.

Horizontal Complementarity Between Trade and Security Cooperation: West Africa on the Rise

ECOWAS' decision to venture into conflict management was largely informed by the serious implications that violent conflicts could have on trade and trade relations in the region. A longstanding senior staff of ECOWAS[4] interviewed had this to say:

> … the civil war in Liberia went a long way in turning ECOWAS' attention to establish and strengthen security mechanisms. The link was drawn to the devastating effect the conflict could have on trade and the eventual disruption of the region. There is always a strong link between the two. Over the years, we have seen what happened in Cote d'Ivoire and the transnational nature and effects of conflicts in the region. No investor wants to invest in a conflict-ridden region.

Conflicts also have direct negative impact on trade and the economy of neighbouring countries. The influx of refugees into and the intermittent attacks on Guinea by insurgency groups in Sierra Leone in the 1990s created a sense of economic hardship and insecurity that gravely affected the confidence of investors in the stability of Guinea.[5] A similar trend was associated with the crisis in Côte d'Ivoire. UNDP states that "since instability in Côte d'Ivoire started in the late 1990s, the cumulative trade losses for intra-West African Economic and Monetary Union (WAEMU) trade are estimated at close to $9 billion" (UNDP 2011: 1). The preceding observation underscores the fact that no matter the size of an economy, its disruption by armed conflict will have direct negative impact on its neighbours and the wider region. Thus, there is a strong connection between trade, trade relations, security and growth and development in a region.

The ability of ECOWAS to recognise and make a good attempt at addressing intra-state and regional security crises has contributed significantly towards stabilising the region and promoting trade and security. However, the region is still affected by diverse challenges. A border management expert in Ghana[6] identified some of the challenges as follow:

> Trade and security relations at the local level are still evolving and need to be carefully looked at if trade and security relations are to be strengthened in the region. This is because border security personnel are ill-trained and not familiar with ECOWAS trade protocols and movement of people. So, instead of promoting trade, they discourage it. Economic security and welfare of West Africans relies heavily on their ability to trade across nations and that is weak at the moment and in need of careful attention.

The preceding comments highlight one of the fundamental shortcomings of ECOWAS trade and security mechanisms: their lack of focus and complementarity towards resolving the root causes of conflicts. While ECOWAS has established robust conflict prevention and management mechanisms, it appears it is predominantly concerned with resolving conflicts as a means to remove obstacles to further economic integration. At the same time, not enough effort seems to be made to use trade cooperation as a tool to remove some of the structural and deeply rooted causes of violent conflicts in the region. This needs to change in order to enable the region to continue to rise and overcome the pervading obstacles to human insecurities.

What ECOWAS requires is investment in monitoring and follow-up mechanisms among member states to ensure compliance with policies. As a matter of necessity, member states should comply with protocols and policies of the Commission and should train and have their officials roll them out fully. Studies such as that of the Mano River Union's (2016) have indicated how women traders are ill-treated and discouraged from participating in cross-border trade in the ECOWAS region. Additionally, the lack of communication and knowledge on existing protocols, markets and business opportunity in the region affects the potential for traders to plan and take advantage of such opportunities. This requires investment in awareness raising and sensitisation activities on trade regulations, training in business skills and investment, mapping of opportunities and information on markets.

ECOWAS should also address another major challenge in the region: its poor road and transport infrastructure. In a global study, Yildiz Kara (2008: 88) states that a well-functioning transport infrastructure and services could provide "opportunities in terms of access to local and international markets, access to basic social services such as education or healthcare, and access to livelihood opportunities particularly in the transport industry". The lack of livelihood opportunities and social mobilities often serve as root causes of conflicts in West Africa. Thus, better transportation link, in the context of regional trade liberalisation schemes, could contribute to overall conflict prevention efforts.

Ultimately, ECOWAS needs to develop multi-layered approaches that would compel member states to promote good governance, human rights and the rule of law, which have direct relationship with access to economic and livelihood opportunities for citizens within the member states. A member of the parliament of Guinea[7] sums up this line of thinking:

> The key to trade and security in West Africa is good governance. Without good governance nothing will work. ECOWAS needs to encourage its member states to open the socio-economic space for all and importantly provide service-oriented leadership. The different countries need to invest in their people and that would improve security and strengthen trade in the region. People are poor, hungry and desperate in Guinea, Sierra Leone, Nigeria and every other country in the region and trade and security would be forever threatened if the context does not change.

Conclusion

Since its establishment in 1975, ECOWAS has succeeded in strategically positioning itself as one of the most effective RECs in Africa. Though established on the need to strengthen economic integration and cooperation, it has expanded its focus to regional security in order to address the challenges posed by the brutal conflicts that threatened regional trade and security between 1989 and the 2000s. Since then, it has used both diplomatic and military measures to manage and contain violent conflicts within member states.

In the last two decades the Commission has succeeded in introducing several protocols and policies related to trade and security, notably the ETLS and the ECPF. Inasmuch as significant gains have been made in promoting economic integration and movement of personnel and good within the region, there is much more to be done to strengthen trade and security. Key among them is the need to break the Anglophone-Francophone divide and to fully integrate all sub-structures across the divide into the ECOWAS frameworks. Failure to do so will lead to continuous undermining of the progress of ECOWAS in relation to trade and security in the region. An integrated approach that will bridge the sub-regional divides will go a long way in maximising the trade, security and political potentials of ECOWAS. It will provide the Commission with the resources, political will and space it requires to efficiently and effectively function. This will consequently impact positively on peace, security, growth and development in the region, thereby allowing the region to rise to its potential. In addition, member states should comply with the protocols and principles of ECOWAS and demonstrate political will by fully domesticating and implementing them. This should be complemented with the sensitization of government officials and other stakeholders on the protocols. The lack of sensitization and training of border security officials and other actors contribute to their shabby and unfair treatment of cross-border traders and normal travellers.

Finally, while ECOWAS has succeeded in using diplomatic and other measures in mitigating violent conflicts and military coups d'état, it appears to be struggling with the application of a regional approach in tackling the structural causes to conflicts. It is expected that the full implementation of the ECPF's Plan of Action will go a long way in overcoming both existing and emerging security threats to peace and security in the region. This has to be complemented with member states willingness to promote governance, human rights and the rule of law in their respective countries. A shift from practices that marginalise and anger sections of a society will contribute significantly in strengthening peace, security and trade in the region.

Notes

1. The fifteen countries were Sierra Leone, Guinea, Liberia, Ghana, Nigeria, Senegal, Cote d'Ivoire, Benin, Togo, Mali, Gambia, Guinea Bissau, Niger, Cape Verde and Mauritania.

2. Interview conducted in Abuja on 18 January 2019.
3. Interview conducted in Abuja on 17 January 2019.
4. Interview conducted via Skype on 3 March 2019.
5. Based on interview with a staff of the Ministry of Finance of Sierra Leone in Freetown on 3 April 2019.
6. Interview conducted in Accra, Ghana on 21 February 2019.
7. Interview conducted via Skype on 12 April 2019.

References

Adkission, Stephen C. 1984. Integration in West Africa: An empirical Examination of ECOWAS. Published thesis, Portland State University.

Aggad, Faten, and Luckystar Miyandazi. 2017. Understanding ECOWAS Efforts in Promoting a Governance Agenda. ECDPM Policy Brief.

Aljazeera.com. 2019. New African Currency: Will the 'ECO' Replace the CFA Franc? See https://www.aljazeera.com/ajimpact/african-currency-eco-replace-cfa-franc190711162229142.html.

Annan, Nancy. 2014. Violent Conflicts and Civil Strife in West Africa: Causes, Challenges and Prospects. *Stability: International Journal of Security and Development* 3 (1): Art. 3. http://doi.org/10.5334/sta.da.

Bangura, Ibrahim. 2016. We Can't Eat Peace: Youth, Sustainable Livelihood and the Peacebuilding Process in Sierra Leone. *Journal for Peacebuilding and Development* 11 (2): 37–50.

Bangura, Ibrahim. 2017. A Call for Constructive Engagement: Youth, Violence, and Peacebuilding in the Mano River Basin Area. Special Issue: African Youth—Generation Next for Peacebuilding? Kujenga Amani, African Peacebuilding Network, USA.

ECOWAS. 1975. *Treaty of the Economic Community of West African States (ECOWAS)*. Abuja, Nigeria: Economic Community of West African States (ECOWAS).

ECOWAS. 1979. Protocol Relating to the Movement of Persons, Residence and Establishment. Economic Community of West African States, Abuja, Nigeria.

ECOWAS. 1986. Supplementary Protocol on the Second Phase (Right of Residence) of the Protocol on Free Movement of Persons, the Right of Residence and Establishment. Economic Community of West African States, Abuja, Nigeria.

ECOWAS. 1990. Supplementary Protocol A/SP 2/5/90 on the Implementation of the Third Phase (Right of Establishment) of the Protocol on Free Movement of Persons, the Right of Residence and Establishment. Abuja, Nigeria.

ECOWAS. 1993. Revised ECOWAS Treaty. ECOWAS, Abuja, Nigeria.

ECOWAS. 1999. *Protocol Relating to the Mechanism for Conflict Prevention, Management, Resolution, Peacekeeping and Security*. Abuja, Nigeria: Economic Community of West African States.

ECOWAS. 2001. Protocol on Democracy and Good Governance, Supplementary to the Protocol Relating to the Mechanism for Conflict Prevention, Management, Resolution, Peacekeeping and Security. Abuja, Nigeria.

ECOWAS. 2008. *The ECOWAS Conflict Prevention Framework*. Abuja, Nigeria: Economic Community of West African States.

ECOWAS. 2019. ECOWAS Launched Plans of Action for Its Conflict Prevention Framework. Economic Community of West African States. See http://www.ecowas.int/ecowas-launches-plans-of-action-for-its-conflict-preventionframework/.

ECOWAS and United Nations Economic Commission for Africa. 2015. ECOWAS at 40: An Assessment of Progress Towards Regional Integration in West Africa. ECOWAS and the United Nations Economic Commission for Africa (UNECA).

Edeko, Sunday Atawodi. 2011. The Proliferation of Small Arms and Light Weapons in Africa: A Case Study of the Niger Delta in Nigeria. *Sacha Journal of Environmental Studies* 1 (2): 55–80.

Engel, Jakob, and Marie-Agnès Jouanjean. 2015. Political and Economic Constraints to the ECOWAS Regional Economic Integration Process and Opportunities for Donor Engagement. Overseas Development Institute, UK.

Francis, David. 2013. *The Regional Impact of the Armed Conflict and French Intervention in Mali*. Oslo, Norway: Norwegian Peacebuilding Resource Centre.

Kara, Yildiz. 2008. Trade as a Tool of Diplomacy and Global Security. *Perceptions* 13 (2): 65–90.

Karaki, Karim, and Elke Verhaeghe. 2017. Understanding ECOWAS Trade and Trade Facilitation: Advancing Economic Integration One Hurdle at a Time. European Centre for Development Policy Management.

Kwaja, Chris. 2012. Confronting the Challenges of Small Arms and Light Weapons. *West Africa Insight*.

Mano River Union. 2016. A Study on the Effects of the Ebola Virus Disease on Female Entrepreneurs Along Border Regions of Liberia and Sierra Leone. Freetown, Sierra Leone.

Omeje, Kenneth. 2007. Conflicts in West Africa. In *Sorting Out the Mess: Wars, Conflicts & Conflict Management in West Africa*, ed. W. Feichtinger and G. Hainzl, 1–38. Vienna: Druck und Endfertigung.

Rogan, James et al. 2016. Young People's Participation in Peacebuilding: A Practice Note. Inter-Agency Network on Youth Development Working Group on Youth and Peacebuilding.

Sierra Leone Telegraph. 2019. West Africa Gets a New Currency—It's Called the ECO. Freetown, Sierra Leone. https://www.thesierraleonetelegraph.com/west-africa-gets-a-new-currency-its-called-the-eco/.

United Nations Development Programme's Regional Bureau for Africa. 2011. The Conflict in Cote d'Ivoire and Its Effects on West African Countries: A Perspective from the Ground. United Nations Development Programme, Nairobi, Kenya.

CHAPTER 8

Trade and Security Cooperation in the SADC Region: Optimising the Developmental Role of Paradiplomacy

Nolubabalo Lulu Magam

Introduction

Paradiplomacy is concerned with the engagement of subnational governments in international relations, which stimulates curious interests given the established practice that such engagements are traditionally the prerogative of central governments. It is a growing field of academic research and system of administration. At a practical level, paradiplomacy finds its operational parameters in decentralised systems of administration. Due to the impact of globalisation on the evolution of systems of governance, there has been a growing shift in how political and administrative responsibilities are shared among different spheres of government, centres of power and a variety of stakeholders. Such sharing of responsibilities or a devolution power to other centres of government has been credited with providing subnational governments with a certain amount of freedom to shape their own developmental trajectory. Importantly, an

N. L. Magam (✉)
University of KwaZulu-Natal, Durban, South Africa
e-mail: magamn@ukzn.ac.za

K. Omeje (ed.), *The Governance, Security and Development Nexus*,
https://doi.org/10.1007/978-3-030-49348-6_8

extensive array of research affirms that paradiplomacy holds significant developmental potentials.

This chapter explores the role and potentials of paradiplomacy as a tool for regional trade and security cooperation among the 15 member states of the Southern Africa Development Community (SADC). The chapter argues that the SADC region needs to put in place legal and institutional mechanisms that allow for the development of paradiplomacy among its member states. The role of South Africa to this end cannot be understated, as it is one country in the region with a "well developed" paradiplomacy.

The chapter examines discourses, policies and practices of regional economic and security cooperation among the SADC countries and their impact on the overall development of the region. Martinez-Vazquez (2011: 2) posits that most subnational governments have grown disenchanted with the performance of centralised policies and they also fail to see the direct benefits of a supranational institution like SADC. The concept of paradiplomacy and how it's potential for development and security cooperation can be maximised within the SADC region in the context of globalisation is discussed. Among other things, an efficient use of paradiplomacy will help to promote regional socio-economic and human development which is one of the primary objectives for the establishment of SADC.

SADC Trade and Security Cooperation: Legal and Institutional Framework

SADC was founded on 1 April 1980 and originally known as the Southern African Development Coordination Conference (SADCC) but was later changed to SADC in 1992. Ruled by the opprobrious apartheid regime, South Africa was not part of the original SADCC. It was only after the dismantling of apartheid in 1994 that South Africa was admitted into SADC. The organisation's goals among other things include promoting development by improving economic growth through regional integration and cooperation; and enhancing governance at a regional level. Other areas of cooperation and integration underpinning the formation of SADC include promoting the values of democracy and ensuring regional peace and security. There are also the goals of development of infrastructure and services, cooperation in the areas of trade and industry, finance and investment; food, agriculture and natural resources, as well as improving social and human development in the region (SADC 2001: 9).

Given its disproportionately strong economic base and military power, South Africa occupies a vital hegemonic position in the SADC region. Many SADC countries such as Swaziland, Lesotho, Malawi, Zimbabwe, are substantially dependent on the South African economy for goods and services and there persists a high level of labour migration from the SADC countries and elsewhere in Sub-Saharan Africa to South Africa. In fact, the Lusaka Declaration of 1980 that set up the defunct South African Development Coordination Conference (SADCC) aimed to harness the different resources, capabilities and strengths of its member state as a means to reduce their economic dependence on the then Apartheid South Africa and to promote the members' development (Thornhill et al. 2002: 187).

Essentially, economic development in the form of trade cooperation and promoting security and peace are at the core of the concerns of SADC. As such, the SADC, driven by the aforestated objective, has promulgated several protocols and policies[1] aimed to inter alia achieve its regional developmental goal of eradicating poverty and promoting economic growth through cooperation. Through these diverse institutional processes, the region has enjoyed significant growth in political, economic and security cooperation (SADC, 2018).

In its Revised Regional Indicative Strategic Development Plan 2015–2020, for instance, some of the organisation's achievements are clearly presented. Despite a recorded growth and progress in terms of regional economic and security cooperation, the regional body still faces several challenges. One of such challenges in Magakwe's (2013) view is that while the regional body has a multiplicity of goals and objectives, there is however a problem of clarity regarding the content and implementation of these said goals and objectives. Similarly, Saurombe (2012) suggests that there is a challenge with regard to "how SADC Member States are willing to subject themselves to supranational governance as provided for by the Treaty and implemented by the key institutions that also derive their mandate from the Treaty" (2012: 1). A posteriori, it can be suggested that some of the challenges faced by the regional body are as a result of the uneven developmental and economic powers of member states. Consequently, it becomes an onerous task for such states to commit to the objectives and goals of the body. Consequently,

Saurombe (2012) opines that one of the ways to surmount such challenges is for SADC to develop a specialised technical ability that allows it to achieve its aims and objectives. For Magakwe (2013), one of the ways SADC can achieve its objective and address some of its challenges of implementation is for individual member states to include the different protocols and treaties into their respective national plans and budget priorities.

Again, it is suggested that in order to understand and evaluate the value of regional trade relations and security and peace cooperation, the institutional or the policy framework that guides the programmes needs to be critically assessed (Schreiner and Baleta 2015). Such a critical assessment according to these scholars helps to provide an understanding of the constraints and opportunities for promoting an integrated decision-making process at a regional level. The SADC Treaty is described as the overarching legal framework for cooperation in the region. The implication of this is that the Treaty of the South African Development Community firstly provides the legal structure of the organisation through a clear articulation of the organisation's status. The Treaty also articulates the values, goals and responsibilities of Member States. Membership, the organisations institutions, procedural issues that pertain to areas of cooperation between member states and cooperation with other regions and organisations are also delineated in the treaty. In addition, financial issues, conflict resolution and other practical matters like sanctions, withdrawal and dissolution are also stated in the Treaty (SADC Treaty 1992).

The main objectives of the Treaty to reiterate, includes achieving economic development, peace and security, and economic growth; poverty reduction; enhancement of the standard and quality of life of the peoples of Southern Africa and "support the socially disadvantaged through regional integration" (SADC 2015). Article 22(1) of the SADC Treaty stipulates that member states should "conclude a series of protocols with clearly stipulated objectives and scope as well as institutional mechanisms to address the specific issues that underlie cooperation and integration" (Schreiner and Baleta 2015: 95). "In order to ensure this, the SADC Treaty also makes provision for the formulation of subsidiary legal instruments such as protocols giving specific mandates to various SADC institutions. A total of twenty-three protocols have so far been formulated" (Saurombe 2012: 457).

Institutions, legal instruments and protocols have effectually been put in place to ensure that regional integration takes an appropriate and efficient trajectory that allows it to realise its goals and objectives. These legal instruments, institutions and protocols importantly find their operational parameters or derive their mandates from the SADC Treaty (Saurombe 2012). In the subsequent subsection, the chapter shows that SADC as a regional body has enjoyed several reforms and restructuring that have been geared towards improving coordination and communication within SADC. More so, this is believed to be necessary for the optimisation of the values and benefits of regional cooperation and integration (Schreiner and Baleta 2015; Saurombe 2011).

SADC's Economic and Security Institutions: Key Reformations

The SADC as a regional body has enjoyed significant institutional restructuring aimed at improving the values and benefits of regional cooperation (Saurombe 2012). One of such restructuring was done in order to address some of the challenges faced by the body in the course of its transition from SADCC to SADC. The focus was essentially on the restructuring of its institutions with a major objective to increase the efficiency and effectiveness of SADC policies and programmes and to implement a more coherent and better coordinated strategy to eliminate poverty in the region (SADC 2005). Moreover, the restructuring led to:

> the grouping of 21 sectors into clusters under four Directorates at the SADC Secretariat. At the national level, SADC National Committees now coordinates their respective individual Member State interests relating to SADC. At the regional level, an Integrated Committee of Ministers (ICM) was created to coordinate the work of different clusters. The new structure also includes the Troika system and the Organ on Politics, Defence and Security. (DIRCO 2004)

As a prop to the institutional restructuring, the regional body also developed two road maps which are "the Regional Indicative Strategic Development Plan (RISDP), the anchor of the SADC Development Agenda, and the Strategic Indicative Plan for the Organ on Politics, Defence and Security (SIPO), the linchpin of a safe environment for the attainment of the SADC Development Agenda" (SADC 2005: 11).

Through the RISDP, the developmental agenda, as well as the plans and methods of achieving economic and human development are clearly stated; while the SIPO serves as a strategic plan to promote formal inter-state cooperation in security and peace. In effect, with the launch of the RISDP and SIPO in 2004, SADC sought to "provide strategic direction with respect to the institution's programmes and activities and have a direct bearing on improving the lives of citizens in the region. They are also intended to make effective use of the opportunities for development that globalization presents, while containing the adverse effects of global trends" (ibid.).

Moreover, like the RISDP and SIPO has been lauded for some of their achievements and further critiqued for their limitations. According to van Nieuwkerk (2013: 146):

> achievements under the SIPO include the establishment of the SADC Mutual Defence Pact, launch of the SADC Standby Force (SSF), integration of the Southern African Regional Police Chiefs Cooperation Organisation (SARPCCO) into the Inter-State Defence and Security Committee (ISDSC), establishment of the Regional Early Warning Centre as well as the SADC Electoral Advisory Council (SEAC) and a mediation unit.

Despite the recorded achievements, there is still room for improvement as it is further reported that SIPO also faces a challenge of poor implementation. "A key challenge is the failure of SIPO to produce a business plan that will enable it to address its 130-plus objectives; and no serious effort was made to develop strategies for operationalising the Organ" (ibid.).

Evidently, it can be deduced that some of the impediments to the actualisation of the economic (trade) and security aims and objectives of SADC has been a problem of coordination and implementation. There are *defacto* institutions and legal frameworks that have been put in place to facilitate an effective regional economic and security cooperation. The challenge of implementation provides an avenue for the promotion of paradiplomatic activities; as such an activity falls within a decentralised system like the SADC's. Saurombe (2011: 458) agrees that "SADC placed particular emphasis on a decentralised institutional arrangement. This was a deliberate avoidance of supranational institutions. This ensured that Member States are the principal actors in the formation and implementation of policy decisions".

Essentially, paradiplomacy can become an important feature of such a system because by allowing subregional governments (of SADC member states) a leeway or a *de jure* structure to directly engage with the subnational governments of Member states, there are diverse developmental benefits that could accrue from such. Firstly, it is widely acceded that the aim of decentralisation or devolution of power is to promote direct democratic participation, ensure effective delivery of services, as well as foster economic development. This is also in tandem with the Saurombe's (2011: 313–315) argument that several institutions "are authorised by the Treaty and the Protocol on Trade, among other things, to harmonise the political and social economic policies of Member States, and to encourage popular participation in the activities of SADC and the implementation of SADC initiatives". Paradiplomacy as this chapter argues should be mainstreamed into one of the SADC's institutions in order to optimise the security and economic goal of the organisation.

Paradiplomacy and Regional Cooperation: A Developmental Outlook

In a dossier released in 2011, SADC reports that:

> while SADC recorded some remarkable achievements, difficulties and constraints have also been encountered. These include lack of institutional reforms for effective transformation from SADCC into SADC, lack of synergy between the objectives of the Treaty on the one hand and the existing SADC Programme of Action and institutional framework on the other, and finally lack of appropriate mechanisms capable of translating the high degree of political commitment into concrete programmes of community building and integration. (SADC 2005: 10)

Similarly, in a more recent revision of the RISDP, it came to the fore that moderate progress has been recorded with regard to enhancing SADC intra-regional trade and economic diversification. "This was due to limited capacities to produce and to trade effectively and competitively. The review therefore pointed to an urgent need to frontload industrialisation so as to bring about socio-economic transformation in SADC Member States" (SADC 2017: ii). It is thus within the purview of these efforts aimed at addressing the plethora of constraints encountered by SADC on "the restructuring of its institutions ... to implement a more coherent and better coordinated strategy to eliminate poverty in the region" (ibid.), that the discussion on the developmental value of paradiplomacy can be contextualised.

The first use of the word paradiplomacy is found in Ivo Duchacek and Panayotis Soldatos who describe paradiplomacy as the direct engagement in international activity or relations by "sub-national actors (federated units, regions, urban communities, and cities) supporting, complementing, correcting, duplicating or challenging the nation-states' diplomacy" (Duchacek 1990: 17). Globalisation is identified as one of the push factors for the growth of this phenomenon. Through globalisation, we have witnessed a growing shift in competition between subnational actors other than the age-long competition between sovereign states. Globalisation and the concurrent need for economic growth and developmental needs, influence the involvement of subnational entities in the diplomatic process. Inherent in the preceding position is the view of paradiplomacy as a "policy capacity" enjoyed by subnational actors in a world that is growing increasingly global.

Pluijm and Melissen (2007: 7) suggest that the implication of globalisation for the involvement of subnational entities in the diplomatic process is as a result of a growing grey area in the international and national political sphere. An international issue such as global warming has become a national one as "droughts threaten crops, while national issues like defense becomes international issues as nuclear weapons threatens countries around the world". Consequently, this creates an avenue for SubNational Governments (SNGs) and other non-state actors to get directly involved in the economic, cultural and political responsibility of the central state. Globalisation influences the growth of paradiplomacy as it creates an opportunity or to some extent, places a mandate on subnational entities to share in the "burden" of the state.

Pluijm and Melissen (2007) have argued that globalisation influences the involvement of subnational entities, not simply for economic and developmental reasons, but also for survival in a changing world. From available indications, "the foreign relations of SNGs (provincial, regional, state, municipal or city governments) have also evolved in intensity and sophistication, a trend that is reflected in the emergence of networks of SNGs attempting to influence global policy debates in areas such as sustainable development, aid effectiveness and global economic governance" (Nganje 2014: 89).

Magone (2006) sees paradiplomacy emerging as a way for subnational entities to cope with the thrust of globalisation. Milani and Ribeiro (2011) further suggest that through globalisation, there is a definition of "new modalities in the management of internationalization processes being deployed by states, business, social players and also subnational political entities". Paquin and Lachapelle (2005) view globalisation as giving a thrust to the advancement of paradiplomacy. According to these authors, regions and cities provide an array of advantages that define the issue of investment. Regions compete to garner private investments and positioning of decision-making centers. This inventive competition encourages innovation and an efficient collective allegiance.

In stressing the influence of globalisation on the evolution of paradiplomacy, Porter (1990: 622) asserts that:

> internationally successful industries and industry clusters frequently concentrate on a city or a region, and the bases for advantages are often intensely local while the national government has a role in upgrading the industry, the role of the state and that of the local government is potentially as great or greater.

As Kuznetsov (2015: 102) opines, "due to the universal and engrossing nature of globalisation, we can assume that the factor of globalisation has an impact on the flourishing of paradiplomacy everywhere across the world, but definitely the strength of this variable varies in degree for different regions". Effectually, the extent to which globalisation influences the evolution and the practice of paradiplomacy in different regions in the world may vary considerably, it however remains a salient and pertinent variable (ibid.).

Magone (2006) describes how decentralisation gave the thrust for paradiplomacy. According to him, decentralisation promotes the emergence of paradiplomacy strictly in the economic sense as subnational entities "can be regarded as flexible enough structures to build efficient networks for economic growth". Pluijm and Melissen (2007) consider paradiplomacy as a "form of decentralisation of international relations' management, choosing cities as the key actors".

Such a practice in the eyes of some scholars is an infringement on the central role of a state's Ministry of Foreign affairs. However, Pluijm and Melissen (2007: 9) submit that such an arrangement does not mean that the diplomatic route of subnational governments and that of the central government take different routes "but rather along the same route although in a different car". The functioning logic here is that, both the central government and the subnational entities engage in the pursuance of their interests in different but not conflicting manners. A crucial element in diplomacy is the axiom that a state's diplomatic relationships are geared towards pursuing their national interests. It is tenable to extend this element to subnational governments' involvement in the diplomatic process.

Other factors cited for the development of paradiplomacy includes (but are not limited to) insufficient effectiveness of the central government in foreign relations. In the purview of a supranational body like the SADC, it can be argued that paradiplomacy is ostensibly important because "subnational governments often have more experience, knowledge and resources for some types of international activities" (Kuznetsov 2015). This also concurs with Magone's (2006) "economic consciousness" logic, which suggests that subnational governments have both the capacity and resources to foster their interests in the international scene without relying on the central government. While Magone uses this to examine the growth of paradiplomacy in the context of regions seeking autonomy, the logic is also relevant for understanding the growth of paradiplomacy in centralised states or among supranational bodies.

In the study by Pluijm and Melissen (2007: 11), paradiplomacy is conceptualised as the "institutions and processes by which cities engage in relations with actors on an international political stage with the aim of representing themselves and their interests to one another". Remarkably, the notion of promoting interests stands out for the authors as a reason for cities/subnational entities to engage in paradiplomacy. According to the scholars, cities engage in city to city diplomacy as a means of serving the interests of their city and community (ibid.). They also view citizen activism, a situation where the citizens of a particular city encourage their representatives to engage in specific diplomatic activities like global warming initiatives as another reason for the growth of paradiplomacy.

Pluijm and Melissen further speak of cities engaging in paradiplomatic activities as an act of solidarity with other cities. According to the scholars, cities can have:

> "idealistic" motives for engaging in diplomacy. Although in many of those cases self-interest plays a role as well, solidarity can be said to be an important reason for becoming involved. Many of the city-twining projects with

> South African townships in the late 1980s, for example were set up by Western cities to show their solidarity with the black population in South Africa in the fight against apartheid. (Pluijm and Melissen 2007: 15)

Again, an increase in economic and other forms of interdependence has been said to increase the probability of cooperation among states. Globalisation and the evolving international system have heightened relations between state and non-state actors in what Keohane and Nye refer to as the multiple channels of contact. These channels gave a platform for local and subnational governments to engage in economic activities with their counterparts in a globalised economic world (Keohane and Nye 1977).

Micheal Smith (2001) further opines that due to globalisation, there is a system of "Interdependence", where states cooperate with their counterparts due to their shared and common interest. Because of states corporation, stability is ensured in the international system. However, globalisation has diluted the cultural and economic frontier that existed between states. It has paved way for subnational governments to pursue their economic interests across borders. Porter (1990: 622) remarks that the concentration of industries in cities serves as an advantage for local governments to pursue external diplomacy, while it is the responsibility of the national government to ensure that the city-based industries grow and develop, implying that the role of the local government is arguably greater.

The Nexus Between Decentralisation and Paradiplomacy

The leitmotif for decentralisation is instructive in understanding the growth of paradiplomacy, especially in Southern Africa. A central claim averred here is that through decentralisation, regional actors grew to play more important roles in the global scene (Magone 2006). Nganje (2014: 2) describes the role of decentralisation in promoting paradiplomacy as a "de-velopment-oriented cooperation among actors at the sub-state level". Impliedly, a growing understanding of the role a broad spectrum of actors play in the promotion of development cannot be ignored or excluded (Nganje 2014). A logical and linear connection between decentralisation and paradiplomacy can thus be established. The advent of a decentralised form of cooperation "can be traced to the intersection of two distinct but interrelated processes: efforts to improve the delivery and impact of official development assistance (ODA) on the one hand, and the evolution of the international relations of local governments on the other" (ibid., 3).

In Milani and Ribeiro's (2011) approach, the link between decentralisation and paradiplomacy is situated in the globalisation discourse. These authors expound the term globalisation politics to argue that the role of the state no longer has a monopolistic claim to the conduct of international affairs. Their argument suggests that decentralisation is not merely a form of power devolution but contemporary a necessity. This view is couched in the idea that "globalisation opens unprecedented breaches in power equations" among states and sub-state actors.

Basically, the growth of paradiplomacy is more of a response to globalisation politics which can also be said to be responsible for the growth of regional bodies. This view correlates with the idea that the growth in globalisation provides an impetus for the increasing role of subnational governments in international relations.

Again, the developmental aim of decentralisation cannot be minimised. Different conceptualisations or descriptions of decentralisation place their emphasis on different aspects of decentralisation (Malan 2005). Despite the possible contradictory hypotheses that may arise from the different conceptualisations of decentralisation, there is a nuanced agreement in each perspective that the central aim of decentralisation is to promote the efficiency of government service provisions so as to enhance development.

A practical definition of decentralisation has been proffered by the United Nation. According to the world body:

> Decentralization is commonly regarded as a process through which powers, functions, responsibilities and resources are transferred from central to local government and/or other decentralized entities. In practical terms, decentralisation is a process of striking a balance between the claims of the periphery and the demands of the centre. Decentralization, when appropriately structured, provides an arrangement through which critical issues (such as those of national unity and indivisibility, how to safeguard national interests and ensure coordinated and even development, equity in the distribution of resources and local autonomy) can be recognized. (United Nations Development Programme 2015)

A striking and relevant point from the UN's definition of decentralisation is that while decentralisation refers to a form of power devolution, it nonetheless allows subnational entities some room to manoeuvre and have some level of independence in the ways that enable them seek to promote their separate development. This viewpoint had been earlier canvassed by scholars like Kincaid (1990: 52) who and the latter argued that:

> Unlike the foreign policy of states, regional diplomacy does not seek to represent broad general interests or to be comprehensive in coverage. Regions do not have sovereign governments able to lay down their definition of the "national interest" and to pursue it in a unified and coherent manner. Regions are complex entities containing a multiplicity of groups which may share common interests in some areas but be sharply divided on other issues. Even where there are strong devolved governments, they cannot simply lay down a line to be followed by all but must seek to bring together independent actors around specific programs and issues. They must fit their own activities into a world dominated by national governments and transnational organizations, which they can rarely challenge head on but must work around or with.

Intrinsic to Kincaid's viewpoint is the fact that since decentralisation allows for subregional entities to look for and engage in their separate development, it provides a fillip for paradiplomacy, which creates a platform for subnational entities to be able to engage in international affairs with the sole aim and end of promoting the well-being of their constituents. Fundamentally, decentralisation, be it administrative or fiscal, provides an incentive for subregional governments to become key players in the international arena. It is pertinent to affirm that this engagement does not intend to impugn or interfere with a state's sovereignty. It is an activity that rather seeks to promote the interests of regions that would otherwise have been overlooked by a central government.

Paradiplomacy and Regional Development in South Africa

South Africa is one of the countries in the SADC region that has an extensive array of paradiplomatic activities. These forms of cooperation vary in their scope and nature. The cooperation takes the form of Memoranda of Agreements in the field of sports, education, science and technology and agriculture, among other things. The province of KwaZulu-Natal (RSA), for instance, has engaged in various forms of paradiplomacy that include diverse memoranda of agreements between the country and other subnational governments across the national borders (Africa and beyond). The province has also enjoyed several International visits and meetings, "receiving international delegates in the province, joining transnational networks for subnational governments such as the 'The Climate Group', hosting international events such as COP 17 (Conference of Parties of the United Nations Framework Convention on Climate Change)" (Magam 2018: 162). The province also hosts more than 10 consulates (including Spain, US, Nigeria, Mozambique, Lesotho, Portugal, Germany, etc.).

Like the province of KwaZulu-Natal, the Western Cape Province and Gauteng are other provinces that have been actively engaged in paradiplomacy. It is important to highlight that most of the paradiplomatic activities of these two provinces have been with other provinces outside the SADC regional block. According to Magam (2018), the reason for such targeted engagement with other provinces outside the regional bloc is because they seek investments and the targeted countries are perceived to have the potential to invest in their provinces. Clearly, it is difficult to surmise the financial and developmental benefits of paradiplomacy in the country. However, there are estimations that have been supplied by different provinces. According to the Gauteng Head of treasury, due to the province's engagement in paradiplomacy, there has been a significant growth in the provincial GDP. It is estimated that the province's GDP enjoyed an exponential increase from R500billion in 2004 (about US$35.10 million) to more than R800billion in 2016 (US$56.10 million). Gauteng has signed at least 25 development and investment-related Memorandum of Understanding (MOUs) with several international counterparts (GPG 2016). The broad indication here is that paradiplomacy positively correlates with an accelerated economic growth, and has several socio-economic advantages (Magam 2018).

In addition, Maputo and KwaZulu-Natal province have had relations of some sort in past. In 2005 the two provinces signed an MOU, and in 2011, the premier of KwaZulu-Natal and the Governor of Maputo met in Maputo to discuss among other things, matters of mutual interest, reviving the expired MOU and tapping into various areas of collaboration–trade investment promotion, tourism, transport and economic development. It is worth mentioning that in June 2018 the Maputo–Catembe bridge funded to the tune of US$785 million by the Chinese government (as a loan to the government of Mozambique) was opened by the Member of the Executive Council (MEC) of Economic Development in KwaZulu-Natal Mr Sihle Zikalala and the President of Mozambique

Filipe Nyusi (*The South African*, 2018). This indicates the importance of subnational provincial governments in diplomacy. The MEC in his speech noted that: "This bridge will boost both countries' economy and create more jobs as it will enhance trade opportunities which will make it easier for exports and imports between the two countries".[2]

The bridge falls within the African Continental Free Trade Area Agreement and will expectedly enhance development between Maputo and KwaZulu-Natal. Initiatives such as these can be done through paradiplomacy between provinces in the SADC region. Sister City relations, which also form part of paradiplomacy, are widespread in Africa. Precisely, the eThekwini Municipality (KwaZulu-Natal) has active relations with several cities in the African continent. These include Mombasa, Bulawayo, Maputo, Oran, Libreville and Alexandria.[3] The areas of cooperation include Sports and youth development; economic development and trade and investment promotion; educational support, skills transfer and sharing of skills and models of good practice and environment support. Evidently, the practice of paradiplomacy in the SADC region and the continent at large is rife and has the potential to enhance regional development.

Despite the overarching developmental potential of paradiplomacy, the practice of it in South Africa for instance has been fraught with some constitutional and institutional ambiguities. In South African, the Constitution (1996) does not "specifically spell out a foreign policy role for provincial governments; it is clear that it does forbid certain limited activities which are beneficial to the province at large and the country as a whole" (Magam 2018: 137). Importantly, however, most of the engagements of South African provinces in international relations fall within the purview of the country's overall foreign policy trajectory.

In procedural terms, when provinces seek to engage in paradiplomacy, they will need the approval of the National Executive. "It is only through the National Council of Provinces (NCOP) that they can participate in this process, as a collective" (ibid.). Essentially thus, "the Constitution does not prevent provinces from participating in international relations, but it still does not provide a clear guideline on what is the jurisdiction of provinces in this regard. Therefore, the interest of the provinces should be in tune with that of the country" (Magam 2018: 137).

In providing clarity to the above argument, Magam (2018: 138) reports that:

> A classic example is the case in which the Mayor of Tshwane paid an investment related visit to the capital of Taiwan in flagrant violation of South Africa's one China policy. Such paradiplomatic activities in most part are driven by the internal political dynamics – considering that the mayor stems from the main opposition party – could sometimes result in serious diplomatic spats thereby exposing the fluidity of paradiplomatic activities by provinces. "The mayor has elected to take time out of his personal leave to honour an invitation from the mayor of Taipei to explore possible investment opportunities".[4] It is clear that although provinces can and do undertake paradiplomacy, the national department of international relations remains the gatekeeper of the country's external relations.

In order to promote the practice of paradiplomacy among SADC member states, this study considers Kuznetsov's (2015) six channels of paradiplomacy quite pertinent. Kuznetsov (2015) suggests that there are six channels that can be used to promote and enhance paradiplomacy. He describes these channels as the most suitable activities to measure the active involvement of subnational governments in paradiplomacy. The channels are:

- Establishing a special regional department or ministry responsible for international relations.
- Opening permanent overseas offices for paradiplomacy.
- Officially visiting regional provincial governments and subnational entities.
- Participating in various subnational exhibitions and forums on paradiplomacy.
- Working within regional and transborder networks.
- Working within official central government delegations.

These channels can be adopted by SADC to promote paradiplomacy among its member states. SADC already has an established institutional structure. The above six channels could be added to the roles of either of the following regional institutional frameworks in SADC:

1. The SADC Committee of Ambassadors and High Commissioners
2. The Sectoral and Cluster Ministerial Committees
3. The Standing Committee of Senior Officials.

If we take the Sectoral and Cluster Ministerial Committees, for instance, it is made up of ministers from each Southern African Development Community (SADC) Member State. "These committees are directly responsible for overseeing the activities of the core areas of integration, monitoring and controlling the implementation of the Regional Indicative Strategic Development Plan in their area of competence, as well as providing policy advice to the Council" (SADC 2011: 3).

Some of the clusters involved in this Committee include:

- Ministers responsible for Trade, Industry, Finance and Investment;
- Ministers responsible for Infrastructure and Services;
- Ministers responsible for Food, Agriculture, Natural Resources and Environment;
- Ministers responsible for Social and Human Development and Special Programmes (HIV and AIDS; education, labour; employment and gender);
- Ministers responsible for Politics, Defence and Security and
- Ministers responsible for Legal Affairs and Judicial matters (SADC 2011).

The above-stated Committees have direct or indirect role with promoting regional socio-economic development and they can bear the responsibility of strengthening paradiplomacy and ensuring that there is synergy across all stakeholders (member states, departments, municipalities and the different central governments).

Conclusion

The chapter has among other things broadly interrogated the current trajectory and impacts of regional trade and security cooperation. It argues that the regional body SADC has established appropriate structures and frameworks for regional cooperation in trade and security in accordance with its founding vision and mandate. However, many practical challenges have been encountered, notably the problem of coordination and implementation of the regional body's aims and objectives. Among other things, there is the persistent challenge of uneven development among member states, notwithstanding the fact that several protocols and strategic plans on trade and security have been adopted by SADC to help in achieving some of its set goals and objectives. This chapter highlighted and discussed the potential benefits that paradiplomacy presents as an instrument that could help SADC advance regional cooperation and development.

The chapter describes paradiplomacy as sub-state entities' engagement in international relations. Intrinsic to this conception is the growing understanding that the state is no longer the sole player in the field of international diplomacy. Globalisation is one of the key drivers of paradiplomacy. Essentially, globalisation has *inter alia* brought in a new form of constructive economic competition between subnational actors which thrives alongside the age-long competition between sovereign states. As a regional body, SADC operates a decentralised form of power-sharing and decision-making which potentially favours and positions paradiplomacy as a suitable instrument for the attainment of SADC's goals.

Notes

1. Some of these protocols and treaties include the SADC Protocol on Trade which aims to enhance trade and economic cooperation among member states. Others include the Protocol on Finance and Investment; Protocol Against Corruption, the SADC Regional Indicative Strategic Plan (RISDP), etc.
2. Information provided by the office of the Premier, KwaZulu-Natal Provincial Government.
3. The revenue generated from these cooperation is not available, most of these relations are ongoing and the specific areas of cooperation are centered on knowledge sharing (information provided by the HOD of International and Governance Relations eThekwini Municipality—2 June 2019).
4. Extracted from an article in *The Citizen Newspaper*, dated 28 December 2016 titled: "Msimanga's Taiwan trip causes a diplomatic Stir" by Virginia Keppler.

References

DIRCO. 2004. Southern African Development Community (SADC) History and Current Status. http://www.dirco.gov.za/foreign/Multilateral/africa/sadc.htm. Accessed 12 April 2019.

Duchacek, Ivo. 1990. Perforated Sovereignties: Toward a Typology of New Actors in International Relations. In P. Soldatos and J. Michelmann, Eds. *Federalism and International Relations: The Role of Subnational Units*. New York: Oxford University Press, 1–34.

Gauteng Provincial Government (GPG). 2016. Annual Report for 2015/2016. Available from https://provincialgovernment.co.za/department_annual/413/2016-gauteng-office-of-the-premier-annual-report.pdf.

Keohane, Robert, and Nye Joseph. 1977. *Power and Interdependence*. Boston: Little Brown.

Kincaid, John. 1990. State and Local Governments Go International. *Intergovernmental Perspective* 16: 6–9.

Kuznetsov, Alexander. 2015. *Theory and Practice of Paradiplomacy: Subnational Governments in International Affairs*. New York: Routledge.

Magakwe, Jack. 2013. The Activities of the Southern African Development Community in Relation to Its Purpose Statement. Unpublished Master's degree dissertation. University of South Africa, Pretoria.

Magam, Nolubabalo. 2018. Paradiplomacy in South Africa: The Role of Interest and Identity in the International Relations of KwaZulu-Natal Province. PhD thesis, University of KwaZulu-Natal, South Africa.

Malan, Liliane. 2005. Intergovernmental Relations and Co-operative Government in South Africa: The Ten-year Review. *Politeia* 24 (2): 226–243.

Magone, José. 2006. Para-Diplomacy Revisited: The Structure of Opportunities of Global Governance and Regional Actors. Paper presented at the International Conference on the International Relations of the Regions: Sub-National Actors, Para-Diplomacy, and Multi-level Governance, at https://paradiplomacia.org/upload/downloads/66fc7ecc666b857d415ee890307ab79cjosemagonefinal.pdf, accessed January August 2019.

Martinez-Vazquez J, 2011. *The Impact of Fiscal Decentralization: Issues in Theory and Challenges in Practice*, Asian Development Bank.

Milani, Carlos, and Ribeiro Maria. 2011. International Relations and the Paradiplomacy of Brazilian Cities: Crafting the Concept of Local International Management. *Brazilian Administration Review* 8 (2): 21–36.

Nganje, Fritz. 2014. Paradiplomacy and the Democratisation of Foreign Policy in South Africa. *South African Journal of International Affairs* 21 (1): 89–107.

Paquin, Stephane, and Lachapelle Gerrard. 2005. Why do Sub-states and Regions Practice International Relations. In Loughlin, J. (Ed), *Mastering Globalization: New Sub-State's Governance and Strategy* (pp. 77–89). Oxon: Routledge.

Porter, Michael. 1990. *The Competitive Advantage of Nations*. New York: Free Press.

SADC. 1992. SADC Treaty. Available from https://www.sadc.int/documents-publications/show/Declaration__Treaty_of_SADC.pdf.

SADC. 2001. Regional Indicative Strategid Development Plan. Available at https://www.sadc.int/files/5713/5292/8372/Regional_Indicative_Strategic_Development_Plan.pdf.

SADC. 2005. Regional Indicative Strategic Development Plan. Gaborone: SADC Press. Available at https://www.sadc.int/files/5713/5292/8372/Regional_Indicative_Strategic_Development_Plan.pdf.

SADC. 2011. Communiqué of 20 May. Available from http://www.swradioafrica.com/Documents/SADCSummit240511.pdf. Accessed 5 August 2019.

SADC. 2015. Summary of the SADC Revised Regional Indicative Strategic Development Plan 2015–2020. Gaborone: SADC Press.

SADC. 2017. Summary of the SADC Revised Regional Indicative Strategic Development Plan 2015-2020. Gaborone: SADC Press. Available at https://www.sadc.int/files/5415/2109/8240/SADC_Revised_RISDP_2015-2020.pdf.

SADC. 2018. SADC Selected Economic and Social Indicators. Gaborone: SADC Press. Available at https://www.sadc.int/files/6215/6630/2592/SADC_Selected_Indicators_2018.pdf.

Saurombe, Amos. 2011. The Southern African Development Community (SADC) Trade Legal Instruments Compliance with Certain Criteria of GATT Article XXIV. *PER* 14 (4): 1–33.

Saurombe, Amos. 2012. The Role of SADC Institutions in Implementing SADC Treaty Provisions Dealing with Regional Integration. *PER/PELJ* 15 (2): 454–569.

Schreiner, Barbara, and Hannah Baleta. 2015. Broadening the Lens: A Regional Perspective on Water Food and Energy Integration in SADC. *Aquatic Procedia* 5: 90–103.

Smith, Michael. 2001. *Transnational Urbanism: Locating Globalization*. Oxford: Basil Blackwell.

The South African. 2018. China Just Built the Longest Suspension Bridge in Africa Connecting Maputo and KZN. https://www.thesouthafrican.com.news/maputo-catembe-bridge-africa-china-kwazulu-natal/. Accessed 10 June 2019.

Thornhill, C., Odendaal, M., Malan, L., Mathebula, F., van Dijk H., and Mello, D. 2002. An Overview of Intergovrnmental Relations in Africa: Southern African Development Community (SADC). Pretoria: SAFOUM Publishers.

United Nations Developmental Programme. 2015. Decentralised Governance for Development: A Combined Practice Note. Available at https://www.undp.org/content/undp/en/home/librarypage/democratic-governance/local_governance/decentralised-governance-for-development-a-combined-practice-note-on-decentralisation-local-governance-and-urban-rural-development.html.

Van Nieuwkerk, Anthoni. 2013. SIPO II: Too Little, Too Late? *Strategic Review for Southern Africa* 35 (1): 146–153.

van der Pluijm, Rogier, and Jan Mellisen. 2007. City Diplomacy: The Expanding Role of Cities in International Politics. *Clingendael Diplomacy Papers* 10: 1–45.

CHAPTER 9

Trade and Security Cooperation in the Arab Maghreb Union Region

Hamdy A. Hassan

This chapter examines the nature of trade and security links among the Arab Maghreb Union (AMU) countries, Algeria, Libya, Mauritania, Morocco, and Tunisia. Since the beginning of the Arab Spring in late 2010, this region has undergone significant political and economic changes, among them, facing new forms of terrorism and violent religious fundamentalism. The basic premise of this study is that the experience of Maghreb regional integration does not fall within the context of the idea of Africa's rise, nor does it motivate or strengthen it. The elimination or limitation of interstate conflicts is a precondition for reviving the AMU. To verify this premise, this chapter discusses intra-Maghreb trade trends and highlights the weakness or lack of political and security cooperation at both the bilateral and collective levels.

Political conflicts, mainly between Morocco and Algeria, have been the main factor impeding and reducing opportunities for integration between North and West Africa. Therefore, the AMU countries, either individually or as a bloc, do not appear to be a major economic partner in the

H. A. Hassan (✉)
Political Science, Zayed University, Dubai, United Arab Emirates
e-mail: Hamdy.hassan@zu.ac.ae

K. Omeje (ed.), *The Governance, Security and Development Nexus*,
https://doi.org/10.1007/978-3-030-49348-6_9

continent's rapid economic growth, at the level of either foreign direct investment or trade. Further, Maghreb countries have failed to formulate effective and efficient security policies to address pressing security challenges across the different historical stages of the AMU experience.

Removing all trade barriers and engaging in a multilateral trading system would allow the AMU countries to establish a regional security framework using diplomatic, political, economic, and even military means. This study builds on the theoretical framework that links a strong negative relationship between conflict and trade. Countries involved in many trade exchanges have fewer conflicts. Conflict also leads to low levels of intrastate trade (El Asmi 2018).

Methodologically, this study is based on qualitative research methods. Accordingly, I relied upon data gathered from books, articles, scientific theses, and reports. Given the nature of the data collected, the study used qualitative data analysis techniques. It is noticeable that the literature, with its different approaches and intellectual orientations, has addressed issues of regional integration in the Maghreb by focusing on certain dimensions in terms of success and failure. One trend in the literature is the focus on AMU's experience in assessing the importance of economic integration among African countries (Testas 1999), although some scholars have placed the Maghreb in the context of the Arab and Middle Eastern regions (Worrall 2017). The second trend is concerned with studying the determinants of intra-Maghreb trade. Despite the efforts of trade openness in the AMU region, economic growth, intratrade, and internal trade continue to lag behind other developing countries in the Middle East, Asia, and Latin America (Abdullah et al. 2015; Bchir et al. 2007). The third trend in the literature addresses the AMU as an example of the important role that small states can play when they choose to form an alliance with each other and in cooperation with the European Union and its constituent regional groupings, such as can be seen in the Euro-Mediterranean partnership. This trend may signal the need to develop a theoretical framework that clarifies the motives and actions of nondominant states and non-state entities in the current international system (Jones 2009). Finally, the fourth trend tends toward the repercussions of the Arab Spring events, calling for a revival of the AMU (Zoubir 2012).

According to the foregoing, the study is divided into four sections. The first section deals with the nature of the AMU and the gap between the dream of the great Maghreb and the deeply conflicted reality. The second section analyzes intra-Maghreb trade trends by revealing the relationship between conflicts and tensions among countries and their impact on cooperation in the trade area. The third section discusses the weaknesses of joint security cooperation initiatives among the AMU countries and the use of alternative initiatives with other parties. The final section is devoted to studying the impact of the Arab Spring on the Maghreb region.

The Dream of the Great Maghreb and the Challenges of the Divided Reality

Integration initiatives between the Maghreb countries have been numerous, beginning with the Tangier conference in 1958, when representatives of the wartime Algerian Liberation Front (FLN) met the Moroccan Independence Party and the new Tunisian Constitution Party to discuss ways to create an economic grouping of North African countries. According to Aghrout and Sutton (1990), many agreements were forged on paper, but "unfortunately, the importance given to these events is inversely proportional to their actual application and effectiveness." In the late 1980s, Maghreb integration opportunities reflected the aspirations of Maghreb countries and societies towards the unity of the Maghreb. Indeed, Morocco, Algeria, Mauritania, Libya, and Tunisia signed the Marrakesh Agreement on February 17, 1989, for the establishment of the AMU.

Apart from the dream of great Maghreb, a variety of economic, political, and security factors led Maghreb countries to work together. With low oil prices and high unemployment rates, the economic crises affecting the Maghreb countries increased sharply in the 1980s, prompting the ruling regimes to seek collective solutions. In the political sphere, since 1988, Algeria has tried to contain both Libya and Morocco through a regional framework that would allow a settlement of the Western Sahara crisis and possibly also confront Egypt's growing role. In terms of security, direct external interference in the security of the region, such as the Israeli attack in October 1985 of the PLO headquarters in Tunis and the US bombing in Tripoli and Benghazi in April 1986, prompted Maghreb countries to build the Union and establish a strong regional bloc in the North African region. According to Article 2 of the Marrakesh Treaty (1989), the AMU aims at:

> strengthening the ties of brotherhood which link the member States and their peoples to one another; achieving progress and prosperity of their societies and defending their rights; contributing to the preservation of peace based on justice and equity; pursuing a common policy in different domains; and working gradually towards achieving free movement of persons and transfer of services, goods and capital among them.

The AMU is made up of several institutions, the most important of which is the Presidential Council (Council of Heads of State). According to Article 6, only the Presidential Council has the authority to make decisions, and these decisions are taken unanimously. Since its establishment in 1989, the Council has convened six times, but has not assembled since its meeting in Tunisia in 1994.

Other political institutions of the AMU include a Council of Ministers of Foreign Affairs, which is supposed to meet regularly to prepare for the sessions of the Council of Heads of State and to examine proposals formulated by subordinate committees and four specialized ministerial commissions; a Consultative Assembly consisting of 30 representatives from each member state that can advise the Council of Heads of State; a Court of Justice, composed of two judges from each member state, set up in Algiers and Nouakchott, respectively; and, the General Secretariat, which was established permanently in Rabat in 1992.

In 1991, the AMU countries agreed upon three steps that would lead to regional integration according to the European Common Market model: (a) establishing a free trade area before the end of 1992. The aim of this phase was to remove tariff and nontariff barriers between member states by taking all legal, administrative, and financial measures to promote an environment conducive to the integration of the Maghreb as well as to institute the necessary agreements to create such a zone and to ratify the remaining joint agreements; (b) forming a customs union before the end of 1995, the purpose of which was to standardize the taxes and customs' duties applied by all parties, institute a uniform tariff for the rest of the countries, and standardize customs regulations and legislation(at the second session in 1990, the council of presidents adopted a set of principles that paved the way to the formation of a customs union); (c) organizing a common market before 2000. The aim of this phase was to formulate a single market system, to constitute a major domestic marketplace in which customs duties and other barriers were abolished, and to facilitate the movement of persons, goods, and services, and capital; (d) creating an economic union: the Maghreb strategy has not defined any entitlement to this goal, but has confirmed that this is performed by unifying economic and social development policies and plans (Behlouli 2014). In this context, member countries negotiated the establishment of a Maghreb free trade area for integration in all areas of economic activity. An agreement between trade ministers was initiated in 2010, but it was never ratified (IMF 2018).

The complex problems among the AMU countries have thwarted them from achieving their desired goals and total integration. The failure of the union states to support each other in times of crisis signaled their obstinance and inability to meet the challenges they faced, such as the blockade imposed on Libya following the so-called Lockerbie bombing incident and the failure of the Maghreb countries to break the blockade and help Libya emerge from its crisis, even by diplomatic means, thus alienating Libyans. On the other hand, the Maghreb countries were aware that it was in their interest to confront Europe, in particular, as a unified group and with one Maghreb voice, despite their preference to enter into bilateral trade relations (Zoubir 2012). Europe negotiated bilateral agreements with each of the southern Mediterranean countries, a policy strengthened by the European Neighborhood Policy of 2003. On the other hand, the United States encouraged Maghreb integration but, like Europe, negotiated separate free trade agreements with each Maghreb country. Morocco was the first to secure such an agreement, in 2004 (Sarkali 2018).

Furthermore, Maghreb countries took advantage of the global campaign against terrorism after the 9/11 2001 terrorist incidents in the United States to increase their regional weight at the expense of their competitors in the region, which reinforced the policy of polarization, especially between Algeria and Morocco. The absence of a unified framework for multilateral security cooperation in the region also pushed Maghreb countries into other subregional structures, such as the United States-led Trans-Saharan Counterterrorism Partnership (TSCTP), the NATO dialogue with Mediterranean countries, and the 5+5 Dialogue, which includes France, Italy, Malta, Portugal, and Spain in addition to the five Maghreb countries (Mohamed 2017).

The Moroccan–Algerian conflict resulted in the loss of mutually guaranteed complementarities between the two countries in terms of trade. In the first two months of 2018, Algeria imported nearly 8036 semi-assembled cars from the Dacia factory in Romania, though this product is easily assembled in the Moroccan Tangier. The same applies to agricultural commodities that Algeria has imported on a large scale from outside the Maghreb region, while many are produced by Morocco (Boukhars 2018). The policy of closing the border between the two countries is undoubtedly costly. From 2005 to 2015, it was possible to double the size of their economies in the event of openness to intra-trade exchange. Instead, the Algerian economy only expanded by 33% and Morocco by 37%, which was not enough to meet the high unemployment rates and severe economic crisis in the two countries.

Intra-Maghreb Trade

Intra-Maghreb trade is much less than the bulk of its business with the rest of the world. Intra-Maghreb trade accounts for less than 5% of its total trade (Tables 9.1 and 9.2), compared to intra-regional trade in Africa at about 16%, Latin America at 19%, Asia 51%, North America 54%, and Europe 70% (IMF 2018). Notably, none of the five countries is using its Maghreb neighbors as a major trading partner. Europe is the main trading partner of the Maghreb countries, reflecting historical circumstances, the nature of commercial goods, and the efforts made by each country to liberalize trade with Europe. Improving the regional integration of Maghreb countries would undoubtedly help to secure greater scales in the economy, expand markets, enhance industrial efficiency, reduce the region's dependence on the outside, and decrease the vulnerability of its economy (Djoumessi and Bala 2017).

According to some estimates, the region loses about 530 billion dollars a year as a result of trade restrictions and legislative barriers (Allouche 2019). The lack of trade complementarity, the great similarity in trade structures, and low export diversification have had a significant negative impact on intra-trade, which in 2015 accounted for only 3.6% of total trade in the region. For example, the complementarity of Algerian and Libyan exports with imports from other Maghreb countries remains very low. Morocco and Tunisia perform slightly better as they are more advanced in diversifying exports from their neighbors, which rely heavily on hydrocarbon and mineral sectors. However, despite efforts to diversify, the range of goods exported from Morocco and Tunisia (textile industry, food industry, electrical and mechanical industries) remains very similar. Indeed, the low trade complementarity between the two has complicated their real efforts to trade more with each other (Boukhars 2018).

Table 9.1 Exports of goods to Maghreb countries (average value in US Dollars) 2013–2016

Client	*2013*		*2014*		*2015*		*2016*	
	Value	*%*	*Value*	*%*	*Value*	*%*	*Value*	*%*
1. Algeria								
Libya	22	0.0	36	0.1	23	0.1	31	0.1
Mauritania	29	0.0	248	0.4	57	0.2	39	0.1
Morocco	1052	1.6	1131	1.9	630	1.8	499	1.7
Tunisia	1649	2.5	1575	2.6	846	2.4	603	2.0
Total	2753	4.2	2990	5.0	1555	4.5	1172	3.9
2. Morocco								
Algeria	209	1.0	210	0.9	197	0.9	236	1.0
Libya	87	0.4	36	0.2	68	0.3	90	0.4
Mauritania	141	0.6	172	0.7	162	0.7	173	0.8
Tunisia	87	0.4	96	0.4	109	0.5	98	0.4
Total	525	2.4	515	2.2	537	2.4	597	2.6
3. Tunisia								
Algeria	486	2.9	619	3.7	558	4.0	668	4.9
Libya	869	5.1	668	4.0	540	3.8	443	3.3
Mauritania	31	0.2	29	0.2	22	0.2	16	0.1
Morocco	192	1.1	180	1.1	180	1.3	169	1.2
Total	1579	9.3	1496	8.9	1300	9.2	1292	9.5

Source Compiled from the AMU official website at http://maghrebarabe.org/wp-content/uploads/2019/03/Commerce-total-Intra-Maghreb.pdf (Retrieved on 20 May 2019)

Notably, Maghreb integration arrangements with partners from outside the region—some of which contain provisions on intra-regional trade—have had a greater impact in real terms. Based on traditional business links with Europe, Maghreb countries are involved in several trade agreements. For example, Algeria, Morocco, and Tunisia, among others, are part of the Euro-Mediterranean Agreement, which established a partnership with the European Union and its members. This partnership aims to remove barriers to trade and investment between the EU and the southern Mediterranean countries and among the southern Mediterranean countries themselves. Morocco and Tunisia signed trade liberalization agreements with the European Free Trade Association (EFTA), which includes Iceland, Liechtenstein, Norway, and Switzerland. Morocco and Tunisia also completed bilateral free trade agreements with Turkey, and Morocco reached an agreement with the United

Table 9.2 Imports of goods from Maghreb Countries (average value in US Dollars)

Client	*2013*		*2014*		*2015*		*2016*	
	Value	*%*	*Value*	*%*	*Value*	*%*	*Value*	*%*
1. Algeria								
Libya	317	0.6	4	0.0	8	0.0	0	0.0
Mauritania	1	0.0	1	0.0	0	0.0	0	0.0
Morocco	218	0.4	217	0.4	215	0.4	270	0.6
Tunisia	489	0.9	517	0.9	458	0.9	431	0.9
Total	1024	1.9	738	1.3	681	1.3	701	1.5
2. Morocco								
Algeria	1284	2.8	1332	2.9	789	2.1	616	1.5
Libya	15	0.0	22	0.0	4	0.0	11	0.0
Mauritania	1	0.0	1	0.0	1	0.0	0	0.0
Tunisia	222	0.5	205	0.4	189	0.5	192	0.5
Total	1523	3.4	1560	3.4	982	2.6	919	2.0
3. Tunisia								
Algeria	1185	4.9	1572	6.3	801	4.0	713	3.7
Libya	409	1.7	56	0.2	19	0.1	30	0.2
Mauritania	1	0.0	1	0.0	2	0.0	3	0.0
Morocco	96	0.4	118	0.5	127	0.6	116	0.6
Total	1691	7.0	1748	7.0	950	4.7	861	4.4

Source Compiled from the AMU official website at http://maghrebarabe.org/wp-content/uploads/2019/03/Commerce-total-Intra-Maghreb.pdf (Retrieved on 20 May 2019)

States.[1] Finally, China's recent Belt-and-Road Initiative (BRI) includes the Arab Maghreb. Although BRI focuses on enhancing economic cooperation through investment in infrastructure, including roads, railways, and energy networks, it also covers broader cooperation, such as trade facilitation and technical assistance. Algeria, Libya, Morocco, and Tunisia have already signed the BRI partnership agreements with China.

Moreover, Algeria has become China's most important partner in the Maghreb. Over the past decade, the value of Sino-Algerian trade has grown dramatically, with Algeria becoming China's largest market in the Maghreb. Meanwhile, China has surpassed France as the largest source of Algerian imports (Khechib 2018).

Impediments to Trade Integration in the Arab Maghreb

Numerous complex factors explain the lack of economic integration among Maghreb countries (IMF 2018). These include: (a) Unfavorable trade and investment policies, trade barriers and tariffs, and nontariff. In general, the average tariffs applied in Maghreb countries are much higher than in the G20 or emerging markets and developing economies. For example, in 2016, the average tariffs in the Maghreb countries were around 14%, compared to 5% in the EU, 4% in the United States, and 10% in China. Algeria is the most protected market, with an average tariff rate of 19%, while in other countries the rates are about 12%. (b) Weak regional infrastructure. The weak regional network in the Maghreb is a major impediment to trade integration. There are four modes of transport among the Maghreb countries: sea, air, road, and railways. Only sea transportation is well developed. The only commercial route that can connect all Maghreb countries is the Cairo—Dakar Highway, but the closure of the Moroccan–Algerian border makes it impossible to transport goods from Libya, Tunisia, and Algeria to Morocco or Mauritania by land. Also, parts of that highway remain incomplete, and there is no bridge crossing the river between Mauritania and Senegal. Though Algeria, Morocco, and Tunisia all have local railways, rail tracks stop at the border.

Maritime transport is the primary means of intra-Maghreb trade, but it mainly serves trade with Europe. Although all Maghreb countries have ports, they do not have large commercial shipping lines among them. Each country has developed its own infrastructure for its ports destined for Europe. There are, therefore, very few direct shipping lines between the Maghreb countries, which transport their goods within the region through third-country ports such as Marseille in France, Almeria in Spain, and even Rotterdam in the Netherlands. Such methods sometimes result in increased freight costs and reduce competitive opportunities for commercial products. Collectively, these factors were part of the push for a commercial orientation outside the region, particularly towards Europe; the recent attempts to move towards sub-Saharan Africa since the Africa Rising narrative post-2000; and the emergence of China as an export market for the Maghreb.

Geopolitical factors such as differences among the Member States, especially between Algeria and Morocco, have hampered regional integration. Threats of terrorism have led to further restrictions on common borders. For example, the long border between Algeria and Morocco has been closed since 1994. Research has shown that severe civil wars such as those in Libya can reduce foreign trade by up to 40% (Saidi 2018). Furthermore, the political economy of some of these states sometimes hampers progress toward regional integration. Indeed, several economic and noneconomic factors have led to limited migration within the Maghreb region, among them, low job growth and thus few employment opportunities for potential migrants in the Maghreb countries. Maghreb migrants often prefer to seek opportunities in more mature markets (especially in Europe). Also increasing competition is coming from African, Chinese, and European workers, who are often hired under contractual arrangements in the context of investment projects. Difficulties obtaining a residence card and work permit limit labor movement. Many Maghreb countries require visas for citizens from other Maghreb countries and the rest of the world. In addition to visa requirements, the length of stay is often limited to 90 days (IMF 2018).

Security Cooperation Between Maghreb Countries

The importance of the political and security dimension was very clear when the Maghreb Union was founded. Therefore, the call for the revival of Maghreb regionalism after the events of the Arab Spring makes the governments in the region aware of the importance of strengthening security under complex geopolitical conditions. Mutual regional support and increased institutional cooperation may be a response to the nature of new security threats to the region. The security of any member country of the Union is based on the security of all the other states—a principle defined in the Marrakesh Treaty. Article 14states: "Any aggression directed against one of the Member States shall be considered as an aggression against the other member States." In addition, Article 15states:

> Member States pledge not to permit on their territory any activity or organization liable to threaten the security, the territorial integrity or the political system of any of them. They also pledge to abstain from joining any alliance or military or political bloc directed against the political independence or territorial integrity of the other member States.

However, over the past two decades, the countries of the region have not been able to establish a strong basis for joint security to counter the dangers of terrorism, organized crime, cyber hazards, and other new forms of threat. The Maghreb is an area of transit for migrants to Europe and a drug trafficking route. The region has also experienced fluctuations in its geopolitical stability as a result of the Arab Spring. The Maghreb countries have tended to foster cooperative approaches with other parties and within alternative political and security frameworks, which were given priority over Intra-Maghreb cooperation. As a result, the AMU has become impotent, ineffective and in a deep state of hibernation (Abdel Fattah and Hamzawy 2016).

It is believed that the absence of cooperation between the Maghreb countries in general and security cooperation, in particular, comes down to tension and rivalry between Morocco and Algeria. Complex issues associated with the contradictory historical and ideological paths of both countries have put them in conflict as has a dispute over the demarcation of borders and the issue of Western Sahara. Furthermore, Algeria politically and militarily supports the Polisario Front, which abides by the principles of decolonization and the rights of the Sahrawi people to self-determination. In contrast, Morocco's claim to full sovereignty over Western Sahara is a direct threat to regional unity. That Algeria was among the supporters for the return of Morocco to the African Union (AU) does not indicate the possibility of a political rapprochement between the two countries. The Algerian argument would be that Morocco's commitment to the principles of the AU means that Morocco must forsake demands for the expulsion of the Sahrawi Arab Democratic Republic from the AU, which in itself would be a tacit recognition of the Sahrawi Republic (Hassan 2017).

This deep fissure between Morocco and Algeria has undermined any serious institutional approach to common Maghreb action. It has also helped generate other factors that perpetuate disintegration and thwarted the production of a common approach to Maghreb issues, including collaboration on security challenges. Each of the two countries seeks to possess regional leadership with the ethos that "to the extent that the strongest party wins in the regional equation, the other party loses." Algeria, for example, is seeking to play a leadership role in all security cooperation in the Sahelian -Sahara region without engaging Morocco.

Inherited borders from the colonial era constitute another impediment to regional integration in the Maghreb, where all countries in the region are embroiled in border disputes: Tunisia–Libya, Tunisia–Algeria, Libya–Algeria, and Morocco–Mauritania. Many of these conflicts have been resolved diplomatically and peacefully. However, the border dispute between Morocco and Algeria remains the most serious of these conflicts, which led to a war between the two countries in 1963. The exact origins of the conflict stemmed from France's withholding of Moroccan territory and its annexation of Algeria during the colonial period. The problem of the Algerian–Moroccan border as well as the Moroccan Sahara issue remain the most prominent factors in the absence of regional integration in the region (El Asmi 2018).

The Arab Maghreb countries are generously spending on their military budget to confront the security dilemma of the region as a whole and in response to the internal threats from each country. Algeria ranks 22nd in the world in terms of military spending, with a military budget of about 9.6 billion dollars in 2018, accounting for 5.3% of the gross domestic product (GDP), the highest rate in Africa (SIPRI 2019). Russia—Algeria's historical military trade partner—was the main beneficiary of increasing military spending by Algeria. Between 2000 and 2011, two-thirds of the required military equipment (by value) came from the Russian market. The Moroccan defense budget is estimated at 3.4 billion dollars and ranks 55 globally. Thus, the military gap between the two countries largely favors Algeria. The tension between them cannot accurately be described as an arms race but reflects the nature of the security dilemma in the region.

Bilateral and Multilateral Security Cooperation Options in the Arab Maghreb

The Maghreb countries, individually and collectively, have security relations with areas in geographic proximity such as Europe, the Atlantic region, and Africa. Terrorism, cross-border organized crime, and illegal migration pose serious challenges to regional and global security. However, the Maghreb region was not a strategic priority on the US foreign policy agenda until September 11. Since the intensification of terrorist activity in the Maghreb, Sahel, and Sahara countries, the United States has become concerned about security cooperation with the countries of the region.

Maghreb countries have moved toward Europe to achieve common security. There are four general levels of security cooperation between the Maghreb and Europe. The first level is multinational and includes the Euro-Atlantic framework and the Mediterranean Dialogue Initiative. The second level of security cooperation with the European Union includes the European Security and Defense Policy, the Good Neighbor Policy, and the Euro-Mediterranean Partnership in the framework of the Barcelona meetings. The third level is bilateral, between a European state and a Maghreb State; and, finally, the fourth subregional level is the security and cooperation initiative within the 5+5 Dialogue (Abdel Fattah and Hamzawy 2016). Undoubtedly, these multiple levels of security cooperation reflect differing strategies dictated by their constituencies and adopted based on their interests and priorities.

US military and security cooperation with Maghreb countries focuses on developing the capabilities of special operations, border security, and counterterrorism. In the case of Tunisia and Morocco, cooperation is accompanied by the provision of programs centered on security sector reform. For Tunisia in particular, the goal of security sector reform is clearly linked to the issue of human rights more than in any other country in the region. Further, Tunisia was the only Maghreb country chosen for the Security Governance Initiative (SGI), a US initiative signed in 2014 with six African partners: Kenya, Ghana, Niger, Mali, Nigeria, and Tunisia. If the United States supports the development of Maghreb partners' capacity to confront extraterritorial threats, the intention is to fight terrorism in the Sahel and Sahara. Slowly but steadily, the United States has succeeded in establishing a security network grouping the Maghreb and Sahel countries (Zoubir 2009).

With regard to cooperation with the North Atlantic Treaty Organization (NATO), all Maghreb countries, with the exception of Libya, have sought to engage in the Mediterranean Dialogue Initiative established in 1994 with a view to greater openness of the alliance to the Mediterranean space and to further contribute to strengthening cooperation to counter cross-border risks. The Mediterranean Dialogue and partnership with NATO serve to promote practical cooperation in a number of areas, including military exercises aimed at improving the capabilities of NATO countries and Mediterranean Dialogue countries; conducting NATO-led operations, including military training courses; confronting new security threats and fighting terrorism through intelligence-sharing (Al-Khazendar 2005).

Security Challenges in the Aftermath of the Arab Spring

The waves of action produced by the Arab Spring led to contradictory paths of transition, many of which manifested as turbulent political and security situations in the Maghreb. State authority in Libya collapsed, opening the door to the proliferation of terrorist organizations such as ISIS and its sisters. Algeria's political landscape became fluid and unclear after President Bouteflika resigned in April 2019. Tunisia is seeking to emerge from the transitional experience by absorbing Islamists into the new system. Morocco is making another course for the success of the Islamists' experience in its alliance with the Royal Institution. Finally, Mauritania presents a model of democratic transition under a military cloak. As with Libya, Mauritania remains a regional threat because its weak political and security structure of the state transforms it into a strategic incubator for the proliferation of security crises that threaten regional stability.

Non-Maghreb security challenges in the region and in neighboring countries have led to the emergence of political groupings and entities to address them. In 2014, the G5 Sahel was established in Nouakchott with five Sahelian countries: Burkina Faso, Chad, Mali, Mauritania, and Niger. The military side of this institutional framework is coordinated by the Chiefs of Staff of the countries concerned. Security is the main objective of this cooperation and is aimed at confronting the threat of jihadist organizations operating in the region (Al-Qaeda in the Islamic Maghreb [AQIM], Al-Mourabitoun, Boko Haram). In addition, G5 Sahel helps prevent some countries in the region such as Mali, Niger, Chad, and Libya from becoming transit routes for drug trafficking and illegal immigration into Europe. However, the G5S excluded two major players in the region: Morocco and Algeria. Polarization in the Maghreb has not abated between these two influential countries and always finds room to assert influence in less powerful countries like Mauritania. Tunisia in the post-Ben Ali era has been trapped between an Algerian neighbor with which it shares a hot security border and has an impact on its internal political issues; and Morocco, a far neighbor that is taking the path of openness to the Tunisian experience in order to attract it to its priorities in the region.

The Arab Spring and the Geostrategic Transformations in the Maghreb

The Arab Spring contributed significantly to the reformulation of policy, principles, and values in the Arab Maghreb countries. The challenge posed by regional winds of change to the states of the region is how they adapt to these transformations without losing their political paradigms. While the trend toward political and constitutional reform has determined the transformation of politics in the Maghreb, the security challenges in the region—in particular, those linked to violent Islamist organizations and other terrorist groups from the Sahel-Saharan States—are fundamental obstacles to a democratic transition. These challenges may justify the need for the Arab Maghreb bloc to be a harmonious and integrated bloc, strengthening its bargaining power with foreign partners, and ensuring high levels of coordination in meeting security challenges (Zoubir 2012).

There is no doubt that events of the Arab Spring in Tunisia and Libya from 2010 and Algeria in 2019 led to clear changes in the regional balance of power. While Qadhafi's ambitions and whims strained Libya's relations with its neighbors, the Maghreb countries tried to contain his radical policies by keeping him in the Maghreb Union system so that they could better control him. The security challenges of the Arab Spring rekindled hopes for reviving the AMU and promoting important geostrategic changes (Aljazeera Center for Studies 2013).

Arab Spring in Tunisia, Egypt, and Libya

Manifestations of the Arab Spring in Tunisia, Egypt, and Libya impelled the ruling regimes in Algeria, Mauritania, and Morocco to initiate political reforms. Thus, in March 2011, King Mohammed VI of Morocco, who enjoys popular support as the "Commander of All Believers," announced important constitutional changes that were overwhelmingly approved by referendum in July of the same year. Bouteflika, President of Algeria from 1999 to 2019, announced on April 15, 2011 that important political reforms would be initiated.

Political Islam in the Maghreb

It is clear that the currents of political Islam have been the biggest winners of these changes, as demonstrated by its *de jure* role (through elections, as in the cases of Tunisia and Morocco) or de facto authority (Libya).

However, the strength of civil society and the non-militarization of politics in the Tunisian situation have afforded the country some control over the political Islam movement. Fearing the contagion of political Islam and its access to power in any form, Algeria has allowed the formation of small political parties, most of which are Islamist, so that they cannot challenge the domination of the ruling party. In Morocco, King Mohammed VI was able to benefit from the long tradition of a powerful central government or *Makhzan* to undermine the authority of the Islamic Justice and Development Party (Sadiki 2016).

Increased Security Risks

The state of strife, turmoil, and chaos in which Libyans have been living since 2011 has affected neighboring countries, particularly Algeria and Tunisia, in various forms. With the collapse of the central government and loss of power over all territories and borders, terrorist organizations and groups have proliferated and various illegal activities, such as smuggling, arms trade, human trafficking, and illegal immigration, have escalated. The Libyan situation presents a clear example of state failure in the face of revival of primordial identity tendencies (notably tribalism), the corresponding fissure in national identity, as well as the rivalry between external actors and stakeholders. This breakdown has compelled Morocco and Algeria to try to play a regional role to contain the effects of the Libyan crisis and assist in the process of state-building. This effort was evident in the Skhirat talks in 2015, which was organized by Morocco under UN auspices to lay the groundwork for forming a national government. However, the political divide in Libya, the apprehension of foreign intervention, and the terrorist challenge of ISIS and its sister networks are three formidable challenges to the process of rebuilding the Libyan state.

Emergence of Regional Polarization Between Morocco and Algeria

Seeking to confront Algerian influence in the region, Morocco has tried to take advantage of the Libyan situation by strengthening its role in the Community of Sahel-Saharan States (CEN-SAD). Morocco has also sought to isolate the Sahrawi Republic in the African Union by adopting a comprehensive policy to lure African countries into withdrawing their diplomatic recognition of the Sahrawi state, as well as to compete with Algeria to gain influence on the continent. On the other hand, Algeria has sought to strengthen cooperation with Sahel countries on its southern border, namely Niger, Mali, and Mauritania, by establishing the Joint Operational Staff Committee—and excluding Morocco from its membership. Algeria maintains that Morocco is not a Sahel-Saharan country—unlike Western Sahara occupied by Morocco—which is located on the Sahel. Thus, Morocco's membership in the committee could constitute Algeria's implicit recognition of Morocco's sovereignty over Western Sahara.

Economic Deterioration

The Maghreb countries, particularly Tunisia and Algeria have seen significant economic deterioration largely due to changes in Libya since 2011. Libya was the second economic partner to Tunisia after the European Union. Tunisia's imports from Libya consisted primarily of oil at a preferential rate, which covers 25% of its total needs. These exchanges have been affected by the ongoing closure of border corridors, an increase in smuggling activity, and the parallel economy. Another factor derives from the impact of the return of Maghreb labor from Libya, which created additional social and economic burdens on their countries of origin (60,000 Tunisian workers returned from Libya, prompting a rise in the unemployment rate that exceeded 18.3% in 2011). Furthermore, the Libyan refugees posed a heavy burden on the host states. According to a report by the United Nations Economic Commission for Africa (ECA), the volume of trade between the Maghreb countries during 2015, accounted for 8.3% of the total trade of these countries, with a financial value of only $2 billion, which is quite below the rate recorded by African countries, at 12% (Kabboush 2018).

The Popular Movement in Algeria

The Algerian regime insistence on the candidacy of ailing President Bouteflika's for a fifth term provoked the second wave of the Arab Spring in Algeria. Many political, economic, social, and psychological reasons are behind these protests, especially stagnation of the political system, the absence of change, the dominant role of the army, the deterioration of the economy, pervasive financial corruption in government spending, tax evasion, and the violation of project specifications. President Abdelaziz Bouteflika stayed in power despite his poor health and beginning in 2013 was unable to deliver a public speech, never represented his country at any international summits and visits, and seldom received any foreign dignitaries. The Algerian movement may be a beacon of hope for new policies that support the integrative orientation of the countries of the region and alleviate tension between Morocco and Algeria.

Conclusion

This chapter has shown that the experience of the integrated Maghreb Union does not fall within the context of Africa Rising, nor does it motivate or strengthen it. Clearly, the primacy of political culture at the level of governing regimes prioritizes competition and even conflict over potential integration opportunities, greatly limiting any added value made possible by the experience of this Union, both to its member states and to African integration in general. One of the main indicators of this understanding is the inability of those states to formulate effective and efficient security policies to deal with pressing security challenges that have arisen throughout the union's various historical stages. This failure has resulted in terrorist proliferation and a rise in organized crime in the Sahel-Saharan region, which extends into the territory of those states as well as into Libya. Stymied collaboration over the challenge of illegal migration has also presented problems. Finally, the inability to develop coordinated policies among these states has been a cause for international intervention to deal with these challenges. Thus, at the security level, the presence of the Maghreb Union in the regional and international spaces is the presence of the crisis, not the presence of an efficient and effective partner. As for the infrastructure of integration, undoubtedly political differences between Morocco and Algeria were the key to impeding the Cairo-Dakar Link Road and to reducing opportunities for integration between North and West Africa. As such, the volume of intra-Maghreb trade has not made any real breakthrough under this Union, which parallels the scale of development of intra-African trade in general. Finally, the states of the Maghreb Union do not appear individually or collectively as a major economic partner in the continent's accelerated economic growth either at the level of foreign direct investment or in terms of trade exchange.

In any case, the accelerating pace of globalization and changes in the local context in the Maghreb countries will affect the nature of the post-colonial state, which has been defining individual and collective political behavior within the political clientelism system. Economic development and the increase in the population of young people will likely make policies of exclusion and marginalization unacceptable. Perhaps as a result, a conversation could take place on key issues such as equal citizenship, social justice, and reshaping the national state structure on new grounds. The experiences of the Arab Spring in Tunisia and Libya in 2011 and Algeria in 2019 provide clear examples. New cooperative partnerships could then be built in the Maghreb space to meet the challenges that have impeded the revival of the Maghreb Union.

Note

1. The US–Morocco Free Trade Agreement, signed on June 15, 2004, is a bilateral trade agreement between the United States and Morocco. The FTA provides improved commercial opportunities for US exports to Morocco by reducing and eliminating trade barriers.

References

Abdel Fattah, Loai, and Zain Al Abdeen Hamzawy. 2016. The Maghreb Countries and the Challenge of Transnational Threats: Security Cooperation Choices. The International Symposium on Cross-Border Security Threats. Oujda: College of Legal, Economic and Social Sciences, Mohamed First University, 282–308.

Abdullah, Norehan, Hussin Abdullah, and Hadi Abuhriba. 2015. The Determinants of Trade and Trade Direction of Arab Maghreb Union. *Journal of Economic Cooperation and Development* 36 (3): 123–148.

Aghrout, Ahmed, and Keith Sutton. 1990. Regional Economic Union in the Maghreb. *The Journal of Modern African Studies* 28 (1): 115–139.

Aljazeera Center for Studies. 2013. *Symposium on "The Arab Maghreb: Current Regional Transformations"*. Doha: Aljazeera Center for Studies.

Al-Khazendar, Sami. 2005. NATO's Mediterranean Dialogue and Arab States: Themes Dimensions and Challenges. *Dirasat: Human and Social Sciences* 32: 638–652.

Allouche, Yasmina. 2019. *Regional Power Rivalry and the Failure of the Arab Maghreb Union*. Istanbul: TRT World Research Center.

Bchir, Hédi, Hakim Ben Hammouda, Nassim Oulmane, and Mustapha Sadni Jallab. 2007. The Cost of Non-Maghreb Achieving the Gains from Economic Integration. *Journal of Economic Integration* 22 (3): 684–722.

Behlouli, Faisal. 2014. The Establishment of the Maghreb Free Trade Area as an Input to Achieve Economic Integration Between the Maghreb Countries in

Light of the Current International Economic Challenges. *Al Baheth Journal* 14: 193–203.

Boukhars, Anouar. 2018. *Maghreb: Dream of Unity, Reality of Divisions*. Doha: Al Jazeera Centre for Studies.

Djoumessi, Emilie K., and Alain P. Bala. 2017. The Analysis of Borders Effects in Intra-African Trade. ERSA Working Paper 701. Cape Town, South Africa: Economic Research Southern Africa.

El Asmi, Rayhana C. 2018. Trade and Conflict: The Case of the Arab Maghreb Union. *Topics in Middle Eastern and African Economies*. Proceedings of Middle East Economic Association 20 (2): 90–103.

Hassan, Hamdy. 2017. Will Algeria and Morocco Ever Make Peace? *The Africa Report*, 82, March.

IMF. 2018. Economic Integration in the Maghreb: An Untapped Source of Growth. No. 01/19. Washington, DC: International Monetary Fund Publication Service.

Jones, Jonathan T. 2009. Challenging Theoretical Notions of Regional Integration: The Arab Maghreb Union, the Euro-Mediterranean Partnership and Arab Regionalism (Master's thesis, American University, Washington, DC). Available at ProQuest Central; ProQuest Dissertations & Theses Global.

Kabboush, Alhwas. 2018. The Maghreb Region and the Responsive Mechanisms to Euro-American Policies After 2010. *Jeel Journal of Political Studies and International Relations* 4 (18) (May): 61–80.

Khechib, Djallel. 2018. *One Belt, Different Aims: Beyond China's Increasing Leverage in the Grand Maghreb*. Istanbul: Humanitarian and Social Research Center (INSAMER).

Marrakesh Treaty. 1989. Article Two of the Treaty Instituting the Arab Maghreb Union (with Declaration), Marrakesh. February 17, Retrieved from https://www.wipo.int/edocs/lexdocs/treaties/en/amu/trt_amu.pdf.

Mohamed, Alkhuluqi. 2017. The Arab Maghreb Union: Reality and Challenges. Barq Center for Research and Studies. Retrieved from https://bit.ly/2VJSmeN.

Sadiki, Larbi. 2016. The Post Arab Spring Reform: The Maghreb at a Cross-Roads. *Digest of Middle East Studies* 25 (1): 109–131.

Saidi, Nasser. 2018. *Trends in Trade and Investment Policies in the MENA Region*. Dead Sea, Jordan: MENA-OECD Working Group on Investment and Trade.

Sarkali, Insaf. 2018. *Economic Factor and the Integration of the Maghreb Union*, 1–21. Istanbul: Egyptian Institute for Studies.

SIPRI. 2019. *SIPRI Fact Sheet, Trends in World Military Expenditure, 2018*. Stockholm: Stockholm International Peace Research Institute (SIPRI).

Testas, Abdelaziz. 1999. Evaluating Participation in African Economic Integration Schemes: The Case of the North African Arab Maghreb. *Journal of African Economies* 8 (1): 108–123.

Worrall, James. 2017. *International Institutions of the Middle East: The GCC, Arab League, and Arab Maghreb Union*. Florence: Routledge Ltd.

Zoubir, Yahia H. 2009. The United States and Maghreb Sahel Security. *International Affairs* (Royal Institute of International Affairs 1944–), 85 (5): 977–995.

Zoubir, Yahia H. 2012. Tipping the Balance Towards Intra-Maghreb Unity in Light of the Arab Spring. *The International Spectator* 3 (47): 83–99.

CHAPTER 10

The Boko Haram Insurgency and Regional Security in the Lake Chad Basin: Understanding the Growth and Development Consequences

Usman A. Tar and Samuel Baba Ayegba

Introduction

This chapter explores the Boko Haram insurgency, the emerging counterinsurgency security architecture in the Lake Chad Basin (LCB), and their overall consequences for growth and development in the LCB states. The chapter argues that despite a plethora of research on resurging threats of violent terrorism and the media's portrayal of Boko Haram jihadism in the Lake Chad region, little is known of the newly envisioned regional security architecture, including its operational cost as well as the consequences of the insurgency and counterinsurgency campaign for growth and development in the light of the Africa rising debate. The chapter also explores the role of geopolitics, and Nigeria's internal contradictions in

U. A. Tar (✉) · S. B. Ayegba
Department of Defence and Security Studies, Nigerian Defence Academy, Kaduna, Nigeria
e-mail: uatar@nda.edu.ng

K. Omeje (ed.), *The Governance, Security and Development Nexus*,
https://doi.org/10.1007/978-3-030-49348-6_10

the current transnational securitization project in the Lake Chad region. In so doing, we attempt to contextualize how the emerging dynamics of counter-terrorism and geopolitics are inextricably intertwined in the current discourse of the regionalization of security arrangements.

The end of the Cold War and the changing nature of armed conflicts and security threats have combined to push the agenda for security regionalization to the forefront. The potential for regional organizations to provide a viable platform for building robust supranational entities has become a visible phenomenon throughout the twentieth century (Flemes and Lobell 2015). The emergence of a new regional security architecture to fight terrorism in the LCB is not totally novel. It is built on an existing regional integration bloc—the Lake Chad Basin Commission (LCBC) founded in 1964. However, recent efforts by some members of the LCBC to create a new regional security architecture, under the aegis of the Multinational Joint Task Force (MJTF), to fight terrorism (as exemplified by Boko Haram Insurgency), has led to a paradigm shift in security regionalization within the Basin. Nevertheless, there are both incentives and challenges that underpin the emerging regional security complex in the LBC. These include among others, historical contradictions, linguistic differences, resource geopolitics, hegemonic politics, and local national politics have also hampered meaningful progress and undermined the basis for erecting robust new security architecture in the region (Tar and Bala 2018).

The Chad Basin in Perspective

The Chad Basin covers almost 8% of the African continent, with an area of about 2,434,000 square kilometres (940,000 Sq. mi). It is ringed by mountains. The Aïr Mountains and the Termit Massif in Niger form the western boundary. The rough terrain of the Chad Basin has given rise to several longstanding challenges—notably conservation, resource conflict, food security, and, more recently, cross-border terrorism. During the last four decades, the Chad Basin has witnessed several violent conflicts, guerrilla wars, warlordism, and militias insurgency stemming largely from the Chadian civil war of the 1980s, followed by armed rebellion and the factional militias in both Niger and the Central African Republic that had emerged to capture the ungovernable spaces created by lack of political legitimacy, leadership squabbles, and political fragmentation that bedeviled states across the region. New waves of insecurity in the

LCB are caused by both structural and existential factors. Structurally, the governance systems in the region have largely remained undemocratic, authoritarian, and externally influenced by neocolonial forces leading to a crisis of legitimacy. Existentially, poor investment in social provisioning in the region has led to crises of food and human security (Tar and Mustapha 2016).

Thus, the Chad Basin has become a veritable ground for the emergence of terrorism and militancy. Most problems are often initially banded as "local" only to later transformed into regional "pandemic." Recently, leaders of the LCBC have begun to articulate a new concept of security involving a more proactive approach that was ready to take initiatives for the first time in multilateral settings. Similarly, mindful of the growing threat Boko Haram poses to French interests in the Sahel, in May 2014, the French President spearheaded the Paris Summit for security with some African leaders, the summit brought together the Presidents of Nigeria, Cameroon, Niger and Chad, as well as representatives from the USA, UK, and the European Union in order to strengthen military and intelligence cooperation to deal with Boko Haram insurgency (Onuoha 2014). This was followed by a second summit at Abuja in May 2016 convened by Nigeria's President Muhammadu Buhari, which will essentially lead to the successful conclusion of ongoing military operations against Boko Haram in the northeast of Nigeria and the LCB. The speedy resolution of the humanitarian crises and forced displacements caused by the terrorist insurgency also dominated the Abuja summit (*Vanguard Newspaper* 2016).

The Upsurge of Terror in the Lake Chad Basin

In the years 2003 and 2004, a group known as the Nigerian Taliban, comprising of people linked with a young self-proclaimed cleric Mohammed Yusuf, tried to establish a semi-secessionist community in the village of Kanama, Yusuf's birthplace. They were allegedly dissatisfied with Yusuf's slow approach to building a community and focus on preaching (*Da'wah*) over violent confrontation. The group clashed with security forces, and its members were either killed or dispersed. The increased attention compelled Yusuf to go into exile in Saudi Arabia, from where he returned and continued to develop his Markaz and wider community. When the police shot and wounded several of the group's members during a funeral procession in June 2009, a furious Yusuf demanded that the responsible officers be prosecuted. When nothing happened, he told his followers to prepare for war. The following month saw clashes between protesters and security forces in several northern Nigerian states. The security forces called in reinforcements, and in the following operation an estimated 800 people, mostly innocent bystanders, were killed. Consequently, Yusuf was arrested, tortured, and executed, something that amplified his followers' pre-existing acrimonies toward the government—this blend of revolutionary resentment and brutality of security forces fundamentally shaped the group's *modus operandi* through a sense of retaliation—in speeches, they have consistently referred to Yusuf's killing (Mohammed 2017).

After the violent clampdown, the state declared that the group was extinct. However, in September 2010 Boko Haram conducted a spectacular jailbreak in the state of Bauchi under a new name, *Jama'atul Ahlus-Sunnah Lidda' Awati wal Jihad* (People Committed to the Teachings of the Prophet and Jihad, JAS), under the leadership of Abubakar Shekau. The group conducted a campaign of assassinations targeting politicians, police officers, and religious and village leaders, in what can be branded as acts of retaliation against people by whom the group felt betrayed. A few months later on Christmas Eve 2010, several bombs went off in the central Nigerian town of Jos and in Maiduguri, which showed that the group had larger ambitions than retaliation and that they were willing to use extreme violence to achieve them (Abubakar 2017).

In May 2013, the Nigerian federal government declared a state of emergency in four Northeast-Nigerian states and initiated a grand military operation against Boko Haram. Boko Haram was put under significant pressure and driven from its urban centers of operation. Through personal networks and a terrorism campaign of intimidation of local communities, the group managed to gain a foothold in rural Borno and the surrounding region. The group's brutal methods affected its popular support negatively, but at the same time, a parallel campaign of violence perpetrated by Nigerian security forces, which included arbitrary arrests, extrajudicial executions, and widespread excesses and violations allowed the group to maintain a local support base or resulted in locals not trusting security forces. Security forces accounted for three-quarters of all violent deaths in Boko Haram affected areas in 2013—the insurgency-terrorism inflicted by Boko Haram was reciprocated with state terrorism, creating a toxic dialectic of violence against the civilian population (Hansel 2017).

Boko Haram's largest massacre occurred in January 2015 in the town of Baga on the shores of Lake Chad, a garrison town for the African Union's mandated MJTF consisting of soldiers from Niger, Chad, Cameroon, and Nigeria. When Boko Haram came to the town in January 2015, its residents assisted the soldiers in trying to repel the attack. After routing the soldiers, Boko Haram took a gruesome revenge on the residents—as many as 2000 people were massacred. Subsequently, the group released two videos—one of the videos featured the group's leader Shekau, who taunted the Nigerian army while he showed captured weaponry and took responsibility for killing the towns' "infidels." In the other video a hitherto unknown person was seen portraying the massacre as self-defense, inviting all Muslims to move to the conquered territory, and ending the video by burning a Nigerian flag. The massacre in Baga could be viewed as a reaction to the significant defeats the group had suffered in the prior weeks. The Nigerian army and supporting forces from the MJTF were gaining momentum with help from local hunters with a tradition for fighting cattle rustlers and road bandits, who had organized self-defense groups, and a private military firm named Specialized Task, Training, Equipment and Protection, which had been contracted by the state (Cocodia 2017).

However, Boko Haram never managed to exploit the initial success and regain the offensive, losing significant parts of their territory throughout 2015. On January 16, 2017, Boko Haram again showed their continued capacity for violence, when three suicide bombers detonated themselves at the University of Maiduguri, killing one professor and wounding 17 students. Among the attackers was a 12-year-old girl (*Vanguard Newspaper* 2017). The presence of young girls and women in Boko Haram suicide attacks, although rare in conflicts in general, has become a hallmark for the group. Suicide attacks have been effectively used by the group to put pressure on security forces, undermine and challenge the legitimacy and authority of the state, intimidate and exhaust the local population, to show initiative when on the defensive and maintain a presence in urban centers, as the attacks in 2017 illustrate. Boko Haram has been able to take advantage of networks of affiliates throughout the region. Northeast Nigeria is part of the old Kanem-Bornu Empire that stretched across Chad, parts of Niger, Cameroon, and Libya. The ethnic majority in these areas is the Kanuri, who are said to comprise most of the Boko Haram members. Boko Haram has likely been able to exploit such linguistic, cultural, religious, and kinship relationships to create networks across the region. In addition, high-ranking members such as Mamman Nur, who is from Cameroon, or Khalid al-Barnawi, who allegedly smuggled cigarettes and cocaine with Al-Qaeda in the Islamic Maghreb (AQIM) commander Mokhtar Belmokhtar, have had existing networks across the region and continent (Gourley 2012).

Since Boko Haram's inception, it has been unclear what the group's main objective is. This has made it very difficult to initiate negotiations with them, in contrast for instance with the Niger Delta Militants in southern Nigeria. The latter had very clear objectives, which basically came down to demand that a much greater share of Nigeria's oil wealth should go to the oil-producing region, environmental remediation, and ending the destruction of the natural environment by the oil companies operating in the Niger Delta region. It was possible for the Nigerian government and multinational oil companies to negotiate with the Niger Delta militias and appease them through different means, including instituting measures to respond to some of their demands and co-opting them with money and job opportunities. Boko Haram's sporadic remarks about fighting to establish sharia-based Islamic state in Nigeria or parts of the LCB do not provide a clear foundation for negotiations (Maiangwa and Audu 2017). Cross-border retreating of insurgents into Chad prompted the Chadian government to join regional collaboration to fight the insurgents. Chad launched counterinsurgency operations that occasionally extended into northern Cameroon and Nigeria territories, and made possible by the signing of bilateral agreements with the two governments. The military operations were aimed to wipe out Boko Haram fighters and camps, resecure the supply routes of the militants and curtail further weaponization of the region. The Chadian-led offensives to dislodge the insurgents complemented the Nigerian military offensives in the subregion, and the Cameroon security forces also carried out similar complementary operations (Nasrullah 2015).

The Boko Haram Terrorists (BHTs) group transformed from being a local terrorist organization, by pledging allegiance to Islamic State in Iraq and Syria (ISIS) on March 7 2015 which was subsequently accepted by the leadership of the ISIS on March 13 2015. They claimed to have established an Islamic State in West Africa (ISWA) comprising parts of northern Cameroun and south-eastern Chad in Central Africa, as well as south-eastern region of Niger and north-eastern parts of Nigeria in West Africa. These areas form the major parts of the MNJTF area of operational responsibility (Nasrullah 2015).

Emerging Regional Security Architecture in the Lake Chad Basin: The MultiNational Joint Task Force (MNJTF)

The end of the Cold War security order has resulted in the relative neglect of armed conflicts in the global South. Following the United Nations Security Council's demand for robust transnational and regional counter-terrorism measures (Heupel 2007), states in the region have increasingly been impelled to act collectively. Against the backdrop of emerging security realities, states within the LCBC with the support of the African Union decided to form a transnational counter-terrorism measure that resulted in the expansion of the mandate of the MNJTF in the LCB. The MNJTF reflects a regional military alliance to coordinate efforts to combat the common threats to their national security posed by the Islamic fundamentalist group. This security architecture, under the ambit of a restructured MNJTF from "international border control" to "counter-terrorism," is driven by the changing dynamics of armed conflict in Africa, in particular the resurgence of violent Islamist terrorism and the geopolitics of regional powers. Reminiscence of the West African security regionalism underpinning ECOMOG in the 1990s, the MNJTF in the LCBC represents a new security frontier.

In the LCB, the geostrategic implications of Boko Haram insurgency have altered the power configuration. This has called for the necessary deployment of a security regimen. As a result of the frequency of security threats posed by Boko Haram, the LCB is undergoing the emergence of a new security order and regional configuration. As a regional power, Nigeria and its neighbors in the region realized the tremendous negative geostrategic consequences of Boko Haram transnational border attacks and demanded for the supply of collective regional security arrangements to decimate the insurgency and their associated criminalities (Tar and Bala 2019).

MNJTF reflects a regional military alliance to coordinate efforts to combat the common threat to national and collective regional security posed by the Islamic fundamentalist terrorist group. This emerging regional security architecture institutionalized a paradigm shift and change of mandate of the MNJTF from "international border control" (1990s) to "counter-terrorism" outfit (2015 +). MNJTF as a platform for African-led multilateral securitization and counter-terrorism has focused solely on interstates security dialogue, bringing together the regional defense Chiefs to coordinate region-wide counter-terrorism measures. Increased threats by Islamic radicalism have led to the integration of counter-terrorism into LCBC emerging regional security agenda (*UN News* 2016, May) (Fig. 10.1).

In January 2014, the four countries revisited the MNJTF originally formed in 1998 to deal with the cross-border security issues and extended its mandate to conduct joint military operations against Boko Haram in the Lake Chad region. At its 14th summit of heads of state and government, held in Chad in April 2012, the LCBC decided to reactivate the force and extend its mandate and operational frontier to include containing the growing regional threats of Boko Haram. The headquarters of that force previously located in the city of Baga in Nigeria's Borno State, fell in the hands of Boko Haram in 2015 (Yoroms 2008).

At the continental level, the MNJTF as regional military coalition to fight Africa's jihadists in the Lake Chad region was endorsed by

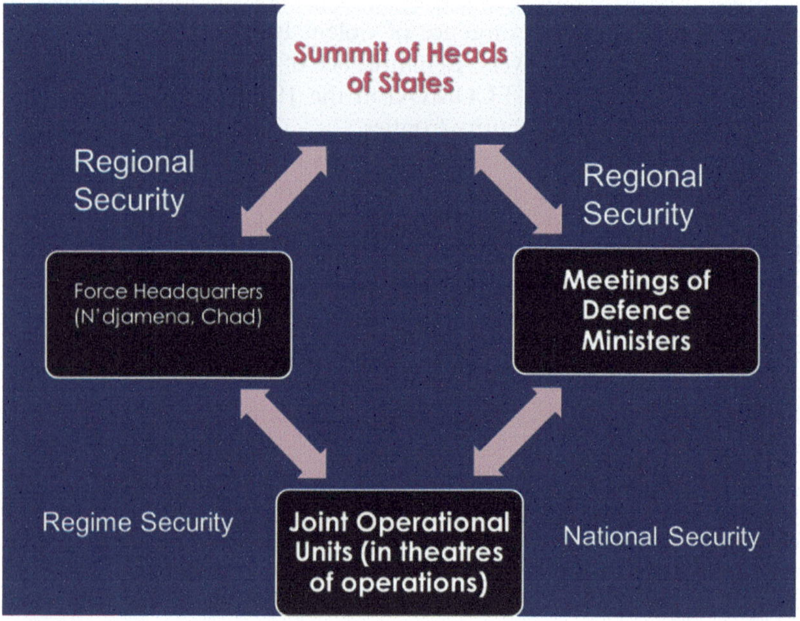

Fig. 10.1 Lake Chad Basin security architecture (*Source* Tar and Mustapha [2017, p. 108])

the African Union (AU) Peace and Security Council (PSC) during its Assembly Summit held on 29 January 2015 in Addis Ababa. The draft concept of operations (CONOPS) for the operationalization of the MNJTF was reviewed by the PSC on 3 March 2015. Member countries of the LCBC were mandated to mobilize forces to fight the terrorist group, which has increased the spate of its attacks in Cameroon, Chad, and Niger. As a follow-up to its decision of 29 January 2015, the PSC held a session on the steps being taken for the operationalization of the MNJTF against Boko Haram by the Lake Chad Basin Countries (LCBC) and Benin (Yoroms 2008).

The AU's authorization of the MNJTF was requested by member states of the LCBC—Cameroon, Chad, Niger, and Nigeria, as well as by a nonmember state, Benin, after a ministerial meeting in Niamey, Niger. It was agreed that the 8700-strong force headquartered in N'Djamena, Chad, would be authorized to exercise a "right of hot pursuit" on Nigerian soil. The LCBC member states agreed that harmonizing their operations is a crucial step in obtaining the United Nations' (UN) legitimization and possible funding for the MNJTF through a UN Security Council Resolution. At a meeting held in Yaoundé, Cameroon, on 5–7 February 2015 experts from the Lake Chad Basin Commission and the AU, with the participation of experts from the Economic Community of West African States (ECOWAS), the European Union and the UN, formally finalized the draft operational plans. The plan outlined the strategic coordination, rules of engagement, and requirements for supporting and sustaining the mission (Théroux-Bénoni 2015).

MNJTF's Strategy

In line with the decisions by the LCBC Member States, the MNJTF's mission is to operate with the AU PSC authority to eliminate BHTs in order to create a safe and secure environment and facilitate the stabilization in the areas by using all the necessary means within its capacity. It is envisioned that the MNJTF should seek and work with the support of relevant bilateral partners as well as regional and international organizations to achieve their strategic mission and mandate.

MNJTF's Mandate

Within the framework of its mandate and in its Area of Operation, the MNJTF is to carry out the following tasks, among others:

i. Conduct security operations to prevent the expansion of Boke Haram and other terrorists' group activities and eliminate their presence.
ii. Facilitate operational coordination amongst the Troops Contributing Countries (TCCs, LCBC member states, Benin, and other stakeholders in the fight against Boko Haram and other terrorist groups, including on the basis of the intelligence collected as well as other relevant African structures and/or those availed by partners.
iii. Conduct patrols and other types of operations in the area of operation.
iv. Conduct operations to disrupt the supply lines of BHTs and other terrorist groups, preventing the transfer of arms and ammunition and other types of support.
v. Ensure, upon request and within the means and capabilities of the MNJTF, the protection of civilians under immediate threat, IDP and refugee camps, humanitarian workers, and other civilian personnel.
vi. Actively search for, and free all abductees, including the young girls abducted in Chibok town of Nigeria in April 2014.

The draft concept memorandum also outlines the establishment of a Central Military Command and joint coordination mechanism that will have control over troops contributed by LCBC members and Benin. A force commander rotating among LCBC members and Benin will hold the operational command and control of the force. Although the AU's decision was to have MNJTF's force size of 7500, during the Yaoundé meeting representatives of Benin, Cameroon, Chad, Niger, and Nigeria announced that they wished to increase the size by 1200 personnel. Nigeria is the largest contributor with 3250 personnel, followed by Chad with 3000 (Agbor and Abdullahi 2017).

To achieve their mission and mandate the MNJTF adopts the following strategies (Yoroms 2008):

i. Carries on and executes security operations to regain full control of the areas under Boke Haram threats and occupation.
ii. Supports the member countries of the LCBC to effectively exercise and maintain state authority in the areas affected by the activities of Boko Haram and other bandit groups and provide protection to the civilian population under immediate threat.
iii. To ultimately ensure that the presence and influence of BHTs is completely eliminated by re-establishing the security conditions for the states to exercise full authority over the areas affected by insurgency activities; assume their responsibilities for the protection of the population, properties and livelihood means as well as regain capacity for addressing regional security and human rights challenges.

The MNJTF Command and Control Framework

The MNJTF Command Structure at Strategic, Operational, and Tactical levels are structured in a hierarchical format. First, at the strategic level, the LCBC in close coordination with the AU Commission, serves as the strategic Headquarters for the MNJTF. Secondly, at the operational level, the Operational Headquarters of the MNJTF is established in N'djamena, Chad and is staffed by personnel from LCBC Member States and Benin. It also comprises relevant bilateral and international partners, particularly from the P3 (USA, UK, and France) through the Centre for Coordination and Liaison (CCL). The MNJTF HQs and its military and civilian staff operate under the authority of the MNJTF Commander. At the tactical level, the MNJTF ground forces comprise of national contingents pledged from the countries affected by Boko Haram and other terrorist groups. The Forces comprise tactical combat units and other units deemed necessary. The MNJTF HQ facilitates the conduct of joint, simultaneous and coordinated patrols, and other types of operations. The three levels structure of the MNJTF is to ensure that each level provides the relevant support to ensure mission success (Yoroms 2008).

Despite its funding limitations, the MNJTF has thus far managed to achieve some successes against Boko Haram. In February and March 2014, the armies of the MNJTF recaptured 36 towns across three states in the northeast of Nigeria. Forces from Chad and Niger were instrumental in expelling Boko Haram from the key towns of Mallam Fatori and Damasak, killing 300 fighters in the process. It is pertinent to note that the emergence of Mohammadu Buhari as Nigeria's President in May 2015 helped to enhance the momentum and political will for a broader regional response to combat Boko Haram. Buhari had made ending the Boko Haram insurgency a key point of his electoral campaign, and shortly after assuming office, he began reforming his command structure, appointing new military service chiefs, and moving counter-terrorism center of operations to Maiduguri, the epicenter of the insurgency. He also increased regional cooperation with its neighbors—Cameroon, Chad, and Niger. In a separate but equally momentous bilateral agreement, Nigeria agreed to allow Chadian troops to enter Nigerian territory to fight Boko Haram, under the right of "hot pursuit" across its borders (Oputu and Lilley 2015).

Challenges and Prospects

The Lake Chad region is currently undergoing the emergence of a new security order and regional reconfiguration in that violent terrorism is threatening regional sociopolitical and economic security and its impact transcends national systems and affects the political stability of the region. Regional powers such as Nigeria and Chad perceived that the geostrategic implications of cross-border Islamist jihadism could only be contained by developing the architecture of cooperative security to manage the latent threats of terrorism. Nigeria appears to be the leading hegemonic power in the Lake Chad Regional Security Complex, but Nigeria's hegemony is challenged by both local and external bottlenecks. Locally, historical animosities and neocolonial linguistic differences between Francophone and Anglophone countries and, in particular, the distrust and mutual recriminations between Chad, Nigeria, and Cameroon persist with regard to perceptions of threat, responsibility, and priorities, which have adversely affected progress toward security regionalization.

Externally, France's undue influence within the West African subregion is a matter of serious concern (Tar and Mustapha 2016). France considers the Lake Chad region as an area of strategic importance, which serves the economic and political interests of Paris. Hence, France's intervention against Boko Haram only began when the group attacked Chad and Cameroun. French planes are known to be carrying out reconnaissance missions on the Nigerian border on behalf of Chad, Niger, and Cameroun, all in the name of pursuing France's strategic goals, something akin to France's support of the Gulf of Guinea countries in their resolve to securing their maritime area against Al-Shabaab (Ismail and Skons 2014).

The geopolitical realities in the LCB region have undermined a robust multinational effort aimed at combating the threats of transnational organized crimes within the region. These geopolitical realities go beyond the traditional discourse of security regionalization and involve factors that are beyond personal and national efforts. These efforts can only be achieved through a solid platform to help address the overwhelming implications of the practical issues that tend to stall the progress and coherence of strong regional security cooperation among the Lake Chad riparian states. Furthermore, the emerging geopolitics of oil on the structure and dynamic of regional balance of power has serious implications to regional stability and the emergence of the new security architecture. For example, the geostrategic competition between Nigeria as a regional hegemon and Chad over the region's oil reserve has triggered power struggles throughout Lake Chad (Didymus 2014).

The key segment of resource-control in the regional power politics is the infusion of "oil geopolitics into an already volatile mix of ecological factors pushing socioeconomic devastation of the region" (Tar and Mustapha 2016: 11). The "regionalization of neo-patrimonial interests and tendencies of accumulation" caused by the discovery and continued exploration of oil in the Chad basin has aggravated the competition among divergent regional actors, which tends to undermine the "counterterrorism and counterinsurgency" (CT-COIN) efforts in the region. This was further projected by the investment interest of powerful politicians in Chad's oil market and their selfish aspiration of having undistracted and exclusive access to oil deposits at the expense of a subregional security cooperation to tame Boko Haram insurgency. In the light of this reality, Tar and Mustapha (2016: 12) have argued that, "the oil wealth beneath the Chad Basin in which some Nigerians and Chadians have made investments is fanning the embers of insurgency in Nigeria. Vested economic interests in the crude oil exploration in the Chad Basin are fuelling the machinery of Boko Haram and its attacks on Nigeria.... Thus, both Nigeria and Chad consider the instability of the region as vital to their geopolitical interests, leading to the securitisation of competing interests that are based on geopolitics."

On the tactical front, adequate intelligence gathering within the Area of Operation (AoO) is lacking due to the absence of dedicated Intelligence Surveillance and Reconnaissance (ISR) assets. In the conduct of their operations, various sectors lack ISR assets which would have provided them with current Boke Haram disposition and probable real time imagery on the ground. Presently, the sectors rely heavily on human intelligence and other sources which may not be instantly available at the time of need. In addition, the CCL at N'Djamena provides some air reconnaissance assistance to MNJTF headquarters. It is however observed that these assets do not have the MNJTF as priority since the same machinery supports the BARKHANE operations in the Sahel region. In addition, the geography and thick largely "uncharted" vegetation of the LCB have proved to be a difficult terrain for joint military campaign. The BHTs have embedded and taken cover in the thick jungles of the LBC; dislodging them would perhaps require more boots on ground, enhanced drone technology, and higher volume of infantry and armory (Agbor 2017).

Other issues include territorial disputes, particularly in the southern shore of the Lake Chad, which has put Cameroon and Nigeria in collision course. The two countries lack an agreed harmonization of security frontier due to a long-running territorial dispute over Bakassi peninsula. Local (national) politics within some member states has also affected the dynamics of regional security in the LCB. For instance, Chad's initial passion in the joint security project has fluctuated between the "expediency" of regional security and the "reality" of regime security (Tar and Bala 2019).

Consequences of the Boko Haram Insurgency and CT-COIN for Growth and Development

Boko Haram insurgency and CT-COIN operations launched to tackle the menace of insurgency have no doubt brought about huge humanitarian crisis in the LCB, with attendant socioeconomic devastation. The LCB remains on the brink of humanitarian and environmental disaster as the Lake shrinks by as much as 90% over the past three decades with most people around having no access to clean water and suffering from avoidable malnutrition (Musa et al. 2008). The Adventist Development and Relief Agency International (ADRA) (2018) Report revealed that, 73% depreciation in the numbers of households who depend on farming as their primary source of income and livelihood depreciated from 56% prior to the insurgency. The depreciation was attributed to the limited access to farmlands because of military restriction and fear of frequent attacks by insurgents. The report further revealed that there are significant changes upwards in the prices of food and nonfood items in the market compared to the same period in 2017. Additionally, skyrocketing food prices created by scarcity and accentuated by the insecurity further compounded the dynamics of food security. For instance, in Borno and Yobe, about one in every five households is extremely vulnerable to price fluctuations as they spend more than 75% of their expenditure on food (ADRA 2018).

In a bid to tackle the resulting humanitarian crisis from Boko Haram insurgency, national governments, international organizations, and foreign partners came up with a regional Humanitarian Response Plan in September 2016 for the four LCB countries worst hit by insurgency, this plan which requires $1.5 billion remains largely unmet. Likewise, at the Oslo Humanitarian Conference on the Lake Chad Region in February 2017, Nigeria, Chad, Cameroun, Niger, and foreign donors pledged $458 m for relief in 2017 and $214 m for 2018. The fallout from this huge counterinsurgency funding by Lake Chad Member countries and the massive financial support being poured into counterinsurgency operations ensures that, human security and investments in infrastructural developments which are necessary for capital investments (including FDI) and economic growth in the Lake Chad Region are relegated to the background.

Similarly, poor security limited pastoralists' access to grazing and triggered early livestock movements, increasing competition for land (Tar and Bala 2019). These situations are further heightened by the scale of environmental insecurity caused by the crisis couple with lingering shrinkage of the Lake Chad. Climate change resulting in droughts has become a recurring feature of the Chad Basin and the occurrence of hydrological drought is in the increase as both surface and groundwater levels are decreasing below average. Desertification is influenced by both climatic and human factors and is regarded as one of the most important climatic changes making huge impacts on environmental sustainability in the LCB. Desertification caused by climate change is still impacting on vegetation cover as there is a general decline and disappearance of large trees and woody species with the disappearance of perennials of the field layer. This is in addition to the continued decline and variability in rainfall recorded within the Basin (Dami et al. 2010).

Dunn's (2018), double-difference study on the impact of Boko Haram insurgency is instructive to the dire environmental impacts of the crisis on the humanitarian and fragile security in the Lake Chad region. The study revealed that there are impacts on community and household resources, fear of attacks naturally prevents caregivers from delivering livelihood activities, health facilities, markets, water, sewage systems, and roads become inaccessible or vandalized. More particularly, civilian populace is subjected to untimely and ill-prepared migration from conflict zones which could make them vulnerable to contaminated or inadequate water, food, and other facilities as witnessed in the North east now. Insurgency and security threats in the LCB block productive and trading activities, thereby hurting the region's ability to meet growing food security needs. Simultaneously, the displacement of millions of people within and across national borders has shifted regional demographic pressures, increasing food insecurity and intensifying the precarious nutrition situations in many parts of the LCB (Lake Chad Basin Desk Review 2016).

Likewise, conflict-related displacement draws people away from their original networks of resilience, communities being physically displaced—migrations often mean people miss out on local-level networking, opportunities for entrepreneurship, or other fundamental survival strategies. Productive activities, including agriculture, fishing, livestock rearing, and the trade of the respective products, have been interrupted by episodes of Boko Haram's insurgency and systemic violence—community assets and food reserves have been destroyed, which contributes to an already severe problem of food security and prevalence of Global Acute Malnutrition (GAM) in parts of the Lake Chad region (Lake Chad Basin Desk Review 2016). No doubt, the economic impact of Boko Haram insurgency in the LCB is multifaceted, as investors unsurprisingly avoid areas identified as likely sources of terrorist attacks. For instance, in Borno and Yobe states in North-East, Nigeria, the flow of economic activities, especially in the areas of beans and fish markets have continued to dwindle due to the fear of terrorist attacks.

According to Apenda and Tough (2015), farmers who produce onions, rice, maize, livestock, pepper, and fish have all fled the LCB, as Baga international market, known for fish trading has been forced to close due to security concerns. In Cameroun, Boko Haram crisis resulted in a 25% drop in cereal production in the northern part of the country in 2016, when compared against the output in 2015. Furthermore, in Adamaoua, food insecurity increased from 19% in early 2016 to 39% in 2015, as about 65,000 Cameroun children under the age of five were thought to be suffering from severe malnutrition (Comolli 2017).

Conclusion

The Chad Basin is evidently a security complex in terms of the broad attributes identified by Buzan and Waever (2003) in theory of regional security complex, which in this context will include sharing the Lake and its resources, interlocking geographical proximity, sociocultural linkages, and shared threats to national and regional security.

Emerging trends suggest that Nigeria, the region's hegemonic power, has been overwhelmed by inherent internal contradictions that have whittled down its power, this is manifested in the inability of the Nigerian government to constructively handle and end Boko Haram revolt within the initial few years of its emergence as a minor internal dissent. Consequently, Nigeria has been brokering the support of countries to put in place a new regional security architecture—the MNJTF, under the aegis of the LCBC. The Task forces have so far worked hard to confront the threat posed by Boko Haram, albeit with modest success. Regional geopolitics and the rough terrain of the Chad Basin have continued to pose a herculean task for the member states of the Chad Basin Commission.

Acknowledgements This chapter draws from Prof Usman Tar's Paper for Workshop on *Security Force Assistance*, jointly hosted by the Kofi Anan International Peacekeeping Training Centre (KAIPTC) and the Peace Research Institute Oslo (PRIO) held at Best Western Hotel Accra on 3–5 September 2019. Prof Tar is grateful to Dr Øystein H. Rolandsen and Nic Marsh of PRIO for their constructive input to the workshop paper.

References

Abubakar, D. 2017. From Sectarianism to Terrorism in Northern Nigeria: A Closer Look at Boko Haram. In *Violent Non-State Actors in Africa: Terrorists*, ed. C. Varin and A. Dauda, 17–47. Rebels and Warlords: Palgrave Macmillan.

ADRA. 2018. *Food Security & Livelihood Assessment Report North-East Nigeria, 30th April*. Adventist Development and Relief Agency International (ADRA). https://reliefweb.int/report/nigeria/food-security-livelihood-assessment-report-north-east-nigeria-april-2018. Accessed on 23 March 2020.

Agbor, T.I., and L.F. Abdullahi. 2017. Taming the Monster: Boko Haram. In *Global Terrorism: The Nigerian Experience in Taming Boko Haram*, ed. M. Mohammed and L.F. Abdullahi, 172–187. Headquarters Nigerian Army: Abuja.

Apenda, I.T., and B.T. Tough. 2015. Terrorism and Boko Haram: Reconsideration of Impacts on World Peace. *International Affairs and Global Strategy* 37: 97–103.

Buza, B., and O. Wæver. 2003. *Regions and Powers: The Structure of International Security*. Cambridge: Cambridge University Press.

Cocodia, J. 2017. Nationalist Sentiment, Terrorist Incursions and the Survival of the Malian State. In *Violent Non-State Actors in Africa*, ed. C. Varin and D. Abubakar, 49–74. New York: Palgrave Macmillan.

Comolli, V. 2017. The Evolution and Impact of Boko Haram in the Lake Chad Basin. https://odihpn.org/magazine/the-evolution-and-impact-of-boko-haram-in-the-lake-chad-basin/. Accessed on 23 March 2020.

Dami, A., F.A. Adesina, and N.O. Adeoye. 2010. The Impact of Drought and Desertification in the Lake Chad Basin Region. *Journal of Environmental Issues and Agriculture in Developing Countries* 2 (2–3): 92–102.

Didymus, J.H. 2014. Boko Haram Crisis and the Regional Geopolitics of Oil. http://ends.ng/boko-haram-crisis-and-the-regional-geopolitics-of-oil-part-1-by-john-thomas-didymus/. Accessed on 23 February 2020.

Dunn, G. 2018. The Impact of the Boko Haram Insurgency in Northeast Nigeria on Childhood Wasting: A Double-Difference Study. *Journal of Conflict and Health* 12 (1): 2–12.

Flemes, D., and S.E. Lobell. 2015. Contested Leadership in International Relations. *International Politics* 52 (42): 139–145.

Gourley, S.M. 2012. Linkages Between Boko Haram and al Qaeda: A Potential Deadly Synergy. *Global Security Studies* 3 (3): 1–14.

Hansel, W. 2017. Boko Haram: Religious Radicalism and Insurrection in Northern Nigeria. *Journal of Asian and African Studies* 52 (4): 551–569.

Heupel, M. 2007. Adapting to Transnational Terrorism: The UN Security Council's Evolving Approach to Terrorism. *Security Dialogue* 38 (4): 477–499.

Ismail, O., and E. Skons. 2014. *Security Activities of External Actors in Africa*. Oxford: Oxford University Press.

Lake Chad Basin Desk Review. 2016. WFP Remote Access Secure Services. Desk Review, April 2016. documents.wfp.org/stellent/groups/public/documents/ena/wfp284135.pdf. Accessed on 11 March 2020.

Maiangwa, J.S., and A.R. Audu. 2017. Civilians in Frontlines: Evolving Grassroots Force for Counterinsurgency Operations in the Lake Chad Basin Region. In *Defence Transformation and the Consolidation of Democracy in Nigeria*, ed. U.A. Tar, 297–318. Kaduna: Nigerian Defence Academy Press.

Mohammed, N.S. 2017. The Niger Delta Avengers, Autonomous Ethnic Clans and Common Claim Over Oil Wells: The Paradox of Resource Control. *African Research Review* 11 (12): 42–55. https://doi.org/10.4314/afrrev.v11i2.4.

Musa, I.K., M. Bila, B. Mana, and C. Mahaman. 2008 Saving Lake Chad. *Proceedings of Sirte roundtable, Lake Chad Basin Commission (LCBC) and International Commission on Irrigation and Drainage (ICID)*, 17 December, Libya. http://afrwg.icidonline.org/save_lakechad.pdf. Accessed on 21 January 2020.

Nasrullah, F. 2015. *The Expanding War in the Lake Chad*. http://fulanisitrep.com/2015/11/19/the-expanding-war-in-the-lake-chad. Accessed on 21 August 2019.

Onuoha, F.C. 2014. A Danger Not to Nigeria Alone: Boko Haram's Transnational Reach and Regional Responses. http://www.library.fes.de/pdf-files/bueros/nigeria/. Accessed on 23 December 2019.

Oputu, D., and K. Lilley. 2015. Boko Haram and Escalating Regional Terror. Retrieved: http://soufangroup.com/tsg-intelbrief-boko-haram-and-escalating-regional-terror. Accessed on 25 December 2019.

Tar, U.A., and B. Bala. 2018. Boko Haram Insurgency, Terrorism and the Challenges of Peacebuilding in the Lake Chad Basin. In *Peacebuilding in Contemporary Africa: In Search of Alternative Strategies*, ed. K.C. Omeje, 142–165. London: Routledge.

Tar, U.A., and B. Bala. 2019. Terrorism, Insurgency and the Challenges of Counter-Terrorism and Counterinsurgency. In *New Architecture for Regional Security in Africa: Perspectives on Counter-Terrorism and Counterinsurgency in the Lake Chad Basin*, ed. U.A. Tar and B. Bala, 267–293. Lanham, MD: Lexington Books.

Tar, U.A., and M. Mustapha. 2016. Emerging Architecture of Regional Security Complex in the Lake Chad Basin. Being a Paper Presented at the *International Conference on Security Regimens in Africa*, organised by CODESERIA, Held at Azalai Grand Hotel, Bamako, Mali, 28–29 September.

Tar, U.A., and M. Mustapha. 2017. The Emerging Architecture of a Regional Security Complex in the Lake Chad Basin. *Africa Development* 42 (3): 99–118.

Théroux-Bénoni, L.A. 2015. The Fight Against Boko Haram Tangled up in Nigerian and Regional Politics. Institute for Security Studies. https://www.issafrica.org/iss-today/the-fight-against-boko-haram-tangled-up-in-nigerian-and-regional-politics. Accessed on 23 September 2019.

UN News. 2016. UN Security Council Demands Boko Haram End All Violence in Lake Chad Basin. *UN News*, 13 May 2016. https://news.un.org/en/story/2016/05/529252-security-council-demands-boko-haram-immediately-end-all-violence-lake-chad. Accessed on 23 August 2019.

Vanguard Newspaper. 2016. Buhari Hosts French President, Hollande, Biya, Others at Abuja Security Summit. *Vanguard New Paper*, 10 May 2016. http://www.vanguardngr.com. Accessed on 23 November 2019.

Vanguard Newspaper. 2017. Terrorized UNIMAID Residents: Eight Boko Haram attacks in Six Months and a Professor Dead. 23 July 2017. https://www.vanguardngr.com/2017/07/terrorized-unimaid-residents-eight-boko-haram-attacks-six-months-professor-dead-unprecedented-siege/. Accessed on 20 March 2020.

Yoroms, G.J. 2008. Counterterrorism Measures in West Africa. In *Understanding Terrorism in Africa: Building Bridges and Overcoming the Gaps*, ed. O. Wofula and B. Annedi, 90–97. Institute of Security Studies: Pretoria.

CHAPTER 11

The AU, RECs, and the Politics of Security Regionalism in Africa

Sabastiano Rwengabo

Introduction

The African Union (AU) faces the challenge of crafting regional peace and security institutions that consolidate sub-continental inter-state cooperation and align it to the singular goal of "Rising Africa", to the desired continental transformation. In 2002, the continental body created the African Standby Force (ASF), a creditable response to the myriad peace and security challenges hitherto facing the continent. The ASF was operationalised via Regional Brigades. Some Brigades are not aligned to pre-existing sub-regional inter-governmental organisations, termed Regional Economic Communities (RECs) in Africa's political lingo. Conceived to be structural constituents of the AU, RECs already handled peace and security issues within their respective regions by the late 1990s (Touray 2005; Franke 2010). The operational disconnect between the ASF and RECs is puzzling and problematic.

During the 2000s, the realisation that Africa must fend for itself in addressing her peace and security problems resulted from the waning

S. Rwengabo (✉)
Research Division, Centre for Basic Research (CBR), Kampala, Uganda
e-mail: rwengabo@u.nus.edu

K. Omeje (ed.), *The Governance, Security and Development Nexus*,
https://doi.org/10.1007/978-3-030-49348-6_11

interest of foreign powers to address Africa's post-Cold War insecurities. There were also misgivings about the motives of western interventions in Africa, especially following the relegation of Somalia after 1991, non-response to a preventable genocide in 1994 Rwanda, and the United Nations (UN)'s slow response to devastating civil wars in Liberia and Sierra Leone where the Economic Community of West African States (ECOWAS) Ceasefire Monitoring Group (ECOMOG) struggled for years before the UN surfaced (Boulden 2003; Jaye et al. 2011). The resulting pan-African desire to find "African Solutions to African problems" sowed seeds of "Africa Rising" to the occasion of taking responsibility to handle its conflict and security challenges. This created incentives for pursuing institutional and structural changes in the AU to enable the AU and regional structures to more effectively respond to conflict and security threats (Touray 2005; Sessay et al. 2009). The Constitutive Act of the AU provided for creation of the AU Peace and Security Council (AUPSC). Under the attendant 2002 Protocol, the ASF was created with Regional Brigades to operationalise the Council's mandate by responding to peace and security threats within regions (AU 2000; AU 2002). Headquartered in Addis Ababa and with a Continental Logistics Base (LOGBASE) in Douala, Cameroon, the ASF's Regional Brigades, which act as rapid-response units, include: East African Standby Force (EASF); ECOWAS Standby Force (ESF); North African Regional Capability (NARC); SADC Standby Force (SSF); and the Economic Community of Central African States Standby Force or Force Multinationale de l'Afrique Centrale (FOMAC) (AU 2010: 37–52). This mechanism constitutes the African Peace and Security Architecture (APSA) (Vines 2013; Van Nieuwkerk 2011; Franke 2009).

These structural changes appeared to indicate an Africa Rising and taking control of her security domain (Rwengabo 2013; AU 2004a, b). Sections of "Africa Rising" scholarship underscores this development, precisely continental formations that constitute the APSA, and recognises the demonstrable political will by which the APSA-founding instruments were developed (Touray 2005; Bah 2010; Van Nieuwkerk 2011). Others underscore Africa's capacity gaps vis-à-vis realisation of these objectives (Kent and Malan 2003; Franke 2009; Vines 2013). Some underscore the limiting influence of state-sovereignty concerns on security cooperation in a continent where states are tenaciously holding onto their highly coveted "meta-political authority" (Rwengabo 2017). Limited effort, however, highlights the challenges this process poses for AU-level assessment of the performance and effectiveness of these Brigades when they have overlapping mandates with RECs' security structures (Rwengabo 2016b).

In this chapter, I combine a governance analytic lens with Principal–Agent views. I view the crafting of regional inter-governmental organisations like the AU and sub-regional RECs as a governance effort to manage resources, opportunities, technologies, relationships, interests, and fears, within a given geo-social space, for the benefit of peoples inhabiting that space. By logical connotation, the Creators of structures can be regarded as Principals and Created structures as Agents, which ostensibly gives rise to a Principal–Agent relationship between the Creators and the Created. Drawing upon literature on the evolution of regionalism in Africa, I question the establishment of the ASF's Regional Brigades with limited consideration for the membership, and the peace and security interests of RECs, which antedated these Brigades. I consider AU-level structures and RECs as levels of governance below the UN but above nation-states, yet the AU is a uniquely placed Principal in and of its own right, which delegates security functions to RECs and Regional Brigades. The irony is highlighted accordingly: while many RECs, such as EAC and ECOWAS, already had security-cooperation arrangements that were not unknown to the AU by the time the Protocol Relating to the Establishment of the Peace and Security Council of the African Union was completed in 2002, the negotiators of the Protocol went ahead and created Regional Brigades without aligning them to pre-existing RECs, specifically in Eastern Africa (AU 2002).

Aware that RECs are touted as sub-regional economic-development structures, I maintain that there is a theoretical, empirical, and acknowledged experiential relationship between security and development, which had necessitated the incorporation of security-cooperation measures within RECs (Rwengabo 2017). AU-level decisions regarding regional security measures under the continental body ought to have been constructed in keeping with already-existing RECs. In accordance with this expectation, a Memorandum of Understanding (MoU) exists between RECs and the AU (AU 2008). While not explaining this disconnect, I show that misalignment between Regional Brigades and RECs results in organisational overlaps and difficulties of assessing performance and responsibility in sub-regional security governance. This overlap is shown in Eastern Africa, where the Regional Brigade, the East African Standby Force (EASF), is not aligned to two RECs that handle peace and security within the region: the East African Community (EAC), and the Inter-Governmental Authority on Development (IGAD). These RECs have security obligations that overlap and seemingly compete with EASF-related security expectations—possibly explaining why the EASF has been slow to metamorphose and less responsive to the region's peace and security issues (Rwengabo 2016b).

The first section of this chapter outlines the analytic perspective used to assess the ironical misalignment of Regional Brigades and RECs. The second draws from a governance perspective to show that the AU and RECs below it are levels of governance theoretically best positioned to address problems at their respective levels. The third examines the EASF and shows why it ought to have been aligned to one of or both RECs in Eastern Africa. The fourth and concluding section summarises main arguments and draws implications.

Regionalism as Governance: An Analytic Perspective

Regionalism revolves around the politics of cooperation between states as sovereign political entities within a given geographical region. The politics of regionalism, therefore, is essentially a politics of allocation of political goods, values, and negotiation of interests within a region. Unlike intra-national regionalism, which consists in domestic hierarchy under federalism and/or decentralisation wherein Central/Federal states retain policymaking and allocation powers over strategic issues, inter-State regionalism demands trading off sovereign powers in exchange for collective benefits. This is why sovereignty bargaining is a central process in regionalism (Rwengabo 2017; Litfin 1997). The incentive to act via regional organisations (ROs) (Abbot and Snidal 1998), therefore, influences the willingness and ability of rational political actors, states, to balance their selfish interests with expectations of collective/shared benefits at a point of [at least minimum] interest convergence. The crafting of cooperation rules—regional Treaties, Agreements, Protocols—and structural formations or organisations to implement these commitments usually results from lengthy political bargaining processes. Bargains are the harbinger of international institutions the effectiveness of which is a subject of debate between neorealist and neoliberal theorists (Baldwin 1993; Jervis 1982; Glaser 1994/1995). Beyond this debate, regionalism has become an indispensable aspect of international politics in a post-World War II world (Acharya and Johnson 2007).

Since 1945, the historical trajectory of regionalism changed for three reasons. First, while pre-1945 alliances and other inter-State cooperation forms were mainly concerned with defence-offence imperatives against enemy State(s), mainly in Europe, post-1945 cooperation was globalised. The League of Nations became the UN, arrogated to itself the mandate of global cooperation, and became the embodiment of global governance for the provision of global political goods. The UN's role evolved beyond security as many agencies handling non-security issues have proliferated. Second, the UN, acknowledging problems which are best addressed at regional than global and national levels, made provisions under Chapter 8 allowing for ROs to emerge in different regions provided they are "consistent with the Purposes and Principles of the United Nations" (UN 1945). Finally, other challenges made it imperative for the UN to decentralise: Cold War challenges; proliferation of ROs in different parts of the world, some without referring to the UN; threats of nuclear war; and increasing global interconnections. These challenges triggered a debate on whether the UN would be efficacious as a universal, security-centred, western-dominated entity or if other governance levels were worthwhile. Pro-regionalism intellectuals within and outside the UN saw ROs as "a natural outgrowth of international cooperation and desirable stepping-stones toward world organisation"; as "indispensable elements in [the UN's] successful growth and functioning" (Wilcox 1965: 789). Opposition from the "universalist" reasoners, who opposed regionalism, was tamed. This gave rise to regionalism as part of international governance in which international organisations are centres of politics and processes of such governance (Karns and Mingst 2009).

The "Governance Perspective", therefore, need not view the UN as a supra-state entity but as an Agent of states, created and assigned to help realise Principals'/States' interests. This is why the "Big Five", who control the UN Security Council, seek to monopolise Veto Power within the otherwise global organisation. From this viewpoint, IOs and ROs are states' constructions in a post-World War II international system. A scholarly body of knowledge, encapsulated in the Journal International Organization, focuses on organised international cooperation. From this perspective, regionalism is a political process of pursuing states' collective regional interests through organised cooperation. ROs and sub-regional organisations are regional mechanisms for inter-State cooperation (Young 1999: 50–132). Much of today's international cooperation takes place below the UN but above the nation-State; in the African context, it occurs below the AU but above the nation-states straddling the African geopolitical landscape. ROs address region-specific problems, which may be difficult or too distanced from all-inclusive IOs like the UN and AU and also beyond states' capacity to unilaterally address (Claude, Jr. 1964; Gitelson 1973; Rwengabo 2017).

The foregoing viewpoint raises three theoretical and empirical implications. First, if IOs and ROs are formed by states, then they are Agents of states through which states act in pursuit of their interests (Abbot and Snidal 1998). Many students of regionalism take this Principal–Agent relationship as a given, giving it inadequate analytic attention. Second, the Principal–Agent Problem is assumed possibly because this economic theory of agency as applied in Political Science seems obvious. Hence, Solingen's (1998) analysis of the role of coalition politics in regionalism; Acharya's (2009) "norm diffusion" thesis; Hemmer and Katzenstein's (2002) study of differential security regionalisms; Mansfield and Solingen's synthesis of "regionalism" (2010); as well as Tavares (2008, 2009), Olonisakin (2011), De Waal (2009), and Franke's (2010) optimism about evolving security cooperation in Africa reflect this link but pay limited analytic attention to the Principal–Agent dynamics of security regionalism.

The challenge of regionalism, from a Principal–Agent perspective, relates to how to create Agent structures that serve Principals' interests at different levels. Multi-level principalhood and agenthood exist in regionalism, which creates decisional and operational difficulties. First, the UN expects organisations like the EU or AU to act "consistent with its objectives and Principles", as though they are UN agents, even when some may pursue independent interests. Second, the UN itself, being an Agent, has difficulties coercing IOs/ROs that are themselves equally states' Agents despite possible unequal positionings of these Agents. Third, a similar problem afflicts security cooperation in Africa: the continental AU with its AUPSC is an Agent for AU member-States at continental level. While mandated by these Principals to operate through sub-regional ROs with wide-ranging mandates, including security, the ROs are also Agents of the same Principals of the AU. The realisation of security objectives expected of the AUPSC requires that delegated responsibilities of the Council are executed by sub-continental Agents, hence creating an Agent acting through other Agents.

Principal–Agent theory assumes a relationship between a Principal and an Agent. In this relationship, the Principal is the actor, the Agent is the means to an end, the channel for action. The Principal acts through the

Agent in pursuit of clearly defined interests. Responsibility for outcomes, that is, effectiveness and efficiency, of action lies not with the Agent but the Principal (Ross 1973; Rees 1985). The Principal is expected to provide material, financial, technological and moral-ethical support and mandate to the Agent to act in desired ways. If the Agent be an independent actor, such as a smaller state (proxy) used by a stronger state (the hegemon) to purse regional interests through that proxy, then a reward mechanism is agreed upon through an Agreement (secret or open, depending on the issue) or other forms of promised support or reward in exchange for the Agent's work.

The Principal may lose control over the process and outcomes of the pursuit when the Agent makes and implements independent decisions. If the Principal has chosen an incentive scheme to maximise expected utility the Agent's utility may not remain unchanged or stationary. Given these challenges, there may be an optimal way of implementing the Principal's desired action by the Agent. But when goal conflict arises between Principals and Agents, the later may have more information, access, and space for manoeuvrability within that situation, than their Principals. This may cause information and power asymmetry between them, sacrificing the Principal's interests at the altar of the Agent's benefits and benefits (Ross 1973; Rogerson 1985; Watermann and Meier 1998). The Problem may also arise when the Agent desires or chooses to pursue other interests beyond the relationship with the Principal but using Agential advantage.

These viewpoints assume unilinear relationships between Principals and Agents. They may be inadequate to complexities and multi-level existences of Principals and Agents, where Agents at one point are Principals at another level, all subject to Core Principles. They do not address the third and fourth source of the problem and how these sources affect decisional and operational imperatives of Principal–Agent relations in international politics. The third source may be the problem of control over the Agent under two conditions: (i) conditions of failure or difficulty in getting an alternative Agent when the original Agent acts unexpectedly, is seen to be incompetent, becomes too expensive in demands and rewards compared to expeted and/or actual returns on the Principal's investment, that is, when the relationship degenerates to what may be here called an "Inefficient Principal–Agent Relationship"; and (ii) inability of the Principal to change the course of the pursuit even if at some point it becomes apparent to the Principal that the outcome is likely to be less rewarding and yet the Agent has to be compensated, herein called "Tied-Up Commitments in Principal–Agent relationships" as reflected in difficulties countries face trying to defect from international agreements: Brexit exemplifies the difficulty of leaving the EU. Even when the original decision was Britain's sovereign decision, the country could not just walk away from the EU. Difficult negotiations have had to follow a referendum in Britain as though the voice of British citizens is inconclusive on Brexit. This Brexit-EU experience raises questions of whether the EU was, in reality, an Agent acting partly on behalf of Britain as one of the Principals, but viewed critically it signals tied-up commitments in principal-agent relationships in which many states find themselves entangled.

The fourth source of the Principal–Agent Problem in regionalism entails multi-level existence of Principals and Agents with competing interests. Typical of international cooperation in Africa, this complexity results from extended chains of delegation, vested and sometimes competing actors' interests, and challenges of information and incentives distortion that afflict other international organisations (Vaubel 2006). In Africa, there are what one may call "sub-Africas" within Africa, sub-organisations within a continental organisation, and states' nested belongings in multiple organisations. In these multiple and interlocking spaces, states are positioned in different levels of Principalhood. A state is a Principal at AU level and at sub-regional level where the AU is expected to be acting through the Agent, the RO. Now the Principal, an AU member-State, appears to be at once a Principal and an Agent. We therefore have what are herein called "Core Principles", then "Mid-Range Principles", and then Agents. Core Principles are member-States of the AU acting through AU structures to pursue common interests. Here, Core Principals can be assumed to have acquired convergence of interest, a minimum requirement in forming international regimes and institutions (Stein 1993) like the AU. Mid-Range Principles are AU institutions, in this case the AUPSC, which, though Agents of Core Principles, are also Principles in relation to sub-continental Agents at regional level, like the EASF, to which the implementation of the APSA is delegated. The Final Agents and Mid-Range Agents are all at once Agents of the Core Principals, the states. These parallelisms and overlaps are to be seen in the ASF's regional unit, the EASF.

The EASF: Parallelism and Overlaps with RECs

From a Principal–Agent viewpoint, the AU, though an Agent, has characteristics of a Principal: delegation powers, oversight over regional actors, and mandate to sanction [non]compliance with continental rules. In this relationship, ROs/RECs like IGAD, SADC, ECOWAS, and EAC, perform security roles that are consistent with continental rules. If RECs already have security-cooperation obligations, AU-level security formations that impact upon RECs ought to be tailored to already-existing structures and processes for efficient allocation of time and resources, operational consistency, mutuality of regional courses of action, and harmonisation of interests. This is crucial because AU-level Core Principals are the same Principals at RECs levels. It follows that the EASF, and RECs in Eastern Africa, IGAD and the EAC specifically, are structurally disjointed. They cannot act as Agents of the middle Principal, the AU as well as of core Principals, the states behind both the AU and RECs. This raises important conceptual and empirical concerns on the politics of security regionalism and "Africa Rising".

In security parlance, the notion of Africa Rising is consistent with the evolution of institutions that address the continent's peace and security problems (AU 2004a, b). The APSA comprises the institutions charged with the task of providing a peaceful and secure environment for Africa's transformation. It is rooted in the Constitutive Act of the AU; the Protocol establishing the AUPSC; and the MoU between the AU and RECs on peace and security cooperation. The Constitutive Act reflects states' consciousness about, and concern with, "the scourge of conflicts in Africa" as a major impediment to the continent's socio-economic development; the "prevalence of armed conflicts in Africa"; and the human and non-human impact of these crises (AU 2000, Preamble; AU 2004b). Undeniably, states in this Act seek to act through AU institutions like the AUPSC, Panel of the Wise, Continental Early Warning System, Common Defence Policy (Franke 2009), and peace and security department for coordination purposes. The created ASF is an agential structure (AU 2000, Art. 11–13). It echos Nkrumah's earlier vision of a pan-African common defence policy and structure (Touray 2005). This neither materialised in Nkumah's Africa which should have been continentally united nor in Nyerere's Africa where RECs would be functional building blocks for continental unity. The Nkrumah-Nyerere challenge had, by the time the ASF was constituted, become more complicated: the issue is no longer regional versus continental unity, but how to harmonise the interests of 54 "Sovereign" states now straddling Africa's regionalised geopolitical landscape.

The ASF is regionalised into Regional Brigades as rapid-response units: EASF for Eastern Africa; the ESF for West African states under ECOWAS; the NARC covering the Arab-Maghreb Union; the SSF for Southern Africa; and FOMAC covering Africa's central region (AU 2010: 37–52). The Brigades are conceived of not as stand-alone structures from the ASF but as its implementation structures. But because they are "Regional" in nature, they are sub-continental, fused with pre-existing, below-OAU/AU structures, the RECs. The AU, then, faces a challenge of coordinating these distinct regional formations under one body. With the exception of the ESF in West Africa, SSF in Southern Africa and FOMAC in Central Africa, the mechanisms for the EASF and the NARC "are not managed by RECs" but are stand-alone structures spanning ROs (AU 2008, Art. 1). These two Regional Brigades raise important questions about pre-ASF regionalism, and whether and why Principal–Agent problems have been overcome. If, as stated in the Constitutive Act (Art. 4), sovereignty, independence, decisional autonomy, sovereign equality, and interdependence must be upheld, then: (i) inter-state relations within the EASF and the NARC ought to be freed from prior commitments under the RECs, or (ii) Brigades and REC sought to be harmonised. This would reduce the Principal–Agent Problem of decisional autonomy, responsibility for [non-]actions and sanctioning mechanisms, but also enable consistency in the regional structuring of the continental ASF.

The EASF consists of Burundi, Comoros, Ethiopia, Djibouti, Kenya, Rwanda, Seychelles, Somalia, South Sudan, Sudan, Tanzania, and Uganda. These countries straddle RECs like the EAC, ECCAS, IGAD, and SADC, as well as the issue-based International Conference for the Great Lakes Region (ICGLR 2004, 2006). The EASF, an ASF structure, displays parallelism and overlap related to coordination between RECs and Regional Brigades. The first challenge here is this: the AUPSC is hard-pressed to meet the objective of promoting peace and security in Africa, because non-interference in states' internal affairs (AU 2008, Art. 4) renders the viability of such a pursuit questionable. This is so despite the existence of "Intervention-Threshold Principles" that grant the AUPSC some intervention mandate "under very limited circumstances", or grave circumstances (Rwengabo 2016b). Were the Council to acquire structures that are autonomous enough to confine states within specified Regional Brigades or security commitments, the Council would be able to attribute failure or success to given Brigades.

The second challenge is the relationship between the EASF and the RECs in Eastern Africa—IGAD, which covers eastern Africa and the Horn, bringing other states in the same regional arrangement with EAC Partner states; and the EAC, which combines IGAD member states (Kenya, South Sudan, Uganda) with SADC founding member, Tanzania. The delinking of the EASF and NARC from RECs may have arisen from the observed challenge of regionalism within Eastern and Northern Africa that antedated the ASF. To this challenge the AU ought to have first paid considerable attention in order to determine whether disconnect between the NARC and EASF from RECs within these respective regions addressed the daunting peace and security question. In Eastern Africa, however, the EASF is independent of IGAD, for it was not fused with pre-existing structures under that REC. It is autonomous from the EAC because it could not be coordinated under the EAC secretariat's Peace and Security Directorate because other states covered by the EASF are not EAC Partner States. Eventually, the EASF is a trans-regional structure. This cobweb edifice creates Principal–Agent challenges in implementing the MoU between the AU, Regional Brigades, and RECs.

Since the APSA's implementation mechanism includes continental, regional, and national structures (Panel of the Wise, Continental EWS, ASF, Military Staff Committee, and a Special Fund), the AUPSC is "a standing decision-making organ" with wide-ranging decision-making powers and functions (AU 2002 Art. 2; Constitute Act, Art. 5[2]). It is Africa's forum for promoting peace, security, stability, conflicts management, and collective crisis response. But the AUPSC implements the AU's Common African Defence and Security Policy (CADSP). It is accountable to the AU Assembly of Heads of States, especially on interventions in grave circumstances. It monitors the APSA's implementation while ensuring that external peace and security initiatives take place "within the framework of the Union's objectives and priorities" (AU 2002, Articles. 3–5). If the AUPSC is a decision-making organ, as the Protocol states, and again a decision-making Agent and implementation mechanism for the CADSP, then its relationship with Regional Brigades is, to a great degree, a Principal–Agent relationship. The question is: to whom does the AUPSC direct its decisional demands—the EASF or RECs?

The third change is that both IGAD and the EAC have security-cooperation arrangements. The role of IGAD in Somalia's post-1991 peace and security crises makes security cooperation under IGAD imperative (Rwengabo 2016a, 2016b). IGAD's role in Sudan and South Sudan, specifically in mediating and resolving post-2005 armed conflicts South Sudan, also demonstrates security-cooperation commitment within the REC. In December 2013, IGAD Heads of State and Government flew to Juba to resolve the ongoing conflict in South Sudan. Lacking impartiality, neutrality, and cohesion due to competing interests between the already-deeply involved Uganda and Sudan over the conflict, IGAD's intervention led to little more than a Cessation of Hostilities Agreement (CoHA) of 9 January 2014 (Rupia 2016: 13). A Troika-imposed agreement followed in 2016, and an IGAD-led Revitalisation Process led to the signing of a peace deal in Khartoum on 12th September 2018. Under the Khartoum deal, Dr. Riek Machar returned to Juba in October 2018 for a peace ceremony that ostensibly marked the end of his armed contestation against President Salva Kiir's government (*Daily Monitor*, Wednesday, October 31, 2018; VoA News, Wednesday, October 31 2018). Interventions under the AfSol—a concept that emerged in 2009 within the ambit of the APSA concerned with the "Elimination of Conflicts in Africa and the Promotion of Sustainable Peace" through AU and sub-regional actors like RECs—have had mixed results judging from South Sudan and Lesotho (Rupia 2016). In both Somalia and South Sudan, the EASF was visibly absent. The REC, IGAD, was left to shoulder the burden in which states, specifically Uganda, which would have deployed under the EASF, were too compromised to constitute the ASF's neutral Regional Brigade. But the demonstrable role of IGAD raises questions on the wisdom behind the provision that the EASF and the NARC "are not managed by RECs" but are stand-alone structures spanning ROs (AU 2008, Art. 1).

Finally, African states have different levels of commitment under different regional structures. Under the EAC, the Treaty and Protocols which are appendages to, and constituent parts of, that Treaty, are binding to Partner States that ratified it almost in equal standing to national constitutions (EAC 1999). New Partner States, such as Rwanda, Burundi, and South Sudan who are latecomers, joined "as is". Even if they take part in negotiations of Protocols, they are Treaty-bound. Prior to the APSA, security cooperation in the EAC had evolved. The MoU on cooperation in defence affairs reached in 1998 (EAC 1998), when Treaty negotiations were still ongoing, was adapted to the Treaty in 2001. The 1999 Treaty (amended 2006, 2007—especially Chapter 23) is explicit on security-cooperation commitments. A Protocol on Cooperation in Defence Affairs replaced the MoU in 2012, and a Protocol on Peace and Security Cooperation was reached in 2012 (EAC 2012a, b). Consistent with continental obligations, the Nairobi Protocol for the Prevention, Control and Reduction of Small Arms and Light Weapons in the Great Lakes Region and the Horn of Africa is also acknowledged in the EAC because it falls under the Bamako Declaration (African Common Position) on the Illicit Proliferation, Circulation and Trafficking of small arms and light weapons (SALWs) (RECSA 2000a, 2000b, 2004; AU/Bamako Declaration 2000). Commitments like UN conventions on terrorism, or the "Dar-es-Salaam Declaration" are not as binding to EAC Partner States as is the Treaty or Protocols; they are respected only to the extent of their consistency with the EAC Treaty.

While EASF decisions are made by the AU Assembly of Heads of States and ministerial Council, with advice from Panel of the Wise, EAC decisions are made by the ministerial Council, indicating lower levels of top-level involvement in decisional processes. EASF-related decisions are dependent on state acceptance than EAC decisions, which, once ratified, become part of national law. Under the EASF, states' willingness, contributions, are more voluntary. There is no institutional pressure to ignite political will. Institutional incoherence under the EASF can be common. The EAC's legislative organ, the East African Legislative Assembly (EALA), however, can legislate and make regional laws that are then subjected to national processes and result in binding commitments. This implies that there is higher institutional pressure, and organisational frameworks, processes, and opportunities, for forcing state action under the EAC than under the EASF (Rwengabo 2016b). This perhaps explains why the EASF could not be constituted to intervene in Somalia as a Regional Brigade: instead, Kenya intervened unilaterally and Uganda and Burundi joined the AU umbrella before Kenya belatedly joined the AMISOM.

Within the EAC, engagements between Defence Attaches and peace and security experts have been taking place since 2001 (Rwengabo 2017) as though oblivious of the Regional Brigade/EASF. By the time the 2013 and 2016 eruptions in South Sudan took place, the EAC boasted of peace and security and defence protocols, a long history of defence, and peace and security cooperation. These opportunities would have been galvanised to assist the EAC's troubled new Partner State. By then the EASF had been being constituted for more than a decade (Vines 2013). The EASF, however, but could not rise to the occasion if not for Uganda's vested interests in the South Sudan conflict then because the Regional Brigade itself has never been fully constituted, tested, and operationalised compared to the periodic military-cooperation activities, such as defence exercises and other confidence-building measures, within the EAC (Rwengabo 2017).

It is difficult to assess the AUPSC's efficacy in creating organisational processes necessary to regionalise the ASF in eastern Africa. Certainly, the Assembly of Heads of States seems to be complacent in retaining this Principal–Agent Problem afflicting security regionalism under the AU. Keeping the EASF separate from the EAC was a serious oversight because of: (i) prior commitments under the EAC and IGAD; (ii) other overlaps under the ICGLR to which Rwanda-Burundi, Uganda, and Tanzania are party; and (iii) ICGRL links to the Democratic Republic of Congo (DRC), hence to SADC and ECCAS. This created stifling nested structures for regional security measures under RECs and issue-specific ROs. Beyond more binding rules, the EAC has relatively more active institutions and processes than IGAD but cannot coordinate EASF activities. The designers of the Regional Brigade, therefore, possibly had limited intent to avoid organisational overlaps, difficulties of assessing performance and responsibility in East Africa's sub-regional security governance. Instead, they linked Principals and Agents in ways that disallow for coherent and coordinated relationships by sanctioning the EASF to straddle countries belonging to various RECs—EAC, ECCAS (Burundi and Comoros), IGAD (Djibouti and Ethiopia, but at that time excluding Eritrea), and SADC (cf. SADC 2001, 2003). From a Principal–Agent perspective, even if peripheral relationships with other RECs were held constant, one still finds that the EASF is structurally disjointed from the IGAD and EAC that would be Agents acting on behalf of the Principal, the AU.

Conclusion: Regional Security Policy and Practice Beyond the Principal–Agent Conundrum

The foregoing analysis raises important questions for the "Africa Rising" debate. Specifically, have the structural transformations of the AU, notably the APSA and the ASF's Regional Brigades, helped the AU to overcome Principal–Agent Problems in security regionalism? The answer requires grasping the imperatives of "Africa Rising": Africa can only rise by taking cognisance of and overcoming the practical challenges hindering the effectiveness of her regional peace and security institutions—and allowing for operational efficacy in implementing continental rules. The starting point is to garner the requisite political will to support and allow these institutions to function. The next is to further strengthen continental and regional institutions, by clarifying their Principal–Agent mandates and providing necessary resources (human, financial, technical, and equipment) for operational efficacy. Limited institutional and political capacities of regional institutions adversely affect their ability to intervene in instances of organised violence. Worse still, the structuring of these institutions makes it difficult for them to operate without igniting contradictory reactions from the very member states constituting them and parallel institutions astride them. Both capacitation and structuring of regional peace and security institutions are political questions which demand decisional foresight. For instance, the structuring of the ASF's Regional Brigades, specifically the way in which the EASF is configured, makes it difficult to mobilise forces and resources within East Africa that would be necessary to achieve enduring peace and security necessary for economic growth and development. As a result, development agendas that have periodically been formulated at continental level since the 1980 Lagos Plan of Action (AU 1980) remain on paper, because Principal–Agent Problems in security regionalism led to practical failures to address the agential factors that provoke and/or prolong spiralling armed conflicts and other forms of organised violence.[1] What has bedevilled the Horn of Africa, Great Lakes Region/Upper Nile Valley, Sahara-Sahel, and Mano River Union may ruin the "Africa Rising" optimism because efforts to develop the continent depend on sustainable peace and security which remain elusive (Williams 2016).

The failure of AU institutions, and their regional replicas, to effectively respond to security threats in different regions calls for caution about the Africa Rising narrative in theory and practice for two reasons. First, structural weaving of security institutions makes it difficult for the ASF to act as a rapid-response force in regions like Eastern Africa via the EASF. This is shown by the failure to muster regional rapid-response to peace and security woes in Somalia and South Sudan today, as well as in Northern Uganda before 2006. This is partly because the Regional Brigade was not aligned with the EAC's peace and security roles. The motives behind instruments and practices of peace and security cooperation within the EAC would create incentives for reconstituting the REC's peace and security infrastructure to operationalise the ASF/EASF (Rwengabo 2017). This paucity of institutional and operational alignment allows opportunistic actors to elude responsibility and hide behind multifarious institutional spaces, hence prolonging conflicts. The conflicting roles of member states in the EAC, EASF, ICGLR, and ECCAS in the conflicts in the DRC is well known. Second, despite the AU's promising peace and security instruments, peace operations around the continent, and the role of external actors in such war theatres as Somalia, [South] Sudan, and DRC, sustainable peace and security has been rendered impractical because of sovereignty provisions and practical evocations of the same principal in Eastern Africa. The role of RECs in responding to peace and security threats, as demonstrated by ECOWAS during the 1990s and early 2000s, and in Mali and Gambia recently, depended on the extent to which RECs are willing and ready to evade sovereignty concerns to address the practical difficulties of restoring peace and security in countries like Liberia and Sierra Leone (Sessay et al. 2009). This is still difficult in East Africa because of limited political goodwill and institutional commitment to disallow sovereignty claims from failing the AU's peace and security roles (Rwengabo 2017).

Three implications—theoretical, empirical, and practical—arise from this analysis and draw attention to questions of handling multi-level Principal–Agent problems in security regionalism under the AU. The theoretical implication is this: why and when do Principals and Agents disentangle themselves from the Principal-Agent Problem related to autonomy, independence, and accountability in a multi-level Principal–Agent relationship? Addressing this question would enrich our grasp of the political imperatives of "Africa Rising" from a security perspective. In a multi-level international-organisational landscape, where Principals and Agents exist at multiple levels, political commitment, necessary for "Africa Rising", may be difficult due to institutional and operational overlaps. Empirically, bargaining strategies and decision-making considerations that informed the ways in which the EASF and NARC were designed need to be exposed. Were there misgivings about misalignment of Regional Brigades with RECs? How did these opinions, if any, underline the ways in which misaligned Brigades would undercut Africa Rising as formulated in the continent's development agendas between the 1980 Lagos Plan of Action and Agenda 2063 (which includes silencing the gun by

2020) (AU 2014), all of which converge on unity, political and economic self-determination, good governance and freedom, progress and collective prosperity?

Finally, the practical implications of the ASF's Regional Brigades that are misaligned to RECs need to be considered. The SSF's intervention in DRC against the M23 and other armed groups partly created cold relations between Tanzania and Rwanda (Rwengabo 2017: 221–224). It may be difficult to make the EAC or EASF deploy in the region when previously afflicted member countries like Uganda failed to allow regional responses to the peace and security problems then afflicting the region. This pessimism is demonstrated by Uganda's failure to cooperate with the EAC's Legislative Assembly to find a regional solution to Joseph Kony's devastating Lord's Resistance Army (LRA) rebellion in northern Uganda. Kenya's initial unilateral intervention in Somalia in 2011, four years after the AU-sanctioned AMISOM intervention had taken off, is equally illustrative of states' hold onto their sovereignty, especially on matters of peace and security (Rwengabo 2017). Given these realities, the Africa Rising narrative needs to take considered cognisance of the failings caused by countries' unwillingness to fully cooperate to resolve the continent's peace and security problems. Is it time, yet, for states to swallow the bitter pill of sovereignty—as shown in Kenya's reference to her right to self-defence as embodied in Article 51 of the UN Charter and sovereignty provisions under AU instruments—to take collective responsibility and overcome practical difficulties of creating functional ASF structures in Eastern Africa? Answering these and similar questions would inform more rigorous assessments of the Principal–Agent travails of "Africa Rising" through AU-level security regionalism. This is crucial in a continent that has witnessed an upward conflict trend since 2010, an increasing role of religious and environmental factors in wide-ranging armed conflicts, increasing occurrences and intensities of popular protests, an "exponential rise" in the use of improvised explosive devices (IEDs) and suicide bombings in terrorism-like attacks, and limited success of militarised responses to these developments (Williams 2017: 33).

Note

1. Some of the factors that led to or prolonged armed conflicts and organized violence in Africa include: ethnicised neopatriamonialism, instrumentalisation of religious extremism, sovereignty concerns, and competition for

natural resources, all involving the interplay of local, regional, and foreign interests (Williams 2016).

References

Abbot, K.W., and D. Snidal. 1998. Why States Act Through Formal International Organizations. *Journal of Conflict Resolution* 42 (1): 3–32.

Acharya A., and A. Johnston, ed. 2007. *Crafting Cooperation: Regional International Institutions in Comparative Perspective*. New York: Cambridge University Press.

Acharya, A. 2009. *Whose Ideas Matter? Agency and Power in Asian Regionalism*. Ithaca & London: Cornell University Press.

African Union (AU). 2000. *Bamako Declaration on an African Common Position on the Illicit Proliferation, Circulation and Trafficking of Small Arms and Light Weapons*. Bamako and Addis Ababa: AU.

AU. 1980. *Lagos Plan of Action for the Economic Development of Africa, 1980–2000*. Addis Ababa: AU.

AU. 2002. *Protocol Relating to the Establishment of the Peace and Security Council of the African Union*. Addis Ababa & Durban: AU.

AU. 2004a. *Framework for a Common African Defence and Security Policy*. Addis Ababa: AU.

AU. 2004b. *Solemn Declaration on a Common African Defence and Security Policy*. Sirte: AU.

AU. 2008. *Memorandum of Understanding on Cooperation in the Area of Peace and Security between the African Union, the Regional Economic Communities and the Coordinating Mechanisms of the Regional Standby Brigades of Eastern Africa and Northern Africa*. Addis Ababa: AU.

AU. 2010. *African Peace And Security Architecture: Assessment Study*. Addis Ababa: AU.

AU. 2014. *Agenda 2063: The Africa We Want*. Addis Ababa: AU.

Bah, A.S. 2010. The Evolution of Regional and Sub-Regional Collective Security Mechanisms in Post-Cold War Africa. In *Cooperating for Peace and Security: Evolving Institutions and Arrangements in the Context of U.S. Security Policy*, ed. Bruce D Jones, Shepard Forman and Richard Gowan, 269–290. Cambridge: Cambridge University Press.

Baldwin, D.A., ed. 1993. *Neorealism and Neoliberalism: The Contemporary Debate*. Columbia: Columbia University Press.

Boulden, J., ed. 2003. *Dealing with Conflict in Africa: The United Nations and Regional Organisations*. New York: Palgrave Macmillan.

Claude Jr., I.L. 1964. *Swords into Plowshares: The Problems and Progress of International Organisation*. New York: Random House.

Daily Monitor. 2018. South Sudan Rebel Leader Machar Returns to Juba After Two Years. 31 Wednesday October, Kampala: *Daily Monitor*. https://www.monitor.co.ug/News/National/South-Sudan-rebel-leader-Machar-returns-Juba-two-years/688334-4830142-uajlxg/index.html, 14 February 2019.

De Waal, A. 2009. Mission without End? Peacekeeping in the African Political Marketplace. *International Affairs* 85 (1): 99–113.

EAC. 1998. *Memorandum of Understanding on Cooperation in Defence Affairs* (adapted to the Treaty, 2001). Arusha: East African Community (EAC).

EAC. 1999. *Treaty for the Establishment of the East African Community*. Arusha: EAC (As amended).

EAC. 2012a. *Protocol on Cooperation in Defence Matters*. Arusha: EAC.

EAC. 2012b. *Protocol on Peace and Security Cooperation*. Arusha: EAC.

Franke, B. 2009. *Security Cooperation in Africa: A Reappraisal*. Boulder and London: First Forum Press.

Franke, B. 2010. Précis of Security cooperation in Africa: a Reappraisal. *African Security Review* 19 (2): 84–96.

Gitelson, S.E. 1973. Can the U.N. be an Effective Catalyst for Regional Integration? The Case of the East African Community. *The Journal of Developing Areas* 8 (1): 65–82.

Glaser, C.L. 1994/1995. Realists as Optimists: Cooperation as Self-Help. *International Security* 19 (3): 50–90.

Hemmer, C., and P.J. Katzenstein. 2002. Why is there no NATO in Asia? Collective Identity, Regionalism, and the Origins of Multilateralism. *International Organization* 56 (3): 575–607.

ICGLR. 2004. *Declaration on Peace, Security, Democracy and Development in the Great Lakes Region (aka: Dar es Salaam Declaration)*. Dar e Salaam: ICGLR.

ICGLR [International Conference on the Great Lakes Region]. (2006). (amended 2012) *The Pact on Security, Stability and Development in the Great Lakes Region*. Bujumbura: ICGLR.

Jaye T., D. Garuba, and S. Amadi, ed. 2011 *ECOWAS and the Dynamics of Conflict and Peacebuilding*. Dakar: CODESRIA.

Jervis, R. 1982. Security Regimes. *International Organization* 36 (2): 357–378.

Karns, M.P., and K.A. Mingst. 2009. *International Organizations: The Politics and Processes of Global Governance*. Boulder, London: Lynne Reinner.

Kent, V., and M. Malan. 2003. The African Standby Force: Progress and Prospects. *African Security Review* 12 (3): 29–46.

Litfin, K.T. 1997. Sovereignty in World Ecopolitics. *Mershon International Studies Review* 41 (2): 167–201.

Mansfield, E.D., and E. Solingen. 2010. Regionalism. *Annual Review of Political Science* 13 (1): 145–163.

Olonisakin, F. 2011. ECOWAS: From Economic Integration to Peace-building. In *ECOWAS and the Dynamics of Conflict and Peacebuilding*, ed. Thomas Jaye, Dauda Garuba, and Stella Amadi, 11–26. Dakar: CODESRIA.

RECSA [Regional Centre on Small Arms in the Great Lakes Region the Horn of Africa and Bordering states]. 2000a. *The Nairobi Declaration on the Problem of the Proliferation of Illicit Small Arms and Light Weapons in the Great Lakes Region and the Horn of Africa*. Nairobi: RECSA.

RECSA. 2000b. *Co-ordinated Agenda for Action on the Problem of the Proliferation of Small Arms and Light Weapons in the Great Lakes Region and the Horn of Africa—SAEM/GLR.HOA/1*. Nairobi: RECSA.

RECSA. 2004. *Nairobi Protocol for the Prevention, Control and Reduction of Small Arms and Light Weapons in the Great Lakes Region, the Horn of Africa, and Bordering states*. Nairobi: RECSA.

Rees, R. 1985. The Theory of Principal and Agent Part I. *Bulletin of Economic Research* 3 (1): 0307–3378.

Rodrigo Tavares. 2008. Understanding regional peace and security: a framework for analysis1. *Contemporary Politics* 14 (2):107–127.

Rodrigo Tavares. 2009. Regional clustering of peace and security. *Global Change, Peace & Security* 21 (2): 153–164.

Rogerson, W.P. 1985. The First-Order Approach to Principal-Agent Problems. *Econometrica* 53 (6): 1357–1367.

Ross, S.A. 1973. The Economic Theory of Agency: The Principal's Problem. *The American Economic Review* 63 (2): 134–139.

Rupia, M. 2016. Regional Intervention in Fragile African states: Comparative Case Studies of South Sudan and Lesotho: Any Lessons Learnt? *AfSol Journal* 1 (1): 1–26.

Rwengabo, S. 2013. Strategic Repositioning in a Hyper-Competitive World: Rising China and Economic Partnership Agreements between European Union and African Countries. *OSSREA Bulletin* X (1): 9–24.

Rwengabo, S. 2016a. AMISOM and African-Centered Solutions to Peace and Security Challenges. *AfSol Journal* 1 (1): 91–138.

Rwengabo, S. 2016b. Institutional Design and the Implementation of the African Peace Security Architecture in Eastern Africa. *Africa Development* XLI (4): 107–138.

Rwengabo, S. 2017. *Security Cooperation in the East African Community*. Trenton, NJ: Africa World Press.

SADC [Southern African Development Community]. 2003. *The SADC Mutual Defence Pact*. Dar es Salaam: SADC.

SADC. 2001. *Protocol on Politics, Defence and Security Co-operation*. Dar es Salaam: SADC.

Sessay Amadu, C., C. Ukeje, O. Gbla, and O. Ismail. 2009. *Post-War Regimes and state Reconstruction in Liberia and Sierra Leone*. Dakar: CODESRIA.

Solingen, E.L. 1998. *Regional Orders at Century's Dawn: Global and Domestic Influences on Grand Strategy*. Princeton, NJ: Princeton University Press.

Stein, A.A. 1993. Coordination and Collaboration: Regimes in an Anarchical World. *International Organization* 36 (2): 299–324.

Touray, O.A. 2005. The Common African Defence and Security Policy. *African Affairs* 104 (417): 635–656.

UN. 1945. *Charter of the United Nations*. New York: UN, esp. Chapter 8.

Van Nieuwkerk, A. 2011. The Regional Roots of the African Peace And Security Architecture: Exploring Centre-Periphery Relations. *South African Journal of International Affairs* 17 (2): 169–189.

Vaubel, R. 2006. Principal-Agent Problems in International Organizations. *Review of International Organizations, Vo.* 1 (2): 125–138.

Vines, A. 2013. A Decade of the African Peace And Security Architecture. *International Affairs* 89 (1): 89–109.

VoA News. 2018. Machar Returns to Juba for Peace Celebrations. Juba: VoA News, Wednesday, October 31, https://www.voanews.com/a/machar-returns-to-juba-for-peace-celebrations/4637235.html, 1 February 2019, report by Waakhe Simon Wudu and Dimo Silva.

Waterman, R.W., and J.M. Kenneth. 1998. Principal-Agent Models: An Expansion? *Journal of Public Administration Research and Theory* 8 (2): 173–202.

Wilcox, F.O. 1965. Regionalism and the United Nations. *International Organization* 19 (3): 789–811.

Williams, P.D. 2016. *War and Conflict in Africa*, 2nd ed. Cambridge, UK: Polity Press.

Williams, P.D. 2017. Continuity and Change in War and Conflict in Africa. *PRISM: A Journal of the Centre for Complex Operations* 6 (4): 32–45.

Young, O.T. 1999. *Governance in World Affairs*. Cornell: Cornell University Press.

PART IV

Specific National Contexts and "the Forgotten Africa"

CHAPTER 12

Ethiopia's Economic Growth in the Context of the Africa Rising Debate

Yohannes Tekalign

Introduction

Africa has been portrayed by the narratives as the "Hopeless Continent" and the "Dark Continent" in the first decade of the new century (*The Economist* 2000, 2007). Nonetheless, this began to change since 2010 by the narratives that have been extolling the continent as "Lions in the Move," "Africa Rising," and "Hopeful Continent" (*The Economist* 2011, 2013).[1] The shift from Afro-pessimist to Afro-optimist narratives has supposedly been driven by the development "successes" of the continent over the past decades. Africa has experienced strong and continuous economic growth since 2000. Its economy grew 4.7% on average annually between 2000 and 2017, making it the world's second fastest-growing economy next to Asia (OECD 2018: 17). Factors that have positively contributed to such notable economic growth and the rising Africa narrative include improved political and macroeconomic (and business) climate, high domestic demand, high commodity prices, an increase

Y. Tekalign (✉)
FDRE Meles Zenawi Leadership Academy, Addis Ababa, Ethiopia

K. Omeje (ed.), *The Governance, Security and Development Nexus*,
https://doi.org/10.1007/978-3-030-49348-6_12

in external financial flows (including foreign direct investment and official development assistance) from US$20 billion in 1990 to overUS$120 billion in 2012, and debt relief (UNCTAD 2014: 2; Zamfir 2016).

However, the economic growth has not been fairly distributed across Africa. Twenty African countries (excluding oil exporters) recorded GDP growth averaged of 5.8% while other countries grew little or slower for two decades since the mid-1990s (Radelet 2016: 7). Ethiopia achieved a remarkable GDP growth averaged of about 10% for over a decade, making it the world's second fastest-growing economy (Obiols 2017). Africa's strong economic growth of the past decades has contributed to reducing poverty and improving people's health and education in the continent. For instance, the proportion of people living in extreme poverty (less than US$1.90/day) fell from 57% in 1990 to 43% in 2012 (Beegle 2016: 4). The share of under-five mortality also dropped by over 50%, malaria deaths by 50%, and deaths related to HIV/AIDS and tuberculosis by over 30% in the past decades (Radelet 2016: 7). Further, the enrollment of children in primary school increased from 55% in 1995 to 74% by 2012 (World Bank 2015). Progresses toward democracy and accountable government, and infrastructure development have also been made in the past two decades (UNCTAD 2014; Radelet 2016).

Despite the economic and social progresses seen in the continent in the past decades, critics of the rising narrative questioned whether Africa is really rising? They rather focused on the development failures across the continent, emphasizing the uneven distribution of economic growth, widespread poverty, and the prevalence of unaccountable and autocratic governments (Brooks 2018; Pillay 2015). There are marked variations across African countries in sustaining economic growth, reducing poverty, and progressing toward democratic governance. Overall, Africa has not been able to sustain the 7% average growth rate required to make significant progress in reducing poverty in the past decades (UNCTAD 2014: 4). Currently, around 43% (i.e., 389 million) of Africa's people live below the extreme poverty line (less than US$1.90/day) (Beegle 2016: 4). Thus, poverty remains a major development challenge of the continent. But the robust economic growth, which is over 7%, in some countries such as Rwanda, Ethiopia, and Mozambique in the past decade have helped them to make remarkable progress on human development (Mukherjee et al. 2017). Ethiopia, for instance, has managed to reduce extreme poverty from 45.5% in 2000 to 23.5% in 2016 (UNDP 2018).

Though the number of electoral democracies in Sub-Saharan Africa increased dramatically from 4 in 1990 to about 23 in less than three decades (Radelet 2016), half of the African governments are still in the autocratic side of the ledger (Siegle 2007). Both the narratives of Africa development "successes" and "failures" have evidently failed to provide the two sides of the continent's stories since neither all Africa countries have succeeded in development nor failed to do so. It is thus important to put individual country cases into the context of Africa rising debate. In this regard, this chapter tries to situate Ethiopia's remarkable economic growth of the past decade within the context of the Africa rising debate.

Contextual Background

Ethiopia is one of the two countries in Africa (the other being Liberia) that has never been colonized.[2] Its escape from the yoke of colonialism nonetheless has not much contributed to its development. Ethiopia has for long encountered several challenges that ruined its development. The frequent war-making by elites to acquire wealth for their expansion or centralization and to tackle hostile and powerful colonial forces (such as Egypt, Italy, and Britain) had for long undermined political and economic development in the country (Geda 2008; Tesfaye 2017). Throughout the nineteenth and twentieth centuries, modernizing emperors (such as Tewodros II, Yohannes IV, Menelik II, and Haile Selassie I) had attempted to consolidate their power to ensure Ethiopia's territorial unity and sovereignty, and to set the pace for its development (Adejumobi 2007). Their modernization zeal was largely based on the idea of creating a centralized strong progressive state through modernizing its administrative apparatus, importing manufactured goods and technologies essential for its consumption, and financial and technical assistance from foreign powers (such as Britain, France, and the USA) (Pankhurst 1968; Zewde 2001).

The process of centralization of state power and modernization of the state apparatus by the emperors mentioned above had culminated by creating Ethiopian modern empire-state by the end of the nineteenth century and an absolute feudal state in the first half of the twentieth century (Zewde 2001). Economic development had for long been constrained by the wars fought in the process of centralization and with colonial powers, and by the feudal system (Pankhurst 1968). Nonetheless, Ethiopia's transition from feudal to "semi-feudal" and "semi-capitalist" state during Emperor Haile Selassie I (1930–1974) had pushed forward the socioeconomic development started earlier (Hiwet 1975).[3] The development plans of the Haile Selassie I regime that encouraged the expansion of industries, commercial agriculture, foreign trade and investment, and the state's tax base, privatization of land accompanied with political stability had contributed to high economic growth since the 1950s (Gebreeyesus 2013; Geda 2008). For instance, between 1960 and 1970, Ethiopia achieved an average annual GDP growth rate of 4.4% (Ofcansky and Berry 1991), which was higher than the average of all African countries combined (Milkias 2011: 61). Productive attempts in expanding modern schools and health facilities were also made during the emperor's period.[4] Nonetheless, the economic growth failed to improve the lives of about four-fifths of the population who lived in poverty (Ofcansky and Berry 1991). This failure together with the uneven development between the center and the peripheries, the recurrence of devastating famine, and the "nationalities question" finally led to the removal of the autocratic imperial regime by popular revolution in 1974 (Tiruneh 1993).

The socialist military regime established afterward (1974–1991) attempted to heal the ills of the past through diverse policy measures. It nationalized all rural land and made "land to the tiller" a reality for the first time in 1975 (Ellis 1988). The regime's social policy also made millions of people literate through massive rural literacy campaign, and enabled the public to have minimal health care through establishing hundreds of health centers (Ofcansky and Berry 1991). But its restriction on the private sector and the market, and its war economy (resource mobilization meant to suppress various rebel forces and an invasion from Somalia in the 1970s) coupled with natural catastrophes (such as drought and famine) militated both against peace and development in the country and led to the overthrow of the regime by a coalition of four ethnic-based rebel forces subsequently named the Ethiopian People's Revolutionary Democratic Front (EPRDF) in 1991 (Gebreeyesus 2013; Tesfaye 2017).[5]

The EPRDF regime has made two significant changes after it assumed state power in 1991. It has reinstated free market economy initially introduced by Haile Selassie I regime but replaced later to a command economy by the socialist regime. This cyclical political process and regime changes are both erratic and violent and invariably has detrimental impact on the economic performance of the country (Geda 2011: 4). Further, the government has restructured the hitherto unitary state into the federal state mainly based on ethnolinguistic criteria aimed at accommodating diversity through devolving power and resources to the lower levels.[6] The peace dividend of the post-Cold War era,[7] the adoption of a developmental state model and market-oriented economy, huge public investment on infrastructure, and high foreign capital inflows (including ODA and FDI) have greatly contributed to Ethiopia's remarkable economic growth of the past decades (NPC 2017; Shiferaw 2017). Its GDP growth average drastically increased from about 1% between 1975 and 1992 to 4.5% between 1993 and 2004, and to 10.9% between 2004 and 2014 (Henze 1989: v; World Bank 2016: 3). Such an impressive economic growth makes the country one of the shining stars in the Africa rising debate.

Ethiopia's Growth Miracle

Ethiopia has been one of the ten fastest-growing economies in the world over the past decades. It has been one of the ten fastest-growing economies in the world (and the sixth in Africa) for the 2001–2010 period.[8] Ethiopia has achieved a double digit economic growth over the past decade since 2000, often referred to as the "Great Run," the "China of Africa." Its average GDP growth rate that exceeded 10% from 2003 to 2013 was "more than four percentage points higher than the average for Africa's 26 other low-income countries" (Donnenfeld et al. 2017: 1). Such rapid economic growth coupled with the government pro-poor policies has enabled the country to make significant progress on human development and poverty reduction. For instance, the share of people living in extreme poverty (less than US$1.90/day) in the country markedly decreased from the world's highest rate 55.3% in 2000 to 33.5% in 2011 and to 23.5% in 2016. Over 5 million Ethiopians have been lifted out of poverty in five-year terms, from 2010/1 to 2015/6. Per capita income also jumped from US$124 in 2000 to US$1608 in 2017 (NPC 2017; World Bank 2016). Further, the overall unemployment and the youth unemployment rates in the country decreased from 26.1 and 35% in 2003 to 17.4 and 22.8% in 2014, respectively (Berhe and Tsegay 2018: 8). Ethiopia is also one of the most equal countries in the world with a Gini index of 0.30 in 2011 (World Bank 2016).

Moreover, the country has achieved most of the Millennium Development Goals by the 2015 deadline. Its HDI value increased by over half from 0.283 in 2000 to 0.448 in 2015. Between 1990 and 2015, life expectancy at birth increased by 17.5 years to 64.6 years; mean years of schooling by 1.1 years to 2.6 years, and expected years of schooling by 5.3 years to 8.4 years (UNDP 2015b).[9] Overall, Ethiopia moved from being the 2nd poorest country in the world by 2000 to the 11th poorest in 2014, and came closer to its goal of becoming a middle-income country by 2025 (World Bank 2016). Its rank on the World Bank's easy-of-doing business index slightly improved from 161 in 2017 to 159 in 2018 from a record low of 104 in 2010.

Ethiopia's rapid economic growth has also been accompanied by a sign of structural change since 2005. The dominant role of the agricultural sector in the economy has slowly been replaced by the industrial and service sectors. For instance, the share of agriculture to GDP decreased from 52% in 2005 to 36% in 2016/7 while the industrial and service sectors increased from 10 to 38% in 2005 to 25 to 39% in 2016/7, respectively (NBE 2013, 2017). Hence, the share of the service sector exceeds a bit that of the agriculture sector, which is a significant shift from two decades ago. Ethiopia has also been one of the ten top recipients of "foreign direct investment" (FDI) in Africa in the past decade and it is now the second-largest recipient of FDI in Africa with 3.6 billion dollars in 2017 (UNCTAD 2018: 11). The economic boom in Ethiopia has also created jobs for millions. For instance, the economy generated 1.6 million jobs through small- and medium-scale enterprises between 2011 and 2015 (AfDB 2015: 13).

Ethiopia's Development Failures

Despite significant progress in socioeconomic development made in the past decades, Ethiopia remains a poor country. Its acclaimed rapid economic growth of the past decade is paradoxically asymmetrical with the socioeconomic position it is currently credited within the world. It is one of the least developed and most populous countries in the Sub-Saharan Africa with over 100 million people.[10] According to UNDP (2015a), Ethiopia is one of the fifteen African countries with the lowest Human Development Index (HDI), and one of the five African countries with the highest multidimensional poverty index.[11] Further, nearly 20 million Ethiopians still live below the national poverty line (NPC 2017: 14). Millions of Ethiopians have also experienced chronic food insecurity yearly due to drought—for instance, on average about 7 million between 1991 and 2003, 4 million between 2003 and 2014, 8.5 million in 2008, and over 10 million between 2015 and 2016 (Asayehgn 2016). To tackle food deficit problem the government has often sought external assistance. For instance, following the El Niño triggered drought of 2016, one of the worst droughts in the country's history that affected over 10 million people, US$1.1 billion aid was required from donors for food assistance.[12]

Furthermore, with over 25% of unemployed urban population between the age range of 15 and 29, which is much higher than overall unemployment, Ethiopia has one of the highest rates of youth unemployment (Central Statistical Agency of Ethiopia 2018). Despite the fact that the overall urban unemployment rate decreased to 16.1% in 2015, it still remains very high and has increasingly become a problem in rural areas too (NPC 2016: 8). Currently, out of the estimated total urban (both males and females) population of 27 million, only 9 million are economically active, 1.5 million (16.9%) are unemployed and nearly one-fourth of which are the youth with the age range of between 15 and 29 years.[13] Unemployment and poverty thus remain to be the major developmental challenges and claimed by the government to have contributed to the recent social unrests that have plagued the country.[14] The state-led rapid economic growth of the past decade has also retarded the democratization process that has been set in motion in the country since 1991.[15]

Ethiopia has an extremely low GDP per capita of US$ 619, which is less than the average for least developed countries (US$ 955), and significantly below half of the average of Sub-Saharan Africa's, US$ 1571.[16] Besides, it is the second-largest IDA-only borrower with an external debt stock of US$ 26 billion in 2017.[17] With about 60% of public debt to GDP ratio in 2018, Ethiopia is one of the most heavily indebted poor countries in the world.[18] The country is also largely dependent on Official Development Assistance (ODA). For instance, the US$ 3.5 billion that it received on average yearly between 2007 and 2011 constituted 50–60% of its national budget (Oakland Institute 2013). Though Ethiopia is the second most populous country in Africa (next to Nigeria), its economy is one of the smallest in the continent with only 1% share of the overall African economy (AfDB 2008). Child and maternal mortality rates are also relatively high in the country despite that they have declined significantly from 101/1000 and 590/100,000 in 2009/10 (MoFED 2010) to 64/1000 and 420/100, 000, respectively in 2016 (NPC 2016). Moreover, the overall adult literacy rate is 49.1%, which is one of the lowest in Africa.[19]

Ethiopia in the Contending Development Narratives: The Balance Sheet

Ethiopia has experienced much sufferings. Between 1961 and 1991, the country was ravaged by one of Africa's longest civil war, which culminated in the separation and independence of Eritrea. Ethiopia has also been struck by frequent famines. The combined incidents of war and famines have resulted in the death and displacement of millions in the country. They have also dislocated the country's economy and development. Central to dislocation tragedy has been the autocratic nature of the subsequent regimes of the country and their misguided development policies.[20] Devastated by civil war and recurrence of drought and famine, Ethiopia was trapped in socioeconomic stagnation for at least two decades (since 1974) before it began to resurge. During the two decades of economic stagnation, Ethiopia's average annual growth rate was about 1%. Poverty and hunger had also been the hallmark of the country in the 1980s.[21] Further, hundreds of thousands of young intellectuals were "liquidated" by the country's military regime during the Red Terror in the late 1970s (Donnenfeld et al. 2017: 10). The Red Terror was a state-sponsored violence against members of competing radical forces mainly the Ethiopian People's Revolutionary Party (EPRP), which instigated terrorist attack known as the White Terror against the military regime's leaders and supporters (Ofcansky and Berry 1991). It was therefore a counteraction to the White Terror.

In a nutshell, Ethiopia, like other Sub-Saharan African countries, has experienced a protracted civil war, military dictatorship, economic stagnation, and widespread poverty in what was commonly referred to as the "lost decade" of the 1980s (see UNDP 1996; Zamfir 2016). The prolonged stagnancy, war, helpless food deficits suffered by Ethiopia between the 1970s and 1990s were part of the narratives that informed the Economist's pessimistic portrayal of Africa as the "Hopeless Continent" in the turn of the new century.

Nevertheless, Ethiopia's reality has significantly changed for good since the 2000s. Its economy has experienced rapid and sustainable growth and has become one of the ten fastest-growing economies in the world over the 2000–2017 period. Such phenomenal economic growth has translated, as indicated above, into tangible improvements in the lives of millions of Ethiopians as the country has made significant progress in human development and poverty reduction in the past two decades.

It is this phenomenal progress that has secured a place for Ethiopia in the Africa rising debate. But it is pertinent to quickly add that Ethiopia remains a poor country grappling with several development challenges notably poverty, high unemployment, food insecurity, commodity dependence, and lack of economic transformation. The mixed narratives of development successes against a backdrop of persistent shortfalls and failures make Ethiopia's real place in the Africa rising debate somewhat paradoxical. On the one hand, its booming economy growth has helped it to make notable progress on almost all human development indicators and poverty reduction in the past decade. But on the other hand, Ethiopia's ranking on the Human Development Index (HDI) has lagged behind most of the low HDI countries. This is partly explained by its rapid population growth and "the difficulty of translating macro-growth into micro-gains" (Veen 2016: 8).

Conclusion

Ethiopia has managed to rise from a protracted civil war, an organized mass violence (i.e., the Red Terror), and a prolonged political and economic stagnation in 1991. It has made significant progress across economic, social, and human development indicators. Such progress has been driven by the country's political stability, improved governance and macroeconomic environment, public investment in infrastructure, and the government policy that poverty is a security (or survival) agenda to be tackled by rapid and sustainable economic development.[22] This development drive has, in turn, motivated the state to mobilize in the forms of development assistance and foreign direct investment billions of dollars, which have been channeled to productive ends, notably human development, public infrastructures, and job creation linked to poverty reduction. Despite the overall progress made in the past decade, Ethiopia is still in the bottom league in global Human Development Index due to some combination of factors. The first is that the country has started development from a low starting point.[23] The second is that Ethiopia's rapid population growth and the inability to translate economic growth to meaningful and widespread impact in the lives of populace. The third is that with the separation of the sea-bound Eritrea in 1993, Ethiopia became landlocked and its landlocked location has incurred for the state a staggering port service charge of about a billion dollar annually, an amount to has progressively grown with the country's economic development.[24]

Furthermore, the state's low revenue generation capacity which presently stands at about 12.5% of the country's GDP is deplorable, especially when compared to the 17% average for sub-Saharan Africa.[25] There are concerns regarding the sustainability of Ethiopia's development success for the key reason that the recorded success has been achieved through a "centralized form of patrimonial governance" by an authoritarian regime. The Ethiopian experience, as some scholars have argued, is a case of "centralized patrimonialism" displacing "competitive patrimonialism," which is the most prevalent trend among Africa emerging democracies (see Booth 2012). A major challenge faced by the Ethiopian government is how to accelerate the country's development and meet the needs of its rapidly growing population based on a political system that has neither demonstrated sufficient capacity to absorb shock nor to responsively manage the unfolding pressure to liberalize the democratic space.

Notes

1. See also the McKinsey Global Institute's publications regarding Africa's progressive economic growth entitled "Lions on the Moves" (2010 and 2016).
2. This is except the forceful occupation of the Ethiopia by Italy from 1936 to 1941.
3. See for the overall socio-economic development made by Emperor Haile Selassie's predecessors Zewde, B. A history of modern Ethiopia, 1855–1991, 2nd ed (2002). Addis Ababa: Addis Ababa University Press.
4. Haile Selassie's most institutions of higher education were located in the capital, as were nine of the empire's twenty secondary schools. Of the country's 620 government elementary schools, 38 were in Addis Abeba, 125 were in Eritrea, and most of the remaining were in the north. He saw 240 medical facilities in 1955 (Markus 1991).
5. The four ethnic-based forces that made up the EPRDF are Tigray People's Liberation Front (TPLF), Amhara National Democratic Movement (ANDM) Oromo People's Democratic Organization (OPDO), and South Ethiopia Peoples' Democratic Movement (SEPDM). See for the detail http://www.eprdf.org.et/web/en/short-history.
6. Article 1 of the FDRE Constitution declares that the state structure is federal, which according to article 46 (1), shall comprise of States whose

borders shall be drawn based on, according to article 46 (2), settlement patterns, language, identity and consent of the peoples concerned. See also about the division of power between the federal state and regional states Article 51 and 52 in the constitution https://www.wipo.int/edocs/lexdocs/laws/en/et/et007en.pdf.

7. This is except the two years Ethio-Eritrean (1998–2000) bloody and costly war that slowed down the pace of the country's economic development.
8. The other five countries in Africa were Angola, Nigeria, Chad, Mozambique, and Rwanda. See "A more hopeful continent. The lion kings?", *The Economist*, 6 January 2011. https://www.economist.com/finance-and-economics/2011/01/06/the-lion-kings.
9. Except MDGs 3 and MDGs 5 Ethiopia has achieved or on track to achieve six of the eight MDGs by 2015 (see for Ethiopia's achievement of the MDGs, UNDP, Millennium Development Goals Report 2014 Ethiopia: Assessment of Ethiopia's Progress towards the MDGs, 2015).
10. With over 100 million population, Ethiopia is currently the second most populous country in Africa next to Nigeria. See for the list of least developed (or poorest of poor) countries at http://www.un.org/en/development/desa/policy/cdp/ldc/ldc_list.pdf.
11. See the list of countries with the lowest HDI and highest multidimensional poverty on the United Nations Development Program's Human Development Report of 2015: hdr.undp.org/sites/default/files/2015_human_development_report.pdf.
12. See about the drought and the US and others assistance at https://ethiopia.usembassy.gov/u.s.response-to-the-ethiopian-drought.html and http://www.unocha.org/el-nino-east-africa.
13. See the Central Statistical Agency data base http://www.csa.gov.et/index.php?option=com_phocadownload&view=category&id=270&Itemid=270.
14. See for this the former Ethiopian PM, Hailmariam Desalegn's comments on the link between the recent social unrest in the country and youth unemployment, poverty and equitable distribution of the wealth of the nation on http://www.fanabc.com/english/index.php/news/item/7415premier-briefs-addis-based-diplomats-on-current-affairs.
15. In terms of progress in democratic transition of emerging countries, Ethiopia's score is one of the lowest. See, for instance, Radelet, Emerging Africa: How 17 Countries Are Leading the Way, 2010, p. 65.
16. See for this the World Bank data http://data.worldbank.org/indicator/NY.GDP.PCAP.CD?end=2015&start=1960.
17. See the World Bank International DEBT Statistics of 2019 http://datatopics.worldbank.org/debt/pdf/ids-2019.pdf.
18. See about Ethiopia's public debt to GDP ratio and its indebtedness at www.gfmag.com/global-data/economic-data/public-debt-per

centage-gdp and www.imf.org/external/np/pp/eng/2016/031516.pdf respectively.

19. See the list of African countries with lowest adult literacy rate at https://www.cia.gov/library/publications/the-orldfactbook/fields/2103.html.
20. See for the details about the civil war and the recurrence of drought and famine in Ethiopia and their consequences on the people and the country's economy, A Human Watch Report entitled as Evil Days: 30 Years of War and Famine in Ethiopia https://www.hrw.org/sites/default/files/reports/Ethiopia919.pdf. Also Kumar, Ethiopian Famines 1973–1985: A Case Study, 1987.
21. For instance, food shortages and hunger crisis in the country led to an estimated 1 million famine deaths from 1983 to 1985. See for this https://www.worldvision.org/disaster-relief-news-stories/1980s-ethiopia-famine-facts.
22. It is explicitly stated in multiple policy documents of the government that poverty is the arc enemy of and threat to the very survival of the Ethiopian state and bringing about rapid and sustainable economic development is a principal means for poverty reduction. See, for instance, Ministry of Information (2002). Ethiopia's Foreign Affairs and National Security Policy and Strategy. Addis Ababa: Ministry of Information. This policy is in effect since 2002; Ministry of Finance and Economic Development (MOFED) (2002). Ethiopia: Sustainable Development and Poverty Reduction Program. Addis Ababa: MOFED. This program laid the foundation for the two 5-year subsequent Growth and Transformation Plans (GTP I (2010–2014) and GTP II (2015–2019)). Both documents are available respectively at: https://www.africaintelligence.com/c/dc/LOI/1415/GTP-II.pdf and planipolis.iiep.unesco.org/upload/Ethiopia/EthiopiaGTP.pdf.
23. See for this UNDP Human Development Report (1991) http://hdr.undp.org/sites/default/files/reports/220/hdr_1991_en_complete_nostats.pdf.
24. See for this Yohannes Tekalign (2017). The Nexus between Ethiopia's Landlockedness and Its Security: The Economic, Politico-Military, and regional Dimensions. Unpublished PhD Dissertation, AAU: Addis Ababa.
25. See for this https://www.ictd.ac/project/practices-challenges-and-prospects-of-public-sector-taxation-in-ethiopia/.

References

Adejumobi, S.A. 2007. *The History of Ethiopia*. Westport: Greenwood Press.

African Development Bank (AfDB). 2008. *Ethiopia: Country Assistance Evaluation, 1996-2007*. Addis Ababa: AfDB, Operations Evaluation Department.

AfDB. 2015. *Development Effectiveness Review 2015: Ethiopia Country Review.* Abidjan: African Development Bank Group (AfDB).

Asayehgn, D. 2016. The Linkage Between Economic Growth and Food Security: An Eclectic Perspective. *Ethiopian Observer.*

Beegle, K. 2016. *Poverty in a Rising Africa.* Washington DC: World Bank.

Beyene, Berhe Mekonnen, and Tsegay Gebrekidan Tekleselassie. 2018. *The State, Determinants, and Consequences of Skills Mismatch in the Ethiopian Labour Market.* Addis Ababa: Ethiopian Development Research Institute (EDRI), Ethiopia.

Booth, D. 2012. *Development as a Collective Action Problem: Addressing the Real Challenges of African Governance.* http://www.institutions-africa.org/filestream/20121024-appp-synthesis-report-development-as-a-collective-action-problem. The Africa Power and Politics Programme.

Brooks, A. 2018. Was Africa rising? Narratives of Development Success and Failure Among the Mozambican Middle Class. *Territory, Politics, Governance* 6 (4): 447–467.

Central Statistical Agency of Ethiopia. 2018. Statistical Report on the 2018 Urban Employment Unemployment Survey. Statistical Bulletin 586, Addis Ababa.

Cowen, T. 2018. *Ethiopia Already Is the 'China of Africa'.* https://www.bloomberg.com/opinion/articles/2018-05-29/ethiopia-already-is-the-china-of-africa. Bloomberg.

Donnenfeld, Zachary, Porter Alexander, Cilliers Jacobus (Jakkie), Moyer Jonathan D., Scott Andrew, Maweni Joel, and Aucoin Ciara 2017. *Ethiopia Development Trends Assessment.* https://papers.ssrn.com/sol3/papers.cfm?abstract_id=3099366. USAID.

Ellis, G. 1988. In Search of a Development Paradigm: Two Tales of a City. *The Journal of Modern African Studies* 26 (4): 677–683.

Gebreeyesus, M. 2013. *Industrial Policy and Development in Ethiopia: Evolution and Present Experimentation.* Helsinki: UNU-WIDER.

Geda, A. 2008. The Political Economy of Growth in Ethiopia. In *The Political Economy of Economic Growth in Africa, 1960–2000: Country Case Studies*, ed. S.A.-P. Benno J. Ndulu, 116–142. Cambridge University Press: Cambridge.

Geda, A. 2011. *Readings on the Ethiopian Economy.* Addis Ababa: Addis Ababa University Press.

Henze, P. 1989. *Ethiopia's Economic Prospects for the 1990s.* Santa Monica: The RAND Publication.

Hiwet, A. 1975. *Ethiopia: From Autocracy to Revolution.* Review of African Political Economy.

Kumar, G. 1987. *Ethiopian Famines 1973–1985: A Case Study.* Oxford: World Institute for Development Economic Research.

Markus, H. 1991. *A History of Ethiopia*. Los Angeles: University of California Press.

Milkias, P. 2011. *Africa in Focus: Ethiopia*. Santa Barbara: ABC-CLIO LLC.

Ministry of Finance and Economic Development (MoFED). 2010. *Growth and Transformation Plan (GTP)*, 2010/11-2014/15 (Draft). Addis Ababa: MoFED.

Ministry of Information (MoI). 2002. *Foreign Affairs and National Security Policy and Strategy of Ethiopia*. Addis Ababa: Ministry of Information, Press and Audiovisual Department.

Mukherjee, Shantanu, Angela Lusigi, Eunice Kamwendo, and Astra Bonini. 2017. Inequality, Gender and Human Development in Africa. In *Income Inequality Trends in sub-Saharan Africa: Divergence, Determinants and Consequences*, ed. G.A. Ayodele Odusola, 245–268. New York: United Nations Development Programme.

NBE. 2013. *Annual Report 2012/13*. Addis Ababa: National Bank of Ethiopia (NBE).

NBE. 2017. *Annual Reports 2016/7*. Addis Ababa: National Bank of Ethiopia.

NPC. 2016. *Ethiopia's Growth and Transformation Plan II (GTP II), Volume I: Main Text*. Addis Ababa: National Planning Commission (NPC).

NPC. 2017. *Ethiopia's Progress Towards Eradicating Poverty: An Interim Report on 2015/16 Poverty Analysis Study*. Addis Ababa: National Planning Commission.

Oakland Institute. 2013. *Development Aid to Ethiopia: Overlooking Violence, Marginalization, and Political Repression*. Oakland: The Oakland Institute.

Obiols, M. 2017. *Countries With Highest GDP Growth In 2017*. https://www.gfmag.com/global-data/economic-data/countries-highest-gdp-growth. Global Finance Magazine.

OECD. 2018. *Africa's Development Dynamics 2018: Growth, Jobs and Inequalities*. Paris: OECD Publishing.

Ofcansky, Thomas P., and Berry LaVerle. 1991. *Ethiopia: A Country Study*. Montana: Kessinger Publishing LLC.

Pankhurst, R. 1968. *Economic History of Ethiopia, 1800–1935*. Addis Ababa: Haile Selassie I University Press.

Pillay, D. 2015. The Global Economic Crisis and the Africa Rising Narrative. *Africa Development* XL (3): 59–75.

Radelet, S. 2010. *Emerging Africa: How 17 Countries Are Leading the Way*. Washington, DC: The Center for Global Development.

Radelet, S. 2016. Africa's Rise—Interrupted? *Finance & Development* 53 (2): 6–11.

Shiferaw, A. 2017. *Productive Capacity and Economic Growth in Ethiopia*. CDP Background Paper No. 34.

Siegle, J. 2007. *Effective Aid Strategies to Support Democracy in Africa*. https://africacenter.org/wp-content/uploads/2016/02/Effective-Aid-Strategies-to-Support-Democracy-in-Africa-Siegle.pdf.

Tesfaye, A. 2017. *State and Economic Development in Africa: The Case of Ethiopia*. New York: Palgrave Macmillan.

The Economist. 2000. The Hopeless Continent. https://www.economist.com/weeklyedition/2000-05-13. 13 May.

The Economist. 2007. The Dark Continent. https://www.economist.com/middle-east-and-africa/2007/08/16/the-dark-continent. 16 August.

The Economist. 2011. A More Hopeful Continent. The Lion Kings?. https://www.economist.com/finance-and-economics/2011/01/06/the-lion-kings. 6 January.

The Economist. 2013. A Hopeful Continent. https://www.economist.com/sites/default/files/20130203_emerging_africa.pdf. 2 March.

Tiruneh, A. 1993. *The Ethiopian Revolution 1974–1987: A Transformation From an Aristocratic to a Totalitarian Autocracy*. Cambridge: Cambridge University Press.

UNCTAD. 2014. *The Economic Development in Africa Report 2014*. New York: The United Nations.

UNCTAD. 2018. *World Investment Report 2018: Investment and New Industrial Policies*. New York and Geneva: United Nations Conference on Trade and Development United Nations (UNCTAD).

UNDP. 1996. *Human Development Report 1996*. New York: Oxford University Press.

UNDP. 2015a. *Human Development Report 2015: Work for Human Development*. New York: UNDP.

UNDP. 2015b. *Millennium Development Goals Report 2014 Ethiopia: Assessment of Ethiopia's Progress Towards the MDGs*. Addis Ababa: UNDP.

UNDP. 2018. *Ethiopia's Progress Towards Eradicating Poverty*. Addis Ababa: UNDP Ethiopia.

Veen, E. V. 2016. *Perpetuating Power: Ethiopia's Political Settlement and the Organization of Security*. The Hague: The Netherlands Institute of International Relations 'Clingendael'.

World Bank. 2015. *Africa Gains in Health, Education, but Numbers of Poor Grow*. http://www.worldbank.org/en/news/press-release/2015/10/16/africa-gains-in-health-education-but-numbers-of-poor-grow. World bank.

World Bank. 2016. *Ethiopia's Great Run: The Growth Acceleration and How to Pace It*. Washington, DC: World Bank Group.

Zamfir, L. 2016. *Africa's Economic GROWTH: Taking Off or Slowing Down?* European Parliamentary Research Service (EPRS).

Zewde, B. 2001. *A History of Modern Ethiopia, 1855–1991*, 2nd ed. Addis Ababa: Addis Ababa University Press.

CHAPTER 13

The Price of Progress: Economic Growth, Authoritarianism, and Human Rights in Rwanda

Aymar Nyenyezi Bisoka and Hilde Geens

Introduction

This chapter shows how large agricultural investments in the fight against poverty have given way to considerable economic growth in Rwanda in the past two decades. However, the rise of Rwanda cannot be sustainable if the lingering tension between democracy and development is not addressed. To support this idea, the chapter illustrates how the ideal of modernity and the debates around economic growth and the fight against poverty are closely interconnected. It takes the Rwandan development model as a case study to illustrate how its modernization project has enabled the country to perform in line with core international objectives of the fight against poverty. Firstly, the chapter summarizes four criticisms of liberal tradition that dominated the economic news on African

A. Nyenyezi Bisoka (✉)
Catholic University of Louvain, Louvain, Belgium
e-mail: aymar.nyenyezi@uclouvain.be; aymar.nyenyezi@ucalouvain.be

H. Geens
NGO Artsen Zonder Vakantie, Mechelen, Belgium

K. Omeje (ed.), *The Governance, Security and Development Nexus*,
https://doi.org/10.1007/978-3-030-49348-6_13

development over the last ten years. Second, from the study of the agriculture and land tenure sectors, the chapter analyzes the way the Rwandan Government has successfully integrated these various economic and political criticisms, in both action and discourse. Furthermore, the chapter demonstrates that these successes are caused by the authoritarian developmentalism of the Rwandan government. Finally, in analyzing aspects of political governance and human rights, the chapter supports the criticism conditioning development to respect for individual rights. This chapter shows that the violation of human rights is a key element that prevents Rwanda to rise sustainably. Authoritarian growth without respect for human rights is not effective because it legitimizes autocrats and does not take into consideration the experiences of the people who have to contribute to this growth.

Since the end of the 1990s and the early 2000s, several African countries underwent a political transition based upon an election-based democracy ideal and a socio-economic program oriented toward the Millennium Development Goals (MDGs). "Good governance" was a focal point in the political transition discourse of both donors and national governments. However, most emphasis was placed on the technocratic aspects of governance, with a strong focus on the fight against corruption and discrimination rather than on protecting civic and political rights. Similarly, the MDGs seemed to have left out human rights targets for the benefit of economic development. Was this due to mere oversight or was it the result of an ideological calculation on the side of the MDGs designers? And can we move from yesterday's MDGs to today's Sustainable Development Goals (SDGs) without revising this omission?

The Rwandan example is an interesting illustration of the "democratic liberalism" model. Whereas the democratic aspect is limited to organizing formal elections and promoting good technocratic governance, the liberalist angle focuses upon the generation of economic growth with a focus on MDG achievements. According to a 2014 UNICEF Report, donors of the MDGs considered Rwanda as a model for development (UNICEF 2014). The report highlights how "macroeconomic stability, the profile of economic growth and [a] convenient choice of sectoral policies" (ibid.: 14) had played a major role in the acceleration of poverty reduction. At the macro-economic level, the report lauded Rwanda's "budgetary policies [aimed] strategically at mobilizing revenues, increasing public investment and distributing social benefits to the increasing population" (ibid.: 17). Next to investment in the agricultural sector, the financial injections, in particular social sectors are considered to be key to reduce poverty, for example, through universal health insurance, free education, and social transfers (ibid.: 22).

However, the 2014 UN Report—together with other similar reports which present Rwanda as a role model—has remained strategically silent on the human, civic, and political rights situation. Yet, the twentieth anniversary of the 1994 genocide—commemorated in 2014—was an important opportunity to reflect on the "democratic liberalism model" adopted by the RPF government since the end of the genocide. Indeed, some reports indicate that the Rwandan Government's "development without politics" approach has had a perverse impact on social cohesion. The Human Rights Watch's Annual Report 2015 mentions remarks that: "Rwanda has continued to make impressive progress in terms of economic and social development, but the government always imposes severe restrictions on expression and association freedoms and tolerates no dissenting voice. The political space is extremely restricted, and civil society as well as independent media is tremendously weak. Real or supposed opponents to the current regime continue to be the target of attacks, whether inside or outside of the country" (HRW 2015).

This chapter aims to shed light on how Rwanda has been able to legitimize its development path, by embedding it within the democratic liberalism model. Its development policies are the foundation of a modernization process in which economic outcomes are more paramount than political liberties. Some refer to the Rwandan political and economic governance model as "developmental patrimonialism" (Booth and Golooba-Mutebi 2012) or as a brand of "market-oriented authoritarianism" (Huggins 2014). Rwanda is not the only country that fits within this pattern. Other African countries like Ethiopia and Uganda for the most part follow a similar paradigm, albeit the Ugandan model seems more tolerant of human rights and public criticism of the government.

Large agricultural investments in the fight against poverty have caused considerable economic growth in Rwanda in the past two decades. However, the rise of Rwanda cannot be sustainable if the tension between democracy and development is not addressed. To further buttress the point, this chapter illustrates how the goal of modernity, the debates around economic growth, and the fight against poverty are closely interconnected. It takes the Rwandan development model as a case study to illustrate how its modernization project has fostered economic performance in line with core international objectives in the fight against poverty. Firstly, the study highlights four criticisms of the liberal tradition that has dominated the economic news on African development over the last ten years. Renowned economists like Jeffrey Sachs (2005), Paul Collier (2007), and Dambisa Moyo (2010) have all defended the dominance of economic liberalism over human rights. William Easterly (2013), on the other hand, defends the idea of "free development," conditioning economic development with respect for individual rights. Secondly, based on the evaluation of the agriculture and land tenure sectors, this study examines how the Rwandan Government has responded to the criticisms of its political and economic development ideologies, in both practice and discourse. Furthermore, this research argues that underlying the rise of Rwanda is the authoritarian developmentalism policy pursued by the state, which sacrifices respect for human rights at the altar of macroeconomic development. But it must be pointed out that the violation of human rights is a key element that prevents Rwanda to rise sustainably. Authoritarian growth without respect for human rights is not effective because it does not take into consideration the privations and hardship of the people who have to contribute to the goal of economic growth. Moreover, authoritarian growth often legitimizes autocrats. The observed non-convergence between political and economic liberalism in the Rwandan case brings us to a broader critique on the modernity ideal implicitly embedded within the MDGs (soon to be transformed into SDGs). Our analysis will question the assumed connection between the ideal of freedom and autonomy (found in the idea of modernity) and economic performance embodied in economic growth and achievement of the MDGs targets (found in the modernization policies).

Economic Development and Poverty Reduction: Neo-Liberal Debates of the Last Decade

The last ten years have generated interesting debates on African development policies, with a particular emphasis on post-conflict settings. These debates have largely been inspired by a more traditional approach to development; assuming that there "is a solution to the problem of poverty, and [that] rich countries have the financial, material, and intellectual resources necessary to develop and apply it" (Gérard 2008). Sachs, one of the main designers of the MDGs, is a fervent defender of this traditional approach to development. In his view, extreme poverty in developing countries can be eradicated if the extremely poor countries escape from their "poverty trap" (Sachs 2005). For Sachs, the "poverty trap" is a result of the demographic pressure hugely exceeding a country's saving capacities, and as a result, a limited connectivity to the production function. A big push through aid from rich countries would allow poor countries to climb the "first stand of the scale of economic development" (ibid.: 73), a crucial step to get out of the trap. The MDGs are designed in line with this liberal logic, based on the primacy of economic development over human rights.

However, Sachs' argument was met with criticism. Collier pointed to the perseverance of poverty traps in countries where a vicious cycle of conflicts reduces all chances for development. This vicious cycle—according to Collier—more likely appears in landlocked countries with bad neighbors, in small countries with bad governance structures, and in countries embedded in a natural resource trap. By identifying multiple development traps, Collier accuses Sachs to base *the fight against poverty* rather exclusively on development assistance. Instead, Collier proposes a mix of financial instruments and aid that are adapted to the specificities of each country. Similarly, Collier criticizes the MDGs for being a one-size-fits-all set of solutions to complex and diverse problems. Due to the broad definition of the MDGs, efforts on the ground are—in Collier's opinion—too fragmented. He therefore proposes to redefine the MDGs in line with the needs of extremely poor countries. However, despite the alarmist first part of his book's title *The Bottom Billion: Why the Poorest Countries are Failing*, the second part, *What can be done about it*, indicates that Collier remains confident about the potential to escape from these development traps. He sees solutions in the opening of commercial markets, the establishment of liberal reforms, and the increase of aid (Collier 2007). For both Collier and Sachs, human rights concerns come second, since they are dependent upon growth and economic development that should be first-order priorities.

These optimistic views of Sachs and Collier are challenged by Dambisa Moyo, who sees little potential in the general development process based upon aid inputs and oriented toward the MDGs. For Moyo, the MDGs are an illustration of "big push thinking" and of the problems of development aid. Moyo considers aid as the cause of all Africa's ills. She stresses how "aid is not the solution, but part of the problem—in fact, aid is the problem" (2010: 47). In attempting to demonstrate the role of aid in the underdevelopment of Africa, she recommends replacing aid by market finance. However, on one point, Moyo seems to agree with Sachs and Collier: development and human rights come after growth, although she doesn't explain how growth will lead to development and human rights.

William Easterly (2013) finally questions the dominance of economic liberalism over human rights, including within the MDGs. Easterly discusses how throughout different historical periods and contexts, similar development techniques have continuously been reproduced. Their failure, for Easterly, lies in the fact that these techniques allow technocrats and autocrats to self-legitimate their domination at the detriment of individuals' freedom. He adds that underdevelopment is first and foremost caused by the unrestricted power of the state over individuals who are both poor and without rights. For Easterly, emphasis should be placed on "*free development*": the promotion and protection of individuals' political and economic rights.

These debates have had a major influence on how developing countries and donors have framed their development policies over the last ten years. In the next part, we will illustrate how the balance between economic development and human rights was set in two specific sectors in Rwanda.

Poverty Reduction in Rwanda: Between Economic Development and Human Rights

Vision 2020 (Government of Rwanda, Finance and Economic Planning 2000) outlines the Rwandan Government's main vision for the country's social and economic future. The policies based upon this vision directly regulate the daily lives of Rwandans and, indirectly, the space for human rights in Rwanda. Vision 2020 identifies three steps for Rwanda to become a middle-income country by 2020: (1) achievement of macroeconomic stability and creation of wealth so as to reduce dependency to aid; (2) conversion of an agricultural economy into a knowledge-based economy; (3) creation of a productive middle class and encouragement of entrepreneurship. This essentially liberal economic agenda is fundamentally oriented to a teleological vision of development in line with the "big push" model of Sachs, and oriented toward the MDGs. It distances itself from Easterly's approach in which economic and social development may emerge out of a positive change in individuals' political and economic rights.

And indeed, a large part of the international community considers the Rwandan post-genocide economic and social reconstruction as a miracle of growth and an economic model for developing countries. Since 2000/2001, several studies about living conditions of Rwandan households (EICV) have showed real economic development and poverty reduction in Rwanda. Between 2004 and 2014, Rwanda has experienced strong real GDP growth; and by 2015, the country had achieved most MDGs. The poverty reduction was limited in the period 2000–2016 (NISR 2012, 2016) but the results of EICV3 showed an impressive poverty reduction for the period 2005–2006 to 2010–2011 (NISR 2015).[1]

This economic track record allows Rwanda to mobilize massive amounts of aid (Ansoms et al. 2018). At the same time, the economic and social progress allows the Rwandan Government to justify the limited space for human rights: "We are accused of not respecting human rights. But more than 90% of Rwandan children are enrolled, and 92% of the population receives health insurance. Are these not human rights?"[2] The same performance-orientated discourse can be found with regard to agriculture and land tenure.

Nonetheless, there are numerous reports on human rights violations and restrictions on freedom of expression and association in Rwanda (HRW 2015: 4). The Rwandan Patriotic Front (RPF) dominates the Rwandan political arena while many members of political opposition have been imprisoned (Reyntjens 2013; Purdekova 2015). The government limits the free functioning of civil society and media. According to HRW, "Government officials have openly expressed their hostility to independent, non-governmental organizations working on human rights" (HRW 2015: 4). Also, the 2015 report of Amnesty International indicates that "freedoms of expression and association in Rwanda continued to be unduly restricted by the authorities. Rwandans were unable to openly express critical views on issues perceived as sensitive by the authorities and the environment for journalists, human rights defenders and members of the opposition remained repressive" (Amnesty International 2015: 3). The promotion of economic growth by the Rwandan government to the detriment of respect for human rights is paramount in several areas of social life. Purdekova (2015: 338–339) argues that "counterposing economic needs and political liberties creates an illusionary trade-off." She convincingly highlights how the depoliticization of development undermines potential contestation and excuses acts of coercion and exploitation, ultimately leading to disempowerment. In the following section, we briefly discuss the process of depoliticization within the agricultural and land tenure, health and education sectors. In addition, we demonstrate how the MDGs have led to economic development through the use of techniques that violate human rights.

Agricultural Sector

Rwanda's current agricultural policies align to the first MDG: eliminating extreme poverty and hunger. The Rwandan government has embedded its agricultural agenda within the liberal agricultural model promoted by the African Union, the World Bank, and the European Union (Ansoms and Rostagno 2012; Nyenyezi 2016).The 2008 World Development Report pleads in favor of a Green Revolution for sub-Saharan Africa (ibid.). The New Economic Partnership for Africa's Development (NEPAD) promotes "the growth of the agricultural sector and economic development at the country level"[3] through national policies and programs of agricultural investment. Rwanda is considered as a model example, as it has successfully integrated this vision within its agricultural policy. The successive Rwandan Strategic Plans for Agricultural Transformation outline the operational framework for agricultural sector development (Ansoms et al. 2018), focusing on agricultural modernization, intensification, professionalization, and enterprise development.

This vision on agriculture is reflected in a policy developed by the Government of Rwanda which aims at promoting monoculture and regional specialization of regional crops, land registration, and consolidation, as well as the commercial orientation in all productive activities (ibid.). The policy package is inspired by the desire to improve efficiency and to achieve economies of scale in food production, with the ultimate aim of contributing to poverty reduction (Ansoms and Rostagno 2012). Through a top-down-controlled network of cooperatives, farmers gain access to credit mechanisms in order to increase their productivity. This meets the visions of Collier and Moyo who plead in favor of stimulating competitive sectors which are open to markets (Collier 2007; Moyo 2010). In effect, for the Rwandan Government, agriculture should be a commercial activity rather than being a subsistence activity. The intent is to create a sector able to consolidate on its comparative advantage in high-value commercial crops, which should allow farmers to compete on free markets, both regionally and internationally (Republic of Rwanda

2004). Some of the techniques used by the Rwandan Government have been contested by a large part of the population, notably with regard to land consolidation techniques and monoculture (Ansoms and Cioffo 2016). Several studies have concluded that, not only this policy is far from respecting the principle of food sovereignty, but also it doesn't provide more food security for the population (Van Damme et al. 2013). Through performance contracts, local authorities have resorted to coercion to impose these techniques to subsistence farmers that are mostly unwilling and for whom these techniques are not appropriate (Huggins 2017a).

Land Sector

International financial institutions (IFIs) have not only highlighted the importance of market-oriented agricultural production, they also place emphasis on the importance of a market-led land reform in order to facilitate the most efficient farmers. In 2007, Collier defended the need for a shift from traditional land management—regarded as inefficient—to modern and individualized land management. This approach aligns with the *maximum growth* school that promotes a neo-liberal land management model—based upon individual land rights—in order to maximize productivity (Huggins 2017b).

The agrarian reform process in Rwanda strongly endorsed a profound reorganization of land rights in favor of land consolidation. According to the 2004 land law (GoR 2004), the consolidation policy aims to increase land productivity (ibid.). Consolidated landholdings allow for the implementation of intensive monocropping techniques on a broad scale. The race toward increasing productivity through "rationalized" land management has several consequences. First, land registration has become mandatory and allows the Rwandan authorities to use the register to impose taxes (ibid.). Second, the reconfiguration of land rights in the wetlands obliged farmers to adhere to cooperative structures if they wanted to secure their land rights. This imposed form of organization was often accompanied with elaborate forms of elite capture, with those better informed or connected capitalizing upon the opportunities provided in this process (Ansoms et al. 2018). But also, in the hills, farmers are increasingly obliged to adhere to specialized cooperatives that produce a single and competitive crop for trade (Ansoms and Cioffo 2016). Although consolidation is presented as voluntary, farmers de facto have no choice when their land is located in the designated area (GoR 2007). Indeed, the land law has granted local administrations the power to confiscate land temporarily or permanently as a response to the failure to "rational exploitation" (ibid., art. 72–77). Performance contracts signed by districts and sector officials commit them to reaching a certain level of crop production and oblige local administrations to make farmers fit into the model (Ansoms et al. 2018).

Rwanda Rising: The Missing Link in the Focus on Economic Performance

This brief sector-based analysis draws attention to the overall picture of the means by which the Rwandan Government pursues growth at the cost of human rights. Growth is considered as a goal in itself that leads to poverty reduction. The MDGs which subordinated human rights to economic growth, incorporated this approach. Social sectors such as agriculture must contribute in achieving the growth objectives through a quest for performance, which often leads local authorities to coerce populations to implement performance contracts (Ansoms et al. 2018). The findings confirm a top-down political choice defended by Sachs (2005) and Collier (2007). This approach originates in the belief of the exclusive capacity of IFIs to provide solutions to the problems of people in the South, through good planning and implementation of public policies by Governmental institutions. This is the promotion of a quick and transition-free teleological vision of development.

To implement these top-down policies, Rwanda does not only rely on the mobilization of its population. The attitude of "good learner" in applying development models financed by important donors such as IFIs is highly rewarding in gaining external funding (Marysse et al. 2007). Again, success achieved in the MDGs is used by the Rwandan Government to justify the limited space for human rights. However, the Rwandan Government adopts the approach proposed by Moyo while emphasizing on considering external aid as temporary resort as Rwandans strives to achieve economic autonomy (Panait and Bisoka 2014).

Rwanda is a developing state (Harrison 2016) that can be described as a developmental patrimonial state in which "the ruling elite acquires an interest in, and a capability for, managing economic rents in a centralised way with a view to enhancing their own and others' incomes in the long run rather than maximizing it in the short run" (Booth and

Golooba-Mutebi 2012: 381). Although Rwanda is often described as a "development miracle" (Mann and Berry 2016) as a result of its strong economic growth (Matfess 2015), macro-economic performance indicators do not always reflect the experiences of populations (Ansoms et al. 2018). Several qualitative studies present evidence of the negative impacts of these policies on local populations (Van Damme 2013; Leegwater 2015; Treidl 2018).

The Rwandan success story underlines the importance of a clearly articulated vision on development based on quantitative measures (Biedermann 2015: 15). Performance strategies are integrated in the administrative system (Booth and Golooba-Mutebi 2012). Within these administrative systems specific objectives and audit procedures presented in performance contracts characterize and feed governance policies by learning through practice and innovation (Biedermann 2015: 9) based on scientific evidence. (Harrison 2016 361). However, those who consider the policies of Rwanda as reactive, problem originated iterative adaptations (par example, Booth 2015), do not consider that these learning processes are characterized by solid top-down governance stemming from a national dialog in which development objectives are discussed in public (Booth and Golooba-Mutebi 2014: 192). However, the imihigo system is often criticized for its coercive character and does not reflect local development priorities (Bugingo and Interayamahanga 2010). Numerous poor citizens have too much fear to express their experiences to the people in power (Mann and Berry 2016: 137). Evidence that contradicts the governmental discourse is contained in the governmental apparatus partly because they are integrated in hierarchical knowledge structures (including skepticism about local practices) at different levels managed by experts (Hasselskog 2015: 158) and partly because programming processes of local authorities are based on approximative classifications and general knowledge (Hasselskog 2015: 163), that lead to standardized solutions (Hasselskog 2015: 157) instead of diversified solutions adapted to local contexts.

The general use of quantitative objectives for planning documents and policies in Rwanda has to be seen in the light of global developmental strategies which focus on calculable results (Hoey 2015; Kelley and Simmons 2015).The detailed activities and objectives are not only used to shape policies but also to highlight successes in order to consolidate donor support to the government (cf. Ansoms and Rostagno 2012; Debusscher and Ansoms 2013: 1124). The capacity of the government to maintain its autonomy in the elaboration of policies is to a large extent based on the capacity to perform and to obtain developmental objectives which gives the governments strong incentives to articulate its successes.

Easterly (2013) strongly rejects this top-down approach of development and advocates linking development to positive changes in individual freedom. In his understanding, whenever there has been a positive change in freedom, development has followed. This approach also leads to questioning the use of state power in achieving performance indicators, as this is the case in Rwanda. In fact, for Easterly, there is a disproportionate use of state power against poor individuals deprived from their rights (ibid.). Hebitterly criticizes that autocrats and technocrats often favor the top-down approach in a process of mutual legitimation. Unlike Easterly, Rwandan authorities consider poverty as a technical problem. For Easterly, developed countries must answer this fundamental question in relation to poor countries: Not "What should we do?" for them, but "How can we make the poor free so as to be able to solve their problems themselves?" (ibid.).

The observations made by Easterly on the ignorance of local contexts by some development economists of IFIs and their complicity with autocrats meets the observations made by Mbembe when he talks about Africa in the field of contemporary knowledge and autocracy in Africa (Mbembe 2000). In effect, Mbembe refers to the concept of "philistinism" to evoke a kind of ignorance, even a deliberate ignorance of Africa justified by the false belief of knowing it, which leads to proposing solutions which then reveal to be ineffective. For Mbembe, it is precisely this lack of historical and contextual knowledge of Africa which proves the fact that academicians—such development economists—pose easy and inclusive questions like: What is Africa? What are the problems of Africa? What needs does Africa have? Subsequently, their answers quickly become a kind of commands made by donors to be necessarily implemented by States,—the autocrats—who then use them to legitimize their brutality and violence.

The MDGs have revealed to be such an easy solution in recent years. We have seen performance contracts put in place in Rwanda and their impact on the everyday lives of Rwandans serve as the basis for international recognition of performance made by the country in terms of MDGs achievement. This situation is neither exceptional for Rwanda nor recent for Africa.

From the structural adjustment plans put in place in 1980s in Africa (Coussy 2006), we witnessed the prevalence of the technician logic of modernization on the prescribed purposes of modernity. However, it is precisely through this external legitimization by technocrats that autocrats have managed to institutionalize some violent practices presumably intended to achieve the prescribed performance by the IFIs (Easterly 2013). Mbembe qualifies this type of practices specific to some African leaders as "command," the way the government forces people by asserting its right on them (Mbembe 2000). Then Mbembe identifies the forms of knowledge which supports the "command" in creating "his various significations" (Mbembe 2000: 140), that it then imposes as determinant matrix "the constitution of any other meaning within [...] societies" (ibid.).

Thus, since 1980, liberal-inspired policies of modernization have nurtured the expectation of progress without reference to its ideals of autonomy and liberty of the people. These policies, currently conceptualized in the MDGs since early 2000, have taken the orientation of economic liberalism while playing a major role: de-politicizing the citizens. In fact, Foucault (2004) and Arendt (1995) explain how liberal development takes the form of government practice dominated by an administrative logic at the cost of the political action. Arendt clarifies that by commanding the political arena, liberalism is causing general depoliticization of individuals through the imposition of the administrative logic (Saint-Pierre 2010). Foucault on the other hand stresses that this depoliticization is channeled by techniques of governmentality (Foucault 2001). Again, with the deployment of liberalism, it is up to the State to not only to deal with politics, but also to calculate, monitor, regulate, and classify the population according to an economic logic. For Arendt, liberalism has transformed modern politics in a "giant administration housewife" (Arendt 1982: 66); "a way of ensuring the satisfaction of vital needs of society and the productivity of free social development" (Arendt 1995: 66–67) on both theoretical and practical levels. For the two authors, economy is the root of such a State reduction to administration, life administration as shown in the Arendian social theorization and the Foucauldian approach. With Foucault, this depoliticization mechanic that emerges with liberalism is infused through governmental action redefinition by the political economy: the market shall no longer be regulated but will impose its truth on the government.

Conclusion

In the criticism of aid and the MDGs by Easterly, denunciation of practices that place economic development before respect of human rights is just not enough. Easterly also detects a discourse which reverses the prevailing logic and makes the means (development programs and policies) devoted to specific purposes (freedom and happiness of peoples), ends in themselves that produce slavery. In this sense, Easterly recovers the long Western philosophical tradition whose major traits have to be illustrated in order to sharpen the critical analysis of the MDGs in Rwanda. This tradition criticizes the misuse of western modernity by a reasoning which enslaves people instead of emancipating them.

In fact, the post-transitional period in Rwanda is part of the process of modernization that is soundly established in all its programs. This modernization is actually unveiled from its questioning of previous modes of management in various sectors of social life and then offers a new way of managing those sectors. This set of proposals is inscribed in what Peemans (2002: 83) calls "new order of things," where, after delegitimizing the techniques of sectoral management in place and considering them as ineffective, he proposes an alternate one which is inscribed in the idea of progress. This pursuit of progress tries to found its legitimization in the idea of rebuilding a new society, by postulating a better material situation for people in this society leading to freedom and happiness of the people (freedom being irreducible to happiness) as postulated by modernization. For the Rwanda case in particular, the MDGs and economic growth have become the goals to accomplish in order to achieve contentment for the people. These goals ought to be achieved through a series of political reforms in various sectors as analyzed above. But, is there any clear link between happiness of the people and the modernization that Rwanda pursues through economic growth and the MDGs achievement?

On several occasions, critical researchers on Rwanda have exploited the question of links between modernization, freedom and happiness of people (Thomson 2013; Reyntjens 2013; Purdekova 2011). They usually notice the difference between promises of modernization in various sectors in Rwanda and the reality on the ground while denouncing the hardship and violence in the process of achieving these promises. The danger of such an approach is however to ignore that, for modernity, hardship and violence are conceivable since the State, the guarantor of the process toward collective well-being, has the monopoly of legitimate violence in order to achieve freedom and happiness of the people. From this point of view, it becomes important to determine the theoretical bases from which it would be more effective to criticize the actions of the State vis-à-vis its modes of legitimizing dependence which are often legality and the defense of the general interest. This is why we opted for a different approach based on a critique of the modernization model of the Rwandan state. In this connection, we have pointed out how this modernization model is far from the idea of modernity, explaining how it has led to the instrumentalization of the ideology of the governing elite to impose domination on the rest of the population. In addition, we have highlighted how the pursuit of the MDGs played a role in this process of using the state's modernization ideology to foster authoritarian control and domination.

Finally, as we have argued in this chapter that economic growth in Rwanda is not sustainable for two reasons: firstly, the fixation on growth statistics which do not necessarily represent the well-being of the poor but instead obscures their plight. The entire growth-oriented fixation process uses a technical language based on numbers which do not reflect the everyday life of the citizens. Secondly is the penchant to use an authoritarian top-down style by the Rwandan government to increases performance. However, this strategy tends to neglect the real objectives of growth, which is human well-being, particularly for the poorest sections of the population. To address the need of the populations trapped in extreme poverty, it is necessary to listen to them and to respect and promote human rights, a process so far discountenanced by the authoritarian development model in Rwanda.

Notes

1. For more detail and criticism of these figures, see Ansoms et al. (2018).
2. *Libération*, 14 September 2011.
3. See http://www.nepad.org, Retrieved on 3 February 2015.

References

Amnesty International. 2015. *Annual Report 2015.*

Ansoms, An, and Donatella Rostagno. 2012. Rwanda's Vision 2020 Halfway Through: What the Eye Does Not See. *Review of African Political Economy* 133 (14): 427–450.

Ansoms, An, and Giuseppe Cioffo. 2016. The Exemplary Citizen on the Exemplary Hill: The Production of Political Subjects in Contemporary Rural Rwanda. *Development and Change* 47 (6): 1247–1268.

Ansoms, An, Giuseppe Cioffo, Neil Dawson, Sam Desiere, Cristopher Huggins, Margot Leegwater, Jude Murison, Aymar Nyenyezi Bisoka, Johanna Treidl, and Julie Van Damme. 2018. The Rwandan Agrarian and Land Sector Modernization: Confronting Macro Performance with Lived Experiences on the Ground. *Review of African Political Economy* 157 (45): 408–431.

Arendt, Hannah. 1982. *Condition de l'homme moderne*. Paris: Calmann-Lévy.

Arendt, Hannah. 1995. *Qu'est-ce que la Politique?* Paris: Seuil.

Biedermann, Zsuzsanna. 2015. Rwanda: Developmental Success Story in a Unique Setting. Centre for Economic and Regional Studies HAS Institute of World Economics Working Paper 213.

Bisoka, Aymar Nyenyezi. 2016. *Invention de la terre et production des anormaux dans le dispositif foncier en Afrique. Pouvoir et résistance à l'accaparement des terres en Afrique des Grands Lacs*. PhD, Université catholique de Louvain.

Booth, David. 2015. Towards a Developmental State Concept That IS Fit for Purpose (In the 21st Century, in Africa). Working Paper. London: Overseas Development Institute.

Booth, David, and Frederick Golooba-Mutebi. 2012. Developmental Patrimonialism? The Case of Rwanda. *African Affairs* 111 (444): 379–403.

Booth, David, and Frederick Golooba-Mutebi. 2014. Policy for Agriculture and Horticulture in Rwanda: A Different Political Economy? *Development Policy Review* 32 (s2): s173–s196.

Bugingo, Irenee, and Reverien Interayamahanga. 2010. *A Study on the Development and Use of Governance Indicators in Rwanda*. Kigali: Institute of Research and Dialogue for Peace.

Collier, Paul. 2007. *The Bottom Billion: Why the Poorest Countries Are Failing and What Can Be Done About It*. Oxford: Oxford University Press.

Coussy, Jean. 2006. États africains, programmes d'ajustement et consensus de Washington. *L'Économie politique* 4 (32): 29–40.

Debusscher, Petra, and An Ansoms. 2013. Gender Equality Policies in Rwanda: Public Relations or Real Transformations? *Development & Change* 44 (5): 1111–1134.

Easterly, William. 2013. *The Tyranny of Experts, Economist Dictators and the Forgotten Rights of the Poor*. New York: Basic Books.

Foucault, Michel. 2001. *Il faut défendre la société. Cours au Collège de France (1975–1976)*. Édition numérique réalisée en août 2012 à partir de l'édition CD-ROM, Le Foucault Électronique.

Foucault, Michel. 2004. *Naissance de la Biopolitique. Cours au Collège de France (1978–1979)*. Paris: Seuil.

Gérard, L. 2008. Réconcilier profits et développement La BoP, une nouvelle normativité pour lutter contre la pauvreté? Observatoire du Management Alternatif, Cahier de recherche, 30 juin 2008—HEC, Paris, 2007–2008, p. 8.
GoR. 2004. *National Land Policy*. Kigali: Ministry of Lands, Environment, Forests, Water and Mines. Government of Rwanda (GoR).
GoR. 2007. *Rapid and Extensive Assessment of Performance Management Contracts—Imihigo*. Ossrea, Kigali, MINALOC and MINECOFIN, July.
Government of Rwanda, Finance and Economic Planning. 2000. *Rwanda Vision 2020*, Kigali, July.
Harrison, Graham. 2016. Rwanda: An Agrarian Developmental State? *Third World Quarterly* 37 (2): 354–370.
Hasselskog, Malin. 2015. Rwandan Developmental 'Social Engineering': What Does It Imply and How Is It Displayed? *Progress in Development Studies* 15 (2): 154–169.
Hoey, Lesli. 2015. 'Show Me the Numbers': Examining the Dynamics Between Evaluation and Government Performance in Developing Countries. *World Development* 70 (June): 1–12.
HRW. 2015. *Annual Report 2015*. Human Rights Watch, USA.
Huggins, Cristopher. 2014. 'Control Grabbing' and Small-Scale Agricultural Intensification: Emerging Patterns of State-Facilitated 'Agricultural Investment' in Rwanda. *Journal of Peasant Studies* 41 (3): 365–384.
Huggins, Christopher. 2017a. Discipline, Governmentality and 'Developmental Patrimonialism': Insights from Rwanda's Pyrethrum Sector. *Journal of Agrarian Change* 17 (4): 715–732.
Huggins, Christopher. 2017b. *Agricultural Reform in Rwanda: Authoritarianism, Markets and Zones of Governance*. London: Zed Books.
Kelley, Judith G., and Beth An Simmons. 2015. Politics by Number: Indicators as Social Pressure in International Relations. *American Journal of Political Science* 59 (1): 55–70.
Leegwater, Margot. 2015. *Sharing Scarcity: Land Access and Social Relations in Southeast Rwanda*. Leiden: African Studies Centre.
Mann, Laura, and Marie Berry. 2016. Understanding the Political Motivations That Shape Rwanda's Emergent Developmental State. *New Political Economy* 21 (1): 119–144.
Marysse, Stefaan, An Ansoms, and Danny Cassimon. 2007. The Aid 'Darlings' and 'Orphans' of the Great Lakes Region in Africa. *European Journal of Development Research* 19 (3): 433–458.
Matfess, Hilary. 2015. Rwanda and Ethiopia: Developmental Authoritarianism and the New Politics of African Strong Men. *African Studies Review* 58 (2): 181–204.

Mbembe, Achille. 2000. *De La Postcolonie: Essai sur l'imagination politique dans l'Afrique contemporaine*. Paris: Karthala.
Moyo, Dambissa. 2010. *Dead Aid: Why Aid Is Not Working and How There Is a Better Way for Africa*. New York: Ferra, Strauss and Giroux.
NISR. 2012. *The Evolution of Poverty in Rwanda from 2000 to 2011: Results from the Household Surveys*. Kigali: NISR.
NISR. 2015. *Results of Integrated Household Living Conditions Survey 2013/14*. Kigali: NISR.
NISR. 2016. *Poverty Trend Analysis Report 2010/11–2013/14*. Kigali: NISR.
Panait, Oana Marina, and Aymar Nyenyezi Bisoka. 2014. L'Agaciro rwandais: Discours post-développementaliste ou usurpation de la lutte postcoloniale? Légitimation et délégitimation d'un discours. In *L'Afrique des Grands Lacs. Annuaire 2013–2014*, ed. Stefaan Marysse, Filip Reyntjens, and Stef Vandeginste, 361–384. Paris, France: L'Harmattan.
Peemans, Jean-Philippe. 2002. *Le développement des peuples face à la modernisation du monde*. Louvain-la-neuve and Paris: Academia-Bruylant/l'Harmattan.
Purdekova, Andrea. 2011. 'Even If I Am Not Here, There Are So Many Eyes': Surveillance and State Reach in Rwanda. *The Journal of Modern African Studies* 49: 475–497.
Purdekova, Andrea. 2015. *Making Ubumwe: Power, State and Camps in Rwanda's Unity-Building Project*. New York: Berghahn Books.
Republic of Rwanda. 2004. *National Land Policy*. Kigali: Republic of Rwanda.
Reyntjens, Filip. 2013. *Political Governance in Post-genocide Rwanda*. New York: Cambridge University Press.
Sachs, Jeffrey. 2005. *The End of Poverty: Economic Possibilities for Our Time*. Penguin Press Hc.
Saint-Pierre, Emilie. 2010. *Au croisement des pensées de Hannah Arendt et de Michel Foucault sur le social, le biopouvoir et la gouvernementalité*, 35. Mémoire de maîtrise, Université du Québec, Montréal, 2008.
Thomson, Susan. 2013. *Whispering Truth to Power: Everyday Resistance to Reconciliation in Post-Genocide Rwanda*. Madison, WI: University of Wisconsin Press.
Treidl, Johanna. 2018. Sowing Gender Policies, Cultivating Agrarian Change, Reaping Inequality? Intersections of Gender and Class in the Context of Marshland Transformations in Rwanda. Antropologia.
UNICEF. 2014. *UNICEF Annual Report 2014: Rwanda*. Paris: UNICEF. https://www.unicef.org/about/annualreport/files/Rwanda_Annual_Report_2014.pdf.
Van Damme, Julie. 2013. Analyse systémique des processus d'innovation dans les systèmes agraires de la region des Grands Lacs basés sur la culture de la banane. PhD dissertation, Université catholique de Louvain.

Van Damme, Julie, An Ansoms, and Philippe Baret. 2013. Agricultural Innovation from Above and from Below: Confrontation and Integration on Rwanda's Rural Hills. *African Affairs* 113 (450): 128–137.
Vandeginste, Stef, Marijke Verpoorten, and Filip Reyntjens. 2014. *L'Afrique des Grands Lacs. Annuaire 2013–2014*, 361–384. Paris: l'Harmattan.

CHAPTER 14

State-Society Relations and State Capacity in Somalia

Abdullahi Mohammed Odowa

Introduction

As one of the first countries in Africa to successfully establish a vibrant, multi-party democracy the country of Somalia was once one of the leading lights on a continent where the rule of dictators and one-party quickly followed the process of decolonization (Abdi. I. Samatar 2016). Endowed with the enormous economic potential of untapped natural resources and an important strategic geopolitical location on the Gulf of Aden, which includes one of the longest coastlines of mainland Africa, Somalia has suffered from political instability, violent conflict, and humanitarian disasters, which have included drought, floods, and famine. Since the collapse of the Siad Barre regime in 1991 and the civil war that followed the country has served as the archetype of a 'failed-state.' This has resulted in Somalia having one of the worst records as measured on human development indices including an average life expectancy of 47 years, adult literacy rate of less than 18%, an infant mortality rate of 132 deaths in every 1000 live births and only 20% of the population having access to health services (UNDP 2001: 19).

A. M. Odowa (✉)
The University for Peace (UPEACE), San José, Costa Rica

K. Omeje (ed.), *The Governance, Security and Development Nexus*,
https://doi.org/10.1007/978-3-030-49348-6_14

The magnitude and protracted nature of the conflict and ongoing cycle of humanitarian disasters have attracted the attention of analysts and academics who have tried to make sense of what has gone wrong with Somali politics and society and attempt to offer solutions based on studies that have employed either traditionalist or instrumentalist theoretical models (Anderson 2012). These traditionalist models typically stress the centrality of the clan system and traditional kinship relationships as part of an effort to explain the origin and nature of the state collapse in Somalia and the challenge facing attempts to rebuild a central government and associated institutions. Furthermore, traditionalists argue that the nature of fragmentation and decentralization of clan system and nomadic/pastoralist way of life of the majority of the Somalis—obviously with the exception of Rahanweyn (Digil and Mirifle) and a group of minority communities who use agro-pastoral or agriculture as the main source of their livelihood—are incompatible with centralized nature of modern statehood, therefore, propose decentralized and negotiated form of statehood (Harper 2012; Kaplan 2010; Lewis 1998a). However, as noted by Abdi. I. Samatar (1992: 626–627) much analysis of the role of clan as the basic unit of society and politics in Somalia remains rooted in an intellectual legacy established during the colonial era and the work of the noted Somali Studies scholar I. M Lewis. This has included according to Samatar a basic failure to recognize that the clan system has not remained unchanged during the political and social transformation which has occurred in Somalia since independence. He notes that those who have adopted a more static or mechanical view of social change in Somali society, and attribute blame for conflict largely on tribal animosities, make the mistake of conflating 'the causes with the consequences of these tragedies' (1997: 687).

In contrast, instrumentalist models approach the issue of the clan system with somewhat more flexibility and place more emphasis on its manipulation firstly by colonial powers and then later by Somali elites both before and after the 1969 military coup (Besteman 1996; Bulhan 2008, Kapteijns 2004; Abdi I. Samatar 1992, 1997, 2000). Nevertheless, as noted by Gaas (2018: 464) the fact that these models offer a more comprehensive analysis of the place and role of the clan in Somali politics and society they have failed to recognize and account for the manipulation of elites by clan actors.

Drawing where relevant to literature based on both traditionalist and instrumentalist models, this chapter adopts the innovative social control model developed by Joel S. Migdal (1988: 29) to advance two main arguments. The first is that the current governance crisis in Somalia is the result of decayed state-society relations that has led to a strong resistance within society to the re-establishment of a centralized state authority. Mistakes in the development and implementation of policy, as well as the abuse of power by colonial authorities and subsequent Somali governments, have eroded public trust in state institutions. This breakdown in relations between state institutions and citizens has also undermined the ability of Somali authorities to mobilize the general population in the face of competition from competing sources of political power, and legitimacy, including traditional leaders, Islamist movements, pirate gangs, and violent religious extremists; included in this last category are Harakaat al-Shabaab al-Mujahideen (aka 'al-Shabaab'), Hizb ul-Islam (defunct) and the so-called 'Islamic State' group. The second argument concerns the need to create legitimate and credible institutions to meet the needs of the population and in order to incentivize an acceptance of their authority, activities, and rules.

In support of these arguments I have used Migdal's illustration of society and its relation to the state as a point of departure to offer brief remarks on the two concepts—that of the state and state-society-relations. This is followed by a brief review of the political history of Somalia during the various eras of colonial rule, civilian government, and military dictatorship. I have made analytical contrasts between periods of Somalia's history when the state's influence and control over society were substantially high and when the phenomena had collapsed and disappeared completely.

Defining the Concepts: State and State-Society Relations

It is necessary to begin with a brief introduction to Migdal's model and its analysis of society. In contrast to other models of macro-level societal change analysis (e.g., center–periphery, great tradition–little tradition, and modern–traditional) Migdal (1988: 29) treats society as a mélange—mix of social organizations—in which a vast array of social organizations—formal and informal—compete for dominance and influence. This model presented by Migdal offers a more conceptually innovative approach to the study of society and its relationship with state institutions than these of other (still) more predominate theories.

According to Migdal, the state is one organization among many competing with and overcoming the resistance of other actors to achieve predominance as the recognized source of legitimate political authority. While in some environments the state can, without engaging in a major confrontation, enforce its rule and undertake major social transformation with ease, in others there are competing sources of power and/or legitimacy. In the latter, different social organizations are in conflict, both violent and non-violent, to shape the 'rules of the game' in the competition between them and their rivals. According to Migdal's model, the currency over which one social organization competes for predominance in a highly competitive and hostile political environment is social control. The ability of one group to increase its social control is determined by the level of compliance, participation, and its ability to confer legitimacy (Migdal 1988: 33).

Since the era of decolonization most countries in Africa have seen the ability of the state to extend its authority and set the 'rules of the game' in this way to have been more myth than reality (Stepputat et al. 2007: 8). While in some cases governing authorities have been forced into negotiating with one, several or even a multitude of other actors in more extreme cases, state institutions have been defeated and dismantled by informal social organizations. In such a context, Migdal's model becomes very useful in analyzing the push and pull forces between different social organizations that are competing for predominance and in an often highly hostile environment. The model also serves to highlight the conditions which can assist the state to uphold a monopoly on power to enforce its rule as well as those that can lead to its defeat and dismantling such as occurred in Somalia.

Conceptualizing the State

While the state has occupied a central place in the field of political science, it has nevertheless remained a messy concept (Mann 1988: 4). This is due in part to the fact that scholars have often adopted definitions beyond the one famously offered by Max Weber; that of 'a human community that successfully claims the monopoly of the legitimate use of physical forces within a given territory' (Weber 1946: 1). However, although these other definitions offer competing concepts of the state most still rest on, directly or indirectly, the four essential components of the population, fixed territory, government, and sovereignty (Grigsby 2009: 56; Grotenhuis 2016: 25; Stepputat et al. 2007: 7).

The concepts of government and sovereignty are closely related and form two critical components of any definition of the state. The government can be defined as the set of differentiated institutions run by staffed personnel; the government is the agency of machinery through which standard policies are determined and by which everyday affairs are regulated and implemented (Grigsby 2009: 56). It is through government that the authority of the state is enforced, whether directly or indirectly, and that the functions of the state (e.g., creation and enforcement of the law) are exercised. Sovereignty can be understood as the main feature of the state that distinguishes it from other social organizations competing for dominance and legitimacy within a given geographically defined area. The concept implies that the authority of the state is recognized by both its citizens and by other states as the only supreme and final legal authority above and beyond which no other legal power exists (Stepputat et al. 2007: 7). It is through the exercising of this authority that the state is able to maintain order within society and prevent other actors and destabilizing forces from undermining its monopoly on the use of force and undermining, if not destroying, its institutions. Without this authority, the state will be unable to ensure its continued existence let along provide good governance or otherwise defend its citizens from either internal or external threats. Mann (1988: 5) identifies two types of powers exercise by the states and their elites, namely, 'Deposit power' and 'Infrastructural power.' The first of these, 'deposit power,' is defined by Mann as a 'range of actions which the elites are empowered to undertake without routine, institutionalized negotiation with civil society groups.' These powers are often immense in more authoritarian regimes and weaker in capitalist democracies. The second power, identified by Mann as 'infrastructural power,' is the 'capacity of the state to penetrate civil society and to implement logistically political decisions through the realm' (Mann 1988: 5). These classifications of state/elite powers offered by Mann offer useful tools to undertake an analysis of the power exercised by the governing authorities that have ruled Somalia across different periods of the country's history. They can also be useful in helping to develop a better understanding how the presence, or indeed absence, of these powers has had on the on state-society relations; a notable aspect of which is how the presence or absence of these powers impacts the capacity of the state to impose, coerce, mobilize citizens.

Moreover, it is essential to note that the administrative capacity of the state, its legitimacy, and its monopoly of power are all closely interlinked and cannot be separated from each other. In other words, weakness in one area can have a negative impact on other characteristics that define statehood. This has been demonstrated by Stepputat, Andersen, and Møller (2007: 8) as follows:

> The state's administrative capacity as well as its ability to uphold a monopoly of violence are thus closely linked to its capacity to raise revenues from society, which in turn is linked to its legitimacy in the eyes of the population, which in turn is linked to the state's capacity to provide services for which it needs both administrative capacity and a monopoly of violence.

It is against this benchmark, or similar, that the capacity of any given state to govern is commonly assessed. While in some countries and even regions of the world the capacity of the state to set and enforce rules or provide moral leadership is taken for granted (e.g., the European Union) this is not a universal experience. For many countries in Africa, the state sovereignty has been fragmented and incomplete. This has resulted in the reduction of the state to one of many actors competing not only for supremacy over its rivals but also at times struggling for survival (Clapham 1996; Krasner 1999; Herbs 1997). In many African states, the crisis of governance affecting the state has also served to undermine its ability to increase the supply of public goods and maintain harmonious social relations between ethnic tribes, clans, faith communities, political factions, and other actors. It is this experience that gives validity to the assessment that revolutionary measures will need to be taken to address the root causes of these crises in governance before affected countries in Africa can be expected to be able to sustainably fulfill either their domestic or international obligations.

State–Society Relations

The concept of state-society relations provides a starting-point to develop a more balanced understanding of the dynamics between the state and society as well as the influence they may have on each other (Migdal 1994: 23; Zhao 2000: 1596). This takes on particular importance in the context of Africa where many of the crises in governance in Africa, both historic and contemporary, can be linked to conflicts based on the nature and dynamics of the relationship between the state and society (Ahmed. I. Samatar 1985: 23). Nevertheless, the concept of state-society relations has remained somewhat elusive and difficult to define. In part, this is due to the significant change that has taken place in the literature on state-society relations that has taken place over the past five decades or so. Prior to the 1970s the concept of state-society relations was a rather insignificant area of interest within the field of sociology before the state and society began to be treated in the literature published in the 1980s as separate but interactive entities (Goodwin 1989; Goodwin and Skecpol 1989; Skocpol 1989). The literature of the period of the 1970s and 1980s can be characterized as having a state-centric focus owing to its focus on the state and analyzing societal factors within the context of the existing state apparatus. In contrast, scholars in the 1990s adopted what could be described as a society centric approach when analyzing the relations between state and society (Linz and Stepan 1996; McDaniel 1991; Migdal 1994). This latter approach presents the state as part of the wider society and posits that each transforms the other as they come into contact (Migdal 1994: 23).

Another factor requiring consideration is the difficulty inherent in attempting to separate the concepts of state and society: the question may be asked 'where does the state end and society begin?' Having an understanding of how the state affects a society and vice versa is, in the opinion of this author, critical for the resolution of the deep-rooted crisis of government affecting many African countries today. Likewise, an appreciation of this relationship can also play a role in supporting efforts to enhance the sovereignty of the state as well as its legitimacy in the eyes of its citizens. My own experience traveling from Somalia, a country in which I have worked and called home since 2005, to the city of Geneva in Switzerland revealed to me that one of the primary factors that sets the two countries apart is the nature and sharp contrast between their respective state-society relations.

While living and working in the city of Hargeisa, the capital and economic hub of the self-declared independent Somali region known as Somaliland, I rarely interacted with either the state or its services. Although relatively peaceful compared to other Somali cities the state and its institutions remain largely invisible to people going about their every-day lives. An example of this concerns the supply of water to the city and its residents. During my stay, I was one of the many inhabitants of Hargeisa who lacked running water in their house and were forced to rely on water trucks. Similarly, security in my local area was not provided by the police but rather private patrols that charged a regular fee of US$5 per house. The poor state of the public education system, both in terms of quality, outcomes, and discipline, also necessitated sending my children to a private school. The invisibility of the state and its inability to provide essential public goods have severed the state from the society. With the gaps left by weak state institutions filled by the private sector the state's sovereignty has suffered and the legitimacy of the government has been weakened in the eyes of the general population. This also affected the state's capacity to collect revenues with a majority of the people unwilling to pay taxes that compelled the government to adopt oppressive and even unlawful devices, such as removing the main doors of people's houses in order to force them to pay taxes.

It was from such an environment in which the condition of state-society relations had deteriorated so badly that I traveled to the city of Geneva for a two-week business trip. On my arrival I was transported to the hotel where I would be staying and on checking-in received a card that I was told to use for the city's public transport system. After a short rest I left the hotel and took a bus to the center of the city. To my surprise there was no conductor on the bus and my attempt to show the driver the card I had been given by the hotel was met with a polite request to just take a seat. I took my seat and in the course of the journey observed how passengers get on and off the bus without any discussion about paying a fare. On returning to the hotel I intimated the receptionist about my experience on the bus and was informed that local residents pay to use public transport either monthly or annually while visitors such as myself have this cost covered by their hotel. While to the receptionist this was a matter of state conventional wisdom, I found this entire experience quite astonishing when compared to how things work in Hargeisa and it left me puzzled about the extreme differences between the two parts of the world.

Ostensibly, the answer to my puzzle is a rather simple one. Local Swiss authorities are able to provide a high-quality service to their citizens in a transparent and professional manner because of the willingness of locals to pay their taxes. This is because unlike in Hargeisa locals in Geneva believe that the state will use these funds in a manner that serves their interests. The benefit to Swiss authorities is that by delivery services in an efficient and accountable fashion their authority and ability to mobilize the local population, whether to obey rules or support government policies, has been greatly enhanced. In contrast, the authorities in Hargeisa and elsewhere in Somalia have proven incapable of delivering basic essential services such as water, security, education, and electricity. This in turn has undermined the ability of Somali authorities to generate the revenue necessary to maintain functional state institutions. The resulting invisibility of the state to ordinary Somali's in their day-to-day life has contributed to the weakening of its legitimacy, authority, and sovereignty to the point that it has become what Jackson (1990) has described as a 'quasi-state.'

Colonial Legacy: Laying the Basis for a Weak State in Somalia

One of the key factors to consider in explaining the root causes of the failure of successive Somali administrations to establish good governance is the continued legacy of Italian, French, and British colonial rule. This issue of the ongoing impact of the experience of colonialism is not unique to Somalia and has been the topic of a significant amount of literature in the field of African studies (Boahen 1987; Brett 1974; Tordoff 2002). And yet even with the passage of more than sixty years since independence the brutal and exploitative nature of the colonial rule, as well as the role it has played in creating division and conflict within and between clans and ethnic groups, remains an important factor to consider when analyzing the current condition of state-society relations in Somalia.

In order to understand this enduring legacy of colonial partition and administration on the Somali people it is necessary to engage in a brief examination of the political and social organization of their pre-colonial society. This history was characterized by two main themes: contact with the outside world and a decentralized clan-based social structure.

As noted by Harper (2012: 14), the proximity of the Horn of Africa to the Arabian Peninsula and its 3000 km coastline has meant that the Somali people have a long history of contact with the outside world. This has included trade with Greeks, Romans, Persians, Ottomans, Indians, and Arabs that long pre-dated the European 'scramble for Africa' (Bulhan 2008: 20). This was not only true for coastal communities but also applied to pastoralists who lived a nomadic or semi-nomadic existence.

These pastoralist communities regularly encountered non-Somali communities during their movement westward toward Ethiopia or south toward what is now Kenya during the search for water and pasture needed to maintain their herds (Harper 2012: 45).

Within the writings of those who have examined the early history of Somalia a common theme has been the description of Somali as a highly decentralized and egalitarian people who lacked any commitment to a centralized authority (Lewis 1992). Here it is worth noting that with the (limited) exception of the Dervish state established by Sheikh Mohammad Abdulla Hassan (called the 'Mad Mullah' by the British) pre-colonial Somali states such as the Hobyo, Ajuran. and Warsangali Sultanates were essentially clan-based projects that failed to establish power bases beyond a single clan and its associated sub-clans. The fundamental base on which this pre-colonial society was organized was the household on which all other social and political organization was built. The harsh nature of the local environment in which resources such as water and pasture were often limited necessitated cooperation between these households in order to limit the outbreak of conflict between clans or even among their own sub-clans (Abdi. I. Samatar 1997: 693–694). Within this system, community elders exercised limited authority because they lacked control over who could or could not have access to communal resources. It was in this environment that the system of traditional Somali law (Somali: *Xeer*) was developed. This system which relied on a mixture of Islamic law and a commitment to precedent allowed elders to resolve disputes and put an end to violent conflicts. Although imperfect, stronger actors have often been able to impose or ignore an unfavorable judgment, this system was the basis on which the moral, political, and economic system of pre-colonial Somali society was based (Abdi. I. Samatar 1997: 694).

Within this system it can be noted that pre-colonial community elders lacked 'Deposit Power' which would have allowed them to enforce their decisions and exercise effective authority over people and resources. Instead, the authority of community elders was based on 'Infrastructural Power' based on Islamic values the moral system which emerged through the development and implementation of the *Xeer* as a system justice, dispute resolution, and de-escalation of conflict.

Unfortunately, as in other parts of Africa, the intervention of colonial powers violently interrupted the natural evolution of the traditional Somali political and legal systems of governance. It is however beyond the scope of this chapter to speculate what type of political system may have developed or to try and provide a detailed exploration of what was close to one hundred years of colonial rule. Conscious of these limitations I shall be concentrating on the enduring legacy of the colonial-era partition of the Somali-inhabited regions in the Horn of Africa and the commodification of the traditional system of government that took place under British, Italian, and French rule.

The partition of the Somali people into five parts that were administered separately by Britain, France, Italy, and Ethiopia has had the obvious effect of preventing one of the largest ethnic groups in Africa from forming their own nation-state. This does not mean that the fragmentation of the Somali people along the lines of clan and sub-clan is overlooked. Instead, it recognizes the fact that the division of the Somali people into the regions of British Somaliland, Italian Somaliland, French Somali Coast (now Djibouti), Ogaden region (now part of Ethiopia), and Northern Frontier District (now part of Kenya) took place without their consent. The imposition of artificially constructed borders by foreign powers not only denied Somali's the right to self-determination as a single people but has also threatened the livelihoods of pastoralists who have had their freedom of movement to search for water and pasture restricted. Following the achievement of independence in 1960, the Somali government would spend much of its meager resources on lobbying to incorporate those predominantly Somali-inhabited regions that lay outside of its borders into its nascent state (Bulhan 2008: 63). The pursuit of this objective would lead to a rise in political tension with the United Kingdom and Kenya as well as three wars with Ethiopia; these included border conflicts in 1968 and 1982, as well as the 1977–1978 Ogaden War (Harper 2012: 53). Other Ethiopian interventions in Somalia have occurred between 1996–2000, 2006–2009, and 2009–present. The ongoing Ethiopian intervention is related to the issue of the historic partition due to concerns by policymakers and defense planners in Addis Ababa about the possibility of violence and instability spilling across the border into the predominantly Somali-inhabited Ogaden regions of their country.

It was the irredentist attempt by the Siad Barre regime to forcibly annex and integrate the Ogaden region of Ethiopia into Somalia that would set in motion a series of events that led to the collapse of the Somali state in 1991 (Harper 2012: 33). Howbeit, the seeds of this conflict were largely sown during the period of colonialism. As noted by Bulhan (2008: 28–29) the decision by the British government to transfer a large Somali-inhabited region of its 'Somaliland Protectorate' to the then Ethiopian Empire under the terms of a secret treaty created not only distrust toward these foreign powers but also hostility. This transfer of territory that occurred without the knowledge or consent of the local inhabitants is part of the root-causes of the post-colonial conflicts between the two states and their correlated interventions.

Moreover, the legacy of the colonial era has had a long-lasting impact on the relations between the Somali state and its citizens. It is worth mentioning that the current border dispute between Somaliland and Puntland administrations of Somalia is rooted in the imposition of artificial borders forced upon the local population in the nineteenth century.

As with the artificial partition of the Somali people by colonial powers, the commodification of the traditional system of government that took place under British, Italian, and French rules has also had an enduring legacy on state-society relations in Somalia. In the pre-colonial era, the work of community elders was largely voluntary and hence possessed limited authority and ability to enforce controls on the use of collective resources. Instead, the social power of elders lay in their social power which was derived from their ability to set and enforce moral and ethical values within their communities. This system was dealt great damage by European colonial authorities who introduced chieftainship institutions that provided incentives to some registered 'chiefs' in order to secure control over the rural and remote hinterlands and their inhabitants. However, although now backed by the power and authority of the colonial regime these 'chiefs' were then seen as their employees which undermined the legitimacy in the eyes of their own communities. In this way creation of a non-indigenous system of chieftainship and the commoditization of traditional systems of governance played a significant role in weakening the foundations of the post-colonial Somali state.

This problem of colonial interference in traditional governance structures in order to control rural and remote areas was not unique to Somalia. According to Herbst (1997: 18) one of the root causes of state fragility in Africa can be traced back to the inability of African states to extend state power into these areas. The decision of the colonial governments to rely heavily on the indirect rule through handpicked and paid chiefs created a governance gap between the majority rural areas and few urban centers in the coastline that still exists to the present day. Since the interests of the colonial governments in the Somali territory were mainly to secure livestock trade from the interior to supply colonial forces in the region and to establish bases in the strategic Somali coast, they had little incentive to fully colonize the region (Bulhan 2008: 22; Harper 2012: 47). Therefore, the colonial states have opted to use indirect rule through appointed chiefs to control the rural population.

Another result of this colonial policy was the creation of a socio-economic gap between urban areas that were the focus of economic investment and activity and the more rural areas of the country, which were seen as too difficult and costly to govern directly. It also had the effect of weeding out elders with integrity and principles, and seen as being hostile or of suspect loyalty, with those willing to put the interests of colonial authorities before those of their communities. This practice had an enduring impact on the traditional system as subsequent Somali governments have also adopted the colonial strategy of misusing the chiefs and other traditional elders for their benefit. The adoption of this practice and other colonial-era practices, made worse by contemporary failures of governance, have resulted in the weakening and distortion of state institutions at the very level of their foundations. In the Somali context, this has resulted in a state and state institutions that are representative of neither indigenous nor Western values.

Civilian Government (1960–1969)

The politics of post-independence Somalia can be divided into two main phases of parliamentary politics (1960–1969), and military dictatorship (1969–1991). Further dissecting each phase it is possible to identify two distinct periods: a brief period (1960–1964 and 1969–1977) in which Somali authorities (both civilian and military) enjoyed a high degree of legitimacy and popular support, hence strong state-society relations, and a second period (1965–1969 and 1977–1991) in which Somali elites failed to develop legitimate and functional institutions by instead opting in favor of clan favoritism, corruption, and nepotism. The result of which was economic stagnation, undermining the legitimacy of central authorities in the eyes of the population, and the deterioration of state-society relations.

In the first years immediately following independence the newly birthed Republic of Somalia, itself a union between British Somaliland and Italian Somaliland (*Somali Italiana*), saw the establishment of lively multi-party parliamentary democracy that stood out among the dictatorships, one-party states, and civil wars that characterized many postcolonial African states (Harper 2012: 53; Abdi. I. Samatar 2016). As previously mentioned, the Somali state in this period enjoyed a high degree of legitimacy and public support. Nevertheless, despite the healthy condition of state-society relations and the ability of the state to exercise robust social control the experience of state-building in this period was unlike that which historically took place in Europe. Whereas in the European experience state-building was established (in most cases) with a brutal force it also included the provision of critical public services to local populations. In contrast, the embryonic Somali state relied mainly on making promises in an effort to gain the trust of its citizens.

Leaders of the major pre-independence political parties as well as post-independence elected representatives attempted to use slogans and rhetoric about modernization in order to persuade citizens to abandon their allegiance to the clan system in favor of nationalism and the 'common interest.' There are several examples dating from around the time of independence and the era of civilian government that demonstrate the (limited) success of these efforts. The first of these was the decision by the decision of Somaliland Protectorate Legislative Council to unite with the newly independent Somali Republic (former Italian Somaliland/*Somali Italia*). The decision to accept the unconditional unification of both former protectorates for the sake of the common interest of all Somali's demonstrated that the forces of clannism and regionalism were no longer exercised a grip strong enough over society to prevent such a merger (Bulhan 2008: 63; Abdi I. Samatar 1997: 697). The second was the election of Mohamed Bihi and Omer Abdirahman. Both from Hargeisa, to the legislative council in the 1960 and 1964 elections. The election of these two men signaled the ability of the people to elect candidates based on merit rather than tribalism. These men were members of the Ogaden and Tumal tribes respectively yet were able to compete and win an electoral contest in a city dominated by members of the Isaaq clan (Bulhan 2008: 63; Abdi I. Samatar 1997: 697). The third example is the generous welcome and accommodation given by the citizens of the newly established Republic of Somalia to their brothers and sisters from other Somali-inhabited territories in Ethiopia, Kenya, and Djibouti who flocked to the new Republic in search of opportunities and freedom (Bulhan 2008: 60). According to Abdi Ismail Samatar

(1997: 698), the relative political stability and strong state-society relations during this period were a result of the unity among the ruling elites as well as the euphoric effect of independence. This is not to say that the brief post-independence period of civilian government was not free from challenges and failings. To the contrary, even the successes mentioned here were achieved in the face of political infighting (including within the ruling party), tensions with neighboring countries over Somali-inhabited regions outside of Somalia and the different experience of colonialism felt by the northern and southern regions of the country all contributed to the undermining of economic reforms and the building of badly needed state institutions (Trunji 2015: 473).

It was therefore unfortunate that elections in 1963 (municipal), 1964, and 1969 (parliamentary) were characterized by fraud, tribalism, corruption, and other illegalities that Bulhan (2008: 62) has termed as 'Klannism.'[1] Abdi Ismail Samatar (1997: 698) has offered a useful description of the corrosive effect that this behavior had at the time Somalia was still in the process of building (already fragile) state institutions:

> The confluence of individualist and clans' tendencies moulded a volatile political and economic environment in which political leaders felt insecure in their tenure at the top of the hierarchy and attempted to exploit it. Consequently, their primary preoccupation was to defend their positions.

The narrow political vision and strategy of survival, at the expense of others, adopted by Somali elites at this time diverted already meager public resources that were needed rural economic resources-livestock, fishery, and agriculture. This also forced the newly established government to rely on foreign aid in order to balance its budget (Laitin 1976: 455). The entrenchment of corruption so early in the state-building process contributed to a rapid decay in state-society relations as the public became disenchanted with the country's political elites. As citizens withdrew their support and trust from the state and its leaders the prospect of reuniting Somali-inhabited regions inside neighboring states also became an increasingly remote prospect; the outcome of which contributed to further erosion of any remaining public trust and support. With this increasing breakdown of state-society relations the likelihood of a catastrophic breakdown and the irreversible crisis became increasingly likely. On 15 October 1969, the assassination of President Abdirashid Ali Shermarke proved to be the final straw with the military then stepping into take power in a coup that was met with the support or else indifference of most citizens.

Military Regime (1969–1991)

Such was the poor condition of state-society relations that in fact the overthrow of Somali's civilian government by the military had been a matter of speculation since 1964 (Trunji 2015: 498). In what would be a bloodless coup the head of the Somali army, General Maxamed Siyad Barre, took power alongside a new governing body called the Supreme Revolutionary Council led by Lieutenant Colonel Salaad Gabeyre Kediye. Taking advantage of the collapse of support for the civilian government the new military regime promised to fight corruption, tribalism, injustice, nepotism, a lack of discipline in the civil service sector as well as ending country's dependence on foreign aid (Bulhan 2008: 175; Latin 1976: 456; Omar 1992: 95). Popular anger and disenchantment fueled by these issues as well as the outrage still felt over the artificial patrician of the Somali people by former colonial powers meant that the coup was met with overwhelming popular support and even jubilation among large sections of the population (Bulhan 2008: 168; Omer 1992: 95; Trunji 2015: 538).

Even though few studies were undertaken during the first decade of military rule, the majority of the small number of assessments undertaken during the early seventies provided evidence for the success of the economic reforms and other efforts to address issues of literacy and the empowerment of women that were undertaken by the military regime (Geshekter 1979; Laitin 1976; Lewis 1972). In his assessment of the performance of the military rule during its first seven years in power, David Laitin (1976) has highlighted several notable achievements. These included improvements in the level of professionalism within the civil service, the closing of socio-economic gaps between urban and rural populations through a large-scale public works campaign (building roads, digging wells, etc.), a campaign to standardize the Somali language and improve literacy, and efforts to improve gender equality; a symbol of this last campaign was Asli Hassan Abade who became the first female fighter pilot in Africa. Nevertheless, Latin notes that despite these efforts the economic performance of the military regime during this period was weak.

The achievements of the military regime during the first five years are undeniable and it can be said that its undertaking of large-scale development projects and successful efforts to exercise social control are demonstrative of it having both 'Deposit' and 'Infrastructural' power. However, by the end of the 1970s the condition of state-society relations under the rule of the military regime had also begun to deteriorate. This was due in large part to the failure of the government's economic reforms, which had largely neglected the country's rural economy, in particular, the livestock, agriculture, and fisheries sub-sectors suffered from neglect and chronic underinvestment (Ahmed.I. Samatar 1987: 873–874).

With the military regime unable to address these problems its ability to exercise effective control over society decreased. As a result, its rule became increasingly repressive as the public gradually withdrew their support when their demands on the state went unfulfilled. Unable or unwilling to try and reenergize its revolutionary program efforts to silence dissent through the use of force were met by an increasing level of failure. During this period the regime focused on securing its remaining power base by engaging in the old and ugly practices of tribalism, nepotism, corruption, and wholesale embezzlement of state resources common among other non-democratic post-colonial African regimes (Omer 1992: 156).

The collapse of state-society relations reached a crisis point in 1980s with the outbreak of an armed rebellion. This was fueled by the defeat of Somali forces in the Ogaden War and the brutal repression of communities belonging to the Isaaq, Majeerateen, Hawiye, and Ogaden clans that were undertaken in response to the formation of clan-based armed opposition groups. Prior to the Ogaden War, the regime had already been forced to abandon its commitment to self-reliance the regime heavily dependent on foreign aid than the civilian government it had overthrown (Laitin 1976: 458). This state of affairs only became worse as the regimes increasingly meager resources were diverted to its campaign to hold on to power through violence and intimidation.

The collapse of the regimes 'infrastructural' its reliance on force and an increasingly narrow clan-based power base had the further effect of destroying the faith remaining in the military as one of the last remaining national institutions that had still enjoyed some popular support. This collapse of support for the regime and the military resulted in popular support for clan-based armed opposition groups (Somali Salvation Democratic Front; Somali National Movement; Somali Patriotic Movement;

and United Somali Congress) even when backed by Ethiopia. Although successful in overthrowing the military regime in 1991 the failure of these armed groups to reach a negotiated power-sharing settlement would plunge the country into a civil war. What remained of the state and its institutions would be destroyed in the vicious fighting and mass displacement that characterized the fighting between these clan-based forces in the period which followed. This not only destroyed what remained of the social fabric of Somali society, already devastated during the last years of the military regime, but the effects of this were made even worse by the effect of recurrent environmental disasters (both drought and flood) which would kill or displace hundreds of thousands of civilians at a time.

Conclusion

While the crisis of governance facing Somalia today is an extreme example of the consequences of state collapse and destruction of state-society relations, the fact is that many other states in contemporary Africa face similar crises of governance and legitimacy. In the case of Somalia, these crises are deeply rooted in policy-failure, corruption, mismanagement, and tribalism. In some other cases (e.g., Nigeria), ethnicity and religion are important drivers of instability and conflict, which further undermine state-society relations. It is therefore an illusion for African states to imagine economic growth alone is sufficient to address deep-rooted social structures and conflict drivers undermining state-society relations as often promoted by major international financial institutions.

As the case of Somalia demonstrates it is critical that states take effective action in order to address the issues and threats which undermine state-society-relations. Although often not sufficient in themselves, to collapse the relationship between the state and its citizens each of these conflict drivers acts corrosively and their combined impact can fuel a spiral of convoluted violent conflict. As a healthy condition of state-society relations is critical for the ability of the state to exercise an effective monopoly of power and mobilize the masses toward common goals it is necessary to put in place policies and strategies to prevent a catastrophic breakdown in legitimacy and trust. Unfortunately, in the case of Somalia, these efforts have often been counter-productive and rather than improving state-society relations have resulted in the further alienation of the state from the general population. This has weakened the impact of both local and international efforts meant to address the crisis of governance in

Somalia. With these efforts either achieving minimal results or oftentimes ending in failure, negative drivers such as tribalism and corruption continue to poison efforts to rebuild state-society relations in Somalia. While it is long overdue to embrace policies that promote justice, inclusion, and equality there is no question that apart from brief periods under civilian and military rule the last hundred years of Somali history has been characterized by self-destructive competition and conflict fueled both by colonial powers and the Somali people themselves. There is a common Somali proverb, '*Millil Korkii Lama Dhayo*,' which can be loosely translated as 'it is wrong to expect a wound to heal faster while treating it superficially.' Evidently, attempts to rebuild or repair state-society relations in Somalia following the failure of colonial and post-colonial civilian or military rule have all at best been perfunctory and superficial. It is clear that the broken and distorted condition of state-society relations in Somalia will require policymakers to go back to the drawing board and take into account the failures of the past if a modern and sustainable Somali state is to be established.

Note

1. According to Hussein, A. 'Klannism' parochialism individualistic approach in which Somali elites manipulate clan system for their power and wealth.

References

Abdi, I. Samatar. 1992. Destruction of State and Society in Somalia: Beyond the Tribal Convention. *The Journal of Modern African Studies* 30 (4): 625–641.

Abdi, I. Samatar. 1997. Leadership and Ethnicity in the Making of African State Models: Botswana Versus Somalia. *Third World Quarterly* 18 (4): 687–708.

Abdi, I. Samatar. 2000. Social Transformation and Islamic Reinterpretation in Northern Somalia: The Women's Mosque in Gabiley. *The Arab World Geographer* 3 (1): 22–39.

Abdi, I. Samatar. 2016. Africa's First Democrats: Somalia's Aden A, Osman and Abdirazak H. Hussein. Bloomington: Indiana University Press.

Ahmed, I. Samatar. 1985. Underdevelopment in Somalia: Dictatorship Without Hegemony. *Africa Today* 32 (3): 23–40.

Ahmed, I. Samatar. 1987. Somalia Impasse: State Power and Dissent Politics. *Third World Quartely* 9 (3): 871–890.

Albert, A. 1987. *African Perspectives on Colonialism*. Lanham, MD: The Johns Hopkins University.

Catherine, B. 1996. Representing Violence and "Othering" Somalia. *Cultural Anthropology* 11 (1): 81–97.
Charles, G. 1979. Socio-Economic Developments in Somalia. *The Horn of Africa* 2 (2): 24–36.
Christopher, C. 1996. *Africa and the International System: The Politics of State Survival*. New York: Cambridge University Press.
Crawford, Y. 1997. *The African Colonial State in Comparative Perspective*. New Haven: Yale University Press.
David, D. 1976. The Political Economy of Military Rule in Somalia. *Modern African Studies* 14 (3): 449–468.
David, M. 2012. Clan Identity and Islamic Identity in Somalia. CEADS Papers Volume 2: Somalia 4. November. Retrieved 20 May 2019, from https://apps.dtic.mil/dtic/tr/fulltext/u2/a574116.pdf.
Dingxin, Z. 2000. State-Society Relations and the Discourses and Activities of the 1989 Beijing Student Movement. *American Journal of Sociology* 105 (6): 1592–1632.
Edwin, A. 1974. *Colonialism and Underdevelopment in East Africa*. London: Heinemann.
Finn, S., A. Louise, and M. Bjørn. 2007. Introduction: Security Arrangements in Fragile States. In *Fragile States and Insecure People? Violence, Security and Statehood in the Twenty-First Century*, ed. L. Anderson, B. Møller, and F. Stepputat, 3–20. New York: Palgrave Macmillan.
Grigsby, E. 2009. *Analyzing Politics: An Introduction to Political Science*, 4th ed. London: Wadsworth.
Hussein, A. 2008. *Politics of Cain: One Hundred Years of Crises in Somali Politics and Society*. Bethesda, MD: Tayosan International Publishing.
Ioan, M. 1972. Somalia's Leaders Go Forward with Confidence. *New Middle East*, 51 December.
Ioan, M. 1998. Doing Violence to Ethnography: A Response to Catherine Besteman's "Representing Violence" and "Othering Somalia". *Culture Anthropology* 13 (1): 100–108.
Jeffrey, G. 1989. Colonialism and Revolution in Southeast Asia: A Comparative Analysis. In *Revolution in the World-System*, ed. T. Boswell, 59–78. New York: Greenwood Press.
Jeffrey, H. 2000. *States and Power in Africa: Comparative Lessons in Authority and Control*. Princeton, NJ: Princeton University Press.
Jeffrey, G., and S. Theda. 1989. Explaining Revolutions in the Contemporary Third World. *Politics and Society* 17 (4): 489–509.
Joel, S. 1988. *Strong Societies and Weak States: State-Society Relations and State Capabilities in the Third World*. Princeton, NJ: Princeton University Press.

Joel, S. 1994. The State in Society: An Approach to Struggles for Domination. In *State Power and Social Forces*, ed. J.S. Migdal, A. Kohli, and V. Shue, 7–34. Toronto: D VMilkman.

Juan, J., and C. Alfred. 1996. *Problems of Democratic Transition and Consolidation: Southern Europe, South America and Post-Communist Europe*. Baltimore: Johns Hopkins University Press.

Lidwien, K. 2004. I.M. Lewis and Somali Clanship: A Critique. *Northeast African Studies* 11 (1): 1–23.

Max, W. 1946. *Politics as a Vocation*, ed. H.H. Gerth and C. Wright Mills. New York: Oxford University Press.

Michael, M. 1988. *States, War and Capitalism: Studies in Political Sociology*. Oxford: Blackwell.

Mohamed, H. 2018. Primordialism vs Instrumentalism in Somali Society: Is an Alternative Needed? *Journal of Contemporary African Studies* 36 (4): 464–483.

Mohamed, O. 1992. *The Road to Zero: Somalia's Self-Destruction*. London: HAAN Associates.

Mohamed, T. 2015. *Somalia: The Untold History 1941–1969*. Leicester: Looh Press.

René, G. 2016. Nation and State. In *Nation-Building as Necessary Effort in the Fragile States*, ed. R. Grotenhuis, 25–44. Amsterdam: Amsterdam University Press.

Robert, H. 1990. *Quasi-States: Sovereignty, International Relations, and the Third World*. Cambridge: Cambridge University Press.

Seth, K. 2010. Rethinking State-Building in a Failed State. *The Washington Quarterly* 33 (1): 81–97.

Stephen, D. 1999. *Sovereignty: Organized Hypocrisy*. Princeton: Princeton University Press.

Theda, S. 1985. Bringing the State Back in Strategies of Analysis in Current Research. In *Bringing the State Back In*, ed. B. Peter, R. Dietrich, and S. Theda, 3–37. Cambridge: Cambridge University Press.

Tim, M. 1991. *Autocracy, Modernization and Revolution in Russia and Iran*. Princeton, NJ: Princeton University Press.

United Nations Development Programme. 2001. Human Development Report. Retrieved 2 May 2019, from http://hdr.undp.org/sites/default/files/somalia_2001_en.pdf.

William, T. 2002. *Government and Politics in Africa*, 4th ed. New York: Palgrave Macmillan.

CHAPTER 15

Emerging from the Doldrums? Governance and Politics in Eritrea

Redie Bereketeab

Introduction

The Eritrean state is born out of thirty-year liberation struggle. Following the demise of Italian colonialism, instead of exercising the right to self-determination and decolonisation, it was forcibly tied with Ethiopia through UN-sponsored federation. The Emperor Haile Selassie aborted the federation that was put in force in 1952, just after ten years, in 1962. The Eritreans embarked on protracted liberation war in 1961 to exercise the right of self-determination. Thirty years of bloody war against twenty times bigger enemy, supported, first by the USA and later by the USSR, ended when the Eritrean People's Liberation Front (EPLF), victoriously marched into Asmara the capital of Eritrea in May 1991, wiping out the 2nd Division of the Ethiopian army based in Eritrea. After two years of interim period, popular referendum was held and with resounding, yes vote, Eritrea became de jure independent in 1993. A lone struggle of fifty years (twenty years of political struggle and thirty years of armed struggle) embedded Eritreans strife for state formation. Certainly, this historical

R. Bereketeab (✉)
The Nordic African Institute, Uppsala, Sweden
e-mail: redie.bereketeab@nai.uu.se

K. Omeje (ed.), *The Governance, Security and Development Nexus*,
https://doi.org/10.1007/978-3-030-49348-6_15

genealogy shaped the behaviours and characteristics of the post-liberation Eritrean state and its relations with the international community.

The one thing that most significantly shaped the national psyche of Eritreans is the attitude of the so-called international community. In the Eritrean psyche the behaviour and act of the international community, particularly, Western powers are inundated with betrayal double-standard, isolationism and unjust treatment of Eritrea. This perception has induced stark suspicion, mistrust and abhorrence of the international community by Eritreans. Eritreans could count a litany of betrayals and unjust treatment by the international community. The first of these betrayals is the tying of Eritrea to Ethiopia, instead of granting it the right to exercise self-determination and decolonisation, a right granted to all European colonised territories in Africa. The second betrayal was the inaction of the international community when the federation was abrogated arbitrarily by Emperor Haile Selassie in spite of the fact that the federal arrangement put the sole responsibility of change of status on the international body that created the federation, the UN. The third betrayal was during the thirty-year liberation struggle where the international community never showed interest or empathy to provide political, moral, diplomatic, legal and material support; it never even expressed abhorrence against atrocities committed by Ethiopian regimes (Habte Selassie 1989; Yohannes 1991). The fourth betrayal occurred during the implementation of Eritrea—Ethiopia Border Commission (EEBC) verdict on border demarcation that was mediated and authored by UN, OAU, EU and USA who were also witnesses and guarantors of the Agreement, following the 1998–2000 Eritrea—Ethiopia war (Algiers Agreement 2000a, b). When Ethiopia rejected the final and binding International Court of Arbitration verdict, the witnesses and guarantors, instead of respecting their commitment to make sure the verdict was implemented in accordance with the Algiers Agreement, simply ignored it to appease Ethiopia. The fifth betrayal of Eritrea by the international community is connected with the imposition of sanctions on the aggrieved party (Eritrea) based on what Eritreans perceive as trumped up allegation that the Eritrean government was, among other things, "backing Al-Shabaab militants in Somalia, as well as other movements attempting to undermine the Ethiopian state" (Plaut 2018). All these perceptions of betrayals and double-standard have shaped and dictated Eritreans engagement with, and behaviour towards the international community. They also would help to explain Eritrea's place in the Africa rising narrative.

This chapter seeks to examine and analyse the post-liberation political trajectory of Eritrea. It interrogates the post-liberation state-building challenges and intricacies, as well as problems of transformation from the phase of national liberation struggle to post-liberation civic governance. It examines the role of the international community in these challenges of transition and transformation. It contends that the litany of betrayal, double-standard, isolation and unjust treatment of Eritrea over seventy years of history by the international community, particularly the big powers, has left an indelible impact on the Eritrean psyche, which impels Eritreans not to trust the external world. This in turn informed the problematic relation between Eritrea and international community in the last twenty years. Moreover, the study argues that a clash of contradictory ideologies underpins the diverging views of today's Eritrea. How do all these impacts on Eritrea vis-a-vis the Africa rising narrative?

Challenges of Transition from National Liberation Movement to Civic Government

The primary challenge the national liberation movement (NLM) faced in its post-liberation reconstruction and state-building is the transformation from national liberation political culture to post-liberation civic political culture of governmentality (Pool 2001). A highly successful NLM encountered a real uphill task in the post-liberation dispensation and responsibilities. Indeed, its success turned into a burden (Bereketeab 2007a). It has proven to be a formidable task to go through the necessary transformation from liberation movement to a conventional political organisation of a state. This is because the NLM pursued the same *modus operandi* as it did during the liberation struggle in its exercise of power in the post-liberation space, which now encompasses the whole society. There is a strong tendency that liberation movements always try to shape and reshape the larger society in the image of the miniature society they created in the liberation cosmology (Melber 2007; Southall 2013; Bereketeab 2018). As David Pool (2001: 159) aptly put it, "Instead of Eritrea making the EPLF, EPLF had been vigorous in making Eritrea in its image. State-building continued in the trajectory of the front-building we have analysed." National liberation struggle by its very protracted nature develops a unique political culture that might not be conducive to post-liberation civic governance, operation and culture. The NLM indeed constructed a miniature society in the liberated part of Eritrea (Bereketeab

2007b, 2016). It is that miniature society which imposed itself on the bigger society. This engendered two parallel societies.

The characteristic features of national liberation culture include high centralisation, hierarchically structured system, high secrecy, selflessness and sacrifice, absolute loyalty and obedience of members (Connell 1993; Wolde Giorgis 2014). All these necessary conditions of survival and victory of the NLM are compressed into what is known in the national liberation parlance as democratic centralism. Democratic centralism, in its concentrated application and *modus operandi* subscribes to military order where subordinates are permitted to raise questions only after executing an order. In a war setting and military operation, this could mean individuals have the right to raise questions after death.

Undoubtedly, these cultural attributes served the NLM well, contributing to the success of the liberation struggle (Pool 2001; Connell 1993), but proved highly problematic in the post-liberation phase, in the establishment of civic governance, democratic state-building and construction of national institutions. The post-liberation reality required a different culture, civic political culture and national institutions separate from the NLM. It also required opening the political space to include other stakeholders and sectors of society besides the liberators. In addition, a new set of agenda of the political economy of the running of state is required. Unfortunately, the liberators were convinced that only they could shoulder the post-liberation state reconstruction responsibility. Based on this perception, they set the agendas and priorities that were to constitute the central values of the post-liberation state. The selection of priorities elevated certain values, while ignoring others. The selected central values could be summarised in three grand objectives and programmes. These were (i) nation-building, (ii) socio-economic development, (iii) national unity (Government of Eritrea 1994; National Charter 1994). Other values such as democracy, social, political and civic rights, press freedom, plural political system and economic liberalisation were subordinated to the core values. Moreover, these values were buttressed by a national liberation ideology that underscored socialist ideals such as social justice, equality, equitable distribution of national resources, bridging the gap between urban and rural spheres, state ownership of key national resources, bolstering collective identity and heavy involvement of the state in the political economy. To achieve these goals the society was to be mobilised, organised and act in unison, in the same manner it did to realise independence. This perception was the underpinning doctrine of the national service introduced in 1994 and enlisted Eritreans between 18 and 40 years of age for mandatory military service. Self-reliance that ensured liberation would also serve the post-liberation reconstruction. This constituted an antagonistic stance to the neoliberal ideology that was establishing itself as the dominant force in the post-Cold War global structure.

By distancing itself from neoliberalism the liberators embarked on guided democracy and piecemeal socio-economic transformation. The post-liberation government, perhaps to the disappointment of many, did not rush into elections, opening the political sphere for competitive pluralism, allowing vibrant private media, private market-orientated economic system, etc. Regarding the economic system, the choice became a mixed one with heavy emphasis on the role of the state. The state is seen as the primary source of service provision and distributor of national resources and therefore ought to have strong stake in the national economy. National institution-building and institutionalisation progressed at a very slow process. Some works of institution-building and institutionalisation at local and regional levels took place. At a national level however the national assembly that constituted the central committee of the PFDJ, with minor adjustment, continued as transitional legislation. It was expanded in 1996 when it served as the constituent assembly to approve the draft constitution that has been in the process of drafting since 1994 (Bereketeab 2009; Habte Selassie 2003). The new constitution was endorsed in 1997, but before it could be implemented war broke out between Eritrea and Ethiopia (in May 1998) that completely altered the implementation prospect. Since then the country has been run by an undeclared state of emergency.

From the foregoing analysis, it is indicative that the post-liberation transformation project was rightly or wrongly embedded in national, regional and international structures and realities. Apparently, this configuration of actors and structures was, either not properly understood, or intentionally misunderstood by the external world, when the post-liberation, and post-second war development in Eritrea is evaluated.

The painstakingly slow process of transformation, institutionalisation and democratisation encountered another problem, the war that engulfed the whole nation. Any prospect of opening the political space was postponed indefinitely. As the war raged, everything was geared towards the war that was interpreted as saving the nation and preserving national sovereignty. This struggle for survival further truncated the political space and curbed many rights of the people. As a consequence of the second war, a division within the national leadership aggravated the political crisis. Hence, the issue of the state rising to its potential, was for obvious reasons, compromised and perpetually deferred.

The Second War with Ethiopia

The second war between Eritrea and Ethiopia (1998–2000) came as a surprise and shock to many. Many, including the leaders of the two countries described the war as meaningless. Moreover, the real cause of the war also became a source of confusion and debate. The two countries diverged in their assessment of the real cause of the war, which made it very difficult to reach a durable solution. For Eritreans the underlying cause is the inability of Ethiopians to reconcile with the independence of Eritrea, whereas for Ethiopians it was caused by Eritrea's economic non-viability to exist as a sovereign state (Tadesse 1999; Abbay 2001). No matter what the cause was, the consequence was colossal. The human, economic, political and diplomatic consequences were immense, particularly for Eritrea.

In terms of human cost, the two-year war took the life of 70,000–100,000 soldiers from both sides. The Eritrean government announced on 20 June 2003, the day of commemoration of national liberation war martyrs, that 19,200 Eritrean soldiers were killed in the war. Millions of civilians were displaced, and many Eritrean women were raped by Ethiopian soldiers when they occupied a big chunk of Eritrean territory in 2000. Tens of thousands of Eritreans and Ethiopians of Eritrean origin were deported from Ethiopia in an inhuman way (Legesse 1999; Klein 1998). Billions of Dollars' worth of property was destroyed. Eritrea's economy was hard hit, the indication of which was economic growth plummeting from a rate of 6–7% between 1991 and 1997, to below zero in 2000 (Hanson 2000). Military expenses skyrocketed as both states spent billions of dollars in running the war and buying warplanes, tanks and artilleries.

Finally, a ceasefire was signed on 18 June 2000 and a comprehensive peace agreement in December of the same year known as the Algiers Agreement which was brokered by UN, AU, EU and the USA who also comprised the witnesses and guarantors. One of the provisions of the Peace Agreement was establishment of Eritrea-Ethiopia Border Commission (EEBC) mandated to delineate and demarcate their common border, which was to be final and binding. The witnesses and guarantors assumed the responsibility of overseeing the implementation of the EEBC verdict and in the event that one or both parties reneged from their commitment, they will be referred to the UNSC with the possibility of the international body invoking a UN Charter Chapter Seven enforcement action (Algiers Agreement 2000a, b).

Once the EEBC announced its verdict in April 2002, however, Ethiopia rejected it because it awarded the territorial flashpoint of the war, the village of Badme to Eritrea. Ethiopia, calling it unjust, illegal and irresponsible and requested for renegotiation, while Eritrea reiterating its final and binding nature and demanded its complete and unconditional implementation (Reid 2009). The parties stuck with their positions and the witnesses and guarantors abdicating their responsibility, hence a no-war no-peace situation reigned that lasted until July 2018. Senior US officials under the President Obama administration, particularly, Assistant Secretary of State Jendayi Frazer and US Ambassador to the UN Susan Rice, systematically and persistently, tried to use threats and blackmails to change EEBC verdict in order to appease Ethiopia. Indeed, when all threats and blackmails failed, Rice succeeded in placing Eritrea under UN sanctions in 2009 (Cohen 2013). UNSC Resolution 1709 called for weapons embargo, freezing assets and travel ban on civilians and military leaders and associated business people (UNSC 2009). Eritrea's relation with the West, particularly the USA, successively deteriorated. The Eritrean government openly accused the USA of double-standard on the failure to implement the Algiers Agreement, while the USA accused the Eritrean government of failure to cooperate with the international community. The USA, bent to isolate the Eritrean government, completely ignored the Algiers Agreement and the no-war no-peace situation generating bitterness among Eritreans. The position taken by successive US administrations is that everything is the fault of Eritrean government and therefore, the government has to be punished.

This further reinforced the Eritrean sense of betrayal leading the well-proven strategy of mobilising and organising the people to defend the nation. The proclamation of the Warsay-Yekealo development programme in 2002 where every capable person is required to render mandatory services for the development and survival of the nation was introduced. The post-liberation generation was, therefore, in the same way as the liberators have done before them, required to make high sacrifices where the individual's rights, interests and privileges were subordinated to the perceived survival of the collective. This induced international uproar, spurring accusation of violations of human rights, slave labour and turning the entire country into an open prison, further aggravating the hostile relations between Eritrea and the international community. This led the Eritrean state to create impregnable fortresses in order to ensure the survival and sovereignty of the state, a project that had extreme political and human rights consequences.

Sanctions, Isolation and Siege

The souring of Eritrean relation with the USA was cleverly exploited by the TPLF-dominated EPRDF government in Ethiopia. The Ethiopian government conducted offensive diplomacy to isolate Eritrea. Ethiopia not only succeeded in getting away with the violation of the International Court of Arbitration verdict, but also succeeded in mobilising the neighbouring countries and international community to isolate the Eritrean government. The Ethiopian government succeeded in pilling criminal accusations against the Eritrean government that was uncritically accepted by the international community. These criminal accusations included that Eritrea was financing, training and arming the Somali terrorist group Al-Shabaab that controlled greater part of war-torn Somalia following the Ethiopian invasion of the country in December 2006. However, simple logic would disprove the accusation, notably how could Eritrea which has no land border with Somalia evade the surveillance capacity of the internationally assisted regional peacekeepers and penetrate the Somali air space, sea front and land space to freely aid Al-Shabaab as purported? Other allegations include that Eritrea was planning to bomb the AU Summit in Addis Ababa, in 2011, and that Eritrea was supporting armed Ethiopian rebels to destabilise their country (while evidence of the Ethiopian government's support to Eritrean rebels to destabilise their own country was completely overlooked by the international community). Ethiopia was the main source of information to the Somali-Eritrea Monitoring Group (SEMG) established by UNSC to monitor Security Council's decision on violations. The Ethiopian allegation that Eritrea was planning to bomb the AU Summit in Addis Ababa was strangely believed by the SEMG and reported to the UNSC.

Eritrea was, therefore portrayed as a threat to peace, security and stability of the region and the world in general. The UN Security Council imposed sanction on Eritrea in 2009 and 2011 (UNSC 2009; Bereketeab

2013). The reason for the first sanction was Eritrea's alleged support for the Somali terrorist group Al-Shabaab, while the second set of sanctions was imposed in connection with the Djibouti-Eritrea conflict. Following a brief military confrontation between Eritrea and Djibouti, and Djibouti's accusation that Eritrea has occupied its territory, UNSC order Eritrea to vacate, although Eritrea never accepted the accusation. UNSC Resolution 1709 thus included sanction on Eritrea for not withdrawing from "Djiboutian territory" (UNSC 2009). The allegation of Eritrea's support to Al-Shabaab was never proved. The SEMG in its annual report, for several years, could not find any evidence that Eritrea supported Al-Shabaab. Despite the organ established by the UNSC itself, report of no evidence however, the sanctions continued, until November 2018, when the new Ethiopian leader Prime Minister Abiy Ahmed pushed for its repeal. Expediently, Ethiopia and the USA branded Eritrea a rogue state that undermined peace and security of the Horn of Africa region.

Finally, violation of human rights was added to the litany of criminal allegations against Eritrea. The UN Human Rights Commission Rapporteur, Sheila B. Keetharuth, Report of the Commission of Inquiry on Human Rights in Eritrea (A/HRC/32/47), using dubious methodology, compiled a report based on information extracted from some five hundred refugees, mainly members of Eritrean opposition groups in the Diaspora, and neighbouring countries (Ethiopia, Somalia and Djibouti), alleging perpetration of gross human rights violations by the Eritrean government. The report claimed that the Eritrean government might have committed crime against humanity since 1991 and recommended that it should be referred to the ICC. Djibouti and Somalia initiated the idea that UNHRC should investigate the human rights record of the Eritrean government. The report was debated in UNHRC, in Geneva, and UN in New York, but was rejected. The Eritrean government saw it as another ploy by Ethiopia and the USA acting through proxies to continue the sanctions and isolation of Eritrea.

Eritrea was convinced that it was the USA who were behind the sanctions against them. Eritrea was also convinced that in a bid to evade compliance with the International Court of Arbitration border verdict, Ethiopia concocted all the allegations to punish their arch enemy. The TPLF-dominated EPRDF's critical role in the US global war on terror secured it unswerving support from successive US Administrations. The unflinching position of the Eritrean government to the EEBC border verdict unnerved US officials and spurred coordinated TPLF/EPRDF government and US campaign of demonisation, isolation, siege and regime change policy against Eritrea. Both Assistant Secretary of state Jandyi Frazer and US Ambassador to the UN Suzan Rice were culprits in the policy (Bolton 2007; Woldemariam and Yohannes 2007; Cohen 2013). The regime change policy ultimately failed, and following the 2018 Ethiopia-Eritrea rapprochement, all the allegations against the Eritrean government evaporated and the sanctions were lifted.

International Relations: Clash of National Liberation Ideology and Neoliberal Ideology

The discourse on post-liberation Eritrea is dominated by two strands. The first emanates from a national liberation ideology and another from neoliberal ideology. The government and sympathisers primarily promote the former, while neoliberal critics advance the latter. On the one hand, you have an image of the Eritrean government that fought for thirty years and against all odds achieved independence and still tries to meet its governance obligations to the people while having to contend with the opposition and double-standard of international neoliberal forces. Following liberation, the Eritrean government has against all odds been involved in rebuilding a state that was torn by two brutal wars and a hostile external environment, and have nonetheless achieved impressive success in education, health care, provision of potable water, roads, infrastructures, constructing grand dams and bridging the gap between rural and urban. The Eritrean government was commended by the UN for meeting a number of the MDGs, notably in primary education (MDG2), gender equality (MDG3), child mortality (MDG4), maternal health (MDG5), HIV/AIDS, malaria and other diseases (MDG6) (UN 2014; UNECA 2015). The government was even awarded a certificate of commendation for its achievements in health (UNDP 2014).

On the other hand, we have a picture portrayed by neoliberal-oriented scholarships, activism, media and human right community, presenting Eritrea as the North Korea of Africa, an obnoxious police state, a garrison state, a brutal dictatorship and an open-air prison, etc. (Tronvoll and Mekonen 2014; Plaut 2016; van Reisen and Mawere 2017). It is a profound mystery how a tiny country like Eritrea could provoke such strong sentiments of horror and resentment. Is Eritrea really as odious as portrayed by the powerful Western states' propaganda machinery, media, scholarship and civil societies? With reference to the connotation of police state, a Ugandan researcher visited Eritrea in 2018, and wrote a piece titled, "Eritrea, the 'Police State' Where there are No Cops to Be Seen"? The researcher reported that in every office he visited and every place he frequented he did not come across any police officers on duty, yet there was such an idyllic atmosphere of order, safety and normalcy (Golooba-Mutebi 2018). Some of the reasons that spurred such highly sensational depictions of Eritrea as a police state are: the mass flight of Eritrean youth through dangerous and murderous routes where thousands lost their lives; imprisonment of opponents, journalists, national service evaders, religious minority groups and the phenomenon of endless national service. Reading and watching deplorable situation of Eritrean youth going through excruciating experiences of death, torture, human and organ trafficking in the Sahara and Mediterranean Sea, of course, invokes some moral opprobrium. The critical question is however if this diatribe helps to explain and analyse the root causes of the problem.

In addition, to being highly sensational and exaggerated, the diatribes lack historical contextualisation as they fail to address the real historical, structural, national, regional and international factors underlying the production and reproduction of youth exodus, among other problems. Nonetheless, they indicate a pattern of narrative about Eritrea dominant in the neoliberal world. This neoliberal world powers seem bent on shaping the world along neoliberal values, norms and social formation. Societies that do not conform to their paradigm are to be remoulded if necessary by hook or crook. Regimes perceived to be less accommodative of the paradigm should be removed by the now familiar mantra of regime change. Violent regime change is often preceded by a systematic campaign of demonisation and vilification. Once the discursive ground is laid, it becomes easy for military intervention to possibly follow. Iraq, Afghanistan, Libya and Syria are some examples of countries where this strategy has been applied. In the case of Libya, "Gaddafi was so thoroughly demonised that the wildest accusations about his likely (or, as many claimed, certain) future conduct would be believed whatever his actual behaviour" (Roberts 2001: 17). It has now become a fashionable *modus operandi* in the West to first unleash concerted campaigns of demonisation and calumny as a precursor to the violent regime change. Sections of mainstream Western media, activists and scholars have perfected the strategy such that criticising it has become perilous.

In the case of Eritrea too, the self-fulfilling prophesy of the failed and inevitable collapse of a "criminal" state was carefully choreographed.

The concerted campaigns are intended to create conditions that produce a failed and ultimately collapsed state. This means that the proponents and conspirators work hard on their invented project for their prophesy to be realised. Respected scholars such as Gerard Prunier have fallen victim of propagating the self-fulfilling prophesy. In a speech he delivered in 2011 to the Association for the Study of Middle East and Africa, titled "Eritrea! The Real Story," Prunier portrayed an image of Eritrea as a rogue state and its government as a criminal mafia organisation. Among the derogatory phraseologies he used in describing Eritrea include: "hell on earth," and "national slavery" (referring to the national service). He also conjured an image of Eritrea as "establishing of half-way house in the Red Sea Islands for Arab sex buyers in order to sell weapons and support extremist Islamic groups like Al-Shabaab"; "training Tamil Tigers in India for money"; "receiving money from Al Qaeda in order to sell weapons to Hamas and Al-Shabaab." In describing the Eritrean system Prunier claimed that the Soviet Communist system was democratic when compared to that of Eritrea. Practically Prunier presented the Eritrean government as an international network of smugglers, money launderers and criminal syndicates. Some of the sources for his information by his own admission were "Ethiopian intelligence agents." If a renowned researcher like Professor Prunier could make such preposterous claims without any guided investigation, it becomes understandable when gullible pedestrians are lured into believing the neoliberal media-sponsored representations and image of a monstrous Eritrea.

This critique does not however exonerate the Eritrean government from any wrongdoing. To the contrary, the government bears a huge responsibility for bringing Eritrea into international disrepute. The reasons why people are leaving Eritrea en mass is because of unbearable hardship. In particular, the indefinite national service has become intolerable. Intolerance to dissenting views, arrests and repression of opponents, failure to implement the national constitution and hold democratic elections, as well as suspension of the national assembly are some of the evident failures of the Eritrean government. As already explained, governments of neighbouring countries, and the wider international community also share great responsibility in ruining the reputation and economy of Eritrea.

Eritrea Rising?

The assessment of whether Eritrea is rising or not could only make sense against the incredible struggle for survival that spans over two decades. At independence, in 1991, the country was completely destroyed as a result of the thirty-year war. The EPLF (Eritrean People's Liberation Front) led government faced a daunting task of reconstruction of the economy, infrastructure, state institutions, schools, health facilities, housing and provision of basic services. It began from scratch. In terms of institution-building, sovereignty and state-building it immediately embarked on organising a referendum that took place in April 1993 to dress the military victory with popular and legal attire (Habte Selassie 2003; Tesfai 1999). This was followed by transforming itself into the People's Front for Democracy and Justice (PFDJ) that occurred in its third congress in 1994 (EPLF 1994). A constitutional drafting process was finalised in May 1997 (Habte Selassie 2003). Through participatory democracy the general population deliberated on the constitution drafting process through public discussions, seminars, workshops and symposiums (Habte Selaasie 2003).

In further, consolidating the state-building process redrawing of administration regions occurred in 1996 that morphed into six regions (Tesfai 1999; Bereketeab 2012). Education as a vector of socio-economic transformation was given high priority and reportedly registered consistent growth over the years, the total number of students at all levels, in 1991, was 186,000, by 2007 this figure was almost quadrupled to reach 700,000, and tertiary education also increased from one university to eight university college (Rena 2008).

In reconstruction, immediate activities took place in building schools, clinics, dams, water catchments, terraces, seaport, airports, electrical installations, public houses, forestations, agricultural projects, renovation of main roads and feeder roads, renovation of decaying industries and building new ones (Bereketeab 2009). The military institute of Sawa served as the centre of nation-building and development where the national service programme draftees were turned into development workers (Nielsen 2002). These reconstruction activities constituted the foundation of the post-liberation socio-economic rehabilitation, and indeed the outcome was impressive. Annual economic growth until 1997 was estimated to be between 5 and 7% (Hanson 2000; World Bank 2004;

Rena 2007). The second war from 1998 to 2000 and the subsequent no-war no-peace situation changed all this.

As explained, the last twenty years have been marked by the struggle for survival. Nonetheless, despite the isolation, sanctions and siege, Eritrea has achieved impressive socio-economic development. Following the rapprochement between Eritrea and Ethiopia, a new era has been ushered in that looks beyond basic survival, and potentially presents significant opportunity for rising. Eritrea possesses several strategic advantages that could help to jump-start economic growth. The first of these advantages is its strategic location. Eritrea's location in the strategically important Red Sea and its more than one thousand kilometres of coastline is a huge advantage that could be harnessed for growth and development. With the end of the 20 years of military confrontation and return of predictable peace in the region, Eritrea would be able to channel its strategic locational advantage to strengthen its growth potential. Following the commencement of the 2018 rapprochement, Eritrea is poised to regain its strategic importance to landlocked Ethiopia as the most cost-effective outlet to the sea for import and export trade. Ethiopian economy has been the fastest-growing economy in Africa for more than 10 years and therefore a resuscitation of the Eritrean seaports of Massawa and Assab will help to boost international trade for Ethiopia and Eritrea and *ipso facto* their national revenue bases.

The second advantage is its population. The Eritrean government is adept at mobilisation of the population which over the years of hostilities has been utilised, not only for defending the nation, but also for rebuilding it. Despite its many shortcomings, the national service that was introduced in 1994 served as effective mechanism of mobilising and organising the labour force. Impressive projects such as big dams, roads, schools, clinics, forestation, bridges; and agricultural projects were built through the national service programme. Recruitment into the public sphere including education, health, civil service, and many other aspects of national life are also managed by national service. Without the national service (which many detractors brand as slave labour), Eritrea might not have survived the enormous challenges it faced in the last twenty years. This, of course, does not mean that the national service is a perfect programme. To the contrary there are many problems with the national service programme which have already been highlighted.

A third asset or advantage of Eritrea is that it has a relatively corruption-free public space. Many foreign missions based in Asmara and international guests who have visited the country in the last few years have testified to the relative absence of corruption in the country.[1] Related to the virtual absence of political corruption is the dedication and selflessness of the Eritrean leadership. The monthly wage of government Ministers is between US$300 and 400, while that of the President is between US$500 and 600. The simple lifestyle of the political leadership, who generally reside among common people—driving old cars, sharing the comparable living standard with the people—are some of the qualities of the Eritrean leadership rarely found among other Africa countries.

The government's ideology of self-reliance is one of the driving principles used in mobilising and inspiring the citizens to make maximum sacrifices and render selfless services for the purpose national development. Many cases of the Africa rising narrative have been achieved on the backdrop of massive external borrowing and a rising national debt profile. The case of Uganda is a good example where leading international financial institutions (the World Bank and IMF have over the years pumped in billions of dollars, thereby dictating the economic growth and Uganda rising narrative (Wiegratz et al. 2018). For instance, according to IMF (2019), Uganda's public debt for 2018 is 41.3% of GDP, to this could be added western aid. A fourth advantage is that Eritrea is blessed with significant natural resource endowment. Due to a history of protracted wars, the prospecting and exploitation of Eritrea's natural resources has not been seriously conducted. Eritrea has huge untapped natural resources such as gold, silver and copper mines in Bisha and Zara regions. Eritrea is in the process of finalising the production of a world class Potash Colluli mining in the Danakil (Southern Red Sea Region). Recently, the UNDP in the aftermath of a funded independent Report on Eritrea, issued a statement that Colluli mining would support Eritrea's sustainable development goals, economy, agricultural productivity, training and employment (UNDP 2019). The Colluli deposit in Eritrea is believed to be the largest in the world. The UNDP funded Report shows that the mines have a potential of over 1 billion tonnes of high-grade potassium deposit and an approximate of 200 years life span.

Conclusion

The story of modern Eritrea has largely been about struggle for survival, perseverance and resilience. It is a history of suffering, tragedy, injustices and maltreatment. In more than seventy years and particularly over the last two decades, Eritreans have shown immense resilience and perseverance to achieve and preserve their independence, but in the process have also sustained immense despair and confusion. This unique feature would explain the persistent international portrayal of Eritrea in contradictory and ambiguous terms. On the one hand, Eritreans have demonstrated a unique quality of defying great odds, and on the other hand, they have paid immeasurable sacrifices and pains rarely found in most African countries. In this context, Eritrea has often been misunderstood in recent and contemporary international history. During its liberation struggle, Eritrea was completely ignored by the international community, and during the last twenty years of survivalist struggles as a sovereign state, it has been perceived as odd, arrogant, rigid, undiplomatic and perhaps most dismally, as a state that inflicts continuous suffering of its own people. This image is reinforced by the tragic scenes screened by international media of desperate Eritrean youth migrants to fortress Europe that has occasionally perished in the Mediterranean Sea.

Eritrea is indeed an epitome of contradictory behaviours and images. On the one hand, it is a state borne out of epic sacrifices, neglect and unjust treatment, trying to furiously assert its independence and existence. On the other hand, is a hegemonic neoliberal world that never tries to extend a compassionate hand, not willing to understand, or admit and remedy the unjust treatment of Eritrea, which is the source of its suffering; yet ready to tame it, subordinate and force it into submission. The politics of subordination and forcing Eritrea into submission necessitates the demonisation and vilification of the leadership.

Now the state of no-war no-peace is over a great opportunity has opened for Eritrea to focus on improving its internal development. Using its locational advantage and natural resource endowment, Eritrea has great potential to rise.

Note

1. Interviews with EU Ambassador to Eritrea until 2016, Ambassadors of Germany, Italy, South Africa, head of mission of the US Embassy to Eritrea; and UNDP staffs. The interviews were conducted in 2015 and 2017, in Asmara, Eritrea, by the author.

References

Abbay, Alemseged. 2001. Not with Them, Not without Them: The Staggering of Eritrea to Nationhood. *Africa* LVI (4): 459–491.

Algiers Agreement. 2000a. Agreement on Cessation of Hostilities Between Ethiopia and Eritrea. Organisation of African Unity, 18 June.

Algiers Agreement. 2000b. Agreement Between the Government of State of Eritrea and Government of Federal Republic of Ethiopia. Algiers.

Bereketeab, Redie. 2007a. When Success Becomes a Liability: Challenges of State Building in Eritrea (1991–2005). *African and Asian Studies* 6 (4): 395–430.

Bereketeab, Redie. 2007b. *Eritrea: The Making of a Nation, 1890–1991*. Trenton, NJ: Red Sea Press.

Bereketeab, Redie. 2009. *State-Building in Post-Liberation Eritrea: Challenges, Achievements and Potentials*. London: Adonis & Abbey.

Bereketeab, Redie. 2012. Re-examining Local Governance in Eritrea: The Redrawing of Administration Regions. *African and Asian Studies* 11: 1–29.

Bereketeab, Redie. 2013. The Morality of the U.N. Security Council Sanctions Against Eritrea: Defensibility, Political Objectives, and Consequences. *African Studies Review* 56 (2): 145–161.

Bereketeab, Redie. 2016. *Revisiting the Eritrean National Liberation Movement, 1961–91*. Trenton, London, New Delhi, Cape Town, Nairobi, Addis Ababa, Asmara, Ibadan: The Red Sea Press.

Bereketeab, Redie (ed.). 2018. *National Liberation Movements as Government in Africa*. London and New York: Routledge.

Bolton, John. 2007. *Surrender Is Not Option: Defending America at the United Nations*. New York: Simon & Schuster.

Cohen, Herman J. 2013. *Time to Bring Eritrea in from the Cold*. African Argument.org.

Connell, Dan. 1993. *Against All Odds: A Chronicle of the Eritrean Revolution*. Trenton, NJ: Red Sea Press.

EPLF. 1994. A National Charter for Eritrea: For a Democratic, Just and Prosperous Future. Approved by the Third Congress of the Eritrean People's Liberation Front (EPLF), Nacfa, February.

Golooba-Mutebi, Frederick. 2018. Eritrea, the 'Police State' Where There Are No Cops to Be Seen? http://www.eastafro.com/2018/09/04/eritrea-the-police-state-where-there-are-no-cops-to-be-seen/. Accessed 1 March 2019.

Government of Eritrea. 1994. *Macro Policy Document*. Asmara: Government Press.

Habte Selassie, Bereket. 1989. *Eritrea and the United Nations*. Lawrenceville, NJ: Red Sea Press.

Habte Selassie, Bereket. 2003. *The Making of the Eritrean Constitution: The Dialectics of Process and Substance*. Lawrenceville and Asmara: Red Sea Press.

Hanson, Göte. 2000. *Eritrea 1999: A Bleeding Country That Never Kneels Down, Country Economic Report 2000: 5, Department of Economic and Institute for Economic Research*. Lund: Lund University.

IMF. 2019. World Economic Outlook database. https://www.imf.org/external/pubs/ft/weo/2019/01/weodata/download.aspx.

Klein, Natalie. 1998. Mass Expulsion from Ethiopia. Report on the Deportation of Eritreans and Ethiopians of Eritrean Origin from Ethiopia, June–August.

Legesse, Asmerom. 1999. The Uprooted: A Scientific Survey of Ethnic Eritrean Deportees from Ethiopia Conducted with Regards to Human Rights Violation. Part Two, by Prof. Asmerom Legesse on Behave of Citizens for Peace in Eritrea. Asmara, Eritrea, 22 February 1999.

Melber, Henning. 2007. *Transitions in Namibia: Which Changes for Whom?*. Uppsala: Nordic Africa Institute.

National Charter. 1994. A National Charter for Eritrea: For a Democratic, Just and Prosperous Future. Approved by the Third Congress of the Eritrean People's Front (EPLF). Nacfa, February.

Nielsen, Soren Walther. 2002. *Reintegration of Ex-Fighters in Highland Eritrea: A Window into the Process of State Formation and Its Lines of Social Stratification*. Roskilde: Roskilde University.

Plaut, Martin. 2016. *Understanding Eritrea: Inside Africa's Most Repressive State*. London: Hurst and Company.

Plaut, Martin. 2018. Why Sanctions on Eritrea Are Being Lifted and What it Means. *Africa Arguments*, 14 November. https://africanarguments.org/2018/11/14/eritrea-sanctions-lifted-what-it-means/.

Pool, David. 2001. *From Guerrillas to Government: The Eritrean People's Liberation Front*. Oxford, Athens: James Currey and Ohio University Press.

Prunier, Gerand. 2011. *Eritrea!! The Real Story*. ASMEA: Association for the Study of the Middle East and Africa. https://www.youtube.com/watch?v=Vg-PHUI0bWc. Accessed 13 February 2019.

Rena, Ravinder. 2007. Higher Education in Africa: A Case of Eritrea. *New Delhi: Journal of Educational Planning and Administration* 21 (2): 125–140.

Rena, Ravinder. 2008. Education in Eritrea: Developmental Challenges. *International Journal of Scientific Research in Education* 1 (1): 41–53.

Reid, Richard. 2009. *Eritrea's External Relations: Understanding Its Regional Role and Foreign Policy*. London: Chatham House.

Roberts, Hugh. 2001. Who Said Gaddafi Had to Go?. *London Review of Books*. https://www.lrb.co.uk/v33/n22/high-roberts/who-said-gaddafi.had-to-do. Accessed 8 January 2019.

Southall, Roger. 2013. *Liberation Movements in Power: Party and State in Southern Africa*. Woodbridge, Rochester and Scottsville: James Currey and University of KwaZulu-Natal Press.

Tadesse, Medhanie. 1999. *The Eritrea-Ethiopia War: Retrospect and Prospect. Reflections on the Making of Conflicts on the Horn of Africa, 1991–1998*. Addis Ababa: Mega Printing Enterprise.

Tesfai, Alemseged. 1999. Issues of Governance in the Eritrean Context. In *Post-conflict Eritrea: Prospects for Reconstruction in Development*, ed. Martin Doornbos and Alemseged Tesfai. Trenton, NJ, and Asmara: The Red Sea Press.

UN (United Nations). 2014. Health Millennium Development Goals Report: Innovations Driving Health MDGs in Eritrea. Abridged Version. UN/Ladavicius.

Tronvoll, Kjetill, and Daniel R. Mekonnen. 2014. *The African Garrison State: Human Rights & Political Development in Eritrea*. Woodbridge and Rochester: James Currey.

UNDP. 2014. Eritrea Health MDGs Report 2014. http://www.er.undp.org/content/eritrea/en/home/library/mdg/eritrea-health-mdgs-report-2014.html. Accessed 4 March 2019.

UNDP. 2019. Analysis of the Potential Contributions of the Colluli Potash Project to SDGs in Eritrea.

UNECA. 2015. *MDG Report 2015. Lessons Learned in Implementing the MDGs*. Addis Ababa: ECA Publications.

UNSC. 2009. *Security Council Imposes Sanctions on Eritrea over Its Role in Somalia, Refusal to Withdraw Troops Following Conflict with Djibouti*. New York: UNSC.

van Reisen, Mirjam, and Munyaradi Mawere (eds.). 2017. *Human Trafficking and Trauma in the Digital Era: The Ongoing Tragedy of the Trade in Refugees from Eritrea*. Mankon, Bamenda: Langaa Research & Publishing CIG.

Wiegratz, Jörg, Guiliano Martiniello, and Elisa Greco (eds.). 2018. *Uganda: The Dynamics of Neoliberal Transformation*. London: Zed Books.

Wolde Giorgis, Andebrehan. 2014. *Eritrea at a Crossroads: A Narrative of Triumph, Betrayal and Hope*. Houston, TX: Strategic Book Publishing.

Woldemariam, Yohannes, and Okbazghi Yohannes. 2007. War Clouds in the Horn of Africa. *Sudan Tribune*, 12 November.

Yohannes, Okbazghi. 1991. *Eritrea, a Pawn in World Politics*. Gainesville: University of Florida Press.

CHAPTER 16

The Giant of Africa? Explaining the Nigerian Governance, Security, and Development Paradox

Bashir Bala and Usman A. Tar

Introduction

The global economy is argued to have reached the Fourth Industrial Revolution anchored on the application of technologies (new digital and automated) in production, distribution, and other chains of service delivery. This significant change in global economic outlook suggests that there are open opportunities for emerging markets to improve their productivity and get into the loop of global cost competitiveness for their products and development (Oxford Business Group Report 2020a). With about 200 million people, Nigeria has the largest population and also the largest economy in Africa; the country has the world's 10th largest proven crude oil and the 9th largest natural gas reserves (Oxford Business Group

B. Bala
Institute of Strategy and Security Studies, University of Exeter, Exeter, UK

U. A. Tar (✉)
Department of Defence and Security Studies, Nigerian Defence Academy, Afaka, Kaduna, Nigeria
e-mail: uatar@nda.edu.ng

K. Omeje (ed.), *The Governance, Security and Development Nexus*,
https://doi.org/10.1007/978-3-030-49348-6_16

Report 2019a; UK DfID 2019). With an expanding middle class and the global population projection of the country set to reach 300 m by 2030 and 400 m by 2050, Nigeria is seen to potentially provide growth for Fast-Moving Consumer Goods (Oxford Business Group Report 2020b). Nigeria is therefore a significant emerging and investment partner for global competitiveness and in the best place to reap the opportunities of global new industrial technologies for governance, development, and security. It is important to stress from the standpoint of certain political, economic, and sociodemographic base factors, Nigeria is arguably seen as the giant of Africa. These factors, include *inter alia* Nigeria's population, GDP size, continental leadership aspiration, the country's role as a major Troop Contributing Country (TCC) for UN operations (Kuna 2005; Gani 2005; Alli 2006) as well as the sterling contributions of Nigeria's military to regional peacekeeping, democratic stabilization and peacebuilding, especially in West Africa (Frank and Ukpere 2012; Ajayi 2013; Toyin 2015).

However, Nigeria has continued to struggle with Boko Haram terrorism and insurgency in the North east, economic sabotage on its strategic oil facilities and infrastructure in the Niger Delta and the menace of cattle rustling and armed banditry in the north central and west geopolitical zones. Despite huge natural resources, the country has, according to Global poverty projections by the Brookings Institution in 2018, overstepped India as having 87 million people on less than $1.90 a day compared to India's 73 million and thus the largest population of people leaving in abject poverty (Okoi 2019). The missing link associated with these poor development and insecurity indices is lack of good governance as abundance of resources cannot guarantee security and development when there is absence of active commitment to political governance (Akahalu 2014). It is against this backdrop that this chapter aims to examine the prevailing challenges to governance, security, and development in Nigeria. Following this introduction section is an exploration of the governance, security and development nexus in Nigeria, the subsequent sections provide a sectoral analysis of Nigeria based on the performance of key sectors, as well as the key challenges of security and development in the country.

Security, Governance, and Development in Nigeria

The emergence and evolution of Boko Haram terrorism and insurgency has largely altered security calculations in Nigeria by further bringing to the fore the cost and inadequacy of good governance to manage security. The series of unabated bombings carried out by the sect coupled with the hostage-taking dimension added to their tactics have, in a larger context, pinpointed the free operating space they exploit. This is not surprising because as Adebakin and Raimi (2012) have pointed out even public and private establishments such as residential areas, places of worships like churches and mosques, markets, and telecommunications masks are not spared by Boko Haram attacks. The consequences of these attacks and the human and material resources employed to mitigate the menace naturally exerts a heavy burden on economies and development of developing countries like Nigeria (Adebayo 2014). The economic impact of terrorism if left unchecked has the potency of causing tremendous investor apathy that would result in low Foreign Direct Investment.

As recently witnessed in Nigeria, the insurgency has negatively impacted the regional economy where several Lebanese, Indians, and other expatriates who have established profitable businesses had to either close down their businesses or relocate to other regions of the country. This largely resulted in the reduction of activities in the areas of tourism, banking, and hospitability services management in North-East Nigeria. Similarly, the border towns that used to be beehive of fruitful business activities have equally been destroyed or vacated for fear of terrorism and insurgency. The level of insecurity this has created has resulted in making investment in key areas of the economy more unattractive and increases the cost of doing business "either through direct loss of goods and properties or the cost of taking precautions against business risks and uncertainty" (Achumba et al. 2013: 82). Invariably, the connecting factor between insecurity and business remains a huge challenge for business activities to flourish in North-East Nigeria.

Another dimension of this is the inability of the government to combat the menace of terrorism and thus provide a fertile and secure environment for businesses and investors to enjoy returns on their risks and uncertainty. According to Ewetan and Urhie (2014), the inability has resulted in wanton destruction of lives, properties, and economic activities which has brought inter-ethnic resentment and mistrust in Nigeria and this in the short and medium run, have negatively affected economic growth and development parameters. In the meantime, the present government soft approach of rebuilding and reconstructing the North-East through the North East Development Commission (NEDC) is a step in the right direction. However, these efforts of rebuilding infrastructure and facilities destroyed by insurgents naturally divert national resources by imposing a financial strain on the government at various levels. Thus, as Bamidele (2012) observed, Boko Haram terrorism and insurgency has put on a negative string on Nigeria's attainment of sustainable development.

In the North West, cattle rustling and armed banditry surfaced in the light of scourging threat pose by Boko Haram in the North-East. The menace is breeding in the region as cattle and livestock rearing remain the major preoccupation of people and overall, agriculture remains the mainstay of the regional economy. Cattle rustling and armed banditry, as Okoli and Okpaleke (2014) have observed, have emerged as a core national security quagmire. Many available reports have indicated how killing, maiming of cow owners, destruction of their properties, and pillaging of cows have proliferated. For example, Bashir (2014) quoted the Chairman of the Kaduna State Chapter of the Miyyeti Allah Cattle Breeders Association asserting that between 2013 and 2014 about 7000 cattle were rustled from commercial and traditional herders in Northern Nigeria. In most cases, it was reported that the cattle rustlers and armed bandits did also rape women, kill children, cart away livestock and burn down houses (Egwu 2015; Olaniyan and Yahaya 2016; Abdulazeez et al. 2018). The dangerous dimension to the evolution of the menace is kidnapping innocent people for ransom which has continued to be a significant threat to sustainable development in Nigeria (Ngwama 2014; Badiora 2015; Suleiman et al. 2015). The impact of kidnapping on the socioeconomic development and security of the region and Nigeria at large is huge. The impacts include threats to public safety, sabotage of economic activities for fear of abduction, negative perception of Nigeria at the international stage, and endangering of potentials for investment and sustainable growth and development (Okoli and Agada 2014).

In Nigeria's South-South region particularly Niger Delta housing an important wetland and coastal maritime ecosystem, the complex nature of militancy, resource conflict, and pipeline vandalisation have continued to retard developmental efforts. The construction of pipeline network in the region was done at strategic locations that will allow for effective exploration, production, and distribution of oil and gas products from the oil-rich Niger Delta to other parts of Nigeria. However, despite the government's efforts in ensuring the safety and security of laid pipes and other oil and gas strategic economic activities, Iwayemi (2008) and Akinro et al. (2008) observed that, the safety and functionality of those pipelines is being compromised by vandals who damage and rupture them in order to tap crude oil. Moen (2012) and Onouha (2008) also added that the strategic importance of these pipelines to the Nigeria's political economy remains high due to their relevance in security and development in Nigeria. However, the long range of employment and the insufficient security coverage of the pipelines have made them vulnerable to attacks by militants. By implications, the damage and rupture of the pipelines often result in massive cost of repairs and maintenance, poor fuel supply for electricity generation, oil spillage on diverse waterways, reduction in government revenue and huge impact on the socioeconomic wellbeing and stability of Nigeria (Alawode and Ogunleye 2011). Regardless of the primacy of combating oil pipeline sabotage, it is noteworthy that the menace is a serious threat to national security particularly for a country like Nigeria that heavily depends on oil exports. The losses from crude oil theft facilitated through pipeline sabotage is monumental such that in 2014 alone, Nigeria was listed as a country where 400,000 barrels of crude oil were stolen (Kim 2016; Nwachukwu 2018). Similarly, up to 3.8 trillion Naira were recorded as losses by both Nigerian government, domestic and transnational oil companies from crude oil theft in 2016 (Okoromadu 2018). The huge losses from the menace therefore suggest the need for good governance and security that will ensure combating oil theft in Nigeria through such efforts as deployment of technology to monitor activities around pipelines and their precincts as well as adequate Special Forces for aerial surveillance.

Development, Governance, and Security in Nigeria: A Sectoral Analysis

Agriculture

Globally, the agricultural sector provides an uplift to the growth and development of a country's economy through four major anchors, namely, product, factor, market, and foreign exchange contributions. For this reason, governments in many developing countries like Tanzania, Liberia, Rwanda, and Nigeria have realized the need to strengthen the sector through various policies and programs (Ewetan et al. 2017).

In Nigeria, the export economy is largely oil-centered. However, the agricultural sector has been an important component of the national economy in the past one or two decades as it provides opportunities for employment generation, poverty alleviation, and substantial contribution to the aggregate growth of the economy (Izuchukwu 2011). In recent times, the Nigerian agricultural sector has recorded steady growth and contributed to macroeconomic stability notwithstanding the recent recession the economy was plunged in and the global oil market price volatility. The decades of the oil export boom (beginning from the 1970s) witnessed a great neglect of the agricultural sector in the country, but the trend has been gradually changing in recent years with the growing policy emphasis on diversification of the economy. Nigeria has vast arable land and an expansive network of diverse production base that incubates high-value cash crops capable of boosting the country's agricultural export, development, and investment (Oxford Business Group 2019b).

One of such essential cash crops is rice which according to the UN Food and Agriculture Organisation, Nigeria is one of its largest producers with small-scale farmers accounting for 80% of rice production and a trending consumption pattern that rose by 4%, representing an increase of 6.7 million tonnes during 2017/2018 season (Oxford Business Group 2020c). Agricultural export receipts was $687.7 million (N212.7 billion) in 2016, representing 4% of total trade with Tin Can Island at Lagos' Apapa Port alone recorded a 160% increase in agricultural exports in 2017. The National Bureau of Statistics reports that agricultural exports indicate a growing trajectory, maintaining a steady rise on quarter-by-quarter basis to 54.9% in the fourth quarter of 2017 and year-on-year trend of 170.9%. The NBS reports that agricultural exports rose by 63.8% quarter-on-quarter in the first quarter of 2018 to $236.8 million (N73.24 billion), representing a 24% increase year-on-year. Prime agricultural exports included fermented cocoa beans at $75.3 million (N23.3 billion), sesame seeds at $86.2 m (N26.7 billion), and raw cocoa beans at $19.5 million (N6 billion). Other agricultural exports included cocoa butter, frozen shrimp, hibiscus flower, and rubber. The parameters of export performance have made significant manifestations with "the free on board value of agricultural commodities shipped from Tin Can Island soared by 402.2% in the first quarter of 2018 to N29.2 billion ($94.4 million), with the total volume of exports jumping by 558.5% over the same period to 45,462 tonnes" (Oxford Business Group 2020b).

In the past, successive administrations in Nigeria have initiated flurry of projects, policies, and programs to change the stagnant trajectory of the country's economy through enhancing agricultural output. These included the Economic Empowerment and Development Strategy (NEEDS) I and II (2001–2007), Seven-Point Agenda (2007–2010), Food Security Strategy Document in 2009, Land Resources Policy to guide sustainable use of agricultural lands, National Agricultural Mechanisation Policy, National Cooperative Development Policy, and the National Seed Policy and National Policy on Integrated Rural Development (NPIRD). The NPIRD could have particularly bolstered the potentials of the sector as its objectives were tailored toward attaining sufficient infrastructure, coordination, management and empowerment of the rural population and the economy through wealth creation and integration to national development. Despite the attempts made by governments through these policy interventions, the agricultural sector was still blighted by a plethora of setbacks that include poor investment by the private sector and land tenure and ownership severities (Olomola and Nwafor 2018). Other challenges are stringencies on agricultural research and extension program, ineffective access to credit and incentives, poor infrastructure and facilities, high rural-urban migration as well as poor implementation strategies for policies and projects. It is in the light of these challenges coupled with the acclaimed potentials of agricultural exports and the declined oil revenues that hit the country's economy in 2015 that the President Buhari's government initiated efforts to seek economic diversification and agricultural development as support mechanisms for macroeconomic stability, non-oil growth, economic growth, and development.

Evidently, the present government and its immediate predecessor have initiated various projects aimed at augmenting the dividends of agricultural sector. These projects are fourfold and are framed within the context and objective of providing mollifying measures and special subsidy packages to farmers. One of such packages is the Agricultural Transformation Agenda's (ATA) e-Wallet system initiated in 2014 as a mechanism through which bankrolled electronic vouchers are given to farmers for agricultural inputs. These e-vouchers were delivered directly to the farmer's mobile phones and they used them to purchase inputs directly from agribusiness dealers. This program, according to the US Department of Commerce's International Trade Administration (2019), has proven to be more effective and efficient in eliminating corruption in the program and in enabling small-scale farmers easy access to requisite resources.

In a similar vein, the Presidential Economic Diversification Initiative (PEDI) was introduced in July 2017 and it supported the revival of waning industries (particularly textile and core agro-processing). The initiative provides access to credit, reduces bureaucratic bottlenecks, and attracts investment in the agribusiness sector. There is also the Presidential Fertilizer Initiative (PFI) which was launched in December 2016 as a Public-Private Partnership in Nigeria. This initiative was a strategic partnership between the Federal Government of Nigeria and Morocco led by the Nigerian Sovereign Investment Authority (NSIA) and the Fertilizer Producers and Suppliers Association of Nigeria (FEPSAN) (Toromade 2018). At the commencement of PFI, phosphate and potash were sourced from the international markets in Morocco and Europe, respectively, while urea and limestones were procured from local farmers in Nigeria. It was within the dividend of the initiative that a single plant was able to produce 50,000 metric tonnes of fertilizer in the first year and this was sold to farmers at ₦14,000 ($24.04) per bag and subsequently, the cost was reduced ₦8000 ($16.5) per 50-Kg bag to ₦5500 ($11.4) per 50-Kilogram bag in 2017 due to reactivation of more fertilizer-blending plants (Olomola and Nwafor 2018).

The commitment by President Buhari to refinance the Bank of Agriculture (BOA) and the Bank of Industry (BOI) with N15 billion and additional N10 billion, respectively, is also a step in the right direction (Adanikin 2019). However, the government has not yet complied with the African Union (AU) Maputo Declaration on Comprehensive Africa Agriculture Development Program (CAADP) in July 2003, to earmark 10% of the annual budget to develop the agriculture sector and ensure food security in member countries. This integral initiative will be good for the attainment of food sufficiency, boosting agribusinesses and in the long run, will provide streams of middle-income earners so that insecurity due to poverty and unemployment will become a thing of the past. Similarly, the rural farming areas are presently blighted by cattle rustling, armed banditry, and kidnapping that have forced rural–urban movement in unprecedented scale and the situation has left several farmlands uncultivated and thus dwindling the fortunes from the agricultural sector.

Petroleum Sector

The Nigerian petroleum sector accounts for about 10% of Federal Gross Domestic Product (FGDP) and the oil and gas export revenue accounts for 86% of total export revenue (OPEC 2020). In 2017, oil alone accounted for approximately 56% of state revenue and 85% of export revenue (Cohen 2019). The contribution of the oil sector to aggregate oil export revenue appreciated higher in 2011 at 8.5% and from 2011 to 2018, and it has continued to slow down and reached a lowest point in 2016 when the export revenue nosedived to 2.5% at $45 per barrel. This trend is captured in Fig. 16.1.

Crude oil production including natural gas liquids and condensates was 1.82 mbd (56.4 million barrels) in May 2019. This clearly indicated a decline of 0.01 mbd compared with what obtained in April 2019 where the production stood at 1.92 mbd (57.6 million barrels). Crude oil export declined to 1.37 mbd compared to 1.47 mbd in April 2019. In the second quarter of 2019, the price of Nigerian oil rose to US$73.70 per barrel from US$73.03 per barrel in the first quarter of the year which represents an increase of 0.9% (CBN 2019). The increase in the price of oil then was partly attributed to the ongoing conflict in the Middle East and more particularly, the various economic and diplomatic sanctions imposed on

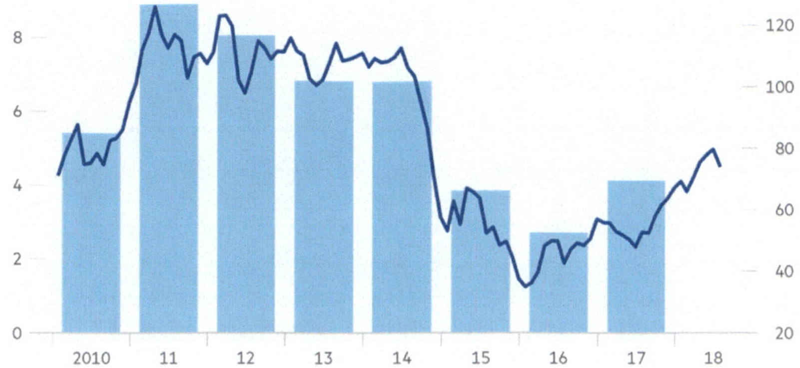

Fig. 16.1 Nigeria's diminishing oil revenues (*Source* Bloomberg [2019])

Iran by the US. Moreover, oil production averaged 1.7 million barrels a day in the first nine months of 2018, 600,000 barrels short of the 2.3 million barrels per day on which the Nigerian budget for the year was based (Dulue and Bala-Gbogbo 2019). Fig. 16.2 indicated this reality where Nigerian oil production fluctuated across a decade of oil-refining imports.

There is no doubt that the present administration is making effort toward reforming the sector with the unbundling of Nigerian National Petroleum Corporation (NNPC), potential establishment of modular refineries, reconstruction of existing refineries, and recall of various oil well licenses and concessionaires. The effort to revitalize the sector is thus driven by its vulnerability to external shocks in a competitive oil market which Katsouris (2019) argues is influenced by US sanctions on heavy crude and US shale dominance in light sweet crude. The Nigeria's downstream oil sector is also challenged by the dysfunction of the four major refineries which have a capacity of 445,000 b/d. These refineries have been underperforming due to a combination of infrastructural decay and pipeline sabotage and vandalism. Gupte (2019: 46) refers to the issue of infrastructural decay as "technical problems arising after years of neglect." Over the years, the refineries have experienced petro-rentier criminality

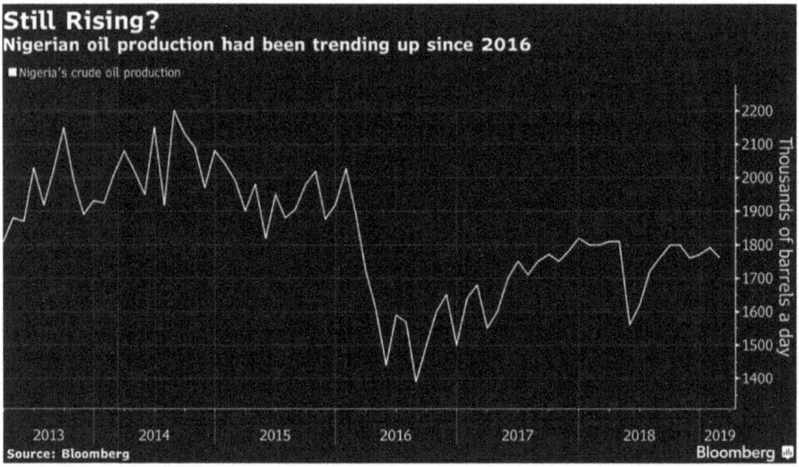

Fig. 16.2 Oil production in Nigeria, 2013–2019 (*Source* Bloomberg [2020])

perpetrated by militants and state agents in the form of oil thefts, plundering, and cannibalization of facilities resulting in massive developmental costs (Okoli 2019a, b). The poor state of the refineries has compelled the government to barter up to 330,000 barrels per day of crude production for gasoline refined elsewhere which indirectly divests revenues that could have been used for provision of public utilities (Gupte 2019). In order to avoid the loss of revenue by heavy import bill, the construction of privately owned Dangote refinery needs to be hastened and the state and federal government needs to provide the needed support for the operational efficiency of the 600,000 b/d Dangote refinery in Lagos. This refinery will help to curb the country's importation of refined oil and other petroleum products.

Manufacturing

The manufacturing sector contributes hugely to modern economy as a catalyst for boosting foreign exchange capacity, generating employment, and increasing productivity relative to export expansion and import substitution (Opaluwa et al. 2010). The Nigeria's manufacturing sector encompasses thirteen distinct activities such as oil refining, food and beverages, cement, tobacco, footwear, textile, apparel, wood and its product, paper products and pulp. Others include chemical and pharmaceutical products, non-metallic products like rubber and plastic products, electric and electronics, iron, steel, basic metal, motor vehicles and assembly as well as other manufacturing activities (NBS 2019). The nominal GDP growth of the sector in the first quarter of 2019 stood at "36.45% (year-on-year) or 27.52% points higher than the rate recorded in the corresponding period of 2018 (8.93%), and 2.88% points higher than in the preceding quarter" (NBS 2019: 48). The quarter-on-quarter contribution of the sector to nominal GDP was recorded at a growth rate of 2.88% and the overall sector's contribution to nominal GDP during the first quarter of 2019, witnessing a growth rate of 11.32%. The percentage of the sector's contribution in the quarter was higher than what obtained from the sector in the first and fourth quarters of 2018 where real GDP growth in the sector stood at 9.28% in the first and 10.11% in the fourth quarter (NBS 2019).

Over the past two decades, the country's manufacturing sector has witnessed shocks despite several policies and measures that are seemingly palliative lunched and initiated by successive governments. Even the present administration of President Buhari has implemented wide-ranging initiatives in manufacturing activities in segments like cement, automobiles, agro-processing, and bio-fuels through the ERGP (Oxford Business Report 2019c). The prolonged decline of the sector is practically attributed to its import-dependent posture which has made it susceptible to both internal and external shocks, thereby exposing the weak competitiveness of the sector. The weakness of the sector has also been occasioned by low local value addition, loosened backward integration, poor forward integration, and inefficient employment generation potentials of local manufacturing firms (*The Vanguard Newspaper* 2019). Congestion in the Apapa Port in Lagos State which is a vital import and export channel is also another major bottleneck affecting the growth of many manufacturing firms. The absence of an immediate integrated plan to decongest the port often results in delays and high clearance costs for the manufacturing industry in Nigeria (McAllister 2019). All these factors have continued to impact negatively on the sector's contribution to the economy and development process. Therefore, creating enabling measures that would provide conducive environment as a springboard for the growth of local production is important. In this regard, the reduction in the cost of goods transfer from ports to factories, dredging of the various ports outside Lagos State to decongest Tin Can and Wharf ports and the need to revisit the Nigeria Industrial Revolution Plan (NIRP) which provides the mandate and modalities on review of backward integration policies to encourage local production and infrastructural gaps are important needs toward developing the sector. Once these steps are taken, the sector will provide high yields on investment for the Nigerian economy (Oxford Business Report 2019c).

Tourism

The tourism sector is one of the world's fastest-growing economic sectors, especially in many developing countries (Yusuff and Akinde 2015; Edgell Sr 2016; Khoshnevis Yazdi et al. 2017). The contribution of the sector to the Nigerian economy can be analyzed using both micro and macroeconomic aggregates. Bankole (2002) argues that at the micro level, consideration is given to direct and indirect impact of tourism. The direct impact is assessed on such activities as accommodation, entertainment, food and beverages, transport and shopping by tourists. The indirect impact on the other hand, is assessed based on revenue from food and beverage suppliers, manufacturers, suppliers, airport facilities, telephone and postal, gas and electric services. The macro analysis "estimates the extent to which tourism revenue is a factor in offsetting or adding to a deficit on merchandise trade, or in reducing the current account deficit, and thereby improving the overall balance" (Bankole 2002: 75). Furthermore, directs impact of tourism sector are recently calculated in a model that aggregate tourism consumption spending by target population of tourists both within and outside the target region. The model equally encompasses the gross value added to the economy by the tourism sector as profits, wages, salaries, rent, and interest. It also aggregates the total effects of the sector in terms of economic contribution by adding the flow-on effects in the target region supported by demand generated by tourism spending plus employment generated by the sector and subsidiary tourism sector (Wood et al. 2006; Driml and McLennan 2010; Zuruba et al. 2015). The Nigerian tourism sector is enriched with diverse cultures and sites that have severally been cited as the main reason why tourism should be a major booster of Nigeria's foreign exchange earnings (Nwanne 2017). Across the six geopolitical zones are rocks, springs, waterfalls, lakes, game reserves, and zoos as necessities for the creation of tourism services (Bankole 2002). The tourism assets include Obudu Cattle Ranch, Yankari Game Reserve, the Osun Osogbo Groove, Ogbunike Cave, Idorin Hills, Mambila Plateau, Oguta Late, and Olumo Rock among several others yet to come to limelight (Ovat 2003; Nwanne 2017). During the 61st United Nations World Tourism Organisation Commission for Africa (UNWTO-CAF) Conference in Abuja on 4 June 2018, Yemi Kale, the Statistician-General of the Federation and Chief Executive Officer NBS disclosed that tourism sector in Nigeria has great potentials as it gradually begins to harness and affect several sub-sectors of key productive sectors (*Premium Times* Online Newspaper 2018). This is evident by the sector's key contributions to nominal GDP as it accounted for 34% of GDP and about 20% of the nation's employment creation in 2017.

Similarly, in 2016, air travel and tourism in Nigeria for 1.7% to the GDP and in cash flow it generated N1.861 billion according to the 2017 Annual Economic Reports of the World Travel and Tourism Council (WTTC). This alone ranked Nigeria "171st among 185 countries; 180th on the growth rate and 105th on the long-term growth rate index. While Nigeria lags behind, travel and tourism in The Gambia contribute 9% to the GDP, with 63.7% foreign visitors" (Oyebade 2018). However, it is important to note that in the years before 2016, the trend analysis of the sector's total contribution to GDP, visitors' exports and employment generation fluctuated (Yusuff 2016). Despite some moves by the present government to improve the sector, lack of convincing marketing strategy, unhealthy competition among critical stakeholders, poor funding, inefficient infrastructure and facilities and insecurity are some of the challenges impeding the growth of tourism sector in Nigeria (Oyebade 2018; Yusuff 2016).

Challenges of Governance, Security, and Development in Nigeria

Notoriety of Corruption

Since the oil boom of the 1980s, Nigeria is globally acclaimed as a cesspool of corruption which has embedded its political and economic matrix. Eliminating corruption and its vast patronage network which has been core in the country's political culture has been identified as a key (Steven 2016). Corruption in Nigeria comprises of bribery, illegal asset accumulation, political nepotism, illegal campaign financing, money laundering, violations of Procurement Act, lack of financial transparency and accountability in governance (World Bank 1997). These variegated dimensions of corruption have over time been retarding the various sectors of the Nigerian economy and have also been source of concern in the moral compass of the nation's governance. For example, the construction sector believed to be growing rapidly has been bedeviled by inadequate infrastructure projects which Kasimu (2016) attributes to corruption in national governance and diversion of needed resources. Similarly, in terms of security provisioning, corruption has stunted the needed wherewithal to ensure sound and effective security service delivery. This is particularly evidenced by an empirical study conducted by Banini (2020) on the connections between corruption and military effectiveness. The study revealed that corruption in national defense and security architecture has affected military capacity and capability for effective counter-insurgency operation. It is instructive to note that the present government campaign for Treasury Single Account (TSA) has met some resistance from few institutions and its implementation has reduced the scale of unregulated cash flow and leakages in national financial management. However, the TSA has no significant impact on curtailing corruption in terms of bribery, inflation of contracts, and violations of procurement regulations (Salihu 2020). The net impact of this is the endangering of national governance by giving loopholes for corruption to flourish and continue to negatively impede governance and economic initiatives toward national growth and development.

Infrastructure Deficit

The poor state of critical infrastructure that will facilitate growth and development has been at the front-burner of analyzing Nigeria's stunted economic prosperity and the failure to address insecurity. Today, Nigeria's midstream and downstream oil infrastructures are in dire shape than upstream production as the country is capable of producing 2.5 million barrels of crude oil per day despite having more than 40 billion barrels of reserves. As Cohen (2019) rightly observed that in 2018 refining capacity was down by 11% and the country's refineries are currently underperforming below their intended consolidated capacity of 500,000 barrels per day. Similarly, gas infrastructure which also largely located in the supply end of Niger Delta and the demand hubs in Lagos and Port Harcourt has continued to suffer bottlenecks of interconnectivity between both. This has made it difficult for the supply of gas from the eastern hub to the demand hub in western half. Though there is a contract worth US$400 million awarded in 2012 for the construction of new east-west 48-inch, 127 km interconnector pipeline called Obaifu-Obrikum-Obem (OB3). This contract has suffered major setbacks and inability to achieve milestones and deadlines (Eweje 2019).

The poor state of road networks in Nigeria is also a key infrastructural barrier that has diminished the availability of trucks as consumer goods heavily rely on road transport system. Similarly, as the economy has expanded coupled with the population explosion, the port system is both obsolete and moribund. The present government has done remarkably well in terms of rail transport system, however, no evident effort is made to dredge various ports outside Lagos to decongest Tin Can and Wharf and equally lower the cost of transporting goods from ports to factories (Adekoya 2019). In the long run, poor state of road and gas infrastructure has been a stumbling block to generation of more revenue for the government by affecting production capacity. It has also affected security provision as militants, terrorists, and armed bandits mostly operate in rural areas where access to their hideouts is an issue. This has largely affected quick responses to complex emergencies in Nigeria.

Insufficient Electricity Generation Capacity

The inadequate supply, cost, and access to reliable energy and power have remained one of the key infrastructural barriers affecting Nigeria's development. Access to power remains a major economic and social challenge in Nigeria with about 90 million citizens lacking access to power supply (Oxford Business Group 2019b). Energy and power generation is also a huge burden on local manufactures as the absence of reliable grid power has been a core limitation on the cost competitiveness of Nigerian products in both the local and export markets. Though the national power regulatory agency has been unbundled and the power sector privatized, there is still the need for creating a secure and enabling regulatory environment for more capable private investment in power generation.

Conclusion: Nigeria's Leadership Claims and Disputed Regional Hegemony in Africa

It is imperative to consider the continental hegemonic claim and its associated disputation which has put Nigeria on a map of aspiration for African leadership and claiming to be the giant of Africa. The position and status of giant of Africa were never conferred on Nigeria by its African counterparts who are all emerging markets making strides in the socioeconomic development of their people. Evidenced from the ongoing socioeconomic and political malaise Nigeria is grappling with, it is safe to suggest that the quest for African leadership is a way too far for the Nigerian government. It is on record that the humanitarian fallout of Boko Haram terrorism and insurgency in Nigeria can distinctly be ascribed to the exponential migration and internal displacement of Nigerians from Northeast to other parts of the country and even Libya and Europe. In 2016 alone, Nigerians were the largest number of desperate migrants crossing the Mediterranean Sea to Europe and in that year about 37,000 Nigerians scaled through the perilous journey to Italy alone (Kanu et al. 2019). The continual resuscitation of Boko Haram group in the face of several claims of defeating its kinetic operations has continued to question the military capacity and capability of Nigeria as one of the major Troops Contributing Countries for UN peacekeeping operations. The threats to its internal security occasioned by widespread kidnapping and proliferation of small arms and light weapons due to the porosity of its borders have also questioned Nigeria's readiness to provide adequate security for its citizens which will be imperative for making a strong claim to the leadership of the African continent in security, governance, and multifaceted development.

No doubt, the African RECs have three decisive regional hegemons comprising Nigeria in the ECOWAS West Africa, South Africa in the SADC region, and Egypt in the Arab Maghreb. Nigeria has the advantage of a large growing population that provide massive market for financial flows, substantial oil endowment/export, and the largest GDP on the continent. But in terms of human security that provide the requisite platform for economic prosperity and development, both South Africa and Egypt are well ahead of Nigeria. For example, South Africa presently prides itself as the most industrialized country in Africa and is one of the leading powers in the continent even in terms of defence and security provision. The country has private military and security industry that is robust and productive, providing complementary and combat support to their commercial sector and the government (CIA 2011; Mahr 2017; Bloomberg 2019). On the other hand, Egypt has a leading military firepower that continues to project its foreign policy objectives and defence diplomacy amidst an empirical condition of relatively stable internal security. However, a recent report by Carnegie Endowment for International Peace has postulated otherwise (Miller 2018). The report argues that Egypt under President Al-Sisi has failed to reverse the internal state decay bedeviling the country and it has lost the regional hegemonic capacity in the Middle East. The report further asserts that Egypt now has no sufficient wealth, military power, and the administrative efficiency to influence events and outcomes in the region, except in Libya and Gaza. The dissipation of the country's soft power in the region and its lack of expeditionary capability to deploy military might outside its borders—all potentially point to its lack of military operational readiness.

On the economic front, the few emerging market currencies have been hit harder by the spread of coronavirus occasioned by divestment amidst riskier assets, lockdowns, a slump in tourism and factory closures, and lower demands for exports. These countries are Ghana, Egypt, Kenya, and South Africa even though the Egyptian Pound recently appreciated against the US Dollar based on the benchmark for emerging market currencies and its increasingly overvalued pattern (El-Tablawy and Wallace 2020). Moreover, the monetary easing, social safety nets, expensive medical procurements, and fiscal stimulus embarked upon by these governments amidst the pandemic disease crisis have meant more pressure on their currency (Dzawu 2020). South Africa in particular, has its economy slumped into second recession in two consecutive years as power shortage weighed on national output and business confidence and sustainability. This has mounted pressure on the country's Central Bank to cut interest rates as annual GDP shrank by 1.4% in the fourth quarter of 2019. The contraction in its economy means that the most industrialized country in Africa recorded an abysmal economic growth rate of 0.2% representing the lowest since the global financial crisis of 2008 (Naidoo and Mbatha 2020). Though Nigeria is not saved from the looming recession as fall in oil prices ramped up pressure on its economy impelling a recent currency devaluation against the Dollar (Adekoya and Jeremiah 2020). The country's high cost of governance has persisted in spite of negative volatility of oil prices at the global market, which is most unhealthy for governance and development. Despite the uncertain economic climate, Nigeria remains the largest economy in Africa and with a fast-growing population, which if gainfully skilled and employed, could become an advantage for the country in addressing some of the country's security, governance, and development challenges.

To address the plaguing insecurity and attain development, good governance in Nigeria must encompass and promote effective anti-corruption crusade that will ensure financial transparency and accountability at all levels and across all sectors. The African Development Group (2019) has acknowledged that the federal government has made some efforts with institutional and governance reforms by implementing the Integrated Financial Management and Information System and the Integrated Payroll and Personnel Information System. However, more needs to be done also to improve on fiscal prudence and public procurement processes that will stop corruption particularly in security provision. Though Nigeria has made improvement in banking, telecommunication and airline industry, the agriculture, power, transportation and manufacturing sectors have continued to suffer infrastructural deviancies (Joseph 2009). There is therefore the need for more provision of facilities and infrastructure that will aid agricultural value chains and facilitate production of domestic goods at a relatively cheaper cost. On electricity generation, the 2017 Power Sector Recovery Program which provides several reforms related to prioritizing investment, development of new sources of energy, and funding to upgrade and expand the existing regional grid and other generating opportunities needs to be holistically revisited. By so doing, Nigeria will be able to address the plethora of governance, security, and development challenges and prosperously emerge as the undisputed "giant of Africa".

References

Abdulazeez, A., A. Ibrahim, and S. Saifullah. 2018. The Incidence and Impact of Cattle Rustling in Some Rural Communities of Katsina State, Nigeria. *FUDMA Journal of Sciences* 2 (2): 288–296.

Achumba, I.C., O.S. Ighomereho, and M.O.M. Akpor-Robaro. 2013. Security Challenges in Nigeria and the Implications for Business Activities and Sustainable Development. *Journal of Economics and Sustainable Development* 4 (2): 79–100.

Adanikin O. 2019. Budget: 16 Years After, Nigeria Fails to Implement Maputo Declaration on Agric, Food Security. Featured News, *International Centre for Investigative Reporting (ICIR)*, 28 December. https://www.icirnigeria.org/author/oadanikin/.

Adebakin, M.A., and L. Raimi. 2012. National Security Challenges and Sustainable Economic Development: Evidence from Nigeria. *Journal of Studies in Social Sciences* 1 (1): 1–30.

Adebayo, Anthony A. 2014. Implications of 'Boko Haram' Terrorism on National Development in Nigeria: A Critical Review. *Mediterranean Journal of Social Sciences* 5 (16): 480–489.

Adekoya, F. 2019. Nigeria: Despite Growth, Manufacturing Sector's Contributions to GDP Remain Static. *The Guardian*, February 13 (Lagos). https://allafrica.com/stories/201902130064.html.

Adekoya, F., and K. Jeremiah. 2020. FG Proposes Budget Cut as Projected Oil Price Heads for $20. *The Guardian Newspaper*, March 10. https://guardian.ng/news/fg-proposes-budget-cut-as-projected-oil-price-heads-for-20/.

African Development Group. 2019. *African Economic Outlook 2019, Macroeconomic Performance and Prospects Jobs, Growth, and Firm Dynamism, Integration for Africa's Economic Prosperity*, February 13. Addis Ababa: Africa Development Bank.

Ajayi, Adegboyega I. 2013. Military Regimes and Nation Building in Nigeria: 1966–1999. *African Journal of History and Culture* 5 (7): 138–142.

Akahalu, Uchenna A. 2014. *Interrogating Frustration-Aggression from Environmental Degradation in the Niger Delta Conflict*. A Doctoral Thesis for the Award of PhD in International Relations at the Nottingham Trent University, United Kingdom.

Akinro, A.O., D.A. Opeyemi, and I.B. Ologunagba. 2008. Climate Change and Environmental Degradation in the Niger Delta Region of Nigeria: Its Vulnerability, Impacts and Possible Mitigations. *Research Journal of Applied Sciences* 3 (3): 167–173.

Alawode, A.J., and I.O. Ogunleye. 2011. Maintenance, Security, and Environmental Implications of Pipeline Damage and Ruptures in the Niger Delta Region. *Pacific Journal of Science and Technology* 12 (1): 565–573.

Alli, Warrisu O. 2006. The New ECOWAS Strategy for Conflict Resolution: A Case Study of Côte d'Ivoire. *Nigerian Journal of International Affairs* 32 (2): 87–112.

Badiora, Adewumi I. 2015. Regional Differences and Developmental Implications of Security Challenges in Nigeria: The Case of Kidnapping. *African Security Review* 24 (1): 55–62.

Bamidele, O. 2012. Boko Haram Catastrophic Terrorism: An Albatross to National Peace, Security and Sustainable Development in Nigeria. *Journal of Sustainable Development in Africa* 14 (1): 32–44.

Banini, Daniel K. 2020. Security Sector Corruption and Military Effectiveness: The Influence of Corruption on Countermeasures against Boko Haram in Nigeria. *Small Wars & Insurgencies* 31 (1): 131–158.

Bankole, A. 2002. The Nigerian Tourism Sector: Economic Contribution, Constraints, and Opportunities. *Journal of Hospitality Financial Management* 10 (1) Article: 71–89.

Bashir, M. 2014. Hopes for an End to Cattle Theft. *Daily Trust Newspaper*, February 21. www.dailytrust.com.ng/daily/feature/33468-hopes-for-an-end-to-cattle-theft.

Bloomberg. 2019. Emerging Trends, Drivers and Challenges in the Private Security Services Market 2019–2023, September 27. https://www.bloomberg.com/press-releases/2019-09-27/emerging-trends-drivers-and-challenges-in-the-private-security-services-market-2019-2023-technavio.

CBN. 2019. *Economic Report*, May. Central Bank of Nigeria (CBN). https://www.cbn.gov.ng/Out/2019/RSD/November%202019%20Economic%20Report%20Published.pdf.

CIA Directorate of Intelligence. 2011. South Africa: Internal Security Apparatus. Central Intelligence Agency, Government of the United States of America (USA).

Cohen, A. 2019. Will President Buhari Rescue Nigeria's Oil and Gas Sector? *Forbes*, March 8. https://www.forbes.com/sites/arielcohen/2019/03/08/will-president-buhari-rescue-nigerias-oil-and-gas-sector/#3a5b18c433da.

Driml, S., and C. McLennan. 2010. *Handbook on Measuring the Economic Value of Tourism to National Parks*. Australia: Cooperative Research Centre (CRC) for Sustainable Tourism Pty Ltd.

Dulue, M., and E. Bala-Gbogbo. 2019. Nigerian Oil Region Crisis Threatens Buhari's Economic Plans. *Bloomberg*, March 12. https://www.bloomberg.com/news/articles/2019–03-13/nigerian-oil-region-crisis-threatens-buhari-s-economic-plans.

Dzawu, M.M. 2020. Virus-Stricken African Currencies Are Set for Even More Pain. *Bloomberg*, March 27. https://www.bloomberg.com/news/articles/2020-03-27/virus-stricken-african-currencies-are-set-for-even-more-pain.

Edgell Sr., D.L. 2016. *Managing Sustainable Tourism: A Legacy for the Future*. London and New York: Routledge.

Egwu, S. 2015. The Political Economy of Cattle Rustling in Contemporary Nigeria. In Report Presented at the Centre for Democracy and Development's Research Validation Meeting Held at Dennis Hotel, Abuja on Thursday 28 May 2015, Vol. 28, 13–48.

El-Tablawy, T., and P. Wallace. 2020. Egypt's Red-Hot Currency Continues to Rise as Inflows Pick Up. *Bloomberg*, 14 January. https://www.bloomberg.com/news/articles/2020-01-14/egypt-s-red-hot-currency-continues-to-rise-as-inflows-pick-up.

Eweje. A. 2019. *The Nigerian Oil and Gas Upstream Report*. Lagos, Nigeria: A Publication of Afrinvest West Africa.

Ewetan, O., A. Fakile, E. Urhie, and E. Oduntan. 2017. Agricultural Output and Economic Growth in Nigeria. *Journal of African Research in Business & Technology*. https://www.semanticscholar.org/paper/Agricultural-Output-and-Economic-Growth-in-Nigeria-Afolabi-Ogundele/ae8ce7e6f118d75923 5e89ba6fef46b98c8ad087.

Ewetan, Olabanji O., and E. Urhie. 2014. Insecurity and Socio-Economic Development in Nigeria. *Journal of Sustainable Development Studies* 5 (1): 40–63.

Frank, Etim O., and Wilfred I. Ukpere. 2012. The Impact of Military Rule on Democracy in Nigeria. *Journal of Social Sciences* 33 (3): 285–292.

Gani, Y. 2005. Nigeria and Security in Africa. In *Nigeria and the Development of the African Union*, ed. A. Akinterinwa Bola, 229–243. Ibadan: Vintage Publishers.

Gupte, L. 2019. *Nigeria's Oil Reforms in Limbo: Africa's Oil & Gas Scene After the Boom*. Oxford: Oxford Energy Forum.

Iwayemi, A. 2008. Nigeria's Dual Energy Problems: Policy Issues and Challenges. *International Association for Energy Economics* 53 (1): 17–21.

Izuchukwu, Oji O. 2011. Analysis of the Contribution of Agricultural Sector on the Nigerian Economic Development. *World Review of Business Research* 1 (1): 191–200.

Joseph, R. 2009. *Economic Transformation and Developmental Governance in Nigeria: The Promise of the Obama Era*. Washington, DC: Brookings Institution.

Kanu, I.A., M.B. Bazza, and I.O. Omojola. 2019. Boko Haram and Forced Migration: A Focus on the Northeast and Lake Chad Basin. *Nnadiebube Journal of Education* 4 (2): 24–41.

Kasimu, M.A. 2016. Good Governance as an Anti-Corruption Tool: Nigerian Construction Industry Perspective. *Journal of Environmental Sciences and Policy Evaluation* 6 (1): 34–45.

Katsouris, C. 2019. *Buhari's Second Chance at Oil and Gas Reform in Nigeria*. Chatham House, April 4. https://www.chathamhouse.org/expert/comment/buhari-s-second-chance-oil-and-gas-reform-nigeria#.

Khoshnevis, Yazdi S., Salehi K. Homa, and M. Soheilzad. 2017. The Relationship Between Tourism, Foreign Direct Investment and Economic Growth: Evidence from Iran. *Current Issues in Tourism* 20 (1): 15–26.

Kim, I. 2016. *Crude Security: Oil, Armament, and Alliance*. Doctoral dissertation, The George Washington University, USA.

Kuna, Muhammed J. 2005. The Role of Nigeria in Peace Building, Conflict Resolution, and Peacekeeping Since 1960. In *Workshop on Nigeria and the Reform of the United Nations,* Organised by Centre for Democratic Development, Research and Training, Hanwa, Ahmadu Bello University, Zaria, 11 June 2005, 1–9.

Mahr, K. 2017. High South African Crime Rates and Low Faith in Police Boost Private Security in Guateng. *Financial Times*, May 13. https://www.ft.com/content/ab7600e4-2068-11e7-b7d3-163f5a7f229c.

Manufacturing Sector in 20 Years: Our Position—LCCI. 2019. *Vanguard Newspaper*, May 31. https://www.vanguardngr.com/2019/05/manufacturing-sector-in-20-years-our-position-lcci/.

McAllister, C. 2019. Industry & Mining: From The Report: Nigeria 2019. *Oxford Business Group*. https://oxfordbusinessgroup.com/nigeria-2019/industrymining.

Miller, A. 2018. Security, Human Rights, and Reform in Egypt. Carnegie Endowment for International Peace. Testimony: US House Foreign Affairs Committee. https://carnegieendowment.org/2018/07/24/security-human-rights-and-reform-in-egypt-pub-76943.

Moen, S. 2012. *Managing Political Risk: Corporate Social Responsibility as a Risk Mitigation Tool. A Focus on the Niger Delta, Southern Nigeria*. Doctoral dissertation, Stellenbosch University, Stellenbosch.

Naidoo, P., and A. Mbatha. 2020. South Africa's Second Recession in Two Years Adds Pressure to Rates. *Bloomberg*, March 3. https://www.bloomberg.com/news/articles/2020-03-03/south-african-economy-slumps-into-second-recession-in-two-years.

NBS. 2018. Tourism Contributes 34% to Nigeria's GDP, Generates 20% Employment. *Premium Online Newspaper*, June 5. https://www.premiumti

mesng.com/entertainment/naija-fashion/271174-tourism-contributes-34-to-nigerias-gdp-generates-20-employment-nbs.html.

NBS. 2019. Nigerian Gross Domestic Report (Q1 2019). National Bureau of Statistics. https://nigerianstat.gov.ng/download/937#:~:text=Quarter%20on%20Quarter%2C%20growth%20was,the%20fourth%20quarter%20of%202018.&text=Transportation%20and%20Storage%20sector%20grew,and%2011.95%25%20in%20Q3%202018.

Ngwama, Justice C. 2014. Kidnapping in Nigeria: An Emerging Social Crime and the Implications for the Labor Market. *International Journal of Humanities and Social Science* 4 (1): 133–145.

Nwanne, C. 2017. A Look at Nigerian Tourism Industry in 2017. *The Guardian Newspaper*, December 30. https://guardian.ng/saturday-magazine/a-look-at-nigerian-tourism-industry-in-2017/.

Nwachukwu, Amanzee C. 2018. Curbing Crude Oil Theft. *Pipeline Oil & Gas Magazine*, August 7. https://oglinks.news/nigeria/news/curbing-crude-oil theft.

Okoi, M. 2019. *The Paradox of Nigeria's Oil Dependency*. South African Institute of International Affairs, Centre for International Governance Initiative. https://www.africaportal.org/features/paradox-nigerias-oil-dependency/.

Okoli, Al C. 2019a. *Oil Pipeline Vandalism in the Niger Delta: Need, Greed and Grievance Factors*. African Centre for the Constructive Resolution of Disputes (ACCORD). https://www.accord.org.za/conflict-trends/oil-pipeline-vandalism-in-the-niger-delta/.

Okoli, Al C. 2019b. Cows, Cash and Terror: How Cattle Rustling Proceeds Fuel Boko Haram Insurgency in Nigeria. *Africa Development* 44 (2): 53–76.

Okoli, Al C., and F. Agada. 2014. Kidnapping and National Security in Nigeria. *Research on Humanities and Social Sciences* 4 (6): 137–146.

Okoli, Al C., and Francis N. Okpaleke. 2014. Cattle Rustling and the Dialectics of Security in Northern Nigeria. *International Journal of Liberal Arts and Social Science* 2 (1): 109–117.

Okoromadu, F. 2018. Nigeria: Beyond Owning an Oil Well License. *All Africa*, October 21. https://allafrica.com/stories/201810210024.html.

Olaniyan, A., and A. Yahaya. 2016. Cows, Bandits, and Violent Conflicts: Understanding Cattle Rustling in Northern Nigeria. *Africa Spectrum* 51 (3): 93–105.

Olomola, Aderigbibe S., and M. Nwafor. 2018. *Nigeria Agriculture Sector Performance: A Background Report for the Nigeria 2017 Agriculture Joint Sector Review*. A Publication of Food Cluster Security Under the Theme: Agriculture, Early Recovery, Livestock, Livelihoods, Food. Security. https://fscluster.org/nigeria/document/nigeria-agriculture-sector-performance.

Onuoha, Freedom C. 2008. Oil Pipeline Sabotage in Nigeria: Dimensions, Actors and Implications for National Security. *African Security Studies* 17 (3): 99–115.

Opaluwa, D., J. Umeh, and A. Ameh. 2010. The Effect of Exchange Rate Fluctuations on the Nigerian Manufacturing Sector. *African Journal of Business Management* 4 (14): 2994–2998.

OPEC. 2020. *Nigeria Facts and Figures*. Organisation of Petroleum Exporting Countries. https://www.opec.org/opec_web/en/about_us/167.htm.

Ovat, Okey O. 2003. Tourism and economic development in Nigeria: An Empirical Investigation. *Global Journal of Social Sciences* 2 (1), 33–44. https://www.ajol.info/index.php/gjss/article/view/22765.

Oxford Business Group. 2020a. *Nigerian Demand for Rice Imports Drives Focus on Domestic Underproduction*. https://oxfordbusinessgroup.com/analysis/rice-and-fall-demand-rice-rising-domestic-underproduction-and-over-reliance-imports-need-be.

Oxford Business Group. 2020b. *Agriculture Exports in Nigeria Increase*. https://oxfordbusinessgroup.com/analysis/leveraging-growth-agricultural-exports-are-although-various-hurdles-still-need-be-overcome.

Oxford Business Group. 2020c. *Global Economies Prepare for the Next Industrial Revolution*, Country Report, Nigeria. https://oxfordbusinessgroup.com/overview/high-gear-economies-around-world-are-preparing-opportunities-and-challenges-brought-about-3.

Oxford Business Group Report. 2019a. *Nigerian Domestic Market Supports Producers of Fast-moving Consumer Goods*. https://oxfordbusinessgroup.com/analysis/domestic-moves-major-manufacturers-fast-moving-consumer-goods-have-been-supported-expanding-domestic.

Oxford Business Group Report. 2019b. *Country Report—Utilities in Nigeria*. Retrieved from https://oxfordbusinessgroup.com/nigeria-2019/utilities.

Oxford Business Group Report. 2019c. *Industry and Mining—Nigeria 2019*. https://oxfordbusinessgroup.com/nigeria-2019/industry-mining.

Oyebade, W. 2018. Why Nigerian Tourism Sector Lags Behind Amid Huge Potential. *The Guardian*, September 12. https://guardian.ng/features/why-nigerian-tourism-sector-lags-behind-amid-huge-potential/.

Salihu, H. 2020. Combating Corruption in the Nigerian Civil Service: An Empirical Assessment of Treasury Single Account (TSA) Policy. *Journal of Money Laundering Control* 23 (1): 267–280.

Suleiman, A., E.L. Jackson, and J. Rushton. 2015. Challenges of Pastoral Cattle Production in a Sub-humid Zone of Nigeria. *Tropical Animal Health and Production* 47 (6): 1177–1185.

Steven, P. 2016. *Moral Economies of Corruption: State Formation and Political Culture in Nigeria*. Durham, NC: Duke University Press.

The U.S. Department of Commerce's International Trade Administration. 2019. *Nigeria Country Commercial Guide: Nigeria—Agriculture*. https://www.export.gov/article?id=Nigeria-Agriculture.

Toromade, S. 2018. Five Agriculture Initiatives by President's Administration He Wants you to Know About. *The Pulse*, April 24. https://www.pulse.ng/news/local/buhari-5-agriculture-initiatives-by-presidents-administration-he-wants-you-to-know/9sjkcnl.

Toyin, O.S. 2015. The Impact of Military Coup D'état on Political Development in Nigeria. *International Journal of Business and Social Science* 6 (10): 194–202.

UK DFID. 2019. *Find out How the UK will Respond to Opportunities and Challenges: What is Being Achieved for the UK and Who We are Working with*. UK Department of International Development (DFID). https://www.gov.uk/world/organisations/dfid-nigeria Accessed on 15 February 2020.

World Bank. 1997. *Crimes in Nigeria, Helping Developing Countries Combat Corruption: The Role of the World Bank*. New York: Oxford University Press.

Yusuff, Mulkat A. 2016. Performance Assessment of Tourism Sector as a Vital Tool of Economic Growth in Nigeria. *International Journal of Academic Research in Business and Social Sciences* 6 (10): 143–150.

Yusuff, Mulkat A., and M.A. Akinde. 2015. Tourism Development and Economic Growth Nexus: Nigeria's Experience. *European Journal of Hospitality and Tourism Research* 3 (4): 1–10.

Wood, D., J. Glasson, J. Carlsen, and D. Hopkins. 2006. *Economic Evaluation of Tourism for Natural Areas: Development of a Toolkit Approach*. Gold Coast: Sustainable Tourism Cooperative Research Centre.

Zuruba, H.H., A. Ionescua, and V.D. Constantina. 2015. Emerging Markets Queries in Finance and Business: Measuring the Economic Impact of Tourism in European Emerging Markets. *Procedia Economics and Finance* 32 (1): 95–102.

CHAPTER 17

The Conflicts in the DRC: Wider Ramifications for the African Great Lakes Region

Joseph Lansana Kormoh

Introduction

This chapter explores the politics, history and complexities in the conflicts in the DRC and their wider implications on the Africa Great Lakes Region within the context of the 'Africa rising' debate. While scholars have discussed the dynamics of conflicts in the Great Lakes Region in more general terms (mainly focusing on causes and effects), this chapter attempts some delineation of the conflict in the DRC and its wider implications on the entire region. Evidently, while some African countries such as Ethiopia, Rwanda, Seychelles and Uganda, to name but a few, are on the trajectory of growth and have made marked economic development progress, the armed conflicts in the DRC have continued to pose serious threats to peace, security and development in the country, with significant resonance for the larger Africa Great Lakes Region.

J. L. Kormoh (✉)
Department of History and African Studies, Fourah Bay College, Freetown, Sierra Leone

University of Bradford, Bradford, UK

K. Omeje (ed.), *The Governance, Security and Development Nexus*,
https://doi.org/10.1007/978-3-030-49348-6_17

According to Khadiagala (2006), the name 'Great Lakes Region' (GLR) was derived from the freshwater lakes and river basins within Central and Eastern part of Africa. However, the term now refers to a region with interlinked conflicts and common fundamental problems that emanate from post-colonial challenges to state and nation building. The Great Lakes Region can be defined within the wider context of that regional entity categorised by the International Conference of the Great Lakes Region (ICGLR) which are Rwanda, Burundi, Democratic Republic of Congo (DRC) and Tanzania, and for the purposes of this chapter the definition of the Great Lakes Region has incorporated other interlinked geo-political spaces that extend to Kenya, Uganda, Zambia, Central African Republic (CAR), South Sudan, and Sudan, which have all helped to complicate the already constructed socio-political, historical and the economic landscape of the region.

The Great Lakes Region is arguably a region of too many complexities emanating from the nature of conflicts that have rendered the whole region vulnerable to external influences. Due to the fact that the region constitutes a complex network of political and economic interactions, there are also enormous implications for security, peace and governance. The region is blessed with abundant mineral resources, forestry and agricultural land. Kenneth Omeje summarises the ecological system of the Great Lakes Region as follows:

> From biodiversity to solid minerals and human talents, this geo-political space is endowed with abundant natural and cultural resources. Some of the world's most ecologically diverse freshwater systems, sub-tropical rainforests, savannah grasslands, and temperate highlands with immense extractive, agricultural, and touristic value are found in the Great Lakes region. In addition, it is culturally and linguistically diverse, comprising population groups with rich and dynamic historical, religious, economic, political, and legal traditions that have both endured and been transformed by internal and external factors. (Omeje and Hepner 2013: 1)

However, the region with all the natural resources can best be described as a paradox—a contradiction of itself as it is beset by 'striking contrasts and continuities' (Omeje, ibid.). It is a bizarre case of dying of thirst in the abundance of water when one considers that the DRC for example is the leading world producer of most of the world's most important mineral deposits such as diamonds, cobalt petroleum, copper, silver and coltan.

Paradoxically, the vast natural resources of the DRC have been part of the driving factors of armed conflict in the country, often attracting vested regional and international interests.

It is my argument in this chapter that in spite of its deplorable conflict history, the Great Lakes Region has a great potential for development, peace and security given its enormous rich natural endowments, which could be constructively harnessed to transform the region. I also argue that while the conflict in the DRC may seem complex with many internal and external complications, yet they are by no means insurmountable. With a visionary national leadership and strong regional cooperation, the conflict issues could be systematically addressed to create the necessary opportunity for the DRC to emerge as a prosperous country. A careful look at the Joint World Bank-IMF Debt Sustainability Analysis of September 2019 lends credence to this bullish viewpoint. The report details the deterioration of the DRC economy between 2014 and 2017 but ends on a positive note that gradual progress was noticeable between 2018 and 2019.

> From 2014 to 2017, the Congolese economy deteriorated sharply in the wake of a commodity price shock and a political crisis. The sharp fall in the price of copper — which accounted for over 50 percent of total exports of goods and services— between 2014 and 2016 and the uncertainty caused by the delay in holding general elections hurt economic growth, exports, and fiscal revenues, unleashing a spiral of currency depreciation and inflation. By the end of 2016, the price of copper had lost 45 percent of its value relative to 2011. Furthermore, donors stopped providing budget support because of delays in conducting the presidential elections. Government deposits at the BCC were largely depleted by the end of 2016 and the fiscal rule of no BCC financing of the budget—introduced in 2011—was breached. Domestic arrears were also rising. The end-of-period inflation rate rose to 23.6 percent in 2016, driven, at least in part, by central bank financing of the fiscal deficit. Foreign reserves dropped from about 6 weeks of imports in January 2016 to less than 2 weeks by end-2017. The exchange rate depreciated by 71 percent between end-2015 and end-2017, the largest depreciation in SSA over that period. Conversely, the current account deficit narrowed modestly to 3.1 percent of GDP in 2016, as a decline in imports compensated for dwindling exports. All this induced a fall in GDP growth from 6.9 percent in 2015 to 2.4 percent in 2016 and 3.7 percent in 2017.

On the greener side of the analysis, the report submits that:

> Since 2018, the economy has started to recover. Supported by a rebound in commodity prices, GDP growth was 5.8 percent in 2018, while 12-month inflation has fallen sharply to less than 5 percent and the exchange rate has stabilized. Strict budgetary discipline led to overall fiscal surpluses in 2017–18 and a balanced position is projected for 2019. (World Bank-IMF 2019: 2)

It is observable that the complications created by armed conflicts in the Great Lakes Region have greatly undermined the development of the region and made the security situation fluid for regional integration. Lemarchand (2009: x) argues that it is not possible to actually grasp the deep-rooted causes of the recent conflicts in the DRC without having to reflect seriously on the implications of the conflict within a regional context. Consequently, the author submits that it is only through a regional lens that one can bring into focus the violent patterns of interaction that form the essential backdrop to the spread of bloodshed within and across national boundaries (Lemarchand 2009: x). The violent conflicts in the region tend to expand geographically and their epicentre shifts from one locus to another over time (Kanyangara 2016).

At the regional level, the African Great Lakes Region has throughout its post-independence history been the scene of several violent conflicts that have spilled over across borders. Thus, shortly after the genocide in Rwanda, the DRC became the hub of one of the nastiest wars which has been characterised by heinous crimes against humanity ever recorded in the history of armed conflicts in Africa since World War II. This is due to the fact that there has been spiralling and sometimes overlapping conflicts in Burundi, Rwanda, Uganda and the Democratic Republic of Congo (DRC) (Salehyan and Gleditsch 2006: 335–366). A clear understanding of the causes of the persistent wave of violence in the DRC is largely dependent also on a clear understanding of the geographical configuration of the region. This is so because the conflicts in the region are dynamic and complex as they involve multiple and interlocking regional and international actors (Ansorg 2011).

A Brief Historical Background of the Conflicts in the DRC

The transition from colonial rule to independence in the Congo could be best described as a political stillbirth which only delivered a nation that has ever since been characterised by one violent conflict after another. In essence, armed conflicts have continued to remain the main feature of the Congolese history since the 1960s. The conflicts in the Democratic Republic of Congo (DRC) which was then christened Zaire after decolonisation date as far back as the occupation of this 'jurisdiction' by King Leopold of Belgium and their eventual colonisation. This colonisation project of the Belgians institutionalised corruption and the establishment of a criminal enterprise that availed itself of national resources for personal enrichment, brutal repression of the demands of the people for political freedom, and social divisions along ethnic and regional lines (Lemarchand 1964; Young 1965; Young and Turner 1985).

It is thus important to point out that it was partly as a result of this tragic history, that the DRC experienced a difficult and unstable post-independence era, marked by rebellions and secessionist wars starting in 1960 (Young and Turner 1985; Nzongola-Ntalaja 2002; Kisangani 2012). The wars of the 1960s and 1970s are critically important for understanding the conflicts in modern day DRC and for thinking about workable strategies for resolving them and consolidating peace (ECA 2015).

The conflicts in the DRC had its roots in strong ideological differences manifested between the main post-independence leaders. It initially bothered on the issue of self-determination where the first Prime Minister Patrice Lumumba advocated for a complete independence of the Congo which was totally independent of any ideological ties with the west. The other side of the political divide would prefer to maintain their patrimonial ties with the former colonial Belgian overlords. This school was represented by Moise Tshombe. Lemarchand (1964), Meditz and Merrill (1994), and Ndikumana and Kisangani (2005), among others, have spoken so eloquently about this ideological disagreement to warrant any further elucidation here.

The most important thing to point out here is that this ideological antagonism was the key cause of the Eastern rebellion of 1964–1966 which was led by a pro-Lumumba coalition headed by Gbenye and Gizenga, with other key actors including Laurent Kabila who would later resurface as leader of the 1996 anti-Mobutu rebellion (Lemarchand 1964; Nzongola-Ntalaja 2002). The ideological disputes caused political chaos following independence and were the key motivation behind the assassination of Lumumba, and the installation of pro-Western Mobutu Sese Seko in power (ECA 2015). Ludo De Witte (2002) in his research uncovers a network of complicity spreading from the Belgian government to the United Nations and the CIA regarding the assassination of Patrice Lumumba. The ECA thus concludes that 'this course of events dramatically changed the country's destiny, sowed the seeds of regional and ethnic antagonism, and instituted the long reign of dictatorial, autocratic, and kleptocratic regimes' (ECA 2015: 12).

In addition to internal disagreements among the political elite about the configuration of the state, especially the choice between federalism and a centralised state, the period under review was characterised by strong antagonisms along regional and ethnic lines. Moreover, the refusal on the part of the former colonial masters to 'hands off' the politics of the young nation further exacerbated the already fluid situation in the country. It was a classic case of giving the bull to someone and still holding on to the rope. Thus, it is important to point out that this was meant to serve a dual beneficial purpose for the former colonial powers. In the first place, the former colonial masters were still interested in the massive strategic minerals in the country and second, and perhaps also most important at the time, was the geopolitical interests of the western powers who used the DRC as a base in the fight against the expansion of communism in Africa. Thus, the conflicts in the DRC have always had both internal and external dimensions (Lemarchand 1964; Young 1965; Ndikumana and Kisangani 2005).

Many of the external influences emanated from the establishment of a system of colonial administration that was based on fraud and exploitation which institutionalised state-condoned criminality; this ugly colonial legacy has also perpetrated and there has been theft of national resources for personal enrichment of the rulers—a practice that was passed on from King Leopold II to the Belgian colonial administration and to the post-independence regimes (Nzongola-Ntalaja 2002; Kisangani 2012). A major aggravating factor is the fact that instrumental in the treatment of national identity which has been one of the dangerous potent forces in the conflicts in the DRC. In this way, the wars in the DRC have been associated with ethnic identities and poorly regulated exploitation of the natural resource sector that has become the terrain for competition among local as well as foreign state and non-state actors seeking to capitalise on the regulatory vacuum and insecurity (ECA 2015). As in other cases like Sierra Leone and Liberia where resources were not the cause of conflicts per se, in the DRC also, in the absence of strong institutions to ensure effective regulatory oversight and protection of human rights, the exploitation of natural resources has become both an incentive for rebellion against the state as well as a fuel of the war machinery (Nzongola-Ntalaja 2002; Kisangani 2012).

As was the case in many colonial territories in Africa, the colonial powers in their greed and selfish pursuits of their own benefits went ahead and created artificial boundaries which hitherto did not exist before the advent of colonial rule. This arbitrary boundary delimitation by the colonial powers brought into close communion diverse ethnicities within these new borders. They went ahead to redraw an ethno-cultural map which was further exacerbated by their discriminatory policy of divide and rule. In particular, the institutionalised manipulation of nationality laws to target long-time immigrants from Rwanda and Burundi is at the heart of chronic insecurity in Eastern Congo and the spillover of the conflicts into DRC's eastern neighbours (ECA 2015). Thus, it is plausible to argue that the wars in the DRC are indeed more than mere domestic conflicts, but wars that have had devastating regional dimensions.

The Politics of State Suffocation: From Mobutu Sese Seko to Joseph Kabila

The Democratic Republic of Congo is endowed with huge natural resources, including minerals, oil, water, forestry and arable land for agriculture. The country is acclaimed as a world leading producer of copper and cobalt, and it also produces large amounts of coltan (columbite-tantalite), diamonds, silver and petroleum.

2014 estimates have shown that the DRC accounts for 55% of the world's cobalt production (with 45% of world's reserves), 21% of industrial diamonds, and 12% of tantalum (Yager 2014). The mining and processing of minerals represent a substantial share of total domestic production (11.5% in 2012). But it is important to point out that while minerals and oil generate the most attention, other sources are equally important; such as the country's massive endowment in large water reserves, which constitutes an important asset for transport and hydropower generation (ECA 2015). This report states that the DRC has the potential to generate electricity that can feed the entire Great Lakes Region and beyond. This constitutes a potential pillar and incentive for regional integration in addition to being a source of growth and an enabler of economic diversifica-tion in the country and the region (ECA 2015).

Like other conflicts elsewhere in Africa, the abundance of natural resources have been identified as both the cause and intensifier of conflicts in the DRC. It has emerged as a main feature for our understanding and analysis of the conflict in the sense that it supports the argument of 'resource curse'. In general terms it means therefore that natural resources have motivated, fuelled and sustained conflicts in the DRC (Murhula 2006; Laudati 2013). It may also be argued that the DRC fits the literature narratives of the economics of resource-driven conflicts (Collier and Hoeffler 2004; Omeje 2015).

One of the fundamental issues that have emerged in the literature as a major factor that is responsible for the conflicts is that, while the country is heavily endowed with natural resources, they are unequally distributed across her regions. The province of Katanga, for example accounts for 70% of the country's copper and cobalt production. At independence, the province generated 75% of national output and financed 20% of government expenditures (Ndikumana and Kisangani 2005). Also, the Kasaï of the country region, notably dubbed as the 'diamond state', has vast reserves of gem-quality and industrial diamonds. The eastern provinces, especially the two Kivus, have large reserves of gold, coltan and tin (Ndikumana and Kisangani 2005).

In fact, during the early days of independence, leaders of these regions were advocating for secession because they were aggrieved that the central government was using their resources to subsidise central government's expenditures with little benefit in exchange (Meditz and Merrill 1994; Kisangani 2014; Nzongola-Ntalaja 2002; Meriam 1961). Thus, between 1960 and 1963, the first open and physical secessionist war began in the province of Katanga which was then later followed by the Shaba I war in 1977 and Shaba II war in 1978. It is in this context that one must also understand the Kasaï secession war of 1960–1962, as well as the eastern rebellion of 1964–1966 (ECA 2015).

When Mobutu took over the reins of governance in a military coup in 1965, he went ahead to establish a patrimonial and kleptocratic rule which plundered the country for 32 years. 'Corruption, lawlessness and impunity became institutionalised in both public and private spheres' (Omeje and Hepner 2013: 28). He assumed the position of a deity in his own right and expected the Congolese people to view him as such. He harassed his political opponents, and many were eliminated. He was a very corrupt leader who wrecked the economy of the state together with his family and his cronies. Mobutu was not only a terror to his own people, but 'his domineering presence and cold-war related solidarity and support for inept reactionary regimes in the region were a significant security menace' (Omeje and Hepner 2013: 29).

Mobutu's 'Zarianization' of the mid-1970s and the concomitant implications on the economy laid the firm foundation for the events that erupted at the end of the 1990s. These conflicts occurred as a result of the economic deterioration that accompanied Mobutu's gross mismanagement of state resources which led to economic decline (Ndikumana and Kisangani 2005). This economic decline was further compounded by the debt crisis of the 1980s and the drying out of external financial support to the Mobutu regime in the 1990s (ECA 2015). Politically, the Mobutu regime faced a growing and intense domestic opposition agitating for democratic reforms. The discontent was exacerbated by Mobutu's violent repression of political dissidence. The most publicised event was the massacre of university students in Lubumbashi in 1990 (Kisangani 2012).

Mobutu's political decline started becoming manifestly clear with the disengagement of his former western allies in the context of the realities of the end of cold war politics and his inability to suppress domestic discontent. While Mobutu was no longer needed as a strategic ally in the fight against communism in Africa, he was becoming an embarrassment to his former western allies especially in light of his high-handedness in suppressing opposition demands for democratic change and his gross human rights violations (Willame 1997; Nzongola-Ntalaja 2002). Thus, pressed by mounting domestic contestation against his autocratic rule and abandoned by his former western supporters, Mobutu was unable to resist the Kabila-led rebellion (Willame 1997, 1999; Nzongola-Ntalaja 2002).

The Wider Implications of the DRC Conflicts on the Great Lakes Region

The armed conflict in the DRC has had wide-ranging ramifications on not only the country itself but in countries of the entire Great Lakes Region.

The African Great Lakes Region (GLR) has witnessed some of the most intense violence and protracted conflicts of the last half-century. While many of the events were intra-state, the conflict literature is beginning to connect them as part of a conflict matrix in the GLR (Salehyan and Gleditsch 2006). From a regional perspective, the Great Lakes Region has for a long time been a region of conflicts. What makes these conflicts more complex is that, every conflict in the region is interconnected with some other armed conflict(s) in the Great Lakes Region which has had an impact on the economic, political and social spheres of the whole region (Muhereza 2011) Some of the factors that contribute to the interconnectedness of the conflicts in the region include territorial contiguity, trans-boundary resources and trans-national ethnicities, or the interests of the actors and purveyors of conflict (Muhereza 2011). Thus, the point should be stressed here that an understanding and analysis of the conflict in the DRC is only possible when the root-causes of the contemporary conflicts in the DRC are contextualised within the wider regional complications in the Great Lakes Region itself. René Lemarchand puts it quite lucidly that, 'only through a regional lens can one bring into focus the violent pat terns of interaction that form the essential backdrop to the spread of bloodshed within and across boundaries' (Lemarchand 2009: x).

Ostensibly, the DRC's nine neighbours have a high stake in the end of conflicts given the negative impact of these conflicts on their economy and political stability (Lemarchand 2009). Refugee flows, for example account for not only a serious economic burden on the receiving country, but also it poses a threat to political and social stability. The influx of refugees following the Rwanda genocide was a major trigger for subsequent conflicts in the DRC (Lemarchand 2009; Prunier 2009; Kisangani 2012). In addition, the DRC has been continuously used as a launch pad by rebel movements who are opposed to the regimes in Rwanda, Uganda, Burundi and Sudan (Prunier 2004). The major problem with the DRC conflict is that it has a very high and grave consequences on its neighbours.

Practically, political stability and economic development in the DRC has direct consequence and implications for the whole of the Great Lakes Region. Hence, I contend that DRC's geographical location in this region offers enormous opportunities for the emergence of the country as a vector for development and trade that will not only benefit the DRC alone but the whole of the Great Lakes Region. As conflict is literally shared between and among the DRC and its neighbours, I argue that, the transformation of that conflict situation will also share the dividends of peace and economic integration between the DRC and its neighbours. This is so because the conflict in the DRC has been largely influenced by negative externalities which emanate from its neighbours who are using the DRC as a launch pad and a safe haven for rebel movements in other parts of the region such as Sudan, Uganda, Rwanda and Burundi until 2012 (Prunier 2004, 2009; Kisangani 2012).

Conclusion

This chapter has briefly explored the conflicts in the DRC within the wider context of its causes and implications on not only the country but on the Great Lakes Region as a whole. There is no gainsaying the fact that there is a developmental dimension of the conflicts in the DRC and its implications for the whole of the region. Our understanding of the causes of the conflicts is critical for designing strategies to resolve the conflicts and consolidating peace and sustainable development. This is so because the failure of development has created an environment for wars and conflicts. One of the core arguments is that the resolution or end of the conflict in the DRC has a direct positive impact on the growth and development of the country and by extension all the neighbouring countries in the region. Tackling the unresolved regional dimensions of conflict is crucial to the region's progressive development and for achieving human security for all.

The chapter argues that although the conflict in the DRC has had a devastating consequence on the economics, politics and global security, yet the country is gradually and steadily emerging from an adverse protracted economic contraction that was exacerbated by the wars. In agreement with the ECA Report of 2015, growth has recovered and accelerated recently on the back of rising production and prices of minerals, especially copper and co-balt, and inflation has declined rapidly to single-digit levels due to aggressive expenditure compression and exchange rate stability. According to the World Bank's (2016) World Development Report 2016, the annual foreign direct investment in the DRC is about \$2.07 billion. The current development trend is promising and the DRC is on the trajectory of progress, development and security. Notwithstanding the recent growth and development trends, some sections of the DRC, especially Eastern Congo, are still potential breeding grounds for rebel movements and insurgents that could further destabilise the neighbouring countries and the entire Great Lakes region.

References

Ansorg, Nadine. 2011. How Does Militant Violence Diffuse in Regions? Regional Conflict System in International Relations and Peace and Conflict Studies. *International Journal of Conflict and Violence* 5 (1): 173–187.

Collier, Paul, and Anke Hoeffler. 2004. *Greed and Grievance in Civil War*. Oxford: Oxford University Press.

De Witte, Ludo. 2002. *The Assassination of Lumumba*. London: Verso.

ECA. 2015. *Conflicts in the Democratic Republic of Congo: Causes, Impact and Implications for the Great Lakes Region*. Addis Ababa: Economic Commission for Africa (ECA).

Joint World Bank-IMF Debt Sustainability Analysis. 2019. Prepared jointly by Staffs of the *International Development Association (IDA) and the International Monetary Fund.*

Kanyangara, Patrick. 2016. Conflict in the Great Lakes Region: Root Causes, Dynamics, and Effects. *Conflict Trends*, 2016/1.

Khadiagala, G. 2006. *Security Dynamics in Africa's Great Lakes Region*. London: Lynne Rienner.

Kisangani, E. 2012. *Civil Wars in the Democratic Republic of Congo, 1960–2010*. Boulder: Lynne Rienner.

Kisangani, E. 2014. US Policy in the Great Lakes Region. In *US-Africa Relations: From Clinton to Obama*, ed. C.R. Veney, 115–147. Lanham: Lexington Books.

Laudati, A. 2013. Beyond Minerals: Broadening 'Economies of Violence' in Eastern Democratic Republic of Congo. *Review of African Political Economy* 40 (135): 35–50.

Lemarchand, Rene. 1964. *Political Awakening in the Congo*. Berkeley: University of California Press.

Lemarchand, Rene. 2009. *The Dynamics of Violence in Central Africa*. Philadelphia: University of Pennsylvania Press.

Meditz, S.W., and T. Merrill. 1994. *Zaïre: A Country Study*. Washington, DC: The American University.

Meriam, A.P. 1961. *Congo: Background of conflict*. Evaston, IL: Northwestern University Press.

Muhereza, Frank Emmanuel. 2011. The Regional Implications of Conflicts on Political, Social, and Economic Development in the Great Lakes Region. Centre for Basic Research, Kampala. Paper presented at the International Conference on Regional Dimensions of Conflicts in the Great Lakes Region, held at Hotel La Mada, Nairobi, 12–14 September.

Murhula, John Katunga. 2006. Minerals, Forests, and Violent Conflict in the Democratic Republic of the Congo. In *Environmental Change and Security Program Report*, vol. 12, 12–18. Washington, DC: Woodrow Wilson Centre.

Ndikumana and Kinsagani. 2005. Conflicts in the Democratic Republic of Congo: Impact, and Implications for the Great Lakes Region. United Nations Commission for Africa (ECA), Addis Ababa, Ethiopia.

Nzongola-Ntalaja, G. 2002. *The Congo from Leopold to Kabila: A People's History*. London: Zed Books.

Omeje, Kenneth. 2013. Theorizing the Conflicts in Eastern Congo. In *Identités, ressources naturelles et conflits en RDC*, ed. Germain Ngoie Tshibambe, 27–44. Paris: L'Harmattan.

Omeje, Kenneth. 2015. Natural Resource Rent and Stakeholder Politics in Africa: Towards a New Conceptualization. *Commonwealth and Comparative Politics* 54 (1): 92–114.

Omeje, Kenneth, and Tricia R. Hepner. 2013. Conflict and Peacebuilding in the African Great Lakes Region. In *Conflict and Peacebuilding in the African Great Lakes Region*, ed. Kenneth Omeje and Tricia R. Hepner, 1–21. Bloomington: Indiana University Press.

Prunier, G. 2004. Rebel Movements and Proxy Warfare: Uganda, Sudan, and the Congo. *African Affairs* 103 (412): 359–383.

Prunier, G. 2009. *Africa's World War: Congo, the Rwandan Genocide and the Making of a Continental Catastrophe*. Oxford: Oxford University Press.

Salehyan, Idean, and K.S. Gleditsch. 2006. Refugees and the Spread of Civil War. *International Organization* 60 (2) (Spring): 335–366.

The United Nations Secretary General's Report had been requested by the Security Council at its 25 September 1997 meeting of Foreign Ministers on the promotion of peace and security in Africa.

Willame, J.C. 1997. *Banyamulenge et Banyarwanda: Viloences Ethniques et Gestion de l'Identi taire au Kivu*. Brussels and Paris: Institut African-Cédaf & L'Harmattan.

Willame, J.C. 1999. *L'odysse Kabil: Trajectoire Pour un Congo Nouveau?* Paris: Karhala.

World Bank. 2016. World Development Report. The World Bank. https://www.worldbank.org/content/dam/Worldbank/Publications/WDR/WDR%202016/WDR2016_overview_presentation.pdf.

Yager, Thomas. 2014. The Mineral Industry of Congo Kinshasa. The USGS Report. http://minerals.usgs.gov/minerals/pubs/country/2012/myb3-2012-cg.pdf.

Young, C. 1965. *Politics in the Congo*. Princeton: Princeton University Press.

Young, C., and T. Turner. 1985. *The Rise and Decline of the Zairian State*. Madison: University of Wisconsin Press.

CHAPTER 18

The "Africa Rising" Paradox, Human Trafficking, and Perilous Migration Across the Sahara and the Mediterranean to Europe

Anne Kubai

Introduction

Migration is simply the action or process of changing one's place of residence permanently or temporarily. Migration can be voluntary or involuntary, though as some scholars would like to argue, very few people would take the risk of leaving their countries, homes, and communities and migrate to unknown places without being forced to do so by circumstances that are often beyond their control. Often the thin line between migration that is motivated by a sense of adventure and the search for greener pastures is blurred. However, research has shown that for most Africans who seek to migrate to Europe and other places, do so largely

A. Kubai (✉)
School of Historical and Contemporary Studies, Södertörn University, Huddinge, Sweden
e-mail: anne.kubai@sh.se

Research Institute for Theology and Religion, University of South Africa, Pretoria, South Africa

K. Omeje (ed.), *The Governance, Security and Development Nexus*,
https://doi.org/10.1007/978-3-030-49348-6_18

to seek refuge from armed conflicts, poverty, repression, and related challenges. Though for decades, people in Africa have migrated to Europe in search of a better life, in recent years the trends have changed, and the numbers increased with the expansion and internationalization of human trafficking networks, and the growth of the European sex industry.

The Horn of Africa has endured violent conflicts for more than three decades, which triggered migration flows particularly from Ethiopia, Eritrea, Sudan, South Sudan, and Somalia while the recent conflicts in Central and West Africa have catapulted the populations onto the international migration stage in trends and numbers hitherto unseen in the region. The exponential expansion of migration and human trafficking led to the emergence of new routes and migrant flows northwards starting as far as Central Africa, moving northwards across the Sahara toward North Africa, mainly Libya and Egypt. From there, migrants head to the Mediterranean Sea and onward to Europe. The medieval Trans-Saharan trade routes have assumed a new significance and have been brought to life by a trade in human beings.

In the last decade, scholars have paid attention to migration and investigated factors, patterns, trends, economic aspects, and issues regarding citizenship and integration in the countries of destination. However, relatively less attention has been given to the impact on individual migrants and the communities in the countries of origin. This chapter analyzes African migration to Europe against the backdrop of the narrative of an Africa that, in the last decade, is seen to be rising from the ashes of inter and intra-state wars of the 1980s and 1990s, with signs of promising economic growth and the emergence of regional blocs to consolidate these gains.

These gains notwithstanding, history provides useful insights when we recall the phenomenon of slavery and slave trade that linked Africa with the rest of the world through a horrific trade in human beings. To explore the paradox, one would like to recall the images of slave ships that are now relics seen only in photographs in museums, and question whether they have any semblance with the rickety vessels overloaded with human cargo perilously floating across the Mediterranean Sea in the service of international modern slavery and slave trade that is euphemistically referred to as human trafficking (Kubai 2017). One would wonder why human traffickers find a market for humans as commodities in contemporary societies, which pride themselves in the protection of human rights and gender equality. To answer this and similar questions, current causes and trends of migration from Africa should be understood through an intersectional perspective of various global phenomena. In the same vein, this research pays attention to an issue that remains inadequately studied in migration research, namely, the impact of the crisis of Africa's forced displacement and migration on families and communities in countries of origin.

Here, the focus is on the northward route to Europe. Using a variety of examples, I describe the recruitment and the journeys across the Sahara and Mediterranean Sea, with a view to framing migration in the words of those who made the journey from migrants' perspectives, and first-hand experience of the horrors of human trafficking. I employ the concept of "life project" because I believe that it does not only help us to explain the exodus of migrants and refugees from Africa, but more importantly, it furnishes us with the conceptual tool to peep into an individual migrant's life as we wonder why people are persuaded to make these perilous journeys. Here, the use of a migrant's account of the migration process, described in his own unmitigated words, gives the reader a sense of raw first-hand experience of the journey across the Sahara and the Mediterranean. I believe that the contradictions inherent in the notion of "Africa rising" and the paradox of mobility and migration in the twenty-first century are explicit in the interview excerpt presented below. In it, we get insights into some of the key aspects of the "life project" on which an individual or a family embarks and sets out with the goal of reaching their "destiny" in Europe. In addition, this approach allows us to broach the issue of human dignity in the recent migration patterns, while at the same time, keeping in mind the gamut of migration and human trafficking activities, processes, and the impact they can have on individuals and communities.

The data on which this chapter is based were gathered in a large study on African migrants in Europe between 2014 and 2019. This study also benefits from the data collected during the "migration crises" in 2015, when fieldwork was carried out in several key countries of origin, transit and destination in West, North and Horn of Africa and Europe, respectively. Much of the data were gathered through interviews with migrants and survivors of the treacherous journeys in trucks across the sands of the vast Sahara; and on rickety vessels and dinghy boats that floated across the Mediterranean Sea, overloaded with human cargo. These data were complemented with field notes taken by this author during the visits to various detention centers and sites where migrants established temporary camps *en route* to preferred destinations in Europe. The method of listening to migrants' narratives "privileges positionality and subjectivity." However, following Riessman (2002), I find narrative analysis relevant "for the study of the disruptive events" in the lives of African migrants and members of their communities in countries of origin. I use narrative analysis because through their individual accounts, migrants are not only able to reflect on their experiences but also to make sense of them. Here, Bamberg and McCabe (1998: iii) provide useful insights in their observation that:

> With narratives, people strive to configure space and time, deploy cohesive devices, reveal identity of actors and relatedness of actions across the scenes. They create themes, plots and drama. In so doing, narrators make sense of themselves, social situations and history.

In this chapter, I use an in-depth interview excerpt to illustrate the processes of migration and human trafficking; as well as the ways in which local and global, social, political, and environmental factors intersect to shape both the processes and outcomes of African mobility and migration to Europe.

Historical Trans-Saharan Trade Routes Brought to Life by Migration and Human Trafficking

In recent years, the old Trans-Saharan trade routes have assumed a new significance. They are brought to life by a dense network of traffickers and traders in human beings. Like its medieval predecessor, the current Trans-Saharan trade based on migration and human trafficking generates immense wealth for those who control the networks and "take possession" of the "human merchandise." As Shelley (2014: 2) reiterates, "human smuggling and trafficking are two of the fastest growing international organized crime activities and are thought to be the most lucrative forms of organized crime after drug trade. "For instance, the Libyan migration market is estimated at 244 million US dollars annually, mainly used to fund the insurgents and violent extremism, thus contributing to widespread instability in the region" (Williams 2019).

While it is difficult to know the exact numbers—there is a lack of research and paucity of data, particularly on trafficking (Shelley 2014:

5). It is estimated that 80% of the mixed migration cases crossing the Mediterranean are facilitated by migrant smugglers and criminal groups (UNODC 2011).

From West Africa, pick-up and lorry trucks take people from strategic migration route cities in different countries northwards through the hubs in Corte d'Ivoire, Niger, Mali, Chad, Algeria to Libya, from where they cross the Mediterranean to Europe. From the Great Lakes and East Africa regions, Nairobi, Addis Ababa, and Khartoum are busy hubs for migrants moving northwards to Libya and Egypt. From Somalia and Djibouti, others cross to the Arabian Peninsula. The journeys are not as straight as the migration routes look on a map. From the interview narratives with survivors of these treacherous journeys, it could take up to seven or more years to get to the desired destination. It is evident that "for many, the sea journey is just a final step of much longer and often a very dangerous journey that has included passing through areas of armed conflict, crossing deserts, and for some, being held for ransom and tortured or trafficked for sexual or labor exploitation" (UNHCR 2018: 11). Along the way, many things can happen, for instance, migrants can change nationalities willingly or unwillingly if they need papers to cross borders, or when they live for long periods in different countries *en route* to the intended destination. Indeed, the nationality of a person does not make a difference; it does not matter in the process of this complex and dangerous journey. There is no doubt that the current migration and human trafficking flows across the desert and the Mediterranean Sea are inherently linked to the forced displacement crises that Africa has endured in the last two decades. Hence, it is important to pay attention to the issue of forced displacement in the continent.

Africa's Internal Forced Displacement and Refugee Crisis

One of the apparently oblivious causes of migration is the violence attendant to the processes and activities attributed the so-called social economic development in Africa. This is evident in the massive displacement of communities and populations in areas that have been found to possess large quantities of natural resources such as oil. Nigeria's Niger Delta region is a key example where it was recently reported that the communities are experiencing "a slow genocide"[1] as a result of the crude oil pollution of the rivers and huge tracts of farmlands and villages. Other examples of mega development projects which have generated both conflict and displacement of communities living in areas with natural resources include Kenya's large deposits of titanium in the coastal region and oil in Turkana; the expansion of Addis Ababa city; and the construction of hydroelectric dams in different places. Apparently, one of the major challenges is how to exploit the resources and protect the communities in the resource-rich ancestral lands.

Another cause of displacement which has, until recently, received little attention is the changing environmental conditions. A majority of pastoralists living in arid and semi-arid regions of the continent have to endure long periods of draught during which much of their livestock—their main source of livelihood—is lost. In these circumstances, they are forced to move in search of water and pasture for the livestock and often nomadic life is fraught with conflict over scarce resources among different communities. These factors and other incidents of violent conflicts that have ravaged the continent for decades have contributed to the destruction of public infrastructures and militated against social and economic development. They have also precipitated or accelerated forced displacement of large segments of the population. Thus, harsh environmental conditions and conflicts intersect to create a vicious cycle of violence and disaster, leading to forced displacement of populations. It is therefore imperative that the Africa rising narrative takes cognizance of the enduring impact of forced displacement on communities and states.

It is estimated that 84% of the 25 million forcibly displaced persons on the continent come from 8 conflict-affected countries, namely, the Cameroon, Democratic Republic of the Congo (DRC), Central African Republic, Ethiopia, Nigeria, Somalia, South Sudan, and Sudan (Williams 2019) as illustrated in the Tables 18.1 and 18.2.

One of the most remarkable aspects of displacement in the continent is that the countries with the largest populations of IDPs are at the same time hosting large numbers of refugees from neighboring countries. For instance, while many Ethiopians and Sudanese are refugees in the neighborhood, Ethiopia hosts large numbers of refugees fleeing from four of her neighbors who are also hosting Ethiopian refugees. This "double displacement" creates a complex situation with enduring consequences: (a) It is a burden on the already weakened social economic systems in the host countries, and adversely impacts development initiatives. For instance, Uganda hosts the largest number of refugees in Africa and the long-term social economic implications of this are yet to be understood.

Table 18.1 Top eight countries with the highest numbers of IDPs by October 2019

Country	*Number of IDPs in 2019*
DRC	3,081,000
Nigeria	2,500,000
Ethiopia	2,137,000
Sudan	1,997,000
South Sudan	1,900,000
Cameroon	668,000
Central African Republic	642,000
Burundi	328,636
Total	12,283,631

Source Data collated by the author from various sources, including IDMC

Table 18.2 Top ten countries hosting large numbers of refugees by October 2019

Country	*Number of refugees*
Uganda[a]	1,300,000
Ethiopia	905,831
Sudan	900,000
Kenya	553,900
DRC	547,503
Chad	446,091
Cameroon	404,808
South Africa	260,000
Tanzania	206,000
Niger	175,420
Total	4,701,153

Source Data collated by the author from various sources, including IRC, UN OCHA, and UNHCR

[a]In 2019, Uganda hosted 1.3 million refugees from seven countries. See International Rescue Committee: https://www.rescueuk.org/country/uganda?gclid=EAIaIQobChMIvLzb_qGc5gIVF4myCh1uwQB2EAAYBCAAEgIU8PD_BwE#what-caused-the-current-crisis-in-uganda

(b) Displacement impacts regional dynamics, ultimately becoming one of the factors in the conflicts from which the refugees were fleeing in the first place.

There is no doubt that the last decade will go down in history as one that witnessed the most dramatic increase in forced displacement and refugees in the African continent. In addition, some African countries whose citizens are fleeing to seek refuge elsewhere, as well as the countries receiving and coping with large numbers of IDPs and refugees, are in the least developed countries (LDCs) category and extremely poor.

Embarking on the "Life Project": The Journey Across the Desert and the Sea

Migration in many African countries has come to be considered as a matter of prestige, as well as a source of livelihood, an escape from war and conflict, poverty, social inequalities, repression, and the impact of climate change. To many of those who need to leave their homes, migration is conceived as a "life project" as some of the migrants who participated in this study put it. The notion of "life project" is a dominant theme which gives hope and courage to those who set out on a journey to the unknown, as the following excerpt of an interview with a man who 'had made it to Europe' illustrates.

> I was living in constant fear of being followed or being abducted. I decided to tell close friends and my wife about my fear and frustration. They advised me to leave behind my kids and the country I love. I headed to Khartoum where I spent 15 days. In Sudan people believe everything is possible; nothing is impossible in their view and whoever you ask about any process they say it is easy, but they do not say how or when it will be done. They do not give you any idea about the time it will take, they just say "give us a chance and in the coming days be ready with cash at hand". Their main interest is to get Dollars.
>
> I encountered a man who explained that he was an expert in tourism and migration. He said that "within five days you are going to be in Trablus."[3] He promised to secure for me a safe trip and advised me to wait for his call, which I got after two days, asking me to be ready by 8.00 pm. I felt surprised and wagered for a few minutes. He came in a car, picked me up and took me to his centre, where I found 7 men and one woman waiting. He told them to come out and get into the car. We travelled for the whole night, and arrived early in the morning at a place where we found 28 men, women and children laying on the ground in a nomads' hall. At about 2 am the next day, a lorry came carrying barrels of diesel, water and some food items and a man wearing military uniform, shouted "women and children first line and men second line." We did as he commanded, and 51 people got onto the lorry. We were supposed to

be about 110 in this lorry, but the others had been arrested by the police in Khartoum.

The first day was good, we were crossing the world's largest desert – the Sahara. We saw animals, nomads and small trees. You also see human skeletons, plastic water bottles, clothes and shoes scattered everywhere. The heat is above 45 degree centigrade and before our eyes, the sand could rise up like Everest and Himalaya mountains. The lorry gets stuck every hour in the sand, we pull it or dig the tyres out of the sand for hours. You kneel at their (smugglers) feet to get a cup of water after you get burned digging up the desert sand. At midday the drivers cruise suddenly among the big sand mountains to hide themselves. They give you half litter of water and one dry piece of bread under the burning sun.

In the evening of the fourth day, three Toyota Land Cruiser pickups came speeding like wind. The drivers were Libyans in military uniforms, and they drove madly. It was like flying from one sand mountain to another for some minutes. When it lands a person or a gallon of diesel drops to the ground, they never take care of it. If a person falls off the truck, the people shout, and the driver beats us all with sticks and then picks up the person. We lost three strong smart young men on that trip. The friends who died said their last words: "please tell my mother, I will never see you again". We cried and cried in the desert. "This is everybody's destination, they are lucky that we cover them with the soil, but the last of us will not get covered with soil" said a man called Daniel from Keren.

After three days and nights of a perilous journey, we entered a small city in Libya. In this city you realize that you are not a human being anymore. They beat you instead of welcoming you; they tell that you are animals and other bad insults. The next thing they tell you before having anything to eat or to drink is: "tomorrow we have a group of people going to Trablus, if you need to join just transfer your money". Everybody makes a call to anyone who can pay for him, all night you struggle with telephone and bugs. The next day a small number of people have paid, but until everyone pays, there is no way out. After staying ten days in this *hell* custody, all night we hear different gun shots and canons. We have not had a bath or enough food; and you talk in whispering with permission, otherwise they punish all the people.

On the tenth day at 9 pm they called out names of 83 people. A long trailer truck came carrying about 250 quintals of animal feed. They built on it a wooden cave-like structure and put the quintals up on top of it, and secured them with ropes. "Everyone, climb and crimp at the edge of the trailer" shouted the leader. The space is so small, one can only sit with folded legs, and the people are forced to entre crawling on hands. You cannot see who is beside you, one of the leaders turns on a mobile phone light; there is no ventilation to allow in air. First when you climb on the truck, you cannot get air to breath and the children begin to cry, while the mothers and the sick people start to vomit. This journey takes 12 hours, if we do not encounter any obstacles and the truck is in good condition.

After travelling for about 10 hours, the wood tied on the sides of truck started to break and the quintals started falling on our heads. We started to shout and bang on the sides of the truck; the driver left the main road and drove on a rough road for about half an hour and stopped. He could not help us to open the wooden structure that they had built to keep the entrance to the truck sealed. He struggled for some time and finally he called some young men who helped to open it. By this time, we were not normal, we could not even get out of the truck; we could not control our legs, we were dehydrated, we had no sweat left in our bodies.

At every check-point, they ordered us not to make any sound, not to even breathe; every one vomited because of the stress and suffocation. We could not control ourselves; we were tossed about in the truck and we did not care anymore. Anyway, we entered the capital city from where you head to the sea. The first thing you notice in the halls rented by the people smugglers, are address, telephone numbers and names of agents all over the world; You wonder how they are organized mafia.

While we were kneeling and crying to our lord, one man shouted, "hi guys, tell your concerned to transfer to these addresses, from wherever, we are ready to serve, the amount is US$1650 only, the sooner the better, we have bought a new big ship. If you pay sooner, you will go tranquil". This was the best news and we did as they said, but "this is their daily and monotonous play, my friends" said one man who had stayed for 6 months in the imprisonment hall. We stayed for 7 days at the seashore in a house where they keep horses. On the seventh day a very young man from Libya came and told us to stand in a line and he counted twice; then we got into a big truck, which was so high that we had to help one another to go up. After about an hour's drive, soldiers stopped the truck by firing in the air. They took us to their camp and after about 2 hours they took us back to the place where we started. We guessed that it was a trick or they gave a bribe to the commanders.

The next day we were accompanied by a military car to the seashore, to the riverboat; then we sailed on the riverboat to the big ship that they bought for this trip. The boat was 100 quintal capacity and they loaded it with 325 persons. We started to sail, the boat moved like a tortoise, very slowly, the sea was calm and sunny. The captain was from Tunis, he told us that after 15 hours we were going to be at an international line, but we sailed for 48 hours, without knowing which direction we were heading. At midnight on the second day, the engine went off; the captain

> was disturbed, women and children shouted, men raised their voices to the captain and, a few raised their hands in prayer. The captain went into the engine room and after about half an hour, he was joined by some of us who were mechanics. They repaired the broken part and we started to sail again.
>
> Imagine this is the Mediterranean Sea. To cross it by a simple boat with so many people, what I can say is that it is the angles of the almighty God who have been carrying us on their wings. Connection was bad and therefore we could not call the 'concerned' and the captain also could not understand the GPS. He was ashamed to tell us he could not read the GPS. Four people and the captain climbed at the top of the boat and tried to call Red Cross in Italy. They answered the call and we gave them the location, but unfortunately, they said: "sorry we cannot help you. You are sailing towards Tunisia." They advised us to adjust the boat towards the northern direction. We got a call in Italian and I talked with them in broken Italian, they told me a Malta ship was coming to help us and they advised to keep in the northerly direction. On the third day about 9.00am two helicopters passed over us, I think they gave a signal to the ships. The ships came at around 11.00am. The ships took us to Sicily and handed us over to Italian humanitarian agencies. This is Europe, the first world; and what do you think of the barefoot man's last destination and place, where he will find rest and do what is expected of him?[4]

This interview excerpt gives rather graphic details of first-hand experience in trucks overloaded with migrants "rushing north along the sandy roads of the Sahara," (which) "have become iconic images of of international migrant smuggling" (Carling 2016: 25). Carling further warns that though this flow northward is important, "it is only one aspect of the complex and poorly documented landscape of migrant smuggling from West and Central Africa" (ibid.).

The Impact of Migration

From the above excerpt, a number of issues emerge. First, it is clear that migration to escape conflict and the attendant violence and insecurity in countries of origin is facilitated largely by human traffickers who make millions of dollars from the horrific trade of human beings. Second, the perilous journey across the desert and the sea deprives the migrants of all human dignity as they are transported like animals and treated in the most inhumane way by their handlers and others in the trafficking rings, including the military and police in the countries through which their journeys take them. It is evident that they just do not pass through these countries, often they spend months or years *en route*. Many of them die and those who survive are often traumatized for life.

The impact on the welfare of families and communities left behind (Azam and Gurbat 2006) is yet to be understood. For instance, communities which have lost many young able-bodied men through human trafficking and migration are beginning to emerge in parts of Cameroon, where husbands who migrate to Europe to work for long periods become absentee husbands and fathers, creating dysfunctional families. This form of migration has created "women's towns" or villages where the male population is diminishing. Its impact on the children raised in such dysfunctional families is yet to be adequately researched. Furthermore, many families have been impoverished by the high cost of migration processes because they have to raise funds by selling family land and other assets, as well as borrowing money from neighbours and friends to send one of their own to Europe with the hope that he or she will pay back the money and the remittances will lift the entire family from poverty. It is a life investment for such families to put their lives, faith, and hope in one or two of their members. And if disaster strikes in the desert or at sea, they lose the person(s) and they become indebted for the rest of their lives. Therefore "the family, community and country lose out on their earning potential. Further, the criminal activity and corruption associated with trafficking undermine domestic stability and the rule of law" (Williams 2019: 25). Thus, migration destroys the communities' prospects of prosperity, in spite of the claims that the remittances by the African Diaspora is three times more than the total amount of aid given by the donors to the continent. Individual immigrants living in Europe send money to their families to meet the basic needs; they do not contribute to the development of the national infrastructure, which is key to sustainable social and economic development.

Concluding Remarks: The Paradox of the "Africa Rising Narrative"

The last two decades have been marked by modest economic growth for many countries in the African continent. Some countries have also benefited from the process of the consolidation of regional blocs as exemplified by the economic growth rates recorded in the East African region. Huge deposits of oil and other natural resources have been discovered in some of these countries and there are prospects of rapid economic and social development for the East African Economic (EAC) community, which has huge potential to improve trade and mobility of people and goods. This new growth has inspired "much optimism among journalists, economists, business-people and investors" (European Union 2016: 3). The Africa rising narrative was spurred by this sense of optimism as it appeared that the continent was approaching a point where it was going to "turn the page," to take off or rise from the devastating impact of colonialism, and the failed hopes of the post-colonial states' political and national development projects.

However, the Africa rising narrative ignores the fact that neoliberal policies have had two contradictory faces, namely, they have on the one hand simultaneously spurred economic growth; but on the other hand, aggravated social inequality and the vulnerability of the poor in most African countries. Due to the persistence of political instability, violent conflicts, and endemic corruption, the economic growth recorded in many countries is showing no signs of sustainability and the benefits scarcely trickle down to most of the poor. Therefore, hundreds of thousands of people are risking death crossing the Sahara northwards toward Europe. For the desperate migrants, their countries are not rising, and they hardly see any hope of how they could escape the trap of extreme poverty or find peace and safety at home. In view of these observations, one can only agree with McKenzie (2016: 3) that "there is clearly a huge disconnect between the narrative of Africa rising and the images of African migrants risking life and limb to get away from Africa and get into Europe."

Arguably, the Africa rising narrative smacks of a pejorative colonial attitude that calls to mind the notion of the "Dark Continent." Prior to the advent of colonialism, Africa was called the "Dark Continent" and now, the span of time notwithstanding, it is said to be the rising continent. Implicit in the Africa rising narrative, therefore, is the age-old association of the continent with an economic and social slumber. These sentiments are echoed in a World Bank report entitled "Awakening Africa's sleeping giant: Prospects for commercial agriculture in the Guinea Savannah zone and beyond" (Michael et al. 2009). Africa is narrated in these terms without taking into consideration the impact of global forces such as colonial legacies, modern-day slave trade euphemistically referred to as human trafficking, migration, and exploitation of Africa's immense natural resource wealth by the developed countries of the West and

China. Indeed, the exploitation of Africa's natural resources by China and Western multinationals "must be understood in the context of the intertwined global social-economic as well as ecological crisis where capital acts as a spreading virus" (Pillay 2015: 61).

The global dynamics of the post-Cold War dispensation, which inadvertently contributed to the collapse of most dictatorships hitherto propped up by the Cold War principal actors in Africa, have continued to impact the continent in subtle ways. For instance, while the dictatorships are gone, with the late President Robert Mugabe of Zimbabwe being the last of the generation that led the decolonization struggles, the country he ruled for decades has sunk into a deep economic abyss, from which it will take decades to rise. Similarly, after the downfall of the kleptocratic dictatorship of Mobutu Sese Seko in 1997, the DRC with all its natural resources has remained a country where more than half of the national population live below the poverty line. While political and economic issues take primacy in the African development discourses, it is apparent that little attention is given to the fractured social fabric and threats to psychosocial well-being of grassroots communities, which create a deep sense of disillusionment, thus inducing many people to place themselves in the hands of human traffickers.

Furthermore, though the foundations laid by dictators in Africa may have been demolished by democratic movements across the continent in the last decade, the democratization processes are accompanied by political violence attendant to liberation struggles, which contribute to further inequalities that push the citizens out of their countries in search of a better future in Europe. As they risk their lives and embark on the perilous journeys to the unknown, many of them are aware of the risks of death at sea or in the desert. Nevertheless, like the speaker in the reported ethnographic interview above, they follow their "destiny" and those who make it finally say: "This is Europe, the first world …, the destination and place where to rest and do what is expected" of them.

Notes

1. "It is estimated that the consequences of oil spills may kill around 16,000 infants in the Niger Delta annually within their first month of life …" (Bassey Willie, *Daily Trust*, 12 November 2019). A recent study on the impact of oil spills on communities within a radius of 10 kilometers in the Delta region shows that oil spills before conception increase the risk

of neonatal mortality by 38.3 deaths per 1000 live births and the impact is the same across social economic backgrounds and uniform among boys and girls (Bruederle and Hodler 2019: 2). In addition, they point out that the effects of oil spills last several years after their occurrence.

2. During the Ottoman rule (1551–1864), there were two places in the coastal region of Libya known as Trablus Garb (Tripoli in the West) and Trablus Şam (Tripoli in the East). Trablus is still used locally to refer to Tripoli; and the people on the journey described in this interview excerpt, are being taken to Tripoli in order to get on the boat that was going to take them across the Mediterranean Sea to Europe.
3. Interview with an Eritrean migrant 21/09/2015, Boden, Sweden.

References

Azam, Jean-Paul, and Flore Gubert. 2006. *Migrant Remittances and Economic Development in Africa: A Review of Evidence.* University of Toulouse (ARQADE and IDEI) and Institut Universitaire de France. https://core.ac.uk/download/pdf/6376039.pdf.

Bamberg, Michael, and McCabe Allyssa. 1998. Editorial. *Narrative inquiry* 8 (1), iii–v.

Bruederle, Anna, and Roland Hodler. 2019. Effect of Oil Spills on Infant Mortality in Nigeria. CESifo Working Paper Series No. 6653.

Carling, Jørgen. 2016. West and Central Africa. In *Migrant Smuggling Data and Research: A Global Review of Emerging Evidence Base*, ed. Marie McAuliffe and Frank Laczko. Geneva: IOM.

European Parliamentary Research Service. 2016. Africa's Economic Growth: Taking off or Slowing Down? Available online: http://www.eprs.ep.parl.union.eu (intranet).

Internal Displacement Monitoring Center. 2019. http://www.internaldisplacement.org/sites/default/files/publications/documents/2019-IDMC-GRID-spotlight-cameroon.pdf.

Kubai, Anne. 2017. Trafficking of Ethiopian Women to Europe—Making Choices, Taking Risks and Implications. In *Ethiopians in an Age of Migration: Scattered Lives Beyond Borders*, ed. Fassil Demissie. Abingdon, UK: Routledge.

McKenzie, Rex. 2016. The Africa Rising Narrative - Whither development? Economics Discussion Papers 2016–9. Kingston University, London.

Michael, Morris, H. Hans Binswanger-Mkhize, and Derek Byerlee. 2009. Awakening Africa's Sleeping Giant: Prospects for Commercial Agriculture in the Guinea Savannah Zone and Beyond. World Bank Report.

Pillay, Divan. 2015. The Global Economic Crisis and the Africa Rising Narrative. In *Africa Development,* 40(3): 59–75. Council for the Development of Social Science Research in Africa.

Riessman, Catherine Kohler. 2002. Doing Justice: Positioning the Interpreter in the Narrative Work. In *Strategic Narrative: New Perspectives on the Power of Personal and Cultural Storytelling*, ed. Wendy Patterson. Lanham, MA and Oxford, UK: Lexington books.

Shelley, Louise. 2014. Human Smuggling and Trafficking into Europe. A Comparative Perspective. Migration Policy Institute. https://www.refworld.org/pdfid/52f3438d4.pd.

UNHCR. 2018. Desperate Journeys: Refugees and Migrants Arriving in Europe and at Europe's Borders. United Nations High Commissioner for Refugees (UNHCR). https://reliefweb.int/sites/reliefweb.int/files/resources/67712.pdf.

UNHCR. 2019a. DR Congo Emergency. https://www.unhcr.org/dr-congo-emergency.html.

UNHCR. 2019b. Sudan-Factsheet. United Nations High Commissioner for Refugees.

UNODC. 2011. The Role of Organized Crime in the Smuggling of Migrants from West Africa. United Nations Office on Drugs and Crime (UNODC). https://www.unodc.org/documents/human-trafficking/Migrant-Smuggling/Report_SOM_West_Africa_EU.pdf.

Williams, Wendy. 2019. Shifting Borders: Africa's Displacement Crisis and its Implications for Security. Africa Center for Strategic Studies Research Paper No. 8.

PART V

Conclusion and Policy Recommendations

CHAPTER 19

From the Narrative of "Africa Rising" to "How Africa Can Arise": The Macro-Economic Imperatives

Temitope J. Laniran and Kenneth Omeje

Introduction

The notion of Africa as the direct antithesis of progress has begun to change in recent years. The advent of the present millennium has seen a persistent unravelling of the narrative of pathological dysfunctionality hitherto associated with Africa and a gradual paradigm shift to a new narrative that sees Africa as a growing continent with profound possibilities. Proponents of the new narrative have not limited it to just economic growth but have included changes in the political, economic

T. J. Laniran (✉)
Institute of Development Studies, Brighton, UK

Centre for Petroleum Energy Economics and Law, University of Ibadan, Ibadan, Nigeria

K. Omeje
Manifold Crown Consulting, Bradford, UK
e-mail: komeje@manifoldcrown.org

K. Omeje (ed.), *The Governance, Security and Development Nexus*,
https://doi.org/10.1007/978-3-030-49348-6_19

and social structures. The new narrative sees an Africa imbued with enormous economic potentials and the opportunity for a sustainably thriving middle class to emerge which hitherto was almost non-existent. On face evaluation, it seems apparent that the tragedy of Africa as a drag to global growth and prosperity has turned. At the start of 2019, Sub-Saharan Africa (SSA) could boast of six of the world's fastest-growing economies.[1] However, on careful examination, the change in the narrative only represents nominal progress but not necessarily real changes in the lives and living conditions of sub-Saharan Africans (Laniran 2018). While the economic growth figures across the region have been quite impressive and significant, the changing face of global poverty suggests a different narrative. This new face of global poverty perceives the region as the home of some of the world's poorest countries, suggesting the inability of Sub-Saharan Africa (SSA) to convert its growth to improved living conditions for its citizens.

Sachs (2005) aptly remarks that economic prosperity across the globe has mainly been driven by continued scientific and technical progress, as well as accumulation and re-accumulation of capital with neoliberal ideologies. The unprecedented economic progress and poverty reduction achieved by South Korea, Singapore, China, India, Malaysia, Indonesia, Thailand among other Asian countries in recent decades has boosted the support for the potency of neoliberal ideologies in achieving economic growth and reducing poverty. In a similar manner, SSA has continued to show potentials for economic prosperity. Indeed, economic growth is potent in lifting huge proportions of the global poor from extreme poverty but it is neither automatic nor guaranteed (Sachs 2005). The forces of the market alone are not enough in moving people out of poverty. While economic growth is crucial and necessary for moving people out of poverty, it is however not sufficient. Lebaron and Ayers (2013) have stressed the dependence of neoliberal ideologies on capital accumulation and doubted its ability to achieve the much needed economic development in a continent beleaguered by the legacy of widespread and systemic colonial underdevelopment. Writing from a Marxist perspective, Ravallion (2013) explained that in the mid-nineteenth century, some leftist intellectuals and activists held the view that in a predominantly neoliberal world as portrayed by the prevailing global conjuncture, poverty is an inevitable consequence of the dialectical tendency for "the accumulation of capital at one pole", to at the same time, precipitate "the accumulation of misery, the agony of toil, slavery, ignorance and mental degradation at the other" (Marx 1976). Proponents doubted the possibility of a neoliberal-driven economic growth reducing poverty, not because of the moral failure of the poor, but rather because of the impossibility of full employment and the drawbacks of gains (e.g. welfare benefits) by the unemployed. It is believed that the dynamics of institutional failures culminating in market failures and interacting with existing inequalities would obstruct the campaign against poverty.

In view of the foregoing observations, the rest of this chapter explores the rise of neoliberalism in Africa and its dysfunctionalities, the continent's continued reliance on primary commodity exports, the potential of the upcoming African Continental Free Trade Area (AfCFTA), as well as critical policy priorities relevant to ensure that Africa really rises beyond the nominal.

The Rise of Neoliberalism and Its Dysfunctionality in Africa

Neoliberalism originated in the 1930s as an economic philosophy which advocated both state intervention and free markets (seeking to provide a middle path between the perceived failure of classical economics in the 1930s and a Marxist approach); however, this original meaning of neoliberalism has been lost (Pettinger 2018). In contemporary history, neoliberalism is a term commonly used to describe free-market economics, with emphasis on policies associated with free trade, privatisation, price deregulation, a reduced size of government and flexible labour markets, as well as more increasingly, policies of austerity and attempts to reduce budget deficits—usually by cutting government spending on social programmes (Pettinger 2018).

Neoliberalism as an economic philosophy is underpinned by a dominant assumption premised on the existence of perfectly operating market(s) across countries. The original ideology of neoliberalism supported free movement of goods and services, accumulation of capital, market forces, among others. It subsequently expanded to a paradigm that not only signifies an economic policy model, but quite significantly, an encompassing philosophy with vast political, ideological, cultural and spatial ramifications. "By the early 1990s, neoliberalism had become elevated to an epochal phenomenon and was often used as loose shorthand for a prevailing *dystopian zeitgeist*" (Venugopal 2015), which akin to the epic Dystopian novel reveals the vicious cycle of Rise, Zenith and

Decay. This has led to characterisations of neoliberalism as "capitalism in its millennial manifestation" (Comaroff and Comaroff 2000: 298). Saad-Filho and Johnston (2005: 5) posit that "we live in the age of neoliberalism". The transition to this new age has been described as a revolutionary turning point in the world's social and economic history (Harvey 2007). The Global Financial Crisis indicated a new wave of neoliberalism and how it potentially fractures a homogenous theory of neoliberalism as an unwavering and monolithic force of globalisation, rather than a "mobile technology for governing" (Ong 2007: 12). The emergence of Donald Trump as the President of the United States of America, rejections of certain aspects of free trade and globalisation by President Trump, among other neo-conservative leaders in the West; BREXIT[1] and China continued Privatisation while retaining state authoritarianism and socialist control, etc essentially reflect the liquidity and fluidity of neoliberal ideologies in recent times. Neoliberal ideologies have indeed continued to mutate, evolve and adapted to various domestic conditions across the world.

At independence, most African countries had leaders that were quite unsympathetic to neoliberal ideologies. With leaders such as Kwame Nkrumah of Ghana and Julius Nyerere of Tanzania the "immediate post-colonial era" had a legacy of independence, ambitious growth trajectory and a region that worked for its people. By the end of the independence decade, many African countries had already been captured by military juntas or descended to dictatorships that steered the ship of the state towards civil wars, overburdening external debts and economic sanctions.

By the early 1980s, a revitalised brand of neoliberalism that favoured the rise of market deregulation, privatisation and curtailing of the welfare state had taken over most of the advanced world, which ultimately began to extend to Africa. According to Loxley (1990), from the early 1980s about 40 SSA countries had begun pursuing neoliberal-oriented reforms in exchange for loans from the IMF and the World Bank, loans that were marked by inimical conditionalities. These policies were fundamentally economic and were scarcely associated with domestic socio-political or institutional reforms, with the result that military regimes and one party civilian dictatorship remained in power across most of the countries in the region. By the end of the 1990s, it had become apparent to the external financiers of neoliberal economic reforms in Africa popularly known as the Structural Adjustment Programmes (SAP) that the combination of neoliberal ideologies with dictatorial regimes was not delivering the needed economic development to the region but rather led to more debt crises, economic regression or low growth, extreme hardship and sporadic implosion of the state marked by rebel insurrections and outbreak of civil wars. It was against this backdrop that the IMF and World Bank came up with the political conditionalities of SAP which required the loan-recipient states in SSA to adopt multi-party democratic governance, leading to a hurried spate of transitions to democratic rule during the 1990s and early 2000s.

The number of autocratic regimes in sub-Saharan Africa fell from a peak of thirty-six countries in 1989 to only five in 2004. These new democratic regimes had inherited a debt-ridden and sanction laden region with very abysmal growth; where many existed. However, some of these new civilian regimes which were largely sympathetic to neoliberal ideologies embarked on massive economic reforms which led to debt pardons and removal of sanctions. For example, the President Olusegun Obasanjo's civilian administration in Nigeria (1999–2007) brokered a historic debt relief deal in April 2006 that led Nigeria to become the first African country to be free of its debt to the Paris Club, following a final transfer of $4.5bn to the Western creditors that supposedly cleared the way for billions to be spent on reducing poverty.

While there are intellectual foundations to neoliberalism which are linked to neoclassical economic principles that promote competition across countries and regions (Peck and Tickell 2002), it is also seen as a political project that emphasises restoration of class power threatened by income and wealth redistribution (Harvey 2005). This, therefore, implies that there are possibilities for variations in neoliberalism as it is not a condition, but rather a process, which will be experienced by different countries in different forms.

Most economies across the globe today are leaning towards neoliberal ideologies to achieve their growth. The growth in China and India has been driven by productivity with strong institutional regulation. However, some critical studies have revealed the excesses of the neoliberal market to include inequality widening and market failures, hence the need for strong institutions and regulations. An overview of African economies however, tends to present a rather more complex situation, which exemplifies different variations of capitalism and neoliberal development, the vast majority of which are indeed aberrations and dysfunctional models that are antithetical to real development.

Persistence of Natural Resource and Commodity Market Dominance

The trend of rising commodity prices that started at the beginning of the present millennium was followed by a period of extreme volatility towards the end of the first decade of the millennium. Prices are mostly expected to remain around the current range in the immediate and medium-term, as growth in the global emerging markets has mostly slowed down and commodity supply not fully adjusted to the resultant reduction in demand. Economic performance in several SSA countries often trails the commodity market. While the linkages between commodity markets, economic growth and development can be complex, commodity prices, however, provide ample incentives that influence decisions relating to production, consumption, income generation, investment, trade and employment (Fig. 19.1).

According to UNCTAD (2019), nine out of ten sub-Saharan African countries are commodity-dependent. By region, 89% of sub-Saharan African countries are commodity-dependent, compared to two-thirds of the countries in the Middle East and North Africa, half of the countries in Latin America and the Caribbean, and half of the countries in East Asia and the Pacific. On the other hand, only a quarter of countries in South Asia, Europe and the Central Asia region are considered

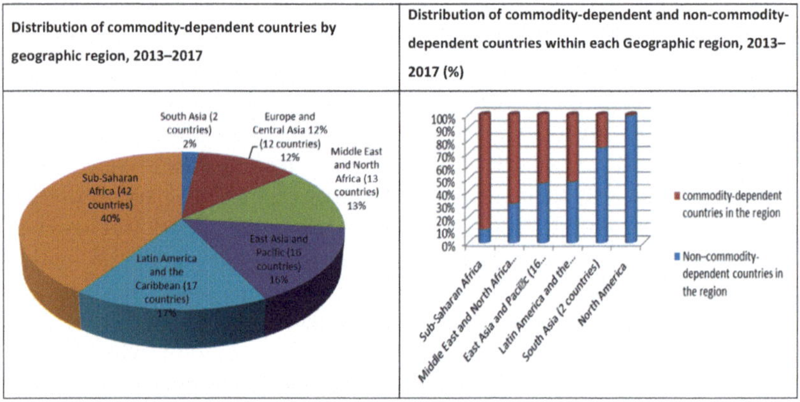

Fig. 19.1 Regional spread of global commodity dependence (*Source* UNCTAD [2019] State of Commodity Dependence)

commodity-dependent, while there are almost no commodity-dependent countries in North America. Even though commodities do not necessarily imply underdevelopment, empirical evidence has, however shown that its continued dependence and failure to achieve structural transformation can be associated with economic challenges. Collier (2003) in discussing the future of Africa highlighted three problems with commodity dependence, namely price shocks, governance and rebellion. In a broader scope, these can be discussed along the lines of price volatility, fiscal regimes and state fragility.

In the case of price volatility, this often undermines development and growth through the channel of export and resultant inability to generate revenue and foreign exchange. Global commodity markets are almost synonymous with volatility as hikes and crashes happen at an almost unpredictable pace. This, therefore, makes planning and economic progress as well as revenue and capital for development quite difficult for SSA countries.

While most of the countries of the world export a mix of different goods, including manufactures and services, most SSA countries depend on a very limited scope of commodities, with most of the exports of the region deviating significantly from global exports due to low-value addition. This exposes them to severe macroeconomic shocks. For other developing regions, such shocks are largely a thing of the past due to export diversification. Collier (2003) has explained that typically, booms do not translate into sustained increases in income; they are mostly missed opportunities as they destabilise budgets. Crashes, on the other hand, produce devastating and long-lasting declines.

Schuktneckt (1999) provides clear evidence that coffee booms lured governments into unsustainable increases in expenditures, which made them find themselves locked into these new patterns after the boom and as such leading to unsustainable debt. It, therefore, becomes important for SSA countries to insulate their economies from adverse effects of volatility by developing value addition processes. Furthermore, there is a need for the adoption of counter-cyclical budgeting to adjust current unsustainable budget structures.

In the case of state fragility, fragile states do not only present some of the most serious and urgent development needs in the world but the most difficult environments for conventional economic theories and assumptions (Chandy 2011). Recent growth in Africa has not been accompanied by sufficient structural transformation, reduction in unemployment levels and adequate inclusivity (AERC 2015). Ostensibly, economic growth in SSA is mostly fuelled by commodity market; correspondingly, there is widespread failure of countries of SSA to drive structural change, reduce unemployment and poverty levels due to challenges of fragility (Laniran 2018). In their study of 36 SSA countries, Mold and Prizzon (2010) argue that the failure of SSA countries to diversify their exports is largely due to inefficiencies and scarcity of technological investment, a problem aggravated by the structural impediments to value addition due to state fragility.

The record of growth in recent years has led to the graduation of about seven SSA economies (including Angola and Nigeria) to middle-income economy status (although the middle-income class is now further divided into upper and lower categories). The experience of these fast-growing economies is mostly consistent with the economic concepts of "convergence" (or the "catch-up effect") and "post-conflict growth rebound" (Staines 2004; UNDP BPCR 2008; IMF 2019). The convergence notion explains the faster growth experienced in poorer economies compared to economies that have achieved a high-income level. The post-conflict growth rebound explains the fast growth that follows sharp drops in GDP, Liberia being an important example of this development (Radelet 2007; Sayndee 2019). Other countries that experienced highly disruptive and destructive conflicts after the end of the Cold War have experienced notable economic rebounds after hostilities ceased (e.g. Angola, Liberia, Mozambique and Sierra Leone).

The economic environment in fragile states mainly characterised by weak human capital accumulation, unstable macroeconomic environment, poor health and educational outcomes, unstable political environment and poor infrastructure is generally not conducive to private sector investment, which is arguably a key driver of growth and job creation. Weak institutions also mean that the ability of the state to deliver services is tenuous—hence, the state cannot hope to substitute for private investment. This observation raises questions relating to the growth experience of the SSA economies given that a majority of the African countries are fragile, war-affected and post-conflict states.

Indeed, the last two decades have seen the economic ascension of the developing world, with GDP growth rates in surplus of those obtained in the developed world. This progression has been particularly evident since the mid-1990s, which has led to tremendous global poverty reduction—thanks to the global impact of China's rapid industrialisation and trade. Chen and Ravallion (2008) have argued that even when the impact of China is omitted from the global sample, poverty reduction is still considerable. The positive development in global poverty reduction is, however far from homogeneous, with many countries, largely in Africa, experiencing little poverty reduction or even increasing poverty. Although some African Countries including Angola, Nigeria, Ethiopia and Rwanda have been among the fastest-growing economies of the past decade, available empirical evidence suggests that Africa constitutes the largest deficit to achievement of the MDG 2015 and the current push towards Sustainable Development Goals (MDG Report 2014; The SDG Centre for Africa 2019). In essence, the growth in SSA has been mostly inefficient.

In the case of fiscal regimes, there are in theory three channels through which commodity dependence can hinder the development of SSA (Laniran,2017). First is the notion of the "Dutch disease". The Dutch disease has various interpretations and the meaning has evolved over time. The term is mostly associated with some natural resource-rich developing economies, but the phenomenon has its origin in critical observations in the Dutch economy in the 1960s when the Netherlands' discovery and production of vast natural gas in the North Sea substantially increased external revenue receipts in the country. Revenue influx made the Dutch Guilder to rise in value, a trend that had a negative knock-on effect on non-oil exports, which became less competitive in the world market, causing a significant drop in capital investment and a corresponding rise in unemployment.[2]

A comparatively different economic condition was observed in Britain during the international oil crisis of the 1970s. Quadrupling of oil price triggered a high level stagflation. British exports (manufactured goods) became less competitive in the international market—an aspect of the Dutch Disease. It became more economically viable for Britain to drill its North Sea oil off the coast of Scotland, and they did, which gradually stabilised the British economy.[3]

Among developing countries, the manifestation of the Dutch disease is comparatively different because most natural resource-rich states do not have an export-based manufacturing sector. As such, a sudden windfall in revenue receipts from primary commodity exports does not necessarily destroy local manufacturing or its export competitiveness (which hardly exists). But it potentially destroys other sectors like agro-forestry production (e.g. the economies of Gabon, Congo and Sudan prior to the commercial production & export of oil). It can also destroy cottage industries and prevent largescale manufacturing from taking off. This form of Dutch disease devastated a number of African oil exporting economies in the 1970s and 1980s, notably Nigeria, Gabon, Angola, Equatorial Guinea, Sao Tome (Sieff 2007). African cash crop exporting economies were also badly affected by a convergence of the Dutch disease and the subsequent crash of the prices of primary commodities in the world market in the 1980s. Most of the African crisis-ridden economies were subsequently bailed out through diverse forms of foreign aid, notably the World Bank and the IMF. Paradoxically, foreign aid seemingly aggravated the African economic crises in different ways akin to the Dutch disease. The large influx of foreign currency in many African economies through balance of payment support loans and humanitarian assistance grants, to a lesser extent, have over the years produced a similar effect typical of the Dutch disease by fostering grand prebendal accumulation through the use of state power (Omeje 2006), a phenomenon that has led critics like Dambisa Moyo (2009) to argue that foreign aid has largely had deleterious effects on growth and development in Africa.

Overall, the Dutch disease allows for a deleterious shunting of "learning by doing process", which is embedded in an incremental development process, thereby engendering resource misallocation, waste and inefficiency (Robinson et al. 2006; Caselli and Cunningham 2009). Furthermore, because the Dutch disease emanates from the "money quantum" available to governments as a result of revenue windfalls often associated with the political economy of resource rent; the phenomenon turns political governance into an overly attractive and lucrative mechanism for prebendal amassing of wealth (Joseph 1987; Sachs and Warner 2001).

It is pertinent to mention that not all resource-rich countries in Africa face the paradox of rentier profligacy and abysmal performance. A few natural resource-abundant economies such as Botswana, South Africa and Namibia have been significantly well-managed economies with accountable and durable governance institutions. While the South African economy has had a substantially thriving manufacturing sector since the Apartheid era, diamond-rich Botswana and Namibia have largely excelled through ensuring fiscal discipline, rule of law and sound macroeconomic management. Both countries have utilised their abundant natural resource wealth to leverage human security and infrastructural development (roads, hospitals, schools, health care, etc), uplifting their countries to upper middle-income status. Since 2010, Botswana in particular has also made sustained progress from the export of raw diamond to value addition in the diamond industry (sorting, cutting, polishing, marketing, etc), thereby triggering a modest value-chain industrialisation, creating more skilled jobs and increasing export revenue. To achieve this tremendous feet, the government of Botswana had to renegotiate its mining and marketing contract with De Beers, its major Multinational investor and joint venture partner in the diamond industry which made De Beers to move its sorting, marketing and Sight holder operations from its London headquarters to Gaborone, the capital city of Botswana in 2013 (Laniado 2017). As part of the government's economic diversification drive, Botswana has prioritised tourism and livestock production (two secondary sectors of foreign exchange earnings) as areas for expanded investment and development. Despite having its own peculiar governance challenges (notably improving government's capacity for generating policy planning statistics, transparency in revenue management, economic diversification, power generation and poverty reduction), it suffices to say that there are some best practices that other natural resource-rich countries in Africa could learn from Botswana, especially the nexus between fiscal discipline, rule of law, sound management and governing for the benefit of the people.

Tax Extraction and Accounting Capacity

Tax extraction and accounting are one of the strategic areas where most of the African countries have weak capacity and ironically have not made an investment priority from a governance perspective. Besley and Persson (2010) have shown that investment in tax capacity determines the maximum feasible level of taxation a state can set. They argue that the tax revenue received from nationals serves as a source of the state's provision of public goods such as health care, effective communication system and public service delivery in general. As a result, an inefficient fiscal regime impedes the number of public goods and development projects that can be provided by the state. This implies that the deliberate decisions of the governing elites to neglect the improvement of the fiscal regimes, not only reduces the level of taxation and revenue they could collect but also limits the scale of public goods and services that could be provided, leading to a decline in human security and development.

A weak fiscal regime would undermine domestic revenue through lower taxes on citizens, and this is based on the assumption that taxation capacity determines the maximum level of taxation that can be set. Therefore, a weak tax capacity translates to low taxes, which reduces the people's ability to scrutinise expenditures of the governing class and demand for accountability. Writing with particular reference to oil-rich rentier states of the Middle East, some theorists of public taxation have argued that the governing elite enjoys an increased probability of retaining power because of the little or no tax burden placed on the populace, a tendency that could also minimise the chances of the citizens demand for democratic representation and accountability (Luciani 1997; Bratton 1998). In the African context, it is apparent that reduced taxation enhances the low provision of public goods in favour of non-productive goods and further incentivises the political elite towards fostering a weakened fiscal regime in the country.

Apart from reduced taxation, other problems associated with tax regimes in Africa are bureaucratic red-tape, unpredictability, widespread corruption in tax administration and taxation without social responsibility, which altogether hinder the country's capacity to attract foreign direct investments (FDI) and the ease of doing business in its jurisdiction. Besides direct taxation in the public sphere, most African countries lack the institutional and technical capacity to level and collect taxes from the private and informal sectors of the economy. In the context of FDI and doing business, many African countries have significantly high corporate income taxes (above 25%)—e.g. Uganda, Tunisia, Zambia, Nigeria, Tanzania, Kenya, South Africa, Namibia, Gambia, Gabon, Burundi, Burkina Faso, DRC, Cameroun, Benin Republic and Central African Republic (Etter-Phoya et al. 2019).[4] The real challenge is that the majority of these countries lack the capacity to effectively audit business investments for taxation purposes and therefore literally depend entirely on their self-declaration of profits for tax assessment with the result that tax evasion/avoidance; transfer pricing for shifting profits, and other under-payment devices are rampant (Mailey 2015; Omeje 2015). Some of the African countries also offer foreign companies a range of tax exemptions often linked to special economic zones, export processing zones and fixed-term post-investment tax holidays, which significantly reduce or eliminate corporate income tax for operating firms. It will require effective reforms and capacity-building to mitigate the observed loopholes and gaps in the individual states' tax systems in Africa.

The African Continental Free Trade Area (AfCFTA): Prospect and Challenges

On 21 March, 2018, 44 African countries out of the 55 member states of the African Union signed the African Continental Free Trade Area (AfCFTA) agreement; twelve additional countries have signed AfCFTA at the time of writing, bringing the total number to 54 countries. The Agreement entered into force on 30 May 2019, 30 days after the required minimum of 22 countries had deposited their instruments of ratification with the African Union Commission. As at November 2019, 27 countries had ratified the Agreement and trading among the ratified countries is scheduled to start on 1 July 2020.

At independence, African countries were largely fragmented and had inadequate capacity (especially, physical and human capital) to utilise their large natural resources for growth and development. Since then African leaders have continued to propose the need for a united market in pursuing the quest for growth and development. Consequently, the idea of "regionalism" has gained traction in recent decades, leading to the formation and revival of Regional Economic Communities (RECs) to foster integration, besides the larger continental body, the African Union (AU). The recent push for the continental free trade agreement which is perhaps one of the most ambitious projects of its kind among developing countries is coming up at a time of emerging scepticism about multilateral trade agreements, especially in the Western world, a tendency that has been fuelled by the emergence of right-wing unilateralist leaders like President Donald Trump in the United States and the UK BREXIT kingpin Boris Johnson in Europe.

Proponents perceive the AfCFTA as an attempt by the African governments to "unlock Africa's tremendous potential" to deliver prosperity to all Africans (UNCTAD 2015; AU 2019). The agreement seeks to create a common continental market that allows free movement of humans, goods, services and capital across the region. Currently, the market size of the continent is about 1.2 billion people with a cumulative GDP of about US$ 3.4 trillion; manufacturing accounts for only about 10% of Africa's GDP (Shihepo 2019). By 2030, the African market size is projected to reach about 1.7 billion people, with a combined and cumulative consumer and business spending of US$6.7 trillion (Mishra 2018). In signing up to the AfCFTA, individual member states have committed to remove tariffs on about 90% of goods at the initial stages, and gradually phase off the remaining 10% over time (Signé 2018). It is expected that the resultant intra-continental trade boost from the agreement will provide a basis for the required type of structural economic change needed to engage the massive unemployed youth population and reduce poverty through the growth of cottage industries, large scale industrial value addition and diversification.

Presently, there are about 8 RECs recognised by the African Union. The Africa Regional Integration Index (ARII) developed by the UNECA, AfDB and AU recognises five indicators of regional integration through which progress among the RECs is measured. These indicators are trade integration, regional infrastructure, productive integration, free movement of people and financial and macroeconomic integration (Lopez 2016). Individual RECs scores on each dimension are ranked on a scale of 0 to 1.

Based on Table 19.1, it is clear that the overall regional integration score for the "trade integration" dimension (0.540) is the highest among the RECs. On the other hand, it is the lowest for "financial and macroeconomic".

In "trade integration", the East African Community (EAC) scores the most (0.780) while the Community of Sahel-Saharan States (CEN-SAD) scores the least (0.353). In "productive integration", the EAC again tops (0.553) the list while the CEN-SAD is at the bottom (0.247). In "free

Table 19.1 African regional integration index, 2016

Regional economic community	*Trade integration*	*Regional infrastructure*	*Productive integration*	*Free movement of people*	*Financial and macroeconomic integration*
CEN-SAD	0.353	0.251	0.247	0.479	0.524
COMESA	0.572	0.439	0.452	0.268	0.343
EAC	0.780	0.496	0.553	0.715	0.156
ECCAS	0.526	0.451	0.293	0.400	0.599
ECOWAS	0.442	0.426	0.265	0.800	0.611
IGAD	0.505	0.630	0.434	0.454	0.221
SADC	0.508	0.502	0.350	0.530	0.397
UMA	0.631	0.491	0.481	0.493	0.199
Average of eight RECs	0.540	0.461	0.384	0.517	0.381

Source Africa Regional Integration Index Report (2016)

movement of people", the Economic Community of West African States (ECOWAS) is the most integrated one with a score of 0.800 and the Common Market for Eastern and Southern Africa (COMESA) is the least with a score of 0.268. It is quite noticeable that some regions have integrated better than others, however, it is hoped that the continental agreement will necessitate faster coordination and integration (Mishra 2018).

The actualisation of the continental integration initiative comes with some prospect and challenges. The prospect includes expanded foreign investments and new markets, reduction in input cost, increased efficiency and ultimately economic growth, employment and poverty reduction. The challenges, on the other hand, include varied levels of economic development and sophistication, competitive pressure, crowding out of SMEs and job losses, environmental depletion and intellectual property theft, among others.

In terms of foreign investment and new market, with the lifting of restrictions, both intra-African and international investors will be attracted to the continent. This will inject the much needed additional capital to stimulate local production and businesses. The new capital will necessitate and drive productivity in the economy. The agreement will give African-owned businesses the opportunity to access new markets which hitherto were almost impossible and thereby lead to diversified products innovations and new products to meet the varied needs of the markets across the continent. In the case of reduction in input cost and increased efficiency, the agreement will ease the access to raw materials across the continent, thereby enabling investors set up industries in other African Countries, particularly for investors in the manufacturing and industrial sector. Further, it will provide platforms for attractive partnerships between multinationals and domestic firms to add value to raw materials, as well as benefit from the spill over effect. Ultimately, it is expected that the actualisation of the continental free trade zone will provide the much needed structural transformation that will boost industrial growth, create jobs and economic growth and ultimately reduce poverty.

On the other hand, the possibility of successfully actualising continental integration is challenged by various factors such as varying levels of economic development and sophistication of the different countries in the continent. For example, about 60% of the cumulative GDP of SSA is accounted for only 2 countries (Nigeria and South Africa) out of over 50 countries, and as such the AfCFTA represents perhaps the most disparate market integration project in terms of income levels of member countries. Furthermore, opening up the economies to allow for a free flow of labour, goods and services by the teeming majority of smaller states (whose economies are mostly still at subsistence agricultural levels) to compete with bigger economies like South Africa and Nigeria can jeopardise the smaller economies through negative externalities such as loss of jobs, un-competitiveness and atrophy of infant businesses, uncontrolled migration in an attempt to search for survival, among others. Moreover, in order to survive keen competition amidst weak governance institutions, many firms could resort to the unsavoury option of producing in environmentally unsustainable ways to reduce cost. Furthermore, the absence of strong institutions and laws to protect against piracy, patency and intellectual property among most African countries could indirectly frustrate investment, research and development.

Another crucial factor that can undermine the actualisation of the continental integration is sabotage. There is a risk of a situation where individual countries will allow inflow of products not produced in their country or within the region to be traded within the continental trade agreement and as such serving as a conduit for external influences such as Europe, China and the rest of Asia. The case of the land border closure between Nigeria and Benin Republic in mid-2019 as a result of the perception of the Nigerian government that Benin republic serves as a conduit for Thai rice despite domestic policy effort to stimulate domestic rice production and ensure the country grows what it consumes. This case has led to agitation across the entire Ecowas framework with countries like Ghana threatening legal action against Nigeria. In essence the risk of sabotage which will almost be inevitable therefore poses a threat to the actualisation of the one Africa market.

Policy Priorities to Capitalise on the Africa Rising Experience

The recent improvement in economic performance experienced in most African countries in the last 2 decades has been made possible largely by improvement in macroeconomic and political stability, growth of the private sector, as well as substantial contributions from export commodities. There have also been some internal structural changes, institutional and sectoral reforms with the objective of stimulating the business environment and encouraging investment. For example, Lin (2011) explains that as at 2010, 28 SSA countries have adopted the Extractive Industries Transparency Initiative with the aim of improving transparency and governance through the verification and publication of company payments and government revenue from oil, gas and mining. In the telecommunication sector alone the continent went to over 400 million mobile phones by 2008 from less than 2 million mobile phones in 1998, making the continent the fastest-growing telecommunications market. Other service sectors such as banking and retail trading have also experienced significant progress. Despite the progress made, most of the export earnings and government revenues still rely on natural resources and primary commodities, and a significant chunk of the growth has been spurred by consumption. It is expected that continued reforms can help diversify and boost export earnings, government revenue and boost productivity and job creation. To sustain progress and address current challenges of unemployment and poverty, the recorded progress need to be backed up by significant structural transformation, deliberately driven by industrialisation. It is therefore imperative for policymakers to identify policy priorities to sustain the progress made in recent decades. Three key policy priorities have been identified to make the recorded progress sustainable, namely deliberate and systematic investments in infrastructures, institution-building and human capital or people development.

Infrastructural Development

Over the past 30 years, electricity per capita output in the continent has scarcely improved. Similarly, less than 20% of the roads have been built among other critical infrastructural deficit, such as railways and seaports to facilitate trade and industrial growth. Many African countries are presently making massive investments in critical infrastructures, albeit with external funding majorly by China. For example, countries like Nigeria, Ethiopia, Zambia, Kenya, etc have intensified efforts aimed at resuscitating, modernising and expanding their highway and railway networks. Other initiatives have focused on developing transnational infrastructural facilities within the RECs, such as the West African Gas Pipeline that seeks to supply gas from Nigeria's Escravos region of Niger Delta area to Benin, Togo and Ghana. It is the first regional natural gas transmission system in Sub-Saharan Africa. According to Sy (2014), Africa needs an estimated US$93 billion per year to develop its infrastructures, with two-thirds required for new physical infrastructure and the remainder for maintenance and operations. Evidently, filling the huge financing deficits in Africa will require alternative sustainable development for financing and blocking of endemic corruption leakages (Laniran 2018).

Institutional Transformation

Clearly, another factor that has contributed significantly to the progress made in recent years on the continent is the gradual push for institutional transformation, a necessary move that has been fraught with enormous resistance and challenges. The push includes the gradual transitions from various forms of dictatorship to civilian democratic rule, with improvements in transparency, governance, property rights, rule of law and the macroeconomic policy environment. The modest gains made towards institutional transformation have provided the necessary foundation required for investor confidence and opened the economy for business in many countries. Over the years, Africa's weak institutional environment has been and indeed continues to be a major impediment to the realisation of the growth and development potential of the continent. The persistence of widespread corruption is one of the factors inhibiting the transformation of the economic growth into development dividends for all citizens of Africa, preventing them from enjoying improved livelihoods and living conditions (Transparency International 2014, 2018).

Despite the observed progress made in institutional improvement, Africa remains for the most part institutionally weak. To achieve sustainable development, Africa's political and economic institutions need massive transformation. There is also the need for sustainable peace and durable mechanisms that foster shared prosperity. This can only be achieved through more inclusive and transparent political institutions that have eluded the region for so long. Robinson and Acemoglu (2012) have argued that the long-term development of countries is largely explained by the existence of inclusive institutions[5] as opposed to extractive institutions,[6] which in turn are a product of critical historical junctures that shaped the nature and development of institutions. This does not mean that countries with extractive political and economic institutions could not achieve short-term economic growth. The problem is that such growth may not be sustainable (Nega and Schneider 2016). Therefore, for the Africa rising experience to be sustainable, there is a need for building more inclusive, transparent and accountable institutions.

People Development

Africa's sustainable growth and development most importantly call for concerted focus on building the people—human capital development. Apparently, the greatest potential for the African region—over and above all its natural resources—is the people of the continent. Unfortunately, there persists a wide contradiction between Africa's population growth and investments in human capital development. Africa currently has the second-largest share of global population—at almost 17% of total global population by continent. Moreover, with about 2.5% growth rate, the continent has the fastest-growing population by region. It is expected that more than half of global population growth between now and 2050 will occur in Africa. The population of sub-Saharan Africa is projected to double by 2050. This implies that there will be an excessive supply of labour readily available for industrial productivity. However, without targeted systematic investment for the provision of quality education and health facilities to create sound intellectual minds that could be gainfully utilised in production, the continent's growing population risks becoming a serious liability. The extent to which decent wage industrial jobs could be created depends heavily on Africa's capacity to equip its burgeoning population with relevant knowledge and skill to participate in a continuously emerging world of digital economy. The type of impactful education and skills training required today for the modern digital economy would necessitate significant changes in the current curricula of most schools and tertiary educational institutions across the continent, as well as massive campaigns to promote schools' enrolment across the region. Africa presently has the lowest HDI mean compared to other continents across the world (Kpolovie et al. 2017). The poor HDI is an indication that the quality of life of the average African needs significant improvement to avoid contemporary population growth being a recipe for spread of diseases, ignorance, poverty and squalor.

Conclusion

Remarkably, proponents of the Africa rising narrative have relied heavily on the recent GDP growth statistics of the continent to optimistically assume that the continent can sustain the recent growth levels by gainfully optimising its numerous potentials Sceptics of the narrative on the other hand dismiss the idea of sustainably a rising Africa under the prevailing local and international political economy as a façade. The sceptics often refer to history to reinforce their argument that this is not the first time such a promising growth bubble has occurred in African economies yet because of its unsustainability the continent continues to lag behind the rest of the world in most development outcome indices. Similarly, the recent and ongoing growth wave is yet to transform into improved living conditions for Africans. Presently, more than half of the continent's population live in poverty. Furthermore, the current growth has only but opened up a new possibility in the economic growth and structural transformation discourse. Upon the emergence of the new Africa rising narrative, quite a considerable number of SSA countries attempted rebasing their GDP in a quest for structural transformation evidence. Significant changes were found in most of their GDP composition, the most notable being that the service sector has grown to presently account for more than half of the GDP of many African economies as against the hitherto dominance of the primary sector. This structural shift, however has not affected the industrial sector, where little or no changes have occurred and in some cases shrinkage was found. Ironically, in spite of the noticeable growth in the service sector, in terms of labour concentration, the bulk of the labour is still engaged in the primary sector. Perhaps, this explains the inability of the observed growth to reduce poverty and create jobs. African countries have mainly continued to sell primary commodities and use the proceeds to consume services. This, therefore, raises question about whether industrialisation is inevitable for advanced development. However, the evidence against the correlation between industrialisation and advanced development remains scanty or almost unavailable. Having said that, we conclude on the note that it is imperative that African policymakers and governing elites capitalise on the marginal gains and impetus provided by contemporary growth and development to address the inherent fundamental challenges of the continent. In particular, there is the urgent need to overcome the structural impediments to the growth of value addition and the industrial sector as a means towards mitigating the staggering unemployment and poverty challenges on the continent to ensure that Africa truly rises.

Notes

1. Britain's Exit from the European Union in 2020.
2. This explanation is partly derived from: Chen James (2019) "The Dutch Disease", 3 July, Investopedia, https://www.investopedia.com/terms/d/dutchdisease.asp; See also: Collier, P. (2008) *The Bottom Billion: Why the Poorest Countries are Failing and What Can Be Done About It.* Oxford University Press.
3. Ibid.
4. Furthermore, information is partly derived from the following sources: World Bank (2019) "Ease of Doing Business Index Report", https://data.worldbank.org/indicator/IC.BUS.EASE.XQ; World Bank (2018) "Doing Business 2019: A Year of Record Reforms, Rising Influence", 31 October, https://www.worldbank.org/en/news/immersive-story/2018/10/31/doing-business-2019-a-year-of-record-reforms-rising-influence.
5. Inclusive Institutions: spread power over a broad swath of society, allowing various groups to be represented and to participate in political decision-making, thereby shaping the economic institutions of their countries. Inclusive economic institutions are characterised by a rule of law that enforces contracts and protects private property rights. This protection incentivises productivity. Inclusive institutions also promote competition and let individuals choose their occupations, thereby making the most efficient use of talent and skill. To achieve inclusive institutions, a country must have stability, a strong central government and pluralistic institutions in which all are represented (Yoe 2019).
6. Extractive Institutions: extractive institutions on the other hand undermine the goal of achieving institutional inclusivity. They are characterised by a small elite (not pluralistic) having all the power and making decisions that benefit and enrich it without concern for the greater population. The government can be led by one absolute ruler, a royal family, or a political party, such as the Communist Party. The economic system is exploited by those in power and exists solely to enrich them. Property rights and rule of law are tenuous or non-existent, and the government either expropriates land and resources or levies high taxes on all production. Either way, the government does not incentivise production or economic growth, and this traps a country far behind those with more inclusive institutions (Yoe 2019).

References

AERC. 2015. Growth in Fragile States in Africa: A Call for Proposals. https://aercafrica.org/growth-in-fragile-states-in-africa/.

AU. 2019. African Continental Free Trade Area (AfCFTA). African Union, January. https://au.int/en/videos/20190101/african-continental-free-trade-area-afcfta.

Besley, T., and T. Persson. 2010. State Capacity, Conflict, and Development. *Econometrica* 78 (1): 1–34.

Bratton, M. 1998. Second Lections in Africa. *Journal of Democracy* 9 (3): 51–66.

Caselli, F., and T. Cunningham. 2009. Leader Behaviour and the Natural Resource Curse. *Oxford Economic Papers* 61 (4): 628–650.

Chandy, L. 2011. *Ten Years of Fragile States: What Have We Learned?* Washington, DC: Brookings Institution.

Chen, S., and M. Ravallion. 2008. The Developing World Is Poorer Than We Thought, But No Less Successful in the Fight Against Poverty. Policy Research Working Paper 4703, World Bank, Washington, DC.

Collier, P. 2003. Primary Commodity Dependence and Africa's Future. In *Annual World Bank Conference on Development Economics* (pp. 139–162). World Bank.

Comaroff, J., and J.L. Comaroff. 2000. Millennial Capitalism: First Thoughts on a Second Coming. *Public Culture* 12 (2): 291–343.

Etter-Phoya, Rachel, Shanna Lima, and Markus Meinzer. 2019. Corporate Income Taxation in the Digital Age: Africa in the Corporate Tax Haven Index 2019, 28 August. https://www.taxjustice.net/wp-content/uploads/2019/08/CORPOR1.pdf.

Harvey, D. 2005. *The New Imperialism*. Oxford: Oxford University Press.

Harvey, D. 2007. *A Brief History of Neoliberalism*. New York: Oxford University Press.

IMF. 2019. IMF: Sub-Saharan Africa Economies Among World's Fastest-Growing in 2019, 13 January. https://africa.cgtn.com/2019/01/14/imf-sub-saharan-africa-economies-among-worlds-fastest-growing-in-2019/.

Joseph, A. Richard. 1987. *Democracy and Prebendal Politics in Nigeria: The Rise and Fall of the Second Republic*. Cambridge: Cambridge University Press.

Kpolovie, P.J., S. Ewansiha, and M. Esara. 2017. Continental Comparison of Human Development Index (HDI). *International Journal of Humanities Social Sciences and Education* 4 (1): 9–27.

Laniado E. 2017. Beneficiation in the Diamond Industry: Botswana. *All Diamond News*, 6 September. https://www.ehudlaniado.com/home/index.php/news/entry/beneficiation-in-the-diamond-industry-botswana.

Laniran, T.J. 2017. Fiscal Regimes In Resource Dependent African States: A Political Economy Game (No. WP/17/037). AGDI Working Paper.

Laniran, T.J. 2018. Capital Flows and Economic Growth: Does the Role of State Fragility Really Matter for Sustainability? In *Financing Sustainable Development in Africa* (pp. 145–173). Cham: Palgrave Macmillan.

LeBaron, G., and A.J. Ayers. 2013. The Rise of a 'New Slavery'? Understanding African Unfree Labour Through Neoliberalism. *Third World Quarterly* 34 (5): 873–892.

Lin, J.Y. 2011. *From Flying Geese to Leading Dragons: New Opportunities and Strategies for Structural Transformation in Developing Countries*. The World Bank.

Lopez, C. 2016. Inching Towards Integration. *International Monetary Fund*, 53 (2).

Loxley, J. 1990. Structural Adjustment in Africa: Reflections on Ghana and Zambia. *Review of African Political Economy* 17 (47): 8–27.

Luciani, Giacomo. 1997. Allocation Versus Production States: A Theoretical Framework. In *The Rentier State*, ed. Hazem Beblawi and Giacomo Luciani, 65–84. New York, NY: Croom Helm.

Mailey, J.R. 2015. *The Anatomy of the Resource Curse: Predatory Investment in Africa's Extractive Industries*. ACSS Special Report No. 3. Washington, DC: African Center for Strategic Studies (ACSS).

Marx, K. 1976. *Capital*, trans. Ben Fowkes. New York: Vintage.

MDG Report. 2014. *Assessing Progress in Africa Toward the Millennium Development Goals*. Addis Ababa.

Mishra, A. 2018. *The African Continental Free Trade Area and Its Implications for India-Africa Trade*. Observer Research Foundation.

Mold, A., and A. Prizzon. 2010. Fragile States, Commodity Booms and Export Performance: An Analysis of the Sub-Saharan African Case.

Moyo, Dambisa. 2009. *Dead Aid: Why Aid Is Not Working and How There Is Another Way for Africa*. London: Penguin Books.

Nega, B., and G. Schneider. 2016. Africa Rising? Short-Term Growth vs. Deep Institutional Concerns. *Forum for Social Economics* 45 (4): 283–308. Routledge.

Omeje, K. 2006. *High Stakes and Stakeholders: Oil Conflict and Security in Nigeria*. Aldershot: Ashgate.

Omeje, K. 2015. Natural Resource Rent and Stakeholder Politics in Africa: Towards a New Conceptualization. *Commonwealth and Comparative Politics* 45 (1): 92–114.

Ong, A. 2007. Neoliberalism as a Mobile Technology. *Transactions of the Institute of British Geographers* 32 (1): 3–8.

Peck, J., and A. Tickell. 2002. Neoliberalizing Space. *Antipode* 34 (3): 380–404.

Pettinger, T. 2018. Neo-Liberalism: Examples and Criticisms, 25 January. https://www.economicshelp.org/blog/20688/concepts/neoliberalism/.

Radelet, S. 2007. Reviving Economic Growth in Liberia. Centre for Global Development (CGD) Working Paper, Number 133, CGD, Washington, DC. www.cgdev.org/files/14912_file_Liberia_Growth.pdf.

Ravallion, M. 2013. How Long Will It Take to Lift One Billion People Out of Poverty? *The World Bank Research Observer* 28 (2): 139–158.

Robinson, J.A., and D. Acemoglu. 2012. *Why Nations Fail: The Origins of Power, Prosperity, and Poverty*. New York: Crown Business.

Robinson, J.A., R. Torvik, and T. Verdier. 2006. Political Foundations of the Resource Curse. *Journal of Development Economics* 79 (2): 447–468.

Saad-Filho, A., and D. Johnston (eds.). 2005. Introduction. In *Neoliberalism: A Critical Reader*. London: Pluto Press.

Sachs, J.D. 2005. Can Extreme Poverty Be Eliminated? *Scientific American* 293 (3): 56–65.

Sachs, J.D., and A.M. Warner. 2001. The Curse of Natural Resources. *European Economic Review* 45 (4): 827–838.

Sayndee, T. Deby. 2019. The Task of Rebuilding Liberia. In *Peacebuilding in Contemporary Africa: In Search of Alternative Strategies*, ed. Kenneth Omeje, 111–124. London: Routledge.

Schuktneckt, L. 1999. Tying Governments' Hands in Commodity Taxation. *Journal of African Economies* 8 (2): 152–181.

Signé, L. 2018. Africa's Big New Free Trade Agreement, Explained. *The Washington Post*.

Sieff, Michelle. 2007. The Dutch Disease in Africa. *The New York Sun*, 6 June. https://www.nysun.com/arts/dutch-disease-in-africa/55946/.

Staines, N. 2004. Economic Performance Over the Conflict Cycle. IMF Working Paper No. WP/04/95.

Shihepo, T. 2019. Africa Has DONE It • 54 Out of 55 Countries Sign AfCFTA. *The Southern Times*, 12 July. https://southerntimesafrica.com/site/news/africa-has-done-it-54-out-of-55-countries-sign-afcfta-27-countries-ratify-agreement-trading-expected-to-start-1-july-2020.

Sy, A. 2014. Shifts in Financing Sustainable Development: How Should Africa Adapt in 2014? In *Foresight Africa*. Washington, DC: The Brookings Institution.

The SDG Centre for Africa. 2019. 2019 Africa SDG Index and Dashboards Report, June. https://s3.amazonaws.com/sustainabledevelopment.report/2019/2019_africa_index_and_dashboards.pdf.

Transparency International. 2014. Sub-Saharan Africa: Corruption Still Hurts Daily Life, 3rd December. http://blog.transparency.org/2014/12/03/sub-saharan-africa-corruption-still-hurts-daily-lives/.

Transparency International. 2018. Corruption Perception Index 2018. Transparency International (TI). https://www.transparency.org/cpi2018.

Venugopal, R. 2015. Neoliberalism as Concept. *Economy and Society* 44 (2): 165–187.

UNCTAD. 2015. The Continental Free Trade Area: Making it Work for Africa. *Policy Brief*, 44. http://unctad.org/en/PublicationsLibrary/presspb2015d18_en.pdf.

UNCTAD. 2019. State of Commodity Dependence United Nations Geneva. https://unctad.org/en/PublicationsLibrary/ditccom2019d1_en.pdf.

UNDP BCPR. 2008. *Post-Conflict Economic Recovery: Enabling Local Ingenuity*. Crisis Prevention and Recovery Report 2008. New York: UNDP Bureau for Crisis Prevention and Recovery. www.undp.org/content/dam/undp/library/crisis%20prevention/undp-cpr-post-conflict-economic-recovery-enable-local-ingenuity-report-2008.pdf.

Yoe, J. 2019. State Institutions and Economic Prosperity. *Monthly Labour Review* 142 (2): 1–5.